# Indian Psychology and Perception

# Indian Psychology of Perception

Rajiv Bhargava

ABD PUBLISHERS
Jaipur ▪ New Delhi

**ABD PUBLISHERS**

**Regd. Off.** "Bony Residency", Gate No. 2
Opp. Tilak Public School, Vishweswariya Nagar,
Gopalpura Road, Jaipur - 302018, India
Ph: 0141 - 2761280, Telefax: 2761381
Email: abdpublishersjpr@gmail.com

**Delhi Office:** 102, 1st Floor, Satyam House,
4327/3, Ansari Road, Darya Ganj,
New Delhi - 110002, India
Ph: 011-45652440

visit us: www.oxfordbookcompany.com

*Distributed By*
**KEYA INTERNATIONAL PRESS LLP**
E-mail: keyainternationalpressllp@gmail.com

Published in India, 2025

Price: ₹ 2500/-



ISBN: 9788183762762



Typeset by Shivangi Computer, Jaipur

Printed and bound in India by Thomson Press Ltd.,
New Delhi

# Preface

The Indian thinkers generally recognize two distinct stages of perception, indeterminate (*nirvikalpa*) and determinate (*savikalpa*). The former is the immediate apprehension of the mere form of an object, while the later is the mediate perception of the object with its different properties and their relations to one another. The former is an undifferentiated and non-related mode of consciousness devoid of assimilation and discrimination, analysis and synthesis. The latter is a differentiated and relational mode of consciousness involving assimilation and discrimination, analysis and synthesis. The former is purely sensory and presentative, while the latter is presentative-representative. In short, the former is abstract and indeterminate, while the latter is concrete and determinate.

Indian philosophers hold the peculiar doctrine that substances alone can enter into direct communion with the appropriate sense-organs in order to form a perception. Thus some sort of direct or indirect relation must be established between the perceptible objects and the appropriate sense-organs. In all kinds of perceptions the objects must be directly or indirectly presented to the consciousness.

Explaining physical basis of perception at the outset, the present book describes various types of perceptions in a lucid manner. In addition, the book also elucidates on illusions, dreams, hallucinations and recognition. Important terms are explained using Sanskrit and English version.

**Rajiv Bhargava**

# Preface

The Indian thinkers generally recognize two distinct stages of perception, indeterminate (*nirvikalpa*) and determinate (*savikalpa*). The former is the immediate apprehension of the mere form of an object, while the latter is the mediate perception of the object with its different properties and their relations to one another. The former is an undifferentiated and non-related mode of consciousness devoid of assimilation and discrimination, analysis and synthesis. The latter is a differentiated and relational mode of consciousness involving assimilation and discrimination, analysis and synthesis. The former is purely sensory and presentative while the latter is presentative-representative. In short, the former is abstract and indeterminate, while the latter is concrete and determinate.

Indian philosophers hold the peculiar doctrine that substance alone can enter into direct communion with the appropriate sense-organs in order to form a perception. Thus some sort of direct or indirect relation must be established between the perceptible objects and the appropriate sense-organs. In all kinds of perceptions the objects must be directly or indirectly presented to the consciousness.

Explaining physical basis of perception at the outset, the present book describes various types of perceptions in a lucid manner. In addition, the book also elucidates on illusions, dreams, hallucination and recognition. Important terms are explained using Sanskrit and English version.

**Rajiv Bhargava**

# Contents

# 1

# The Physical Basis of Perception

## Introduction

The ancient Hindus developed a conception of the nervous system, which is mainly to be found in the medical works of Caraka and Susruta, and in the works on *Tantra*. Caraka and Susruta regarded the heart as the seat of consciousness, but the Tantric writers transferred the seat of consciousness to the brain. Caraka had a clear conception of the sensory nerves (*manovaha nadi*) and the motor nerves (*ajnavaha nadi*). The Tantric writers constantly referred to the centres of different kinds of consciousness. They not only distinguished between the sensory nerves and the motor nerves, but also recognized different kinds of sensory nerves : the olfactory nerves (*gandhavaha nadi*) the optic nerves (*rupavaha nadi*) the auditory nerves (*sabdavaha nadi*) the gustatory nerves (*rasavaha nadi*) and the tactile nerves (*sparsavaha nadi*).

In the philosophical literature of the Hindus, we find an elaborate account of the sense-organs in the treatment of the problems of perception. The different schools of philosophers had different views as to the nature, origin, and functions of the sense-organs. Their views were based mostly on their systems of philosophy, though they advanced certain facts of experience in support of their views. The Hindu accounts of the sense-organs are widely different from those of Western psysiology, because they are based more on metaphysical speculation than on scientific observation and experiment. In the first volume we shall treat of the nature, origin, and functions of the sense-organs without comprehension of which there cannot be an adequate conception of some important problems of the Indian psychology of perception.

## The Nature of the Sense-organs

### *The Buddhist*

The Buddhists recognize six varieties of consciousness; visual, auditory, olfactory, gustatory, tactile, and purely mental. Corresponding to these there are six bases (*asraya*): the organs of vision, audition, smelling, tasting, touch, and consciousness itself and there are six objects (*visaya*) : colours, sounds, smells, tastes, tangibles, and ideas. The preceding moment of consciousness is the basic element of the next moment of consciousness. Thus there are six sense-organs including consciousness. Consciousness is the faculty of intellect which apprehends non-sensuous objects. It is called the mind. It is immaterial and invisible.

Leaving out the mind, there are five sense-organs. They are the end-organs (*golaka*). They are the eye, the ear, the nose, the tongue, and the skin. They are made up of a kind of translucent subtle matter. The five sense-organs are made up of five different kinds of atoms. Thus the sense-organs are material but invisible. They are divided into two classes, viz. *prapyakari* and *aprapyakari* sense-organs. The former apprehend their objects when they come in direct contact with them. The latter apprehend their objects without coming in contact with them. The organs of smell, taste, and touch are *prapyakari;* they must be in immediate contact with their objects. The organs of vision and audition are *aprapyakari* they apprehend their objects at a distance. The Buddhists do not hold with the *Nyaya-Vaisesika* that the sense-organs are different from the peripheral organs, and the visual organ and the auditory organ come in contact with their objects in order to apprehend them.

### *The Jaina*

The Jaina recognizes five sense-organs. They are of two kinds: objective senses (*dravyendriya*) and subjective senses (*bhavendriya*).

The former are the physical sense-organs. The latter are their psychical correlates. They are the invisible faculties of the soul. A physical sense-organ (*dravyendriya*) consists of two parts, viz. the organ itself and its protecting environment. The former is called. The latter is called *upakarana*. Each of these is of two kinds, internal and external The internal organ is the soul itself which is embodied in the sense-organ. The external organ is the physical organ which is permeated by the soul. The internal environment of the visual organ is the pupil of the eye. The external environment is the eyelid. The subjective senses (*bhavendriya*) are of two kinds : *labdhi* and *upayoga*. "*Labdhi* is the manifestation of the sense-faculty by the partial destruction, subsidence, and operation of the knowledge-obscuring karma relating to that sense. *Upayoga* is the conscious attention of the soul directed to that sense." There are five sense-organs : organs of touch, taste, smell, vision, and audition. The tactual organ pervades the whole body. The Jaina does not regard the mind as a sense-organ. He conceives the soul as pervading the whole body. A particular kind of sensepe rception is generated in the soul through that part of it which is associated with a particular sense-organ. Of the physical sense-organs the visual organ is *aprapyakari;* it does not come in direct contact with its objects. On this point the Jaina agrees with the Buddhist. The Jaina holds that the visual organ apprehends objects at a distance with the help of light. But he does not explain the nature of the action of light upon the visual organ. All the other sense-organs are *prapyakari*, they come in direct contact with their objects. But the direct contact may be gross (*sthula*) or subtle (*suksma*). The organs of touch and taste come in contact with gross objects. But the organs of smell and hearing come in contact with subtle objects. The organ of smell has direct contact with minute particles of the object smelt. The organ of hearing has direct contact with merely a kind of motion. Sound is due to the knocking of one physical object against another. It is the agitation set up by this knock. The auditory organ comes in contact with this motion.

### *The Samkhya*

**Vijnanabhiksu says** : "An *Indriya* is the instrument of the Lord of the body or the soul. The essential nature of a sense-organ consists in its instrumentality (in producing cognitions and actions), and in being an effect of *ahamkara* (*egoism*)". Kapila speaks of eleven sense-organs:

five organs of knowledge (*buddhindriya*) five organs of action (*karmendriya*) and the internal organ or mind (*manas*). *Isvarakrsna* also sometimes mentions eleven sense-organs : the sensory organs, the motor organs, and the mind which partakes of the nature of both, and is thus a sensori-motor organ. And sometimes he mentions thirteen sense-organs adding *buddhi* and *ahamkara* to the above list. *Manas, buddhi,* and *ahamkara* are the three forms of the internal organ. The Samkhya recognizes two classes of sense organs: external and internal. It divides the external sense-organs into two classes : organs of cognition (*buddhindriya*) and organs of action (*karmendriya*) The visual organ, the auditory organ, the olfactory organ, the gustatory organ, and the tactual organ are the organs of cognition. The vocal organ, the prehensive organ, the locomotive organ, the evacuative organ, and the generative organ are the organs of action. By these organs of cognition and action the Samkhya does not mean the gross material organs, e.g. the eye, the ear, etc., and hands, feet, etc. By these it means determinate modifications of the indeterminate mind-stuff (*ahamkara* or egoism). The gross material organs, e.g., the eye, the ear, etc., and hands, feet, etc., are the seats of those determinate sensory and motor psychophysical impulses. By the *buddhmdriyas* the Samkhya means the determinate sensory psychophysical impulses which go out to the external objects and receive impressions from them, and by the *karmendriyas* it means the determinate motor psychophysical impulses which react to the objects perceived. The sense-organs are not products of gross matter (*bhautika*) but of *ahamkara* (egoism) which, though not spiritual, may be called mental or psychophysical. Hence, the distinction between the organs of knowledge and the organs of action is ultimately based upon the primary distinction between the sensory and motor mechanisms of the psychophysical organism, by which it knows the external world and reacts to it.

The internal organs are the instruments of elaboration. The mind presides over both the sensory and motor organs. The external senses give immediate impressions of their objects. These discrete impressions are synthesized by *manas* by assimilation and discrimination. Then they are referred to the unity of apperception by *ahamkara*. Then they are determined by *buddhi* which hands them over to the self and reacts to them.

Vyasa refers to two kinds of sense-organs, viz. gross organs and subtle organs. Vijnanabhiksu says that *buddhi* and *ahamkara* are subtle (*suksma*) sense-organs, and the five organs of cognition, the five organs of action, and the central sensory or *manas* are gross (*sthula*) sense-organs. Vyasa says that the five cognitive organs, the five motor organs, and the *manas* which apprehends all objects are the determinative modifications of indeterminate egoism (*ahamkara*). The sense-organs are not the same as their psysiological sites or end-organs (*adhisthana*). The Buddhists wrongly hold that the sense-organs are nothing but the end-organs. They are supersensuous. Aniruddha argues that, if the sense-organs were identical with their physical seats, one whose ears have been cut off would be unable to hear, and one whose eyes are affected with cataract would be able to see. So the sense-organs are not identical with their sites. The sense-organs are not material (*bhautika*) but are products of *ahamkara* (egoism). Aniruddha says that the *Naiyavaisesika* labour under a misconception when they argue that the sense-organs are made up of those material elements which are apprehended by them.

### The Origin of the Sense-organs

According to the Sarhkhya, *Prakrti,* the equilibrium of sattva (essence), *rajas* (energy), and *tamas* (inertia) is the ultimate ground of all existence. Buddhi evolves out of *Prakrti* when the equilibrium of *sattva, rajas,* and *tamas* is disturbed by a transcendental influence of the self (*purusa*) for the sake of which all evolution takes place. *Buddhi* is the cosmic matter of experience : it is the undifferentiated matrix of the subjective series and the objective series. From *buddhi* evolves *ahamkara* (the empirical ego) which gives rise to the eleven sense-organs and the subtle elements (*tanmatra*) of matter under the influence of *sattva, rajas,* and *tamas*? *Isvarakrsna* holds that all the eleven sense-organs evolve out of *ahamkara* by the preponderance of *sattva,* and five *tanmatras* evolve out of *ahamkara* by the preponderance of *tamas* and both the sense-organs and the *tanmatras* evolve with the help of *rajas.* Vacaspatimisra elaborates this view. The cognitive organs (*buddhindriya*) are the instruments of knowledge. So they are endowed with the quality of manifesting objects. They are also capable of quick movement. The cognitive organs quickly move out to distant objects. The motor organs (*karmendriya*) also are capable of quick action. And these properties of illumination and light movement are the distinctive properties of sattva. Hence the preponderating element in the constitution of the sense-organs is *sattva,* though they evolve out of *ahamkara.* The five *tanmatras* also evolve out of *ahamkara;* but the preponderating element in their constitution is *tamas* (*inertia*) because they are extremely inert in their nature. The preponderance of *sattva* in *ahamkara* gives rise to the sense-organs, and the preponderance of *tamas* in *ahamkara* gives rise to the *tanmatras.* But if *sattva* and *rajas* do everything, what is the use of *rajas? Rajas* (energy) is necessary to give impetus to *sattva* (essence) and *tamas* (inertia) to perform their functions. They cannot act without the help of *rajas.* When *rajas* sets them in motion on account of its characteristic property of energizing they perform their functions. Hence, both the sense-organs *sattvic* and the *tanmatras* (*tamasic*) evolve out of *ahamkara* with the help of *rajas.* Aniruddha also holds that the eleven sense-organs are evolved from *ahamkara* under the influence of *sattva.* But Vijnanabhiksu holds that the mind (*manas*) is evolved from *ahamkara* owing to the preponderance of *sattva,* the five cognitive organs and the five motor organs evolve out of *ahamkara* owing to the preponderance of *rajas;* and the five *tanmatras* evolve out of *ahamkara* owing to the preponderance of *tamas.* Balarama holds that all the sense-organs have the preponderance of *sattva* but there are different degrees of its preponderance. The mind arises from ahamkara when sattva is most preponderant; the organs of knowledge arise from *ahamkara* when *sattva* is less preponderant, and the organs of action arise from *ahamkara* when *sattva* is least preponderant.

**The Principal and Subordinate Organs**

The three internal organs, *buddhi ahamkara* and *manas,* are the principal sense-organs, since they apprehend all objects past, present, and future. The external senses are the subordinate organs, since they apprehend only present objects. The former are called gatekeepers, while the latter are called the gateways of knowledge. *Buddhi* is the principal organ not only in comparison with the external organs but also with the internal organs of *manas* and *ahamkara.* Superiority and inferiority depend upon functions; they are relative *terms. Manas* is the chief organ in relation to the functions of the external senses; *ahamkara* is the chief organ in relation to the function of *manas;* and *buddhi* is the chief organ in relation to the function of *ahamkara*. Buddhi is the chief organ for the following reasons. Firstly, *buddhi* directly brings about the experience of the self (*purusa*) while the other senses do it through the mediation of *buddhi*. *Buddhi* is the immediate instrument among all the external and internal senses, and makes over the object to the self, even as among a host of servants some one person becomes the prime minister while the others are his subordinate officers. Secondly, *buddhi* pervades all the sense-organs, and never fails to produce the result in the shape of knowledge. Thirdly, *buddhi* alone is the receptacle of all subconscious impressions (*samskara*). The external organs cannot retain the residua, for in that case the blind and the deaf would not be able to remember things seen and heard in the past. *Manas* and *ahamkara* also cannot retain subconscious impressions because even after their dissolution by means of knowledge of Truth (*tattvajnana*) recollection persists. Hence buddhi has pre-eminence over all. Fourthly, the superiority of *buddhi* is inferred from the possibility of recollection which is of the nature of meditation, the highest of all mental functions. Recollection is the function of buddhi. Thus *buddhi* is the chief organ and all the other senses are secondary organs.

If *buddhi* is the principal organ, why should we not regard it as the only sense-organ and dispense with the other sense-organs? Vijnanabhiksu replies that without the help of the external senses *buddhi* cannot serve as an instrument in all sense-activities, since in that case the blind would be able to see, the deaf would be able to hear, and so on. Kapila holds that the ten external senses may be regarded as different modifications of the chief organ, *manas* owing to the difference of the modifications of the constituent *gunas sattva, rajas,* and *tamas*? Just as one and the same person assumes many roles in association with different persons, so *manas* also becomes manifold, through association with different sense-organs being particularized by the functions of the different senses by reason of its becoming one with the senses. This diverse modification of the mind is due to the diverse modification of the constituent *gunas*.

### The *Vrtti* of the Sense-organs

The Samkhya holds that the sense-organs are *prapyakarl;* they move out to their objects in the form of *vrttis* or modifications, take in their forms, and apprehend them. The *vrttis* of the senses cannot be perceived. But their existence can be inferred from the fact that the sense-organs cannot apprehend their objects without being related to them, even as a lamp cannot illumine objects without being related to them. If the sense-organs be said to apprehend their objects without being related to them, then they may apprehend all objects, distant and hidden. But this is not a fact. Hence the sense-organs must be conceived as moving out to their objects and assuming their forms without leaving connection with the body. And this is possible only by means of a peculiar modification of the senses called *vrtti*. Thus the existence of *vrtti* is established. It connects the senses with their objects. The *vrtti* is neither a part not a quality of the senses. If it were a part it would not be able to bring about the connection of the visual organ with distant objects like the sun. If it were a quality it would not be able to move out to the object. Thus the *vrtti* of a sense-organ, though existing in it, is different from its part or quality. Hence, it is established that the *vrtti* of *buddhi* also is, like the flarne of a lamp, a transformation quite of the nature of a substance which, by means of its transparency, is capable of receiving images of the forms of objects.

### *Susruta and Caraka*

Susruta holds with the Samkhya that there are eleven sense-organs: five organs of knowledge, five organs of action, and the mind , which partakes of the nature of both. The sense-organs evolve out of *ahamkara* under the influence of *rajas* (energy). Caraka also holds that there are eleven sense-organs, five sensory organs, five motor organs, and one internal organ or *manas*. Sometimes he mentions twelve sense-organs : five organs of knowledge, five organs of action, *manas* and *buddhi*? The mind is atomic and one in each body. It is different from the external senses. It is sometimes called *sattva*. Its functions are regulated by the contact of its objects with thc soul. And it controls the functions of the external senses. They can apprehend their respective objects when they are led by the mind. The functions of the mind are the apprehension of objects through the external senses, subjecting them to control, comparison, and ratiocination. Then *buddhi* ascertains the nature of the objects. Certain knowledge is the function of *buddhi*. When *buddhi* has brought about definite apprehension one begins to act, guided by buddhi?

***Caraka says*** : "There are five sense-organs, five materials that constitute the senses, five seats of the senses, five objects of the senses, and five kinds of perception obtained through the senses." Here evidently he speaks of the organs of knowledge. The organs of vision, audition, smell, taste, and touch are the five sense-organs. The materials that enter into the composition of the five senses are light, ether, earth, water, and air respectively. The physical seats of the five senses are the two eyes, the two ears, the nose, the tongue, and the skin. The sense-organs are not the same as the peripheral organs which are their seats. The objects of the five senses are colour, sound, odour, taste, and touch. Visual, auditory, olfactory, gustatory, and tactual perceptions are five kinds of sense-perception. As to the composition of the external senses Caraka seems to be in agreement with the Nyaya-Vaisesika view. But he does not wholly agree with it. According to him one particular element does not enter into the composition of a particular sense-organ; but all the primal elements exist in each sense-organ, though only one element predominates in the composition of a particular sense-organ. Thus light especially enters into the composition of the visual organ, ether into that of the auditory organ, earth into that of the olfactory organ, water into that of the gustatory organ, and air into that of the tactual organ. The particular sense into whose composition a particular element especially enters apprehends that particular object which has that element for its essence, since both partake of the same nature, and one is invested with greater power over the other. Light especially enters into the composition of the visual organ; so it can apprehend colour which has light for its essence. Both the visual organ and colour partake of the nature of light, the former being more powerful than the latter. Hence the visual organ can apprehend colour. Such is the case with the auditory organ and sound, and so with the others. This doctrine of Caraka is kindred to the Nyaya-Vaisesika doctrine. But Caraka does not regard the sense-organs as products of matter as the Nyaya-Vaisesika holds. He traces the origin of the senses to *ahamkara* after the Samkhya. His cosmology is the same as that of the Samkhya. Thus Caraka's views as to the nature, kinds, and functions of the sense-organs are partly similar to the Sarhkhya's view, and partly to the Nyaya-Vaisesika's view.

### The Vedanta

The Samkarite agrees with the Samkhya in recognizing five organs of knowledge, five organs of action, and the internal organ. The Samkhya recognizes three forms of the internal organ, *buddhi, ahamkara* and manas. But the Amkarite admits four forms of the internal organ, *manas, buddhi, ahamkara* and *citta*. Though the internal organ is one and the same, it assumes different forms according to its diverse functions. When it has the function of doubt or undetermination it is called *manas*. When it has the function of determination it is called *buddhi*. When it produces the notion of ego in consciousness it is called *ahamkara*. And when it has the function of recollection it is called *citta*. These functions are different modifications of the same internal organ (*antahkarana*)?

The five organs of knowledge are made up of the *sattvic* part of the unquintuplied material elements. The organs of vision, audition, smell, taste, and touch are made up of the *sattvic* parts of light, ether, earth, water, and air respectively in an uncombined state. The organs of action are made up of the *rajasic* part of the unquintuplied material elements. The organ of speech, hands, feet, the excretive organ, and the generative organ are made up of the *rajasic* parts of ether, air, light, water, and earth respectively in an uncombined state. The internal organs are made up of the *sattvic* parts of the five material elements combined.

The Ramanujist recognizes eleven sense-organs : five organs of cognition, five organs of action, and the mind. The Samkhya admits three internal organs, and the Samkarite admits four internal organs. Both these views are wrong. The so-called internal organs are nothing but different functions of one and the same internal organ, manas. Sometimes the manas is included in the ogans of knowledge.

### The Nature of the Sense-organs

The author of *Vivaranaprameyasamgraha* discusses the nature of the sense-organs:

The Buddhists hold that the sense-organs are the peripheral organs, viz. the eye, the ear, the nose, the tongue, and the skin. It is the sockets (*golaka*) in the body that constitute the sense-organs.

The Mimamsakas hold that the sense-organs consist in the faculty of potency (*sakti*) abiding in the sockets. The mere end-organs do not constitute the sense-organs.

Others hold that the sense-organs are distinct from both the end-organs and their potency, and are distinct substances by themselves.

The Samkarite rejects the first theory on the ground that certain animals (e.g. serpents) can hear, though they do not possess the earhole, and the plants which are believed to be sentient living beings are devoid of end-organs or sockets. For the same reason the Mimamsaka theory also is rejected. The Mimamsaka argues that the Law of Parsimony demands that we should assume the existence of potency (*sakti*) only, and not of the sense-organs endued with a potency. But the Samkarite contends that it is needless to assume the existence of the potency also; the Law of Parsimony, if rigidly applied, will lead us to assume the existence only of the self capable of knowing things in succession. The self is all-pervading; so it can produce cognitions in the end-organs. The Mimamsaka himself admits that the self has modifications of consciousness (*jnanaparinama*) only in those parts of the body in which there are end-organs. Thus, the Mimarnsaka argument ultimately leads to the denial of the sense-organs altogether. So the Mimamsaka doctrine is not tenable. The third theory also is not acceptable. There is no proof of the existence of the sense-organs as distinct substances quite different from the sockets. It may be argued that perceptions of colour and the like are due to the action of the self, and since an action always requires an instrument, the self must require the instrumentality of the sense-organs to perceive colour and the like. This argument is wrong. The reason is over-wide. The self acts upon the sense-organs to incite them to action; but in doing so it does not require any instrument. If it did it would lead to infinite regress. So the third theory also cannot be maintained. But the Samkarite believes in the existence of sense-organs as something different from the peripheral organs on the authority of the scriptures.

### *The Nyaya-Vaisesika*

Gautama establishes the existence of five sense-organs on the following grounds :

In the first place, the existence of five sense-organs is inferred from five distinct functions. Vatsyayana argues that there are five purposes (*prayojana*) of the senses : touching, seeing, smelling, tasting, and hearing. These five purposes require five distinct sense-organs, viz. the tactual organ, the visual organ, the olfactory organ, the gustatory organ, and the auditory organ. Touch is apprehended by the tactual organ, but it does not apprehend colour. So we infer the existence of the visual organ which serves the purpose of apprehending colour. Similarly, touch and colour are apprehended by the tactual organ and the visual organ respectively, but these organs do not apprehend odour. So we infer the existence of the olfactory organ which serves the purpose of apprehending odour. In the same manner, touch, colour, and odour are apprehended by the tactual organ, the visual organ, and the olfactory organ respectively, but these organs do not apprehend taste. So we infer the existence of the gustatory organ which serves the purpose of apprehending taste. Lastly, touch, colour, odour, and taste are apprehended by the tactual organ, the visual organ, the olfactory organ, and the gustatory organ respectively; but these organs do not apprehend sound. So we infer the existence of the auditory organ which serves the purpose of apprehending sound. The function of one sense-organ cannot be performed by another. So the existence of five sense-organs is inferred from five kinds of sense-activities.

In the second place, the existence of the five sense-organs is inferred from the fivefold character of the signs in the shape of perceptions, the sites, the processes, the forms, and the constituents.

First, there are five different kinds of perception, visual, auditory, olfactory, gustatory, and tactual, from which we infer the existence of five sense-organs.

Second, there are five sense-organs corresponding to the five sites (*adhisthana*) or end-organs. The tactual organ, which is indicated by the perception of touch, has its seat throughout the body. The visual organ issuing out to the object as indicated by the perception of colour has its site in the pupil of the eye. The olfactory organ has its site in the nose. The gustatory organ has its site in the tongue. The auditory organ has its site in the cavity of the ear. The diversity of the sense-organs is proved by the diversity of their locations. Things with distinct locations are always found to be distinct as in the case of ears. If the whole body is said to be the seat of all the sense-organs, then deafness, blindness, and the like would be impossible. But if the different sense-organs are held to have different sites, the site of one organ being destroyed, the other organs may remain unaffected so that a deaf or blind person would not necessarily be deprived of all the sense-organs. Thus this theory does not involve any incongruity. This argument shows that the sense-organs are different from their physical seats (*golaka*).

Third, the five sense-organs involve different processes (*gati*). The visual organ, which is of the nature of light, issues out of the pupil and moves out to the objects endued with colour. The tactual organ, the gustatory organ, and the olfactory organ come in contact with their objects resting in their own sites. They do not move out to their objects like the visual organ. The auditory organ also does not move out to its object. Sound travels from its place of origin to the auditory organ in a series of waves. This argument shows that all the sense-organs are *prapyakari*; they apprehend their objects by coming in direct contact with them.

Fourth, the five sense-organs have different magnitudes (*akrti*). The olfactory organ, the gustatory organ, and the tactual organ have the magnitudes of their sites; they are coextensive with their seats. The visual organ, though located in the pupil, issues out of it and pervades its object. Thus it is not coextensive with its site but with the field of vision. The auditory organ is nothing but *akasa* which is all-pervading; still it cannot apprehend all sounds because its scope is restricted by the disabilities of the substratum in which it subsists. The all-pervading *akasa* located in the ear-hole owing to the *adrsta* of a person assumes the role of the auditory organ, and produces the perception of sound through it.

Last, the five sense-organs have their origin (*jati*) in five material elements. The olfactory organ is made up of earth and apprehends smell which is its characteristic quality. The gustatory organ is made up of water and apprehends taste which is its characteristic quality. The visual organ is made up of light and apprehends colour which is its characteristic quality. And the auditory organ is nothing but *akasa* and apprehends sound which is its characteristic quality. There is a community of nature between the sense-organs and their objects. A sense-organ apprehends the distinctive quality of that substance which enters into its constitution. The Vaisesika also agrees with this view.

Gautama does not distinctly mention anywhere that the mind

(*manas*) is a sense-organ. But Vatsyayana points out that Gautamas definition of perception, as a non-erroneous cognition produced by the intercourse of the sense-organs with their objects, inexpressible by words and well-defined, implies that the mind is a sense-organ. If by the sense-organs he means only the external senses his definition would apply only to perceptions of external objects. But Gautama does not give a separate definition of internal perception of pleasure and the like. This shows that his definition covers both external perception and internal perception, and the mind is a sense-organ, Vatsyayana includes the mind in the sense-organs and points out its distinction from the external senses. Visvanatha regards the mind as a sense-organ. He argues that the perception of pleasure must be produced through an instrument just as the visual perception of colour is produced through the instrument of the eyes; and this instrument is the mind (*manas*) which is thus a sense-organ (*karana*). Prasastapada describes the mind as the internal organ (*antahkarana*). He argues that pleasure and pain are not perceived through the external senses, but they must be perceived through an instrument, and that is the mind. Samkaramisra also gives the same argument.

### *The Mimamsaka*

A sense-organ is defined by the Mimamsaka as that which, rightly operating upon its object, produces direct presentations. There are two kinds of sense-organs, external and internal. There are five external organs : the olfactory organ, the gustatory organ, the visual organ, the tactual organ, and the auditory organ. Of these the first four are made up of earth, water, light, and air respectively. So far the Mimamsaka agrees with the Nyaya-Vaisesika. But the Nyaya-Vaisesika regards the auditory organ as of the nature of ether (*akasa*) while the Mimamsaka regards it as a portion of space (*dik*) confined within the ear-hole. There is only one internal organ, viz. the mind (*manas*). The mind is atomic in nature, as proved by the impossibility of simultaneous cognitions. It is called the internal organ, since it operates independently in the perception of the self and its qualities. But in the perception of external objects it acts in co-operation with the external senses, since being an internal organ it cannot come in contact with external objects. It depends upon marks of inference (*lingo*) to produce inferential cognitions, and it depends upon subconscious impressions (*samskara*) to bring about recollection. Thus the

Mimamsaka view of the nature and functions of the sense-organs resembles the Nyaya-Vaisesika view.

**Are the Karmendriyas Really Sense-organs ?**

The Samkhya and the Vedantist hold that the vocal organ, the prehensive organ, the locomotive organ, the excretive organ, and the generative organ are the organs of action (*karmendriya*). They are regarded as sense-organs because they are the instruments which produce the functions of speaking, grasping, walking, evacuation, and sexual intercourse respectively. The function of one cannot be done by another.

But Jayanta urges that if these organs are regarded as sense-organs, many other organs also should be regarded as such. The throat has the function of swallowing food, the breasts have the function of embracing and shoulders have the function of carrying burdens. So they also must be regarded as sense-organs. If it is argued that these functions can be done by other organs also, then it may equally be argued that eating and drinking can sometimes be done by hands and feet, swallowing food by the *anus*, and the grasping of things by the mouth. The functions of the so-called motor organs are sometimes done by other organs also. But the function of one cognitive organ (*buddhindriya*) can never be done by another. A person whose eye balls have been taken out of their sockets can never perceive colour. But a person can grasp and walk a little even with his hands and feet amputated. Besides, walking is not the function of feet alone; it can also be done by hands. If the different parts of the body having different functions in the shape of actions are said to be motor organs, then throat, breast, shoulder, etc., also should be included in the motor organs. Vidyanandin argues that the so-called motor organs are included in the tactual organ. Hence, there is no necessity of supposing the existence of the so-called motor organs.

**Are there Three Internal Organs?**

Jayanta argues that one internal organ, *manas* is quite adequate. It is needless to assume three internal organs, *manas, ahamkara,* and *buddhi*. *Buddhi* is of the nature of cognition, and so it is of the nature of an operation of an instrument. Hence it cannot be an instrument of cognition. *Ahamkara* (egoism) also is an object of cognition so it cannot be an instrument of cognition. Therefore, there is only one internal organ, viz. *manas*? Vidyanandin argues that *buddhi* and *ahamkara* cannot be regarded as sense-organs, since they are modifications of the soul, and results of the sense-organs and the mind. Venkatanatha argues that the so-called internal organs of *buddhi* and *ahamkara* are functions of the mind which is the only internal organ.

**Is the Manas a Sense-organ ?**

Gautama does not include the *manas* (mind) in the list of sense-organs. He mentions it separately among the objects of valid knowledge (*prameya*). Kanada is silent upon the point. But the *Nyaya*-Vaisesika generally regards the *manas* as the internal organ through which we perceive pleasure and pain. The Mimamsakas also recognize the *manas* as the internal organ. They call it the internal organ, since it operates independently in the perception of the self and its qualities. But in the perception of external objects it acts in co-operation with the external senses, since being an internal organ it cannot come in contact with external objects. The Samkhya also regards the manas as an internal sense-organ. Isvarakrsna says that the *manas* is a sensori-motor organ (*ubhayatmakam manah*); it partakes of the nature of both the organs of knowledge and the organs of action. The Vedantists also generally recognize the *manas* as a sense-organ. The Ramanujists regard the manas as the internal organ of knowledge, which is the cause of recollection. They differ from the Samkhya which regards the *manas* as partaking of the nature of both the organs of knowledge and the organs of action. They differ from the Nyaya-Vaisesika in holding that the *manas* is not the organ of internal perception (*manasa-pratyaksa*) since there is no internal perception at all. Samkara admits that the *manas* is a senseorgan because it is distinctly laid down in the *Smrti*. Manu says : "here are eleven sense-organs of which the eleventh organ is the *manas*", Vacaspatimisra also holds the same view. But some Samkarites hold a contrary view.

The authors of *Vedantaparibhasa, Advaitabrahmasiddhi* and *Advaitacintakaustubha* hold that the *manas* is not a sense-organ on the authority of the Sruti. "The objects are greater than the sense-organs, and the *manas* is greater than the objects." In this text the *manas* is given a higher place than the sense-organs. So it cannot be regarded as a sense-organ. The Nyaya-Vaisesika argues that the *manas* should be regarded as a sense-organ, since it is the organ of the perception of pleasure and pain. Perception is always of sensuous origin. There can be no perception without a sense-organ. The author of Vedantaparibhasa argues that the perception of pleasure and pain does not necessarily imply that the *manas* is a sense-organ through which the self perceives pleasure and pain. The perceptual character of a cognition does not consist in its being produced by a sense-organ. In that case, inferential cognition also would be regarded as perception, since it is produced by the mind. The perceptual character of a cognition depends on the identification of the apprehending mental mode with the perceived object.

The Jaina also does not regard the *manas* as a sense-organ. It is called *anindriya*. It is not a sense-organ. Vidyanandin argues that the mind is not a sense-organ because it is different from the sense-organs. The sense-organs apprehend specific objects. One sense-organ cannot apprehend the objects of another. But the mind can apprehend all objects. So it cannot be regarded as a sense-organ. It may be argued that the mind is an instrument (*karana*) of cognition, and so it must be regarded as a sense-organ. But in that case smoke also would be a sense-organ, since it is an instrument (*karana*) of cognition, being a mark (*lingo*) of inference. Hence it is wrong to include the mind in the sense-organs.

## The External Organs and the Internal Organ or Organs

The Samkhya regards the internal organ as threefold in character. It assumes the forms of *buddhi, ahamkara* and *manas* according as its functions differ. Isvarakrsna holds that the external organs can apprehend only the present. But the internal organs can apprehend the present, the past, and the future. Gaudapada makes it clear by examples. The visual organ apprehends only the present colour, neither past nor future colours. The auditory organ apprehends the present sound, neither past nor future sounds. The tactual organ, the gustatory organ, and the olfactory organ apprehend respectively the present touch, taste, and odour, but not past or future ones. This is the case with the motor organs also. The vocal organ utters only present sounds, but not past or future ones. The hands can grasp only the present jars, but not the past or future ones. The feet can walk upon only the present road, but not upon past or future ones. The excretive and generative organs can perform their functions only at present. The functions of the external organs are confined only to the present time. They cannot carry us forward to the future and backward to the past. For this we have to fall back upon the internal organs. The *manas* assimilates and discriminates the present as well as past and future objects. The *ahamkara* refers the present as well as past and future objects to the unity of the empirical ego. The *buddhi* determines the nature of present, past, and future objects. The internal organs bring us into contact with the past and the future as with the present. Vacaspatimisra refers to it in *Bhamati*. He holds that the immediate past and the immediate future should be included in the present owing to their close proximity to it. He seems to believe in the specious present, which is a meeting point of the present, the past, and the future. And this tract of time is an object of sense-perception.

The Nyaya-Vaisesika believes in only one internal organ or *manas*. What is the difference between the mind and the external senses ? Vatsyayana mentions three points of difference. In the first place, the external sense-organs are material, but the mind is immaterial. The mind is not material, since it is not of the nature of an effect, and so does not possess any quality of matter. In the second place, the external senses apprehend only a limited number of objects (*myatavisaya*) but the mind apprehends all objects (*sarvavisaya*). For instance, colours, sounds, tastes, odours, and touch are apprehended by the visual organ, the auditory organ, the gustatory organ, the olfactory organ, and the tactual organ respectively. But all these are apprehended by the mind. It guides all the external senses in the apprehension of their objects and it directly apprehends pleasure, pain, and the like. Vyasa also holds that the *manas* apprehends all objects (*sarvartha*). In the third place, the external senses are of the nature of sense-organs owing to the fact that they are endued with the same qualities as are apprehended by them. For instance, the olfactory organ is endued with the quality of odour, and consequently it can apprehend odour. The visual organ can apprehend colour because it is endued with the quality of colour. The gustatory organ is endued with the quality of taste, and so it can apprehend taste. The auditory organ is endued with the quality of sound, and so it can apprehend sound. And the tactual organ can apprehend touch because it is endued with the quality of touch. But the mind is not endued with the qualities of pleasure, pain, etc., which are apprehended by the mind.

Udyotkara recognizes only the second point of difference between the mind and the external sense-organs. He rejects the other two points of difference. Vatsyayana holds that the external sense-organs are material, but the mind is immaterial. But this is not right. In fact, the mind is neither material nor immaterial; materiality and immateriality are properties of products : what is produced out of matter is material, and what is produced not out of matter, but out of something else is immaterial. As a matter of fact, however, the mind is not a product at all, and as such it can be neither material nor immaterial. Moreover, the auditory organ, which is an external sense-organ, is not material, since it is not a product of matter, but *akasa* itself. So the auditory organ also is neither material nor Immaterial.

But this objection of Udyotkara is based on a misconception of the meaning of the word "material". It may mean either a product of matter (*bhutajanya*) or of the nature of matter (*bhutatmaka*). In the latter sense, the auditory organ also is material, since it is of the nature of *akasa* (ether), though it is not a product of it. In the former sense, all the other sense-organs are material. The tactual organ is a product of air; the visual organ is a product of light; the olfactory organ is a product of earth; and the gustatory organ is a product of water.

Further, Vatsyayana holds that the external senses are sense-organs because they are endued with certain distinctive qualities, but the mind is a sense-organ without being endued with any specific quality. But Udyotkara disputes this point also. For the auditory organ also does not, through its own quality of sound, apprehend a sound exterior to itself, as the other external senses do. For instance, the olfactory organ apprehends an odour exterior to itself, through the odour inherent in itself. But the auditory organ apprehends a sound which is not exterior to itself, but which is actually produced within the ear itself. Hence, Udyotkara concludes that there is only one point of difference between the mind and the external sense-organs; the external senses can apprehend only certain specific objects, but the mind can apprehend all objects. And it is proved by the following reasons. First, the mind is the substratum of the conjunction with the condition of recollection. Second, it is the substratum of the conjunction which brings about the cognition of pleasure and the like. And third, it presides over all other sense-organs.

**Are the External Sense-organs Prapyakari or Aprapyakari ?**

The Nyaya-Vaisesika, the Mimamsaka, the Samkhya, and the Vedantist hold that all the sense-organs are *prapyakari;* they apprehend their objects when they come in direct contact with them. This doctrine is called the doctrine of *prapyakarita*. But the Buddhist holds that the visual organ and the auditory organ are *aprapyakari;* they apprehend their objects at a distance without coming in contact with them. All the other sense-organs are *prapyakari;* they apprehend their objects when they come in contact with them. The Jaina holds that only the visual organ is *aprapyakari,* it apprehends its object at a distance with the help of light without getting at it.

***The Buddhist***

According to the Buddhist, the visual organ is the eyeball or the pupil of the eye (*golaka*), and it can apprehend its object without coming in direct contact with it, because the eyeball can never go out of its socket to the object existing at a distance. According to the Nyaya-Vaisesika, on the other hand, all the sense-organs are *prapyakari,* they can apprehend their objects only when they come in direct contact with them. Thus the visual organ cannot apprehend its object without coming in direct contact with it. The Nyaya-Vaisesika holds that the visual organ is not the eyeball or the pupil of the eye; it is the seat (*golaka* or *adhisthana*) of the visual organ which is of the nature of light (*tejas*); and this ray of light goes out of the pupil to the object at a distance and comes in direct contact with it.

The Buddhist offers the following criticism of the Nyaya-Vaisesika doctrine of *prapyakarita*:

1. Firstly, the sense-organs are nothing but end-organs (*golaka*) which are within the range of perception. They are not mysterious entities behind these peripheral organs. So the visual organ is nothing but the pupil of the eye through which we see visible objects. And the pupil can never go out of the eye to the object, and come in direct contact with it.
2. Secondly, the visual organ cannot come in direct contact with

its object in order to apprehend it, for in that case it would not be able to apprehend an object bigger than itself. But, as a matter of fact, the visual organ can apprehend vast objects like mountains and the like.

3. Thirdly, the visual organ apprehends the branches of a tree and the moon at the same time; it takes the same length of time to apprehend these objects though they are at different distances. If the eye goes out to its object in order to apprehend it, than it must take less time to apprehend a near object, and more time to apprehend a distant object. But, in fact, the eye apprehends the branches of a tree and the moon at the same time, it does not take more time to apprehend the moon than to apprehend the branches; just on opening our eyes we see both the objects at the same time.
4. Fourthly, the eye cannot go out to its object; for if it could go out to its object of apprehension, it would never be able to apprehend objects hidden behind glass, mica, etc., as it would be obstructed by them.

Hence, the Buddhist concludes that the visual organ can never go out to its object to apprehend it; it apprehends its object from a distance without getting at it.

### *The Nyaya-Vaisesika*

Udayana criticizes the above arguments of the Buddhist in *Kiranavali* as follows :

1. Firstly, what apprehends or manifests an object must come in direct contact with it. A lamp manifests an object only because the light comes in direct contact with it. The visual organ is of the nature of light, and so the ray of light must go out of the pupil to the object in order to apprehend it.
2. Secondly, the light of the visual organ issues out of the pupil, and spreads out, and thus can cover a vast object. Hence the field of vision is not co-extensive with the eyeball or the pupil of the eye.
3. Thirdly, it is wrong to argue that a near object and a distant object can be perceived through the visual organ in the same space of time. There must be some difference in the moments

of time required in the apprehension of the two objects, though it is not distinctly felt by us. Light is an extremely light substance, and its motion is inconceivably swift. So even the distant moon is seen just on opening the eyes. Some hold that the light of the visual organ, issuing out of the pupil, becomes blended with the external light, and thus comes in contact with far and near objects simultaneously, so that the eye can apprehend the branches and the moon at the same time. But this is not a correct explanation. On this hypothesis, the visual organ would be able to apprehend those objects which are hidden from our view, e.g. objects behind our back. But it can never apprehend these objects.

4. Fourthly, glass, mica, etc., are transparent by their very nature: and so they cannot obstruct the passage of light. Hence the light of the visual organ can penetrate these substances and apprehend objects hidden behind them. Therefore, the visual organ must be supposed to go out to its object and come in direct contact with it. The Nyaya-Vaisesika does not regard the auditory organ as moving out to sounds, which are held to travel to the ear; either sounds reach the ear in concentric circles of waves like the waves of water or they shoot out in all directions like the filaments of a *kadamba*.

### *The Samkhya*

The Samkhya also holds that the sense-organs are *prapyakari*: they get at their objects in order to apprehend them. All schools of philosophers admit that the organs of touch, taste, and smell come in direct contact with their objects. The Nyaya-Vaisesika holds that the visual organ moves out to its objects, but the auditory organ does not. The Samkhya differs from the Nyaya-Vaisesika in holding that the sense-organs come in contact with their objects through their *vrttis* or functions, and the auditory organ also moves out to sounds through its *vrtti* like the visual organ.

The Buddhists argue that the visual organ does not move out to its object, since we see objects through glass, mica, and crystal; and the auditory organ does not move out to its objects, since we hear sounds at a distance. The Samkhya refutes this view. Kapila urges that the sense-organs do not apprehend objects which they do not reach, because of their not reaching, or because they would reach everything. Aniruddha explains this argument. The sense-organs do not manifest those objects which they do not reach, because they have the nature of manifesting only what they reach, or come in contact with. The visual organ goes out to objects hidden by glass, mica, and crystal in the form of *vrtti*; these substances do not obstruct the passage of the *vrtti* on account of their transparency. The auditory organ is connected with sound by means of its *vrtti* or function, which moves out to it. It does not apprehend sound at a distance without reaching out to it. The sense-organs apprehend objects at a distance by means of their *vrttis*. If it is argued that the sense-organs do not apprehend objects at a distance because they do not reach out to them, as in the case of hidden objects, then it may be pointed out that this disability of the sense-organs (i.e. their not moving out to their objects) would affect not only the cognitions of distant and hidden objects but also those of unhidden objects as well, since the disability must operate equally in both the cases. But, in fact, the cognitions of unhidden objects are never so affected. Therefore, it cannot be maintained that the sense-organs do not reach out to their objects. If, on the other hand, it is argued that the sense-organs apprehend objects even without reaching out to them, then they would apprehend everything which exists within the universe, since there is no distinction in this respect with regard to all things. Hence the Samkhya concludes that all sense-organs get at their objects.

The Samkhya holds with the Nyaya-Vaisesika that the visual organ moves out to its object. But it does not hold like it that the visual organ is made up of light, though it has the power of gliding, since the phenomenon of movement of the visual organ can be explained by its *vrtti* or function. Aniruddha says that the fact that the visual organ moves out to distant objects, like light, and manifests them, leads to the misconception that it is made up of light. But, in reality, the visual organ is related to its objects through its *vrtti* or function. Vijnanabhiksu says that the visual organ, though not made up of light, shoots out to distant objects like the sun by means of its particular modification called *vrtti* without altogether leaving the body, even as the vital air (*prana*) moves out from the tip of the nose up to a certain distance by means of its particular modification called vitalizing without altogether leaving the body.

### The Mimamsaka

Kumarila criticizes the Buddhist and Samkhya theories of auditory perception. The Buddhist holds that the auditory organ apprehends sounds without coming in contact with them. Kumarila contends that in that case all sounds near and distant would be equally perceptible, since they are equal in having no contact with the auditory organ. In that case, both near and distant sounds could be either perceived or unperceived; there would be no sequence in the perception of sounds, near sounds being first perceived and then distant sounds; and sounds coming from different distances would not have different degrees of intensity. This shows that sounds must come in contact with the auditory organ in order to be perceived.

The Samkhya holds that the auditory organ moves out to the region where sounds are produced through the *vrtti*. Kumarila urges that the Samkhya doctrine involves the assumption of two imperceptible things. The so-called *vrtti* or function of the auditory organ is imperceptible, and the movement of the *vrtti* also is imperceptible. It is difficult to conceive how a modification is produced in the auditory organ by a distant sound. The Samkhya may argue that the auditory organ moves out to distant sounds, owing to its all-pervading nature, being a product of all-pervading *ahamkara*. Kumarila urges that this fact would apply equally well to the case of very distant sounds, and hence all sounds would be heard equally well. Moreover, the function of the auditory organ, being immaterial, could not be obstructed by any material obstacles, and hence even intercepted sounds would be heard. Thus the Samkhya theory is untenable. Kumarila holds that sound travels through the air and reaches the space in the ear, and then produces a modification (*samskara*) in it. This theory explains many facts about auditory perception. Sounds are carried to the ear through the air. So when the air is intercepted by obstacles sounds cannot be heard. The air moves along in a certain order of sequence, and hence, we first hear sounds near at hand, and then distant sounds, and near sounds are intense and distant sounds are faint.

### The Vedantist

The Samkarite also holds that the sense-organs are *prapyakari*: they apprehend their objects when they come in contact with them.

Of the five external senses, the olfactory organ, the gustatory organ, and the tactual organ apprehend their objects, remaining in their seats. But the visual organ and the auditory organ go out to their appropriate objects and apprehend them. Even the auditory organ can move outward to sounds because it is the all-pervading ether limited by the ear-hole. Just as the visual organ, which is of the nature of light and very transparent, can move outward to its object and apprehend it, so the auditory organ also, which is of the nature of ether, can move out to its object and apprehend it.

The Samkarite differs from the Nyaya-Vaisesika in his view of the nature of the auditory organ. The Nyaya-Vaisesika holds that a sound is produced somewhere in space and spreads in concentric circles like the waves of water and ultimately strikes the drum of the ear, and thus produces the auditory perception of sound. But the Samkarite urges that if this were the case, we would apprehend the sound as in the ear, and not in the place in which it is generated. But, in fact, we always perceive a sound in such a form as "I hear a sound there" and "not in the ear". This conclusively proves that the auditory organ also, like the visual organ, moves out to the object and apprehends it. The Samkarite thinks that it is unnecessary to assume an infinite series of sounds coming from the original place in concentric or spherical circles to the auditory organ to produce the auditory perception of the original sound. The Law of Parsimony requires that there must be a connection between the sound produced somewhere in space and the auditory organ. And the connection can be easily established by supposing that it is the auditory organ itself that goes outward to the sound and apprehends it. In fact, it is the translucent *antahkarana* (internal organ) which streams out through the orifices of the visual organ and the auditory organ and gets at visible objects and sounds. The Ramanujist also holds the same view. The Vedantists agree with the Samkhya on this point.

## Are the External Sense-organs Physical (*bhautika*) or Psychical (*ahamkarika*) ?

The Nyaya-Vaisesika holds that the external sense-organs are material (*bhautika*) in nature. But the Samkhya disputes this view on the following grounds :

1. In the first place, the sense-organs are *prapyakari;* they

apprehend their objects only when they come in contact with them. If the sense-organs were products of gross matter, they could never go out to distant objects and apprehend them. But, as a matter of fact, some sense-organs (e.g. the visual organ) can apprehend distant objects, and hence they must reach out to them. And they can move out to distant objects if they are products of *ahamkara* (egoism) and as such capable of expansion. So the Samkhya concludes that the sense-organs are psychical, being products of *ahamkara,* and reach out to distant objects in the form of functions (*vrtti*) which are modified into the forms of these objects.

2. In the second place, if the sense-organs were material they would apprehend only those objects which are of their size. But, as a matter of fact, they can apprehend objects which are larger or smaller than themselves. This proves that the sense-organs are not products of matter but of *ahamkara*.
3. In the third place, material objects like lamps, which manifest other objects, also manifest themselves. So, if the sense-organs were material they would be able to manifest not only other objects but also their own nature. But they cannot manifest themselves; the sense-organs are not objects of sense-perception. So they are not material. They are products of *ahamkara*. The Ramanujist also agrees with this view.

Jayanta Bhatta refutes these arguments as follows :

1. The first argument is based on a false assumption. The Nyaya-Vaisesika agrees with the Samkhya in holding that the sense-organs are *prapyakari*; they come in contact with their objects in order to apprehend them. But the sense-organs are not the peripheral organs or the physical seats of eyes, etc. For example, the visual organ is not the pupil but the ray of light (*tejas*) which has its seat in the pupil. And the ray of light can easily stretch out to a distant object and apprehend it, since its motion is extremely swift. So the sense-organs need not necessarily be psychical (*ahamkarika*) in order to get at their objects; they may be material (*bhautika*) and yet *prapyakari*.
2. The second argument also is without foundation. The sense-organs cannot be said to be psychical (*ahamkarika*) because they can apprehend objects bigger or smaller than themselves.

They can do it even if they are material. For example, the visual organ, which is of the nature of light, can expand and apprehend a larger object. The expansion of an object is not the sign of its psychical character.

3. The third argument also is beside the mark. The different sense-organs apprehend different qualities. Every sense-organ does not apprehend all qualities. The sense-organs can apprehend only those qualities of their objects, which inhere in themselves. For instance, smell inheres in the olfactory organ; so it can apprehend only the smell of an object. But it cannot apprehend its own smell. It is by virtue of its own inherent smell that it can apprehend smell in its object. If the sense-organs were devoid of qualities, they would not be able to apprehend anything at all, and they would cease to be sense-organs. Thus the sense-organs can apprehend other objects but not themselves. Hence the Nyaya-Vaisesika concludes that the sense-organs are material.

### Is there only One Sense-organ ?

Some hold that there is only one sense-organ; it appears to be many owing to the difference of *upadhis* or limitations. Kapila refers to this view and criticizes it. Aniruddha argues that though there is a difference of *upadhis* we must also admit that there is a real difference of powers, and if the difference of powers is real, the plurality of sense-organs also is real. Vijnanabhiksu argues that the theory of one sense-organ performing different functions through diversity of powers amounts to the assumption of a plurality of senseorgans, since these different powers also have the character of sense-organs. Hence there is not one sense-organ only.

### Is the Tactual Organ the only Sense-organ ?

Caraka holds that the organ of touch pervades all the sense-organs. They are modifications of the sense of touch. All the sense-organs apprehend their objects when they come in contact with them, and contact is nothing but touch. Thus the sense of touch is conterminous with all the senses. It is perpetually connected with the mind which presides over all the external senses.

Vacaspatimisra refers a similar doctrine to some Samkhyas who hold that there are seven sense-organs : the tactual organ which is the only organ of knowledge and capable of apprehending various objects like colour, etc., five organs of action, and the mind (*manas*).

Gautama also refers to the doctrine that the sense of touch is the only sense-organ and criticizes it. Vatsyayana, Udyotkara, and others elaborate his arguments. Some hold that the sense of touch is the only sense-organ, since all the seats (*adhisthana*) of sense-organs are pervaded by the tactual organ, so that in the presence of the sense of touch there is perception and in its absence there is no perception at all. So the tactual organ is the only sense-organ. This doctrine cannot be maintained on the following grounds.

It contradicts the facts of actual experience. If the tactual organ were the only sense-organ it would be able to apprehend all sensible objects, so that colour would be perceived by the blind, sound by the deaf, and so forth. But, as a matter of fact, the blind can never see colour, the deaf can never hear sound, and so on. Hence the tactual organ is not the only sense-organ.

But it may be urged that the various sense-organs are only special parts of the tactual organ, which is the only sense-organ. The different kinds of sensible objects are perceived through its different parts, so that when these particular parts are destroyed we cannot perceive the corresponding objects. The blind fail to see colours because the particular part of the tactual organ which was located in the eye and was the means of colour-perception has been destroyed. The deaf cannot hear sounds because the particular part of the tactual organ which was located in the ear-hole and was the means of sound perception has been destroyed.

This view is self-contradictory. If the perception of colours, sounds, etc., is held to be brought about by different parts of the tactual organ, then it contradicts the doctrine that the tactual organ is the only sense-organ. Are the so-called special parts of the tactual organ of the nature of sense-organs or not ? If they are, then there are many sense-organs, and the doctrine of a single sense-organ falls to the ground. If they are not, then colours, sounds, etc., cannot be regarded as perceptible by the senses. The hypothesis of a single sense-organ with different parts endowed with different powers amounts to the assumption of many sense-organs.

Further, the tactual organ cannot be regarded as the only sense-organ because, in that case, there would be simultaneous perception of colour, sound, and the like. The soul would come in contact with the mind, the mind with the single sense of touch, and the tactual organ with colour, sound, etc. Thus there would be simultaneous perception of them all. But it is not a fact of experience. Colour, sound, etc., are never perceived at the same time. Hence there is not a single sense-organ which apprehends all kinds of sensible objects,

Moreover, the doctrine of a single sense-organ involves a contradiction. The tactual organ is *prapyakari;* it can apprehend only those objects which comes in contact with it; it cannot apprehend distant objects. But colour and sound can be perceived from a great distance. How, then, can they be perceived through the tactual organ? If they are perceived through it though it does not come in contact with them, it should apprehend touch also without coming in contact with it. Or if the tactual organ can apprehend touch when it comes in contact with it, it should apprehend colour and sound also when it comes in contact with them. It should not operate on touch, colour, and sound in different ways.

But it may be argued that the tactual organ is *prapyakari* in apprehending touch, and *aprapyakan* in apprehending colour and sound. If the tactual organ can apprehend colour without coming in contact with it, it should perceive hidden as well as unhidden colours, which is not a fact; and perception of colour near at hand and non-perception of colour at a distance would remain unexplained. Moreover, if the sense of touch is the only sense-organ, its derangement or destruction would make all perception impossible. But, in fact, we find that though one sense-organ is deranged or destroyed, we can perceive through the other sense-organs. Hence there is not a single sense of touch.

# 2

# Indeterminate Perception and Determinate Perception

## Introduction

The Indian thinkers generally recognize two distinct stages of perception, indeterminate (*nirvikalpa*) and determinate (*savikalpa*). The former is the immediate apprehension of the mere form of an object, while the latter is the mediate perception of the object with its different properties and their relations to one another. The former is an undifferentiated and non-relational mode of consciousness devoid of assimilation and discrimination, analysis and synthesis. The latter is a differentiated and relational mode of consciousness involving assimilation and discrimination, analysis and synthesis. The former is purely sensory and presentative, while the latter is presentative-representative. The former is dumb and inarticulate free from verbal images. The latter is vocal and articulate dressed in the garb of verbal images. The former is abstract and indeterminate, while the latter is concrete and determinate. The former is what William James calls "knowledge of acquaintance" and the latter is what he calls "knowledge-about".

The distinction between indeterminate perception and determinate perception has for centuries engaged the attention of all schools of Indian thinkers, from both the psychological and epistemological points of view. Here we shall attempt a psychological analysis of these two stages of perception from the Indian standpoints.

Though almost all the systems of Indian thought recognize the existence of indeterminate perception and determinate perception, they hold slightly different views about the nature of these two types of perception.

Samkara holds that indeterminate perception apprehends the mere "Being"; it can apprehend neither an individual object nor its properties; it is absolutely indeterminate. The Buddhist holds that perception is always indeterminate; there is no determinate perception; the so-called determinate perception is not perceptual in character. Indeterminate perception apprehends the specific individuality of an object (*svalaksana*) devoid of its generic character and other qualifications. Kumarila, the founder of the Bhatta school of Mimamsa, holds that indeterminate perception apprehends the individual (*vyakti*), which is the substrate of its generic character (*samanya*) and specific character (*visesa*). Prabhakara, the founder of another school of Mimamsa, holds that indeterminate perception apprehends both the generic character and the specific character of its object as an undistinguishable mass. Parthasarathimisra, a follower of Kumarila, holds that indeterminate perception is the immediate apprehension of an object with its multiform properties such as generality, substantiality, quality, action, and name, but not as related to each other. Vacaspatimisra represents the Samkhya view of indeterminate perception as the simple apprehension of an object, pure and simple, unqualified by its properties. The earlier Vaisesikas hold that indeterminate perception is the immediate cognition of the generic and specific characters of its object undifferentiated from each other. The earlier Naiyayikas hold that there is no difference between indeterminate perception and determinate perception except that the former does not apprehend the name of its object. Both of them apprehend substantiality, generality, action, and quality. The later Nyaya-Vaisesika holds that indeterminate perception apprehends an object and its properties as unrelated to each other. The neo-Samkarite also holds that indeterminate perception is the non-relational apprehension of an object which is not necessarily sensuous in character. Ramanuja holds a different view. He regards indeterminate perception as relational apprehension which apprehends the first individual of a class with its generic character in the shape of a structure (*samsthana*) and also its relation to the individual. Thus most of the schools of Indian philosophers admit the existence of indeterminate perception, though they hold different views as to its nature and object. But Madhva and Vallabha, the founders of minor schools of Vedanta, deny the existence of indeterminate perception. They regard all perception as determinate. The Sabdikas also hold the same view. They hold that there can be no thought without language, and hence no nameless, indeterminate perception. No one denies the existence of determinate perception; only the Buddhist holds that the so-called determinate perception is not perceptual in character. We shall consider these different views in detail.

### *Samkara*

According to Samkara, indeterminate perception cannot apprehend any qualifications whatsoever. It cannot apprehend even an object (e.g. mere jar, *ghata*) and its generic nature (e.g. mere *jarness, ghatatva*) unrelated to each other, as some hold for the apprehension of these qualifications presupposes the apprehension of their difference, and difference means mutual non-existence, which is not apprehended even by determinate perception. So it can never be apprehended by indeterminate perception. Non-existence is apprehended by nonperception (*anupalabdhi*). Hence indeterminate perception apprehends the mere undifferenced "Being" (*satta*), which is identical with universal consciousness. Thus Samkara regards indeterminate perception as absolutely indeterminate or devoid of all determinations. It neither apprehends an individual object nor its qualities; it merely apprehends "Being" or existence (*sanmatravisayam*).

### *The Buddhist*

Some hold that indeterminate perception apprehends an object (*visesya*) and its qualifications (*visesana*) but not their relations to each other. But the Buddhist holds that indeterminate perception does not at all apprehend the qualifications of its object, viz. generality, substantiality, quality, action, and name. They are the forms of thought (*vikalpa*). Perception is always presentative and hence indeterminate; it is free from all forms and determinations. It merely apprehends the specific individuality of its object (*svalaksana*) devoid of all qualifications. The so-called determinate perception is not perceptual in character, since it is a presentative-representative process and not produced by peripheral stimulation alone. The recollection of a name intervenes between the purely sensory presentation of an object and the determinate cognition of it as qualified by its name. So the determinate cognition of a qualified object cannot be regarded as a perceptual process.

Thus, the Buddhist agrees with Samkara in holding that indeterminate perception cannot apprehend the qualifications of its object. But he differs from Samkara in so far as he holds that indeterminate perception does not apprehend the mere "Being" but the specific individuality of an object. Hence the indeterminate perception of the Buddhist is more determinate than that of Samkara.

### *The Mimamsaka*

Kumarila holds that immediately after peripheral stimulation there is an undefined and indeterminate perception of an object, pure and simple, similar to the simple apprehension of a baby or a dumb person. It arises purely out of the object itself (*suddhavastuja*). It apprehends only an individual object which is the substratum of generic and specific characters. Even in indeterminate perception there is the apprehension of an object in its two-fold aspect, generic and specific; but there is no distinct apprehension of the generic character as generic, and the specific character as specific. But is it not self-contradictory to say that indeterminate perception apprehends an object, in its two-fold aspect, generic and specific, but yet it cannot apprehend its generic character as generic and specific character as specific ? Kumarila points out that there is no contradiction here. The generic character is common to many individuals. The specific character is peculiar to one individual. The former is inclusive, and the latter is exclusive. Inclusiveness of the generic character and exclusiveness of the specific character are not apprehended by indeterminate perception, since it apprehends only one individual. It cannot apprehend its object as specific, since it cannot distinguish it from other objects; nor can it apprehend its object as generic, since it cannot assimilate it to other objects. It apprehends an object, pure and simple, not as qualified by its generic and specific characters. They qualify the object of indeterminate perception, which is their substratum, but they are not apprehended by it as qualifying its object. All that Kumarila means by mentioning the two-fold aspect of the object of indeterminate perception is to define the character of the object, and to emphasize that its object has a two-fold aspect, generic and specific.

Prabhakara holds that indeterminate perception apprehends not merely the individual object, which is the substrate of its generic and specific characters, but it apprehends also the generic and specific characters of its object without apprehending their distinction. It is not an object of inference; it is felt as perception. The Buddhist is wrong in holding that indeterminate perception apprehends merely the specific individuality (*svalaksana*) since we are distinctly conscious of the generic character (*jati*) in it. Samkara also is wrong in holding that it apprehends merely the generic character (*samanyamatra*), since we are distinctly conscious of the specific character in it. It apprehends the bare nature (*svariipamatra*) of the generic character or community and the specific character or particularity but not their distinction from each other. Community (*samanya*) is inclusive (*anugata*) in character; it is common to many individuals; and particularity (*visesa*) is exclusive (*vyavrtta*) in character; it is confined to a particular individual. The former is the ground of assimilation, and the latter of discrimination. Indeterminate perception is the immediate apprehension of an object with its generic and specific characters. But since it is devoid of assimilation and discrimination it cannot distinguish the two from each other and apprehend the object as belonging to a definite class. Indeterminate perception does not involve assimilation, discrimination, recollection, and recognition.

But how is it that the generic character and the specific character of an object are apprehended by indeterminate perception, but not their distinction ? Prabhakara replies that the apprehension of two different objects does not necessarily imply the apprehension of their difference; the apprehension of the difference between two objects involves an additional factor, viz. the apprehension of the distinctive characters of both these objects. Though indeterminate perception apprehends both the generic and specific characters of its object, it cannot apprehend the difference between the two, because, having a single individual for its object, it cannot apprehend their distinctive characters, viz. inclusiveness and exclusiveness respectively.

But determinate perception apprehends the generic character of its object as generic and its specific character as specific, because it assimilates its object to other like objects and distinguishes it from other unlike objects. But it may be objected that in determinate perception also only one individual object is present to a sense-organ; no other object is present. Hence determinate perception also cannot apprehend the generic character as generic and the specific character as specific, since it presupposes an apprehension of other like and unlike objects which are not present to the sense-organ. Prabhakara replies that the sense-organs, being material and unconscious, cannot apprehend objects; nor can cognitions by themselves apprehend objects; it is the self which apprehends all that can be apprehended. And after indeterminate perception of an object the self remembers some other objects of the same class, from which it differs in some respects, and which it resembles in others, by reviving the subconscious impressions of previous perceptions of these objects. And thus the self comes to have a determinate perception of an object as belonging to a particular class. Indeterminate perception apprehends the bare nature of the generic and specific characters but not the difference between them. But determinate perception distinguishes them from each other and apprehends its object as qualified by them. It apprehends the qualified object and the qualifying properties in the subject-predicate relation.

Parthasarathimisra, a follower of Kumarila, holds a slightly different view. Kumarila holds that indeterminate perception apprehends an individual object (*vyakti*) in which the generic character (*samanya*) and the specific character (*visesa*) subsist. Prabhakara holds that indeterminate perception apprehends both the generic character and the specific character of its object but not their distinction from each other. Parthasarathimisra holds that indeterminate perception is an undifferentiated and non-relational apprehension of an object with its multiple forms and properties, viz. genus, substance, quality, action, and name. Determinate perception breaks up this undifferentiated sensory matrix into its component factors, viz. the qualified object and its qualifying properties, differentiates them from and relates them to each other, and integrates them into the unity of a determinate percept. It apprehends an object as belonging to a particular class (e.g. "this is a cow"), as being qualified by a particular substance (e.g. "this is with a staff"), as being endowed with a particular quality (e.g. "this is white"), as doing a particular action (e.g. "this is going"), and as bearing a particular name (e.g. "this is *Dittha*").

Gaga Bhatta also holds a similar view. He defines indeterminate perception as the apprehension of an object and its properties as unrelated to each other. For instance, it apprehends a jar (*ghata*) and its generic character (*ghatatva*), but not as related to each other. It does not apprehend its object as a qualified substance and its generic character as its qualifying property. Just after the contact of an object with a sense-organ there is the apprehension of the mere individual object in which the generic character and the specific character are not yet differentiated from each other.

Gaga Bhatta's view resembles that of Visvanatha, who holds that indeterminate perception apprehends an object (*ghata*) and its generic character (*ghatatva*) as unrelated to each other. It also resembles the view of Prabhakara, who holds that indeterminate perception apprehends an object in which the generic character (*samanya*) and the specific character (*visesa*) are not distinguished from each other.

Gaga Bhatta holds that indeterminate perception is an object of perception. There is a distinct apprehension that there is something. Some hold that indeterminate perception is an object of inference. It is inferred from determinate perception of a qualified object, which presupposes indeterminate perception of its qualifying properties. Others hold that there is no need of assuming the existence of indeterminate perception to account for determinate perception. The intercourse of an object and its qualifications with the sense-organs is the condition of determinate perception. Indeterminate perception of qualifications is not the condition of determinate perception of a qualified object. Gaga Bhatta holds that indeterminate perception is not an object of inference. It is not merely a logical stage in the development of perception. It is a distinct psychological process. It apprehends an undifferentiated mass of many properties which are not related to the object in the subject-predicate relation.

Gaga Bhatta defines determinate perception as the apprehension of a qualified object, its qualifications, and the relation between the two. This definition closely resembles that of Nilakantha. Gaga Bhatta accepts the neo-Naiyayika definition of determinate perception. Like Parthasarathimisra, he divides determinate perception into five kinds, according as it apprehends an object as qualified by a genus, a substance, an attribute, an action, and a name.

***The Samkhya***

Aniruddha holds that perception is of two kinds, indeterminate and determinate. The Buddhists do not recognize determinate perception. They define perception as a non-erroneous cognition free from imagination (*kalpana*). Imagination is the apprehension of an object as associated with name, class, and other *vikalpas* or categories. And the so-called determinate perception involves such factors of imagination. So it cannot be regarded as perception. Perception is entirely free from imagination. Aniruddha criticizes the Buddhist theory of perception. He urges that the Buddhist definition of perception is wrong. Perception is direct and immediate apprehension of an object. It is produced by conditions of direct and immediate knowledge, not vitiated by any defect. And this direct apprehension or perception is either indeterminate or determinate. Indeterminate perception is the immediate apprehension of an object free from all associations of name, class, and the like. It is purely presentative in character. It is free from representative elements. But determinate perception is a presentative-representative process. It involves the recollection of name, class, etc., of the object, which were perceived in the past and are brought back to consciousness by the law of similarity. The perception of an object reminds us of its name heard in the past; it reminds us of the class to which it belongs, and so on. And this perception of an object as having a particular name, and belonging to a particular class, is called by a special name, viz. determinate perception because it contains an additional factor of representation of name and class.

The Buddhists may argue that the so-called determinate perception involves an element of representation, and so cannot be regarded as perception. But Aniruddha contends that the representative element does no harm to the conditions of perception, nor does it in anyway vitiate the perceptual character of the cognition. The name of an object revived in memory by the perception of it does not vitiate the perceptual character of the determinate cognition. A name is an arbitrary mark of an object. It cannot obscure its intrinsic character. So the determinate perception of an object as bearing a particular name can apprehend its real nature, though it involves the recollection of its name.

Vacaspatimisra also recognizes the distinction between

indeterminate and determinate perception. He defines indeterminate perception as the first act of immediate cognition which apprehends an object, pure and simple, devoid of the relationship between the qualified object and its qualifications. And he defines determinate perception as the definite cognition of an object as qualified by its generic character, specific character, and other properties. Indeterminate perception is the function of the external senses ; they give us a non-relational apprehension of an object unqualified by its properties. Determinate perception is the function of *manas* or the central sensory. It distinguishes the generic character from the specific character, and apprehends its object as qualified by them. The external senses are the organs of indeterminate perception, while manas is the organ of determinate perception. The external senses apprehend an object as merely "this", not as "like this" or "unlike this". Assimilation and discrimination which are involved in determinate perception are the functions of manas.

Vijnanabhiksu also distinguishes between indeterminate and determinate perception. But his view is slightly different from that of Vacaspati. Vacaspati holds that we have indeterminate perception through the external senses, which give us only an unconnected mass of presentations and then we have determinate perception through the internal organ of manas which converts it into a concrete object of perception by assimilation and discrimination. Vijnanabhiksu, on the other hand, holds that we have both indeterminate and determinate perception through the external senses. *Manas* does not play any part in determinate perception. Up to the stage of determinate perception the external senses do everything. Assimilation and discrimination, analysis and synthesis are not the functions of *manas* but of the external senses. Vijnanabhiksu cites the authority of Vyasa, who holds that we perceive an object as endued with generic and specific characters (*samanyavisesatma*) through the external senses. "Bhiksu thinks that the senses can directly perceive the determinate qualities of things without any intervention of *manas* whereas Vacaspati ascribes to manas the power of arranging the sense-data in a definite order and of making the indeterminate sense-data determinate." Vacaspati seems to be in the right. We can hardly ascribe the interpretative processes of assimilation and discrimination to the external senses. They are essentially the functions of *manas*.

## *The Vaisesikas*

Prasastapada holds that just after the intercourse of an object with a sense-organ there is immediate apprehension of the mere form of the object (*svarupamatra*). This is indeterminate perception. It apprehends an object with its generic and specific characters, but does not distinguish them from each other. It is the primal stage of perception. It is not the result of any other prior cognition. It is not of the nature of resultant cognition.

Sridhara clearly brings out the characteristics of indeterminate perception. It is the immediate apprehension of the mere form of an object, which is purely a presentative process, free from all determinations and representative elements. It apprehends both the generic character and the specific character of its object as an indistinguishable mass. It does not analyse its object into its component qualities, generic and specific, distinguish them from each other, and combine them together by a synthetic act of apperception. It apprehends its object with its generic and specific characters, but does not apprehend the generic character as generic and the specific character as specific, since it apprehends a single individual belonging to a class, and cannot therefore assimilate it to other like objects, and distinguish it from other unlike objects. Thus, both generic and specific characters are apprehended by indeterminate perception, but they are not differentiated from each other and recognized as such. It is only at the stage of determinate perception that the generic and specific characters are distinguished from each other, and the object is recognized as belonging to a definite class. If the generic and specific characters were not apprehended by indeterminate perception, they could not be distinguished from each other by determinate perception. Hence it cannot be denied that indeterminate perception apprehends both common and distinctive features of an object. But it cannot recognize them as such because it is a purely presentative process, and consequently cannot revive the subconscious impressions of other individuals perceived in the past. It cannot recognize the generic character of its object as common to the whole class, and its distinctive characters as peculiar to it alone, which distinguish it from all other objects of the same class. Thus Sridhara's view is similar to that of Prabhakara.

Sivaditya agrees with Prasastapada and Sridhara in his view on the nature of indeterminate and determinate perception. He defines the former as the apprehension of the bare nature of an object (*vastusvarupamatra*)) and the latter as the apprehension of an object as qualified by its properties (*visista*). Samkara Misra also agrees with Sridhara. In his view of indeterminate and determinate perception, he holds that in the perception of substances, qualities, and actions there is a determinate consciousness of these individual objects as qualified by their generic characters. And this determinate apprehension presupposes an indeterminate apprehension of the individual objects which are qualified and the generic characters which qualify them. And this indeterminate apprehension is produced by the intercourse of the individual objects (*visesa*) and their generic characters (*samanya*) with the sense-organs. This is called indeterminate perception. It apprehends both common characters (*samanya*) and individual characters (*visesa*) of its object but not the relation between them. It is only at the stage of determinate perception that this relation is apprehended, and a particular substance, quality, or action is recognized as "this is a substance", "this is a quality", or "this is an action". Determinate perception is due to three causes, viz, indeterminate perception of the qualifying properties, intercourse of the qualified object with a sense-organ, and non-apprehension of the absence of connection between the qualified object and its qualifying properties. Thus Samkara misras view is substantially the same as that of Srldhara.

### *The Naiyayikas*

Vatsyayana recognizes a nameless perception which may be called indeterminate perception. An object may be perceived even without an apprehension of its name. When an object is perceived along with its name and their relation to each other it is said to be apprehended by determinate perception. Determinate perception has the same object as indeterminate perception, but it differs from the latter in apprehending an additional factor, viz. the name of its object revived in memory by association. The former is mixed up with the verbal image of the name of its object, while the latter is free from verbal images.

Jayanta Bhatta discusses the different views of indeterminate perception in the following manner :

1. Some (e.g. *Buddhists*) hold that the object of indeterminate perception is the specific individual (*svalaksana*) as distinct from all other homogeneous and heterogeneous objects.
2. Some (e.g. *Samkara*) hold that the object of indeterminate perception is Being which is the summat genus.
3. Some (e.g. *Sabdikas*) hold that the object of indeterminate perception is the word denoting the object, which constitutes its essential nature.
4. Others hold that the object of indeterminate perception is a multiform object qualified by the different forms of quality, action, substance, genus, etc.

Jayanta Bhatta offers the following criticism of the Buddhist view. If indeterminate perception apprehends only the specific individuality of its object, how do its common features suddenly enter into the determinate cognition ? In fact, the consciousness of generality must be already imbedded in indeterminate perception, which is only brought to relief by determinate perception. The consciousness of the class-character must be implicit in indeterminate perception.

Jayanta Bhatta rejects the Vedantist view also on the following ground. Mere "Being" or existence (*satta*) cannot be regarded as the object of indeterminate perception. For, if it apprehends the mere being or bare existence of its object, how can its particular features be perceived ? The existence of an object can never be perceived apart from its different qualities.

Jayanta Bhatta rejects the Sabdika view also on the ground that indeterminate perception can never apprehend the name of its object, since it presupposes the apprehension of the relation of the object to its name, and indeterminate perception, being of the nature of nonrelational apprehension, can never apprehend any relation. Jayanta's criticism will be given in detail later on.

Jayanta Bhatta rejects the fourth view also. It is curious to hold that indeterminate perception has for its objects all the different qualities taken together, viz. quality, action, substantiality, generality, etc. They do not always exist in an object. Sometimes we perceive generality, sometimes substantiality, sometimes action, sometimes quality, and so on. So the object of indeterminate perception cannot be regarded as a multiform object with all its qualifying properties.

Jayanta Bhatta concludes that the object of indeterminate perception is essentially the same as that of determinate perception, the only difference between them lies in the fact that the former is devoid of all reference to a name and hence free from verbal images, while the latter apprehends the name of its object and is thus mixed up with verbal images. Both the types of perception apprehend generality, substantiality, quality, and action. But the former is nameless, dumb, and inarticulate, while the latter is vocal and articulate. Thus determinate perception differs from indeterminate perception only in apprehending the name of its object.

Bhasarvajna defines indeterminate perception as apprehension of the bare nature of an object immediately after peripheral stimulation. Thus he agrees with Prasastapada and Sivaditya. Vasudeva points out that immediately after the intercourse of an object with a sense-organ there is no recollection of its relation to a name and other qualifications. So there is only an immediate apprehension of the mere existence of the object apart from its qualities. And this is called indeterminate perception. Jayasimhasuri points out that immediately after sense-object-intercourse there is an immediate apprehension of the bare existence of an object, which is free from recollection and cognition of time and special properties. But it may be argued that as soon as there is the sense-object intercourse determinate perception emerges into consciousness and we are not conscious of indeterminate perception arising before determinate perception. So there is no indeterminate perception. But Jayasimhasuri urges that we are not distinctly conscious of indeterminate perception arising before determinate perception in our adult experience because, owing to habit, as soon as indeterminate perception arises determinate perception supervenes and shuts out the former from our view. This is the reason why, in our adult experience, as soon as we perceive that an object exists we perceive what it is. But we are distinctly conscious of indeterminate perception in perceiving an entirely new object, where habit does not convert indeterminate perception into determinate perception at once.

Bhasarvajna defines determinate perception as the apprehension of an object qualified by its qualifications such as name, substance quality, action, genus, and non-existence. The concept of name (*samjna*) enters into such a determinate perception as "this is Devadatta". The concept of substance (*dravya*) enters into such a determinate perception as "the man is with a stick". The concept of quality (*gund*) enters into such a determinate perception as "the cloth is white". The concept of action (*karman*) enters into such a determinate perception as "the man is going". The concept of genus (*samanya*) enters into such a determinate perception as "this is a cow". The concept of non-existence (*abhava*) enters into such a determinate perception as "the ground is without a jar".

Varadaraja also holds that indeterminate perception apprehends an object in itself devoid of all qualifications such as name, class, substance, quality, action, and the like; and determinate perception apprehends an object as qualified by these qualifications.

Vasudeva raises an interesting question. What is the organ of determinate perception ? Is it the external sense-organs or the internal organ of *manas* ? Vasudeva holds that if the same external sense-organ apprehends the qualified object (*visesya*) and its qualifications (*visesana*); then this sense-organ is the organ of determinate perception. But if the qualified object and its qualifications are apprehended by different external sense-organs, then the internal organ or manas should be regarded as the organ of determinate perception. For example, the visual organ is the organ of the determinate perception of a white cloth because it apprehends the cloth as well as its white colour. But the *manas* is the organ of the determinate perception of an object with a name such as "this is Devadatta" because "this" is apprehended by the visual organ which cannot apprehend its name, and the name (Devadatta) is remembered by the manas. The *manas* also is the organ of the determinate perception of a fragrant flower because the flower is apprehended by the visual organ, and its fragrance by the olfactory organ. The manas synthesizes the discrete presentations of the flower and its fragrance given by two different sense-organs into the composite percept of a fragrant flower. This is a type of apperception.

Kesavamisra describes the process of perception as follows. The self comes in contact with the manas. The manas comes in contact with a sense-organ. And the sense-organ comes in contact with an object. The sense-organ can manifest an object when it gets at, and is related to, the object. Then immediately after the sense-object-intercourse there arises an indeterminate perception of an object as "this is something". It is the apprehension of the mere existence of the object devoid of all its qualifications such as name, class, and the like. It is followed by determinate perception. It is the apprehension of the object as qualified by name, class, and other qualifications. It apprehends the relation between the qualified object and the qualifications. It connects them together by the subject-predicate relation. Indeterminate perception is vague and abstract. Determinate perception is definite and concrete. The former is the apprehension of an object as something. The latter is the apprehension of an object as having a certain name, as belonging to a certain class, or as having a certain quality.

Kesavamisra raises an interesting question here. There are three factors in the production of an effect. There is an instrument (*karana*); there is an operation of the instrument (*vyapara*); and there is a result of the instrument (*phala*). When a tree is cut by an axe, the axe is the instrument of cutting; the conjunction of the axe with the tree is the operation of the axe; and the cutting of the tree is the result. So in every act of perception there are three factors. When we have indeterminate perception just after sense object contact, the sense-organ is the instrument (*karana*) of indeterminate perception, the sense-object-contact is the operation (*vyapara*) or intermediate agency, and indeterminate perception is the result (*phala*) of the operation. When we have determinate perception after indeterminate perception, the sense-object-intercourse is the instrument (*karana*), indeterminate perception is the intermediate agency (*vyapara*); and determinate perception is the result (*phala*). When after determinate perception we perceive that the object ought to be accepted, or rejected, or neither accepted nor rejected, indeterminate perception is the instrument (*karana*), determinate perception is the intermediate agency (*vyapara*) and the apprehension of acceptability, rejectability, or neutrality of the object is the result (*phala*).

### *The Neo-Naiyayikas*

Gangesa defines indeterminate perception as the non-relational apprehension of an object free from all associations of name, genus, and the like. Visvanatha elaborates the view of Gangesa. He defines indeterminate perception as the apprehension of an object and its generic character as unrelated to each other immediately after the intercourse of a sense-organ with the object. For instance, immediately after the contact of a jar with the visual organ we cannot perceive it as belonging to the class of jars; we perceive the mere jar (*ghata*) and mere jarness (genus of jar, *ghatatva*) without their mutual connection. It is only by determinate perception that we can apprehend the relation between an object and its generic character, and perceive it as belonging to a particular class. According to Visvanatha, indeterminate perception is not an object of perception. It is a non-relational mode of consciousness. It apprehends an object and its generic character but not the relation between them. It does not apprehend any subject-predicate relation. And since it is purely non-relational in character, it cannot be appropriated by the self. A cognition can be appropriated by the self only when it apprehends a property (*ghatatva*) as qualifying an object (*ghata*). For instance, when we have the determinate perception of a jar as qualified by its generic character, we can appropriate it to the self and distinctly apprehend it as our own experience. Here the cognition of the jar qualifies the self-appropriated cognition (*anuvyavasaya*). The jar qualifies the cognition of the jar. And the generic character of the jar (*ghatatva*) qualifies the jar. All these qualifications qualify the self-appropriated determinate perception of the jar. But in indeterminate perception there is no apprehension of any qualification (*visesana*) as qualifying an object (*visesya*). Though it apprehends an object and its generic character, it does not apprehend the relation between them. It cannot apprehend the object as qualified by its generic character. So in indeterminate perception of a jar its generic character is not the qualification (*prakara*) of consciousness; and unless there is a qualification of consciousness it cannot be appropriated by the self and be an object of distinct apprehension. Indeterminate perception is not an object of perception. It is supersensuous and imperceptible.

This argument does not seem to be convincing. Indeterminate perception is vague and indistinct consciousness. How, then, can it be an object of distinct consciousness ? It is simple, immediate, non-relational apprehension. So it cannot be referred to the self. But because it cannot be distinctly felt as the self's experience, it cannot be said that it is not an object of perception.

Annambhatta defines indeterminate perception as the immediate apprehension of an object with its properties without apprehending the relation between them. He defines determinate perception as the apprehension of the relation between the qualified object (*visesya*) and its qualifications (*visesana*) viz. name, genus, and the like.

Nilakantha holds a slightly different view. He holds that indeterminate perception is the mere apprehension of an object (*visesya*) its qualifications (*visesana*) and the relation of inherence (*samavaya*) without their mutual connection. It does not recognize its object as a qualified thing (*visesya*), its qualifications as qualifications (*visesana*) and the relation of inherence as subsisting between the two. The mutual connection among these elements is apprehended by determinate perception. Thus unlike Visvanatha and Annambhatta, Nilakantha makes the relation of inherence also an object of indeterminate perception, though not the connection of this relation with the qualified object and the qualifications. But he agrees with them in regarding indeterminate perception as an immediate sensory presentation of an object.

### *The Neo-Samkarite*

Dharmarajadhvarindra, the author of *Vedantaparibhasa* also holds that indeterminate perception is the immediate apprehension of an object without apprehending its relations; but it may not be sensuous in character. The cognitions produced by such sentences as "this is Devadatta", (*so'yam Devadattah*) "that thou art" (*tattvamasi*) are indeterminate perceptions. Determinate perception is the relational apprehension of an object such as "I know the jar".

But how can these cognitions be perceptual in character, since they are not produced by the sense-organs ? Are they not verbal cognitions (*sabdajnana*) since they are produced by sentences? Dharmarajadhvanndra argues that the perceptual character of a cognition does not lie in its sensuous organ, but in the identification of the apprehending mode (*pramana-caitanya*) with the apprehended object (*prameya-caitanya*) which is capable of being perceived and present at the time of the cognition. And these characteristics of perception are found also in a cognition produced by such a sentence as "this is Devadatta". In this case *Devadatta* the apprehended object, is present to the apprehending mental mode which goes out to the object and identifies itself with its object. So the cognition produced by such a sentence as "this is Devadatta" satisfies all the conditions of perception, and consequently must be regarded as perceptual in character. Likewise in the cognition produced by such a sentence as "that thou art", the cognizing self itself becomes the object of cognition so that there is an identification of the apprehending mental mode with the apprehended object. Hence, this cognition also must be regarded as perceptual in character.

Further, it may be objected : How can the cognition of such a proposition as "that thou art" be indeterminate in character ? Does it not apprehend the relation between the subject and the predicate? Does it not apprehend the meaning of the subject, the meaning of the predicate, and the relation between the two ? If it does not apprehend the relation between the two terms of the proposition, it cannot understand the meaning of the proposition. If it does apprehend the relation between the two, then it cannot be regarded as an indeterminate perception.

Dharmarajadhvarindra says that it is not necessary to apprehend the meaning of the subject, the meaning of the predicate and the relation between the two to comprehend the meaning of a proposition. If we can only understand the intention of the speaker, we can understand the meaning of a proposition. The import ofa proposition, therefore, is not always understood by apprehending the relation between the different parts of the proposition. Moreover, according to the Samkarite, the proposition "that thou art" is an analytical proposition; it is not a synthetic proposition as Ramanuja and Madhva hold. There is no synthetic relation between the subject and the predicate of this proposition; but there is simply an identity of essence or co-essentiality between the subject and the predicate. In this proposition there is no relation of conjunction, inherence, cause and effect, or any other kind of relation (*samsarga*) ; such a proposition is called an *akhanddrtha* proposition, the import of which can be understood without apprehending the relations among its different parts. Hence, the perception of the import of such a proposition as "that thou art" does not apprehend the relation between its subject and predicate; and, therefore, it is non-relational or indeterminate.

Thus, according to the neo-Samkarite, any non-relational consciousness of a presentative character, in which there is an identification of the apprehending mental mode with the apprehended object, be it produced by the sense-organs or not, must be regarded as an indeterminate perception.

Mahadevananda Sarasvati, the author of *Tattvanusandhana* differs from other Samkarites. He does not recognize the distinction of indeterminate and determinate perception. He says that the Vaisesikas divide perception into two kinds, viz. indeterminate perception and determinate perception, and regard the former as nonqualified or non-relational apprehension and the latter as qualified or relational apprehension. But this view is wrong. There is no proof of the existence of nameless indeterminate perception. The Vaisesikas argue that indeterminate perception is inferred from determinate perception as its invariable condition. Determinate perception is the apprehension of an object as qualified by its properties. But there can be no perception of an object as qualified unless there is already the perception of its qualifying properties, which is indeterminate. This argument is wrong. The determinate perception of a qualified object is not produced by the indeterminate perception of the qualifications but by the intercourse of the qualifications with the sense-organs. So the hypothesis of indeterminate perception is gratuitous.

### *Ramanuja*

According to Ramanuja, both indeterminate perception and determinate perception apprehend objects affected with difference. Indeterminate perception is not the apprehension of an absolutely unqualified and undifferenced object or mere "Being", as Samkara holds, nor the apprehension of a qualified object and its qualifications unrelated to each other, as the Nyaya-Vasesika and Mimamsaka hold, but it consists in the apprehension of an object qualified by some difference or qualification. It can never apprehend an object devoid of all difference or qualifications, but of some qualifications. We never perceive an entirely unqualified object, and, moreover, it is impossible for discrimination is the most fundamental condition of all consciousness, and consequently no consciousness is possible without some distinction. We can never perceive an object without apprehending some special feature of the object, e.g. the particular arrangement of its parts (*samsthana-visesa*). We can never perceive a cow without apprehending the peculiar arrangement of her parts, e.g. dew lap and the like. Indeterminate perception must apprehend an object qualified by some qualities, e.g. its generic character in the shape of a particular configuration (*samsthana*) of its parts, etc., because in determinate perception only those qualities which were apprehended by indeterminate perception are remembered and recognized. The only difference between indeterminate perception and determinate perception lies in the fact that the former is the perception of the first individual among a number of objects belonging to the same class, while the latter is the perception of the second individual, third individual, and so on. In the perception of the first cow, there is indeed the apprehension of the class-character of the cow in the shape of her particular configuration, viz. dew lap and the like, but there is no consciousness of this generic character being common to all the cows, since there is no perception of other cows except the first cow in indeterminate perception. But in the perception of the second individual, third individual, and so on, this generic character is recognized as the common character of the whole class. Thus in the indeterminate perception of the first individual there is an apprehension of its generic character in the shape of a particular arrangement of parts, but it is not recognized as common to the whole class. Thus what was indeterminate in the perception of the first individual of a class becomes determinate in the perception of the second individual, third individual, and so on. Hence, the former is called indeterminate perception, and the latter, determinate perception. In indeterminate perception there is the apprehension of the generic character in the shape of a particular structure, since an object having a structure (*samsthdana*) can never be perceived apart from its structure (*samsthana*). In determinate perception we perceive in addition to the object possessing a structure, and the structure itself, the character of the structure as being common to the whole class.

Venkatanatha elaborates the view of Ramanuja. He defines indeterminate perception as perception devoid of recognition, and determinate perception as perception involving recognition. The former is pure perception, while the latter is recognitive perception. The former is a presentative process, while the latter is a presentative representative process. The object of both indeterminate and determinate perception is qualified (*visista*); it is affected with difference. Indeterminate perception does not apprehend an unqualified object as some suppose. We are never conscious of a cognition apprehending an unqualified object. Nor is there a proof of its existence.

It is generally held that perceptions of the dumb, babies, and animals are nameless and indeterminate, and apprehend unqualified objects. Venkatanatha admits that these perceptions are indeterminate and are devoid of the apprehension of names. But he does not admit that they apprehend unqualified objects. Babies and animals do not, of course, perceive objects as having particular names. But they do perceive them as having certain qualities. They never perceive unqualified objects. They react to different objects in different ways. They appropriate those objects which are beneficial to them. And they avoid those which are injurious to them. This clearly proves that they never perceive objects without qualities.

The Naiyayikas, the Mimamsakas and others hold that indeterminate perception apprehends an unqualified object (*avisistavisaya*). But Venkatanatha asks : Does it apprehend an unqualified object because it does not apprehend the qualifications (*visesan*) or the qualified object (*visesya*) or the relation between the two (*visesan-avisesya-sambandha*) ? It does apprehend qualifications. We can never have a cognition without an object. An objectless cognition is a logical abstraction. It is never a concrete fact of experience. And no cognition of an object, pure and simple, without qualifications is possible. So indeterminate perception cannot but apprehend objects with their qualifications. In fact, even the Naiyayika admits that indeterminate perception apprehends objects and their qualifications but not their relation to each other. But what is the nature of this relation ? It is either inherence or *svarupasambandha*. If it is inherence, as the Naiyayika supposes, why should he hold that it is apprehended by determinate perception and not by indeterminate perception? There is nothing to hinder the apprehension of the relation of inherence by indeterminate perception. If it apprehends the qualified object (*dharmin*) and the qualifications (*dharma*) through the sense-organs because of their fitness (*yogyata*) and intercourse with the sense-organs, it may as well apprehend the relation of inherence between them for the same reason. If the relation cannot be apprehended by indeterminate perception it can neither be apprehended by determinate perception. The Naiyayika should not arbitrarily reserve the apprehension of the relation of inherence for determinate perception. If the relation between the qualified object and the qualifications is *svarupasambandha*, then as soon as indeterminate perception apprehends them it also apprehends the relation between them. *Svarupasambandha* is not an external relation. It is internal and constitutive. It constitutes the essence of the terms it relates. So as soon as indeterminate perception apprehends the terms of the relation it also apprehends the relation between them. Thus, indeterminate perception apprehends not only the qualified object and the qualifications but also the relation between them. Both indeterminate and determinate perception are of the nature of relational consciousness. Both apprehend qualified objects. The only difference between them lies in the fact that the former is free from representative elements, while the latter involves memory and recognition.

### *Madhva and Vallabha*

The indeterminate perception, according to Samkara, is a purely non-relational apprehension which apprehends the mere "Being" (*satta*). The Buddhist makes it more determinate by regarding the specific individual (*svalaksana*) as its object. The indeterminate perception of Kumarila also is more determinate than that of Samkara, since it apprehends an individual object in which the generic character and the specific character subsist. Prabhakara and Sridhara make it more determinate, since they make it apprehend the generic character and the specific character as undistinguished from each other. Jayanta Bhatta makes it more determinate, and regards it as a nameless perception which apprehends generality, quality, action, etc. Parthasarathimisra makes it more determinate, since he makes it apprehend an object with its multiple forms such as genus, substance, quality, action, and name, but not in subject-predicate relation. The Samkarite, the Buddhist, the Samkhya, the Mimamsaka, and the Nyaya-Vaisesika regard indeterminate perception as non-relational apprehension. But Ramanuja regards it as relational apprehension, which apprehends the generic character of an object in the shape of a structure (*samsthana*) and also the relation of the structure to the object itself. Indeterminate perception apprehends an object not devoid of all qualifications but as qualified by some qualifications. It apprehends the relation between its object and some qualifications. Venkatanatha also holds that indeterminate perception apprehends not only the qualified object and its qualifications, but also the relation between them. Thus the Ramanujist does not regard indeterminate perception as a non-relational mode of consciousness, as all others hold, but as a relational experience. This is almost a denial of indeterminate perception. But if the indeterminate perception of the Ramanujist has a semblance of indeterminateness, Madhva, Vallabha, and Bhartrhari deny the possibility of indeterminate perception altogether.

The Madhva Vedantist holds that all perception is determinate. He defines perception as the concrete apprehension of an object with its determinate forms. It is of eight kinds. It may be the apprehension of an object as qualified by a substance, or a quality, or an action, or a name, or generality, or particularity, or inherence, or non-existence. Perception is always concrete and determinate; it is never without any form. The Madhva Vedantist does not recognize formless, indeterminate, non-relational apprehension.

The Vallabhite also does not admit the possibility of indeterminate perception. Purusottamaji Maharaja, a follower of Vallabha, says that all knowledge is determinate. All knowledge is in the form of judgement, and all judgement involves a subject-predicate relation. So perceptual judgement also is a determinate relational consciousness involving a subject-predicate relation. Determinate relational consciousness does not presuppose indeterminate consciousness of the terms of the relation. The consciousness of the terms of the relation is as determinate as the consciousness of the relation. For example, determinate perception of a man with a stick (*dandin*) does not presuppose indeterminate perception of the stick, but definite and determinate perception of it. Otherwise the stick can never be used as a term of the relation. "Relational consciousness always demands a definite knowledge of the terms of relation, and definiteness implies determinateness. Indeterminate knowledge is then not a possibility. Knowledge is definiteness and definiteness involves predication."

Purusottamaji Maharaja recognizes two kinds of determinate perception: (i) *visistabuddhi* and (2) *samuhavalarribana*. *Visistabuddhi* is the determinate apprehension of an object as qualified by some properties. It may assume another form called *visistavaisistya-buddhi*. It is the qualified form of determinate apprehension. It apprehends an object (e.g. man) qualified by a qualification (*dandin*) which again is qualified by another qualification (*danda*). *Visistavaisistya-buddhi* is more complex than *visistabuddhi*. Both are determinate and relational consciousness. The former is qualified relational consciousness, while the latter is unqualified relational consciousness. *Visistabuddhi* apprehends the relation between a subject and a predicate. *Visista-vaisistya-buddhi* apprehends the relation between a subject and a predicate, which, in its turn, involves a subject-predicate relation. *Samuhalambanabuddhi* is the determinate consciousness of the relation of a qualified object and its qualification, e.g. a man, a stick, and the conjunction between them. It assumes another form. The determinate consciousness of a collection of objects such as a jar, a cloth, and a pillar is a qualified form of *samuhalambanabuddhi* or combining consciousness. It is called *visista-samuhalambanabuddhi*.

### *The Sabdika*

Bhartrhari and other Sabdikas hold that an object is identical with its name; so when an object is apprehended it is apprehended along with its name. There can be no thought without language. All cognitions are, as it were, interpenetrated by names. Even children and dumb persons perceive objects along with their names known in their previous births. Hence there can be no nameless or indeterminate perception.

Further, the Sabdikas argue that all practical uses and actions follow upon determinate perceptions, hence there is no need of assuming the existence of indeterminate perception.

### The Naiyayika Criticism of the Sabdika View

Vacaspatimisra has elaborately criticized the doctrine in *Nyayavartikatatparyatika*. If objects are identical with their names, as the Sabdika holds, are they identical with the eternal sound (*Sabda Brahma*) or with conventional words which are heard? The first alternative is untenable. We never perceive the identity of sensible sounds with the supersensible eternal sound. The second alternative also cannot be maintained. If objects are identical with their names, then children and dumb persons can never perceive objects, since they never perceive names. It is absurd to hold that they perceive the identity of objects with their names heard in their past lives. Moreover, different cognitions are produced by different objects, and not by different names. A visual perception can apprehend only a colour ; it can never apprehend a sound or a name. Likewise an auditory perception can apprehend only a sound; it can never apprehend a colour. If an object, say, a colour, identical with its name, then a blind man would perceive colour through his auditory organ as he perceives its name through it ; and a deaf man also would perceive a name through his visual organ as he perceives the object through it. But this is absurd.

Hence, Vacaspatimisra concludes that those who have not yet learned the meanings of words, or the relation of words to their objects, must have nameless, indeterminate perception of objects. Even those who are well versed in the meanings of words, have at first a nameless, indeterminate perception of an object, which revives the subconscious impression of its name perceived in the past, and, together with the recollection of the name, forms determinate perception.

Jayanta Bhatta wrongly represents the Sabdika view of perception and criticizes it. He says that according to some, the object of indeterminate perception is the word or name which constitutes the essence of the object. Evidently he refers to the Sabdika doctrine here. The Sabdika holds that all cognitions apprehend objects together with their names; there is no nameless apprehension. Indeterminate perception, which is supposed to be nameless, is impossible. So the Sabdika does not hold that the object of indeterminate perception is the word or name, but he denies the existence of indeterminate perception altogether.

However, Jayanta argues that the Sabdika is wrong in holding that all cognitions apprehend objects with their names because they constitute their very essence. Indeterminate perception can never apprehend the name of an object. If we perceive an object through the visual organ, it is absurd to suppose that we perceive also its name through it. A name can never be an object of visual perception. Moreover, we can never comprehend the meaning of a name unless we apprehend the relation between the name and the object denoted by it. There can never be the comprehension of a name, if the relation between the name and its object has not already been apprehended, or if being perceived in the past it is forgotten, or the residual left by the previous perception is not revived. But in indeterminate perception the relation between its object and its name is not apprehended; nor does it revive the name in memory by association. It is a purely non-relational presentative cognition. Hence it cannot apprehend the name of an object.

Varadaraja also repeats the arguments of Vacaspati and Jayanta. He argues that the Sabdika doctrine, that there can be no cognition of an object without its name, contradicts an actual fact of experience. We do perceive an object even without knowing its name. And even if we know the name of an object, at first we perceive the object in itself, apart from its name, just after its contact with a sense-organ, and then remember its name perceived in the past. The object was perceived in the past, and its name was heard, and the relation between them was perceived. Thus an association was established between the idea of the object and the idea of its name. Now just after peripheral stimulation the object is perceived apart from its name; and then the perception of the object reminds us of its name. And when the name is remembered the object is perceived as qualified by its name. And this is determinate perception. The recollection of the name is due to no other condition than indeterminate perception of the object apart from its name owing to association and revival of the subconscious impression of the name. Thus, determinate perception of an object qualified by its name presupposes indeterminate perception of the object in itself apart from its name.

## Proof of the Existence of Indeterminate Perception

Parthasarathimisra says that the denial of indeterminate perception is contradicted by our experience. Just after the contact of an object with the sense-organ we do experience an immediate cognition of an object devoid of all relations, viz. the relation between the qualified and the qualifications, in which there is not yet a differentiation of the generic characters from the specific characters. If there were no indeterminate perception there would be no determinate perception too. For determinate perception is the apprehension of the relation between the qualified object and the qualifying properties, and the apprehension of this relation depends upon the previous perception of the terms of the relation, viz. the qualified object and the qualifications. Unless these are implicitly known together by indeterminate perception they can never be differentiated from, and related to, each other by determinate perception. Therefore, indeterminate perception must be the invariable antecedent of determinate perception. In the determinate perception of an object we remember the particular class to which it belongs, and the particular name which it bears, which were already apprehended implicitly by indeterminate perception, and refer them to the object present to the sense-organs. If the class and the name were not perceived at all, they could never be remembered. Hence we must admit the existence of indeterminate perception.

The earlier Naiyayikas, Vaisesikas, and Mimamsakas hold that indeterminate perception is an object of perception. But the neo-Naiyayikas hold that indeterminate perception is not an object of perception. There can be no perception of indeterminate perception because there can be no self-appropriation (*anuvyavasaya*) of it. Indeterminate perception is purely non-relational in character; if it were related to the self, it would cease to be non-relational and indeterminate. It can be known only by inference. The determinate perception of an object as qualified by some qualifications presupposes an indeterminate perception of the qualifications of the object, without which there can be no determinate perception. Visvanatha's argument has already been given in detail.

If it is urged that the perception of the qualifications also is determinate, then it would presuppose the perception of the qualifications of those qualifications and so on an infinitum. To avoid this infinite regress we must admit that the perception of the qualifications of an object, which is presupposed by the determinate perception of the object as qualified by the qualifications, is indeterminate.

Janakinatha elaborates this argument further. The cognition of a qualified object (*visistajnana*) presupposes the cognition of qualifications (*visesanajnana*) which is its cause. And this cognition is indeterminate. When we have a determinate perception "this is a jar", the jar (*ghata*) is perceived as possessed of its generic character (*ghatatva*). This perceptual judgement presupposes the cognition of the genus of jar (*ghatatva or* jarness). If there were no cognition of the qualification (jarness) there would not be the cognition of the qualified object (e.g. "this is a jar"). And when there is the cognition of the mere qualification (jarness) there is not yet the cognition of a qualified object. The apprehension of the qualification is entirely indeterminate. This is indeterminate perception. It is presupposed by determinate perception.

It is childish to argue that the determinate cognition of the qualification (jarness) in the past life is the cause of determinate perception of a qualified object in this life, because the cause must be an immediate antecedent of the effect. A cognition in the past life has nothing to do with a cognition in this life.

It is also foolish to argue that the divine cognition of the qualification (*jarness*) is the cause of the determinate perception of the jar, since the two cognitions of the qualified object and the qualification abide in different substrata; they must co-inhere in the same substratum to be related to each other as cause and effect. The cognition of a qualification (e.g. a stick) in one person is not the cause of the cognition of a qualified object (e.g. a man with a stick) in another person.

The determinate recollection of the qualification (jarness) also cannot be the cause of the determinate perception of a qualified object. Even this determinate cognition is not possible without the cognition of qualifications. A determinate cognition is always produced by the cognition of qualifications. And even the determinate recollection is not possible without the previous cognition of qualifications.

The recollection of the qualification cannot be indeterminate. There can be no recollection without previous perception. And if there is no determinate perception of the qualification, there can be no recollection of it. Recollection depends upon previous perception. If it depends upon previous recollection it will lead to infinite regress.

Besides, if the qualification is not remembered, the determinate perception of a qualified object is not possible. And the conditions of the determinate perception of a qualified object being absent, and the conditions of the immediate apprehension of the qualifications (e.g. jar and the genus of jar) being present, there is nothing to hinder the production of the immediate apprehension of the qualifications. And this immediate apprehension is called indeterminate perception.

Let us briefly review the main doctrines of indeterminate and determinate perception. According to the older Naiyayikas, indeterminate perception is the perception of an object without a name, while determinate perception is the perception of an object together with its name. Jayanta Bhatta emphasizes this doctrine in *Nyayamanjari* in unequivocal terms. He says that the object of indeterminate perception is essentially the same as that of determinate perception; the only difference between them lies in the fact that the former apprehends an object without a name, while the latter apprehends an object together with its name; both of them apprehend substance, generality, quality, and action.

But according to Sridhara, Prabhakara, Parthasarathimisra, neo-Naiyayikas, and neo-Samkarites, indeterminate perception is the immediate apprehension of an object and its qualifications without their mutual connection, while determinate perception is the apprehension of an object as qualified by its qualifications with their mutual relations. Indeterminate perception is an undifferentiated and non-relational mode of apprehension, while determinate perception is a relational and discriminative apprehension of an object. In indeterminate perception we are merely conscious of the terms of relations in an object, viz. generality, particularity, substantiality quality, action, etc.; but we are not conscious of the relations among the terms. Indeterminate perception apprehends an object and its qualifications as mere thats, and not as whats, while determinate perception apprehends them as whats. In the language of William James, in indeterminate perception we have a "knowledge of acquaintance" with the "bare immediate natures" without their relations, while in determinate perception we have a "knowledge about" them and of their relations inter se.

## Proof of the Existence of Determinate Perception

The Buddhists deny the perceptual character of the determinate cognition following upon a peripheral stimulation, and regard indeterminate cognition alone as truly perceptual in character. According to them, perception is always indeterminate; the determinate cognition following upon an indeterminate perception cannot be regarded as perceptual in character, since it depends upon the recollection of the name denoting its object, and not upon the direct contact of an object with a sense-organ. Between peripheral stimulation and the determinate cognition of an object there is an intervening factor of the recollection of the name of the object. The determinate cognition, therefore, is not directly produced by peripheral stimulation but by the recollection of the name of its object; it is not a purely sensory presentation but a complex of a sensory presentation and a memory-image; it is not purely presentative but presentative-representative in character.

This objection of the Buddhists is more apparent than real. Peripheral stimulation is the principal cause of the determinate cognition, and the recollection of the name is only an auxiliary cause. Peripheral stimulation by itself cannot produce a determinate cognition; it requires the help of the recollection of the name of the object to bring about a determinate cognition. A determinate cognition is produced by peripheral stimulation, for the sense-organ continues to operate at the time of this cognition, and produces a direct presentation of an object. Thus a determinate cognition is perceptual in character, because it is produced by peripheral stimulation which does not cease at the time of the determinate cognition, and because it consists in the direct presentation of an object, which is not possible without peripheral stimulation. Thus, though a determinate cognition apprehends an object connected with a name, it cannot but be regarded as perceptual in character, because it is produced by peripheral stimulation and brings about a direct and distinct manifestation of its object as an indeterminate cognition.

The Buddhists contend that a determinate cognition is not a direct presentation; it is an indirect cognition of its object, since it is not directly produced by peripheral stimulation. Ridhara argues that cognitions are indirect whenever they are not produced by peripheral stimulation or the contact of an object with a sense-organ, as we find in the case of inferential cognitions. But a determinate cognition is produced by peripheral stimulation; hence it cannot be regarded as an indirect cognition.

The Buddhists may urge that a cognition is non-sensuous or non-perceptual, if it is preceded by recollection, as an inferential cognition; a determinate cognition is preceded by recollection, and hence it is non-sensuous or non-perceptual in character. Ridhara argues that if sensuousness is ever perceived, it is perceived only in a determinate cognition; and hence it cannot be denied. And a determinate cognition is perceptual in character, not only because it is produced by peripheral stimulation, and directly manifests an object, but also because we find in it no such factors as inferential mark and so forth as we find in inference.

The Buddhists contend that it is self-contradictory to assert that a cognition is determinate (*vikalpa*) and, at the same time, a direct presentation (*aparoksavabhasa*). A direct presentation consists in the apprehension of the specific individuality of an object (*svalaksana*) and the specific individuality is apprehended only by indeterminate perception, and not by determinate cognition. A determinate cognition apprehends an object connected with a word; and because a word is not connected with the specific individuality, being a conventional sign for many objects in general, a determinate cognition cannot apprehend the specific individuality of an object. If a word could denote the specific individuality of an object, it would bring about a direct presentation of it even without the operation of the sense-organs, and we should have a perception of it. But, in fact, it does not bring about a direct presentation. Hence a determinate cognition too, which apprehends an object connected with a word, cannot apprehend its specific individuality. And because it cannot apprehend the specific individuality of an object, it is not a direct presentation (*aparoksavabhasa*) and because it is not a direct presentation it is not a distinct cognition or perception (*visadavabhasa*)?

But when we see a cow with our eyes wide open and have a determinate perception such as "this is a cow", is it not a direct presentation (*aparoksavabhasa*) or a distinct perception (*visadavabhasa*)? The Buddhists urge that such a determinate cognition is not really a direct and distinct presentation, but it appears to be so, inasmuch as it borrows a semblance of directness (*aparoksya*) and distinctness (*vaisadya*) from its connection with the immediately preceding indeterminate perception which is a direct and distinct presentation of the specific individuality of its object.

If the directness or distinctness of a determinate cognition following upon an indeterminate perception were not derived from its connection with the immediately preceding indeterminate perception if it were not an adventitious mark of a determinate cognition but its intrinsic character then even verbal and inferential cognitions too, which are not connected with indeterminate perceptions, would be regarded as direct cognitions because they are determinate cognitions. But they are regarded by none as direct cognitions.

Hence only the indeterminate cognition of the specific individual (*svalaksana*) produced by peripheral stimulation is perceptual in character; the determinate cognition following upon an indeterminate perception cannot be regarded as perceptual in nature, since it contains representative elements, and is not of the nature of a direct and distinct cognition. There is only indeterminate perception and no determinate perception.

Parthasarathimisra urges that this doctrine of the Buddhist is anything but satisfactory. When we perceive a cow with our eyes wide open we have a direct apprehension of the cow as a cow, we feel it as a direct presentation. And the directness of this presentation is not an adventitious character of the determinate cognition due to its connection with an indeterminate perception, as the Buddhists suppose, but it is an intrinsic character of the determinate cognition, constituting its essential nature. And it cannot be proved that the directness of the determinate cognition is due to its connection with an indeterminate perception. The Buddhists labour under a misconception that directness or indirectness of a cognition is due to the nature of its object, when they argue that a cognition is direct if it apprehends the specific individual, and a cognition is indirect if it fails to apprehend the specific individual. Were it so, then generality (*samanya*) would always be apprehended by an indirect cognition (e.g. inference), and the specific individual (*walaksana*) would always be apprehended by a direct cognition or perception. But, as a matter of fact, we know generality both by perception and inference, and the specific individual also both by perception and inference. Even the same object may be apprehended both by a direct cognition and an indirect cognition; when it is known through a sense-organ it is known by a direct cognition; and when it is known through marks of inference, and so forth, it is known by an indirect cognition. Hence the directness or indirectness of a cognition is not due to the nature of its object, but to the instrument of the cognition. If the cognition of an object is brought about by peripheral stimulation it is direct, and if it is produced by words, marks of inference, and so forth, it is indirect. When a determinate cognition is produced by peripheral stimulation, even with the help of recollection, we must regard it as a direct cognition or perception, just as an indeterminate cognition produced by peripheral stimulation is regarded as a direct cognition or perception. Hence directness is not the special characteristic of indeterminate perception alone, but also of determinate perception,, since both of them are produced by peripheral stimulation. Though determinate perception is not purely presentative in character being a complex of presentative and representative processes, it must be regarded as perceptual in character, because the presentative element in it preponderates over the representative element owing to peripheral stimulation. Hence we must admit that determinate cognition produced by peripheral stimulation is of the nature of perception.

### The Nyaya-Vaisesika Analysis of a Definite and Determinate Perception

We have distinguished between indeterminate perception and determinate perception. We have found that indeterminate perception is a purely presentative cognition of an object, devoid of assimilation and discrimination, while determinate perception is a complex presentative-representative process, involving a direct perception of an object, and assimilation of it to other like objects, and discrimination of it from other unlike objects reproduced in memory by association. Thus determinate perception involves a presentative element and a representative element. When it is definite and certain, it involves an act of recognition of the particular class to which its object belongs; and it also involves a feeling-tone either pleasant or unpleasant, and also a conative attitude of the self to react to the object for its appropriation or rejection.

### Does Determinate Perception Involve Inference?

Some hold that a full-fledged perception involves an element of inference also. According to them, a complete perception involves the following processes :

1. At first after the peripheral contact of a sense-organ with an object, e.g. a fruit, we perceive the fruit.
2. Then we remember that this kind of fruit (e.g. *kapittha*) gave us pleasure in the past.
3. Then after recollection we have a *paramarsajnana* (knowledge that the middle term, which is an invariable concomitant of the major term exists in, or is related to, the minor term), such as "this fruit belongs to the class of *kapitthas*".

4. After this *paramarsajnana* we infer the pleasure-giving property (*sukhasadhanatva*) of the *kapittha* fruit perceived, such as "therefore, the fruit perceived must be pleasure-giving". The process of inference may be shown as follows :

*All Kaphthas are pleasure-giving ;*

*The fruit perceived is a kapittha :*

Therefore, the fruit perceived must be pleasure-giving.

5. Then after this act of inference, there is another act of inference such as the following :

All pleasure-giving things are acceptable (*upadeya*); the *kapittha* perceived is pleasure-giving, therefore, the *kapittha* perceived is acceptable. And when we have come to know that the fruit perceived is acceptable, the perception of the fruit produced by peripheral stimulation has vanished, and no trace of the perception is left. Therefore a complete act of perception must be regarded as rather an act of inference than an act of perception, inasmuch as the knowledge of the acceptability of the object of perception is the result of inference.

Vacaspatimisra admits that this is the order of the successive steps of a complete perception. At first the perception of the fruit is produced by the peripheral contact of a sense-organ with the object. Then this perception brings about a recollection of the pleasuregiving property (*sukhasadhanatvasmrti*) of this kind of fruit. Then this recollection in co-operation with the intercourse of the sense-organ with the object produces a *paramarsajnana* that "this fruit belongs to the class of *kapitthas*". Then this *paramarsajnana* produces an inferential cognition that "this *kapittha* must be pleasure giving". Then this inferential cognition, in co-operation with the sense-object-contact, brings about the perception that "this *kapittha* is acceptable".

Thus according to Vacaspatimisra, a complete act of perception involves not only an element of recollection but also an element of inference. But he contends that, on this ground, perception should not be identified with inference because the act of inference involved in a complete perception is not independent of sense-perception produced by peripheral stimulation; it co-operates with the peripheral contact of a sense-organ with its object to produce the perception that "the object perceived is acceptable". Though recollection and inference are involved in a complete act of perception, they enter as constituent elements into the perceptive process not independently of peripheral stimulation; they always act in cooperation with peripheral excitation or sense-object-contact, and thus produce, after all, a complex perception which involves memory and inference as integral factors. According to the Nyaya-Vaisesika, whatever mental state is produced by peripheral stimulation or sense-object- intercourse must be regarded as perception, though it involves memory and inference.

Others, however, hold that perception never involves an element of inference. According to them, at first there is a sensuous perception of an object, e.g. a fruit, produced by peripheral stimulation. Then this perception brings about a recollection that this kind of fruit is pleasure-giving. And when this recollection is produced, the initial perception is destroyed; but when it is being destroyed, it produces a definite knowledge that "the fruit perceived is pleasure-giving". And this knowledge of the pleasurableness of the fruit perceived is nothing but the knowledge of its acceptability, because acceptability is nothing but pleasurableness. Hence there is no *paramarsajnana*, or inference in an act of perception. What is the use of postulating an element of inference in perception, which is never experienced? Thus according to some, though perception involves recollection, it does not involve inference.

But it may be objected that pleasurableness of an object cannot be an object of perception, inasmuch as the power of yielding pleasure is imperceptible; so pleasurableness of an object is inferred from the knowledge that it belongs to a particular class of pleasurable objects. Jayanta Bhatta urges that if pleasurableness of an object is known by an inference, then that inference also must be proved by another inference, and so on an infinitum. In fact, there is no supersensible power; hence pleasurableness of an object is known by direct perception.

But when we see an object through the eyes, we do not perceive its pleasurableness through the eyes. How, then, can we perceive that the fruit is pleasurable through the eyes ? Jayanta Bhatta replies that pleasurableness of the object is not perceived through the eyes, but through the mind. Thus there is no need of assuming an inference in an act of perception to know the pleasurableness and acceptability of the object of perception.

# 3

# Objects and Conditions of Perception

## The Objects of Perception

The Nyaya-Vaisesika divides perception mainly into two kinds, viz. external perception and internal perception. External perception is derived through the external senses, and internal perception through the mind. External perception is of five kinds, viz. olfactory, gustatory, auditory, visual, and tactual perception. The objects of these different kinds of external perception are respectively the qualities of odour, taste, sound, colour, and touch as well as their generalities and negations. The objects of internal perception are the qualities of pleasure, pain, desire, aversion, cognition, and volition. Substances can be perceived only by the visual organ and the tactual organ; the remaining sense-organs are capable of perceiving qualities only. Let us briefly consider the objects of these different kinds of perception.

### *Olfactory Perception*

Through the olfactory organ we cannot perceive a substance which is the substratum of odour. We have olfactory perception of odour, the genus of odour, the genus of fragrance, and the genus of bad odour. We can never perceive potential or infra-sensible (*anudbhuta*) odour we can perceive odour only when it is in an appreciable degree (*udbhuta*).

### Gustatory Perception

Through the gustatory organ we cannot perceive a substance which is the substratum of taste. We can perceive taste and the genus of taste through the gustatory organ. But we can perceive taste only when it is in an appreciable degree (*udbhuta*); we cannot perceive inappreciable or unmanifested (*anudbhuta*) taste.

### Auditory Perception

Through the auditory organ we cannot perceive *akasa* (ether) which is the substrate of sound. We can perceive only sound and the genus of sound through the auditory organ. But we can perceive sound only when it is in an appreciable degree (*udbhuta*).

### Visual Perception

Through the visual organ we perceive not only colours but also coloured substances. Appreciable colours (*udbhutarupa*) substances possessed of appreciable colours, separateness, number, disjunction, conjunction, priority, posteriority, viscidity, liquidity, and magnitude are the objects of visual perception. The movement, the genus, and the inherence existing in visible things are also the objects of visual perception. The conjunction of light with visible objects and appreciable colour are the conditions of visual perception. The heat of summer is infra-visible because it has not an appreciable colour; but it is an object of tactual perception because it has the quality of appreciable touch.

### Tactual Perception

Through the tactual organ we perceive substances as well as qualities. Appreciable touch (*udbhutasparsa*) with its genus and substances endued with appreciable touch are the objects of tactual perception. All objects of visual perception other than colour and the genus of colour are the objects of tactual perception. For example, separateness, number, disjunction, conjunction, priority, posteriority, viscidity, fluidity, and magnitude, and also the movements and the universals which subsist in tangible objects are the objects of tactual perception.

## *Internal Perception*

Pleasure, pain, desire, aversion, cognition, and volition are the objects of internal perception. They are perceived through the mind along with the genus of pleasure, the genus of pain, etc. The self also is an object of internal perception. The conjunction of the mind with the self is the condition of the perception of the self. The united inherence of the mind in the self is the cause of the perception of the qualities of the self. But according to the older Nyaya-Vaisesika, the self is not an object of perception but an object of inference; it can be perceived only by the yogi.

## Common Sensibles

There are certain objects which can be perceived through the visual organ and the tactual organ both. Numbers, magnitudes, separateness, conjunction and disjunction, priority and posteriority, motion, viscidity, fluidity, velocity, and their universal essences are both visible and tangible, if they inhere in substances having appreciable colours. These are invisible and intangible in uncoloured or inappropriate substances. Thus certain objects, e.g. colour, sound, odour, taste, and touch are perceived through one sense-organ. Certain other objects, e.g. numbers, magnitudes, etc., are perceived through two sense-organs, viz. the visual organ and the tactual organ. Pleasure, pain, etc., are the objects of internal perception. Existence (*satta*) and the genus of quality (*gunatva*) are perceived through all the sense-organs,

## The Condition of Knowledge

According to the later Vaisesika, the condition of knowledge in general is the contact of the mind or central sensory with the tactual organ. But what is the proof of this ? In dreamless sleep the mind gives up its connection with the tactual organ, which is aerial in nature, and retires into the nerve of *puntat*, which is free from air, where it cannot bring about any cognition. But it may be urged that the mind cannot produce cognition in dreamless sleep because there is no condition of cognition at that time. Supposing that the mind does bring about cognition in deep sleep, what kind of cognition is produced by it? Does it bring about apprehension (*anubhava*) or recollection (*smarana*)? It cannot bring about perception as the conditions of perception are absent. There cannot be any visual perception in dreamless sleep, since there is no contact of the visual organ with the mind. For the same reason there cannot be any other kind of external perception. Nor can there be an internal perception, since there are no cognitions at that time, and in the absence of cognitions there cannot be the perception of the self as well. In dreamless sleep there can be no inference as the knowledge of invariable connection is absent nor can there be analogy as the knowledge of similarity is absent; nor can there be verbal cognition as the knowledge of words is absent. Thus there can be no apprehension in deep sleep as all the conditions of apprehension are absent. Nor can there be recollection in deep sleep as there is no suggestive force (*udbodhaka*) at the time to resuscitate the subconscious traces of previous perceptions. Thus there can be no cognition in deep sleep, either in the form of apprehension or recollection, because the conditions are non-existent. What, then, is the necessity of postulating the contact of the rnind with the tactual organ as the general condition of all knowledge ? Visvanatha contends that it cannot be said that there is no possibility of cognition in deep sleep. For the individual acts of cognition, volition, etc., which are the psychoses immediately preceding deep sleep, can be apprehended during sleep, and the self also can be perceived in relation to these psychoses. And there is no evidence to prove that the psychoses immediately preceding deep sleep are supra-sensible (*atindriya*) nor is there any evidence to prove that those cognitions which immediately precede deep slumber are indeterminate (*nirvikalpa*) and hence supra-sensible (*afindriya*). Hence we must reasonably conclude that there is no cognition in deep slumber, because there is no contact of the mind with the tactual organ at that time, the mind retiring into the nerve of *puritan* which is free from air and consequently free from contact with the tactual organ.

But if the contact of the mind with the tactual organ, which is aerial in nature, is regarded as the general condition of all knowledge, then either visual perception and gustatory perception must involve tactual perception, because at the time of visual or gustatory perception there is the contact of the tactual organ (*tvak*) with an object as well as the contact of the mind with the tactual organ, or there would be no cognition at all, owing to the inhibition of both visual or gustatory perception and tactual perception by each other. To explain this difficulty some suppose that the contact of the mind with the tactual organ is, no doubt, the condition of knowledge in general, but visual perception does not involve tactual perception, because the conditions of visual perception inhibit the emergence of tactual perception. Others, again, suppose that the contact of die mind with the skin (*charman*) and not with the tactual organ (*pvak*) is the condition of all knowledge. According to them, the absence of consciousness in deep sleep is due to the absence of the contact of the mind with the skin, and the absence of tactual perception at the time of visual perception is due to the absence of the contact of the mind with the tactual organ, which is aerial in nature, though there is the contact of the mind with the skin.

## The General Conditions of External Perception

The older Vaisesikas hold that external perception depends upon the following conditions :

1. The object of external perception must have extensity (*mahattva*) or appreciable magnitude. Atoms are imperceptible as they have no appreciable magnitude.
2. The object of external perception must consist of many substances. It must be a composite of many parts (*anekadravyavat*). A mote is perceptible but an atom is not, because the former has magnitude, while the latter has none. A mote has magnitude because it is composed of many parts. An atom has no magnitude because it does not consist of parts. Therefore, an object, in order to be perceived, must not be a simple, indivisible atom, but a composite substance in which a plurality of substances co-inhere. It must be composed of many parts and consequently it must have an appreciable magnitude.
3. The object of perception must have colour (*rupa*). The air is made up of many parts, and so it has an appreciable magnitude. But still it is not perceived through the visual organ because it is devoid of the impression of colour (*rupasamskara*). The term "impression of colour" (*rupasamskara*) means inherence of colour (*rupasamavaya*) or appreciability of colour (*rupodbhava*) or non-obscuration of colour (*rupanabhibhava*). The light of the

eye has colour and magnitude. But it is not visible because there is not appreciable or manifested colour in it. The light of a meteor also has colour and magnitude. But it is not visible in midday because it is obscured by the stronger light of the sun.

The older Vaisesikas hold that manifest or appreciable colour (*udbhutarupa*) is a necessary condition of every kind of external perception of a substance. But the later Vaisesikas hold that manifest or appreciable colour is the necessary condition of visual perception only, and manifest or appreciable touch (*udbhutasparsa*) is the necessary condition of tactual perception, and so on. This is proved by the double method of agreement in presence and agreement in absence. What, then, is the general condition of all kinds of external perception? Either there is none, or it is the possession of a *visesaguna* (distinctive quality) other than sound and those which exist in the self. The *akasa* (ether) cannot be an object of sense-perception, though it is endued with a distinctive quality, viz. sound. The self also is not an object of external perception, though it is endowed with the distinctive qualities of pleasure, pain, cognition, desire, aversion, and volition. So the possession of any other distinctive quality than sound and the qualities of the self may be regarded as the general condition of all kinds of external perception.

The older Vaisesikas may urge that there is a parsimony of hypotheses if colour is regarded as the general condition of all kinds of external perception. But in that case, air would not be an object of tactual perception as it is devoid of colour. If the opponent admits that air cannot be an object of tactual perception, then it may be urged that there is a parsimony of hypotheses even if we suppose that appreciable touch (*udbhutasparsa*) is the general condition of all kinds of external perception. If the opponent contends that on this view a ray of light would not be an object of visual perception as it is devoid of appreciable touch, why should we not admit that it cannot be an object of visual perception, just as the opponent admits that air cannot be an object of tactual perception ? In fact, just as we perceive a ray of light through our visual organ, so we perceive air through our tactual organ; these are the facts of experience; the tactual perception of air is as much a fact of experience as the visual perception of a ray of light. So, neither colour nor touch is the general condition of all kinds of external perception of substances.

The later Vaisesikas agree with the older Vaisesikas in holding that extensive magnitude (*mahattva*) is the general condition of six kinds of perception. Extensity is the cause of the perception of a substance in consequence of its inherence in it. It is the cause of the perception of the qualities, actions, and generalities inhering in substances in consequence of its inherent-inherence or inherence in the qualities, etc., which inhere in substances. It is the cause of the perception of the genus of quality (*gunatava*) the genus of actions (*karmatva*), etc., which inhere in qualities and actions respectively, which, again, inhere in substances in consequence of its inherent-inherence. By *mahattva* we mean proportionate extensity, neither infinite magnitude nor atomic magnitude. Neither all-pervading ether nor atoms are perceptible.

## The Conditions of the Visual Perception of Colour

The older Vaisesikas hold that perception of colour depends on two conditions, viz. co-inherence of many substances (*anekadravyaṣamavaya*) and particularity of colour (*rupavisesa*). We cannot perceive the colour of an atom (*paramanu*) and a binary atomic aggregate or a dyad (*dvanuka*) since an atom does not consist of parts, and a dyad is composed of two atoms only. The colour of an atom and a dyad cannot be perceived, because they are not composed of many substances or a plurality of substances do not inhere in them. Perception, therefore, depends on the co-inherence of a plurality of substances from a tertiary atomic aggregate (just perceptible mott-trasarenu) and upwards in which a plurality of substances co-inhere.

Besides the co-inhesion of a plurality of substances (*anekadravyasamavaya*) there is another condition of the perception of colour, viz. particularity of colour (*rupavisesa*). "Particularity of colour" means particularity abiding in colour. It has three forms, viz. appreciability (*udbhutatva*), non-obscuration (*anabhibhutatva*) and the essence of colour (*rupatva*). We have no visual perception of taste, touch, etc., because they are devoid of the essence of colour (*rupatva*). There can be no visual perception of the light of the eye owing to the absence of appreciability (*udbhutatva*). "Appreciability or manifestness is a kind of universal entity residing in a particular quality of colour, etc., and included in the essence of colour."

We have already seen that according to Visvanatha, conjunction with light (*aloka-samyoga*) and appreciable colour (*udbhutarupa*) are the conditions of visual perception.

## The Conditions of Tactual Olfactory and Gustatory Perception

The older Vaisesikas hold that tactual, olfactory, and gustatory perceptions also depend upon similar conditions. Just as visual perception of colour depends on a particularity of colour (*rupavisesa*) that is, on the distinctive qualities of non-obscuration (*anabhibhufatva*) appreciability or manifestness (*udbhutatva*) or the essence of colour (*rupatva*) so the gustatory perception of taste depends on a particularity of taste (*rasavisesa*) i.e. on the peculiar qualities of non-obscuration, appreciability, and the essence of taste.There are similar conditions also in other kinds of external perception (viz. olfactory and tactual) which also depend upon the co-inhesion of a plurality of substances. Those smells, tastes, and touches are not apprehended, which are infra-sensible or inappreciable to the organs of smell, taste, and touch. In a stone we cannot apprehend smell and taste, because these are inappreciable to the corresponding sense-organs. But in the ashes of a stone we can perceive its smell and taste, because they are there in an appreciable degree. Some hold that we can apprehend the smell and taste of a stone, no doubt, but not distinctly. We cannot perceive the light (*tejas*) in hot water, since it is inappreciable or obscured by touch. Likewise we cannot perceive the colour, taste, and touch in comminuted camphor, *champaka* perfume, etc., owing to their inappreciability. In gold the colour is appreciable; but its whiteness and brightness are much obscured. But it may be urged that gravity inheres in a composite object made up of many substances, which has thus extensive magnitude and colour. But why is it not perceived through the visual organ? It cannot be perceived because the essence of colour (*rupatva*) and appreciability are not existent in gravity. Prasastapada and others hold that gravity is supra-sensible (*atindnya*). But Vallavacarya holds that gravity is not an object of visual perception but of tactual perception.

The Mimarhsaka accepts the Vaisesika view of the conditions of perception. Extensive magnitude (*mahattva*) is the general condition of all kinds of external perception. In the perception of a substance, extensity is a condition through inherence. In the perception of qualities, actions, and universals, it is a condition through inherent-inherence. In the perception of the universals of qualities and actions, it is a condition through inherent-inherence.

Appreciable colour and the conjunction of light with manifest or unobscured colour are the conditions of visual perception. Some hold that extensive magnitude and manifest or unobscured colour are not the conditions of the visual perception of time. The manifest or appreciable touch is the condition of tactual perception.

# 4

# Perception and *Sannikarsa*

## Introduction

In this chapter we shall deal with the different kinds of intercourse of the sense-organs with their objects, acquired perception, and recognition.

Perception is presentative knowledge. And presentative knowledge depends upon the presentation of an object to the self. And most Indian philosophers are of opinion that for the presentation of an object it must enter into some sort of relation with a sense-organ. Perception depends upon some sort of intercourse (*sannikarsa*) or dynamic communion between its object and a particular sense-organ. External perception depends upon the intercourse between external objects and the external sense-organs. And internal perception depends upon the intercourse between the self or its qualities and the internal organ or *manas*. The objects of perception may be material or spiritual substances (*dravya*), their qualities (*guna*), and actions (*karma*) and their generic characters (*jati*). These diverse objects of perception must enter into direct or indirect relation with the external sense-organs or the internal organ according to their nature. Indian philosophers hold the peculiar doctrine that substances alone can enter into direct communion with the appropriate sense-organs; and the qualities, actions, and communities inhering in the substances can enter into communion with the sense-organs through the medium of the substances in which they inhere. And the communities of qualities and actions can enter into communion with the sense-organs through the qualities or actions in which they inhere, which, again, inhere in substances. Thus the abstract qualities are related to the concrete qualities which, again, are related to a substance; and a substance alone can have a direct intercourse with a sense-organ. Thus some sort of direct or indirect relation must be established between the perceptible objects and the appropriate sense-organs. In all kinds of perception the objects must be directly or indirectly presented to consciousness. Let us discuss the different views in connection with the intercourse of the sense-organs with their objects.

### *The Earlier Nyaya-Vaisesika*

According to the earlier Nyaya-Vaisesika, perception depends upon the intercourse (*sannikarsa*) of the sense-organs with their objects. *Sannikarsa* is the function of the sense-organs by means of which they enter into a particular relation with their appropriate objects and bring about the perception of the objects. This intercourse between the sense-organs and their objects is of six kinds so far as our ordinary perception is concerned, viz. (i) Union (*samyoga*) (2) United-inherence (*samyukta-samavaya*), (3) United-inherent inherence (*samyukta-samaveta-samavaya*), (4) inherence (*samavaya*) (5) inherent-inherence (*samaveta-samavaya*) and (6) the relation of qualification and the qualified (*visesanata*). These different kinds of sense-object-intercourse (*indriyartha-sannikarsa*) are illustrated in the following examples :

1. Union (*samyoga*): The perception of a substance (*dravya*) is due to its union with a sense-organ. For instance, in the visual perception of a jar there is a union of the visual organ with the jar. The Nyaya-Vaisesika does not hold with the western psychologists that a substance is perceived through its qualities. He holds a contrary view. According to him, qualities are perceived through the substances in which they inhere.

2.. United-inherence or inherence is that which is in union (*samyukta-samavaya*). The perception of a quality or an action is due to its inherence in a substance which is in union with a sense-organ. For instance, in the visual perception of the colour of a jar there is a union of the visual organ with the jar in which colour inheres.

3. United-inherent-inherence, i.e. inherence is that which inheres in what is in union (*samyukta-samveta-samavaya*). For instance, in the visual perception of the generic character of the colour (*rupatva*) of a jar, there is a union of the visual organ with the jar in which inheres colour in which again inheres the generic character of colour.

4. Inherence (*samavaya*): For instance, in the auditory perception of sound there is the inherence of sound in the sense-organ, viz. the ear-drum which is pervaded by *akasa* (ether), the substratum of sound.

5. Inherent-inherence, i.e. inherence in that which inheres in a sense-organ (*samaveta-samavaya*): For instance, in the auditory perception of the generic character of sound (*sabdatva*) there is the inherence of the generic nature of sound in sound which again inheres in *akasa* (ether) of the ear-drum.

6. The relation of qualification and the qualified (*visesanata*) or (*visesya-visesana-sambandha*): For instance, in the perception of the absence of a jar on the ground, there is a union of the visual organ with the ground which is qualified by the absence of the jar. According to the Naiyayika, inherence (*samavaya*) and negation (*abhava*) are perceived through this kind of intercourse. But according to the Vaisesika, inherence is not an object of perception ; it is an object of inference. So, according to him, negation alone can be perceived through this kind of intercourse. "All that is the object of perception must fall within one or other of these modes of contact. The divergence of modes rests on ontological theories : the eye, for instance, as a substance can come into direct conjunction with another substance, but only indirectly with colour which inheres in that substance, and at a further remove with the class concept which inheres in the colour which inheres in the object with which the eye is in conjunction."

The last kind of the sense-object-intercourse, i.e. *visesanata* is of several kinds which are illustrated below :

(i) **Samyukta-visesanata**: For instance, the visual perception of the absence of a jar on the ground is due to its qualifying the ground which is in direct contact with the visual organ. Thus a negation also must directly or indirectly enter into relation with a substance which is in direct contact with a sense-organ.

(ii) **Samyukta-samaveta-visesanata**: For instance, the perception of the absence of taste in colour is due to its qualifying that which inheres in something in contact with a sense-organ. Here the absence of taste qualifies colour; colour inheres in a substance and the substance is in direct conjunction with a sense-organ.

(iii) **Samyukta-samaveta-samaveta-visesanata**: For instance, the perception of the absence of colour in the generic nature of number is due to its qualifying that which inheres in something inhering in that which is in direct contact with a sense-organ. The absence of colour qualifies the generic nature of number; the generic nature of number inheres in number; number inheres in a substance, and the substance is in direct conjunction with a sense-organ.

(iv) **Samyukta-samaveta-visesana-vtsesanata**: For instance, the perception of the absence of *rasatva* or the generic nature of taste in *rupatva* or the generic nature of colour is due to its qualifying the qualification existing in something inhering in that which is in conjunction with a sense-organ.

(v) **Visesanata**: For instance, the perception of the absence of sound is due to its qualifying the sense-organ, viz. the ear-drum pervaded by *akasa* (ether) which is the substratum of sound.

(vi) **Samaveta-visesanata**: For instance, the perception of the absence of the sound "kha" in the sound "ka" is due to its qualifying that which inheres in the sense-organ, viz. the ear-drum. The absence of the sound "kha" "qualifies the sound" "ka" which inheres in the ether of the ear-drum.

(vii) **Samaveta-samaveta-visesanata**: For instance, the perception of the absence of "khatva" (the generic nature of the sound " kha") in "gatva" (the generic nature of the sound "ga") is due to its qualifying that which inheres in something inhering in a sense-organ. Here the absence of "khatva" qualifies "gatva", "gatva" inheres in "ga"; and the sound "ga" inheres in the ether of the ear-drum.

(viii) **Visesana-visesanata**: For instance, the perception of the absence of "gatva" in the absence of "katva" is due to its qualifying that which qualifies a sense-organ. The absence of "gatva" qualifies the absence of "katva" the absence of "katva" qualifies the ether of the ear-drum.

(ix) **Samyukta-visesana-visesanata**: For instance, the perception of the absence of a cloth in the absence of a jar is due to its qualifying that which qualifies something in conjunction with a sense-organ. The absence of a cloth qualifies the absence of a pot the absence of a jar qualifies the ground; and the ground is in conjunction with the visual organ.

Some people regard either union (conjunction) or inherence only as the cause of perception; and they deny the intervening relationships described above. But the earlier Nyaya-Vaiesika generally admits six kinds of intercourse between the sense-organs and their objects, viz. union, united-inherence, united-inherent-inherence, inherence, inherent-inherence, and the relation of the qualified and the qualification. Substances are perceived through the first kind of *sannikarsa*, qualities, actions, etc., through the second; the genus of qualities, through the third; sound, through the fourth; the genus of sound, through the fifth and the absence of a substance, through the sixth. All objects of perception must depend upon one or other of these kinds of sense-object-intercourse.

***The Later Nyaya-Vaisesika or the Neo-Naiyayika (alaukika sannikarsa)***

In addition to the above six kinds of intercourse, which are called ordinary intercourse (*laukika sannikarsa*), the neo-Naiyayikas recognize three other kinds of extraordinary intercourse (*alaukikasannikarsa*) between the sense-organs and their objects.

Ordinary sensuous perception depends upon one of the six kinds of ordinary intercourse between an external or internal sense-organ and its object. But super-sensuous perception is not produced by any of these six kinds of ordinary intercourse; it is produced by an extraordinary intercourse. The extraordinary intercourse is of three kinds : (1) the intercourse (with all individual objects of a particular kind) through their generic character (*samanya-laksana-sannikarsa*), which brings about the perception of these individual objects at all times and places (2) the intercourse (with an object not present to a sense-organ) through its idea revived in memory (*jnana-laksanasannikarsa*) which brings about an indirect perception of that object; (3) the intercourse (with remote, subtle, past, and future objects) produced by meditation (*yogaja-sannikarsa*) which brings about the perception of these objects. Let us explain these different kinds of extraordinary intercourse.

### *The Intercourse through the Knowledge of Generic Character (Samanya-laksana-sannikarsa)*

Sometimes through the knowledge of the generic nature of an individual we perceive all other individuals of that kind at all times and all places, which are possessed of the same generic nature. In such a case, the knowledge of the generic nature (*samanya*) of an object constitutes the extraordinary intercourse. When, for instance, we see a particular case of smoke with the visual organ, and perceive its generic character (*dhumatva*) there arises in us a perception of smoke of all times and all places. In this perception there is an ordinary intercourse, viz. union (*samyoga*) between the visual organ and the particular case of smoke, and there is an ordinary intercourse, viz. united-inherence (*samyukta-samayaya*) between the visual organ and the generic character of this smoke; but the intercourse between the visual organ and all cases of smoke of all times and all places is not an ordinary one; it is an extraordinary intercourse because there cannot be an ordinary intercourse of the visual organ with all cases of smoke of all times and all places. The extraordinary intercourse consists herein the knowledge of the generic character of smoke (*dhumatva*) which is possessed by all cases of smoke of all times and all places. This kind of intercourse, which consists in the knowledge of a generic character, is called an extraordinary intercourse through the knowledge of a generic character (*samanyalaksana-sannikarsa*).

But what is the use of admitting such an extraordinary perception of all the objects at all times and all places possessed of a generic character, and for that reason, an extraordinary intercourse of the sense-organs with their objects ? It has been urged that the connection between a particular case of smoke and fire was perceived in a kitchen, but not the connection between all cases of smoke and fire, since all other cases of smoke were unperceived at the time and if all cases of smoke and all cases of fire were not perceived through an extraordinary intercourse, then there would not arise any doubt whether all cases of smoke are accompanied by fire; and unless there is such a doubt there can be no inference that this case of smoke is attended by fire, which removes the doubt. According to Visvanatha, when all cases of smoke are brought to consciousness through their generic character (e.g. *dhumatva*) which is perceived owing to its inherence in the smoke which is in conjunction with the visual organ, there arises a doubt in us as to the invariable concomitance between fire and the cases of smoke in other times and places, which are not in direct contact with the visual organ.

It may be objected that if there were an extraordinary intercourse with all objects through the knowledge of their generic character, we should become omniscient, inasmuch as in perceiving an object of knowledge (*prameya*) we could perceive, through the knowledge of its generic character (*prameyatva*), all objects of knowledge of all times and places. But Visvanatha urges that though we can perceive all objects of knowledge through the knowledge of their generic character, we cannot perceive their mutual differences through this kind of intercourse and hence we cannot become omniscient.

### *The Intercourse through Association (jnana-laksanasannikarsa)*

Sometimes an object is not present to a sense-organ, but it is revived in memory; and through the medium of its idea revived we perceive the object. This is called the intercourse through association, which brings about an indirect perception of the object. For instance, when we see a piece of sandal-wood we feel that it is fragrant. What is the cause of this visual perception of fragrant sandal ? Here there is a conjunction of the visual organ with the piece of sandal-wood, which gives rise to the direct visual perception of the sandal; but the fragrance of the sandal cannot come in contact with the visual organ, and so there cannot be direct visual perception of its fragrance. But the visual perception of the sandal brings to consciousness the idea of fragrance by association, which serves as the extraordinary intercourse in the visual perception of the fragrant sandal. This will be explained more elaborately in the next chapter.

There is a difference between the intercourse through the knowledge of generic character (*samanya-laksana-sannikarsa*) and the intercourse through the knowledge of an object revived in memory (*jnana-laksana-sannikarsa*)) though in both there is the intercourse through knowledge. In the former, the knowledge of the generic character (e.g. *dhumatva*) does not bring about the perception of itself but of its substrata, i.e. the individual objects of all times and places (e.g. all cases of smoke), which are possessed of the generic nature. In the latter, the knowledge of an object (e.g. fragrance of sandal) revived in memory does not bring about the perception of its substratum (e.g. sandal) but of the object itself (fragrance).

Some have urged that the visual perception of fragrant sandal may be explained by the intercourse through the knowledge of generic character (*samanya-laksana-sannikarsa*). For instance, when we see a piece of sandal, the visual perception of the sandal reminds us of its fragrance (*saurabha*) perceived in the past, and the generic character of fragrance (*saurabhatva*) which abides in the sandal in the relation of inherence (*samavaya*) and inherent-inherence (*samaveta-samavaya*) respectively. The recollection of the generic nature of fragrance (*saurabhatva*) through the intercourse through the generic character (*samanya-laksana-sannikarsa*) produces in us the perception of all individual fragrances, including the fragrance of this piece of sandal.

To this objection the neo-Naiyayika replies that though through the intercourse of the knowledge of the generic nature of fragrance (*samanya-laksana-sannikarsa*) we may perceive the fragrance of the sandal, we cannot perceive through this intercourse the generic nature of fragrance itself, owing to the absence of the intercourse of the visual organ with fragrance. Had there been the generic nature of fragrance (*saurabhatvatva*) we could have perceived the generic nature of fragrance (*saurabhatva*) through the intercourse of the knowledge of its generic character (*samanaya-laksana-sannikarsa*). But, in fact, there is no generic character of the fragrance. Hence we cannot perceive the generic character of fragrance through the intercourse of the knowledge of its generic character which is non-existent. Thus we must admit that there is another extraordinary intercourse through association (*jnana-laksana-sannikarsa*) to account for our perception of the generic character of the fragrance of the sandal. In illusory perceptions generally there is the intercourse through association (*jnana-laksana-sannikarsa*). For instance, in the illusory perception of silver in a nacre, no silver comes in contact with the visual organ; but still the idea of silver revived in memory by association produces the visual perception of silver.

### *The Intercourse Produced by Meditation (Yogaja-sannikarsa)*

Besides the intercourse through the knowledge of generic character and the intercourse through association, there is another extraordinary intercourse of the sense-organs with their objects, produced by meditation (*yogaja-sannikarsa*). This kind of intercourse again is of two kinds : (1) the intercourse in the perception of a person who is in an ecstatic condition (*yukta*) and (2) the intercourse in the perception of a person who is out of the ecstatic condition (*yunjana*). The nature of yogic perception (*yogi-pratyaksa*) will be fully discussed in a subsequent chapter.

### *The Mimamsaka*

Gaga Bhatta holds that there are three kinds of intercourse between the sense-organs and their objects (1) union (2) united-inherence (*samyukta-samavaya*), and (3) united-inherent inherence (*samyukta-samaveta-samavaya*). Substances are perceived through their union or conjunction with the sense-organs. The qualities, actions, and generalities inhering in the substances are perceived through united-inherence (*samyukta-samavaya*). And the communities of these qualities and actions are perceived through united-inherent inherence (*samyukta-samaveta-samavaya*). So far the Mimamsaka agrees with the Nyaya-Vaisesika. But he does not recognize inherence and inherent-inherence. According to him, sound is not perceived through inherence (*samavaya*) as the Nyaya-Vaisesika holds, because sound is not a quality but a substance; so it is perceived through union or conjunction (*samyoga*) with the ear. And consequently, the generic character of sound also is not perceived through inherent-inherence ; it is perceived through united-inherence like the generic character of any other substance (e.g. a jar). Thus according to the Mimamsaka there are only three kinds of intercourse between the sense-organs and their objects.

Salikanatha, a follower of Prabhakara, holds that there are three kinds of sense-object-intercourse, viz. union (*samyoga*), united inherence (*samyukta-samauaya*) and inherence (*samavaya*).

### The Samkarite

According to the Samkarite, there is no relation of inherence (*samavaya*). Inherence, according to him, is nothing but identity or co-essentiality (*tadatmya*). So the Samkarite recognizes the following six kinds of intercourse between the sense-organs and their objects :

1. ***Samyoga***: For instance, the visual perception of a jar is due to its direct contact or conjunction with the visual organ.
2. ***Samyukta-tadatmya***: For instance, the perception of colour is due to its co-essentiality or identity with something (e.g. a jar) which is in conjunction with the visual organ.
3. ***Samyukta-bhinnatadatmya***: For instance, the perception of the generic character of colour (*rupatva*) is due to its co-essentiality with something (e.g. colour) which is co-essential with that (e.g. a jar) which is in conjunction with the visual organ.
4. ***Tadatmya***: For instance, the perception of sound is due to its co-essentiality with the sense-organ, viz. the ear-drum which is pervaded by ether (*akasa*).
5. ***Tadatmyavada-bhinnatva***: For instance, the perception of the generic character of sound (*sabdatva*) is due to its co-essentiality with something (e.g. sound) which, again, is co-essential with the sense-organ, viz. the ear-drum which is pervaded by ether (*akasa*).
6. ***Visesya-Visesana-bhava***: For instance, the perception of the absence of a jar on the ground is due to the absence qualifying something (e.g. the ground) which is, therefore, possessed of this qualification (e.g. the absence of the jar).

Thus the Samkarite's *samyoga, samyukta-tadatmya, samyukta-bhinna-tadatmya, tadatmya, tadatmyavada-bhinnatva,* and *visesya-visesana-bhava* correspond to the Naiyayika's *samyoga, samyukta-samavaya, samyukta-samaveta-samavaya, samavaya, samaveta-samavaya,* and *visesya-visesana-sambandha* respectively.

**The Other Schools of Vedanta**

The Ramanujist holds that there are only two kinds of sense-object-intercourse, viz. *samyoga* and *samyuktasrayana*. The perception of substances is due to their conjunction with the appropriate sense-organs. And the perception of their qualities is due to the contact of the sense-organs with the substances in which the qualities subsist. The qualities are brought into relation with the sense-organs through the direct contact of their substances with the senses. The Vallabhite recognizes five kinds of sense-object-intercourse, viz. *samyoga, tadatmya, samyukta-tadatmya, samyukta-visesanata,* and *svarupa*. The perception of a jar is due to its contact (*samyoga*) with the visual organ. The perception of the colour of a jar is due to the contact of the visual organ with the jar which is identical with its colour. The internal perception of cognition, pleasure, and other properties of the mind (*svadharma*) is due to the relation of identity (*tadatmya*); there is identity between the mind and its properties. The perception of the absence of a jar on the ground is due to the contact of the visual organ with the ground which is the locus of the absence of the jar. "The locus is perceived by contact, *samyoga,* the negation as a predicate of the locus." The perception of the mental modes (*vrtti*) is due to *svarupasambandha,* they are perceived in themselves without implying any relation beyond themselves.

Janardana Bhatta, a follower of Madhva, refutes all kinds of sense-object-intercourse except union (*sathyoga*). We directly perceive objects and their qualities through the sense-organs. There is a direct contact of all perceptible objects with the sense-organs. And contact implies union. There are no other intervening relations between the senses and their objects. "The *guna* (quality) is identical with the *gum* (substance), and no relation can be conceived among them. Samavdya is refuted as involving an infinite regress and with the refutation of *samavaya,* the forms of *sarnavaya* can have no hold. *Alhava* (non-existence) is directly perceived, and we require no conception of relation."

# 5

# Acquired Perception

## Introduction

In the last chapter we have found that, according to the neo-Naiyayikas, there are not only different kinds of ordinary intercourse between the sense-organs and their objects, but also there are three kinds of extraordinary intercourse. For instance, the visual perception of fragrant sandal is explained by the neo-Naiyayikas as due to an extraordinary intercourse through the knowledge of fragrance, though it is not the proper object of the visual organ. In western psychology such a perception is generally regarded as an acquired perception. And this acquired perception has been analysed by the different schools of Indian philosophers and explained in slightly different ways. According to the Jaina, the so-called acquired perception is a complex psychosis made up of presentative and representative processes mechanically associated with each other and involving judgement and inference. According to the Vedantist also, it is a psychic compound made up of presentative and representative elements integrated together into a compound perception. But, according to the Nyaya-Vaisesika, an acquired perception is a single integral pulse of consciousness which is presentative or perceptual in character, though it is preceded by recollection. The Nyaya-Vaisesika does not admit the possibility of a composite consciousness or a psychic compound of distinct psychic entities. Let us now discuss these different views about acquired perception.

### *The Jaina*

The Jaina holds that the visual perception of fragrant sandal is a case of acquired perception. The visual organ alone cannot produce the perception of fragrant sandal, since fragrance cannot be apprehended by the visual organ. Nor can the visual organ produce this perception, even in co-operation with the recollection of fragrance; for, in that case, odour would be apprehended by the visual organ, which is impossible. The perception of odour cannot be produced by the visual organ. So the perception of fragrant sandal can neither be produced by the visual organ singly, nor in co-operation with the recollection of odour. We have, indeed, an apprehension of fragrant sandal after the operation of the visual organ in co-operation with the recollection of fragrance. But from this it does not follow that it is a simple psychosis of the nature of visual perception produced by the visual organ. In fact, it is a complex psychosis of presentative and representative processes mixed up together. It is a mixed mode of consciousness made up of presentative and representative elements mechanically associated with each other. There is an integrative association of two co-ordinate and co-existent elements, the visual percept of the sandal and the idea of fragrance freely reproduced in memory. The apprehension of fragrant sandal is simply a sum of two distinct psychic entities, the present optic sensation of the sandal plus an image of its fragrance reproduced from past experience by association and integrated together into a complex psychosis. And not only so; it involves a judgement and an inference. Though the sandal is perceived by the visual organ, and the fragrance is reproduced in memory by the law of association, the apprehension of the sandal as qualified by fragrance, or fragrant sandal, involves a process of judgement and an inference. Thus, according to the Jaina, in the acquired perception of fragrant sandal there is a free association of ideas, judgement, and inference. An acquired perception is rather an act of inference than perception, though it depends on both perception and recollection. This account of an acquired perception is similar to the account of the associationist psychology of the west.

### *The Samkara-Vedantist*

The Samkarite also holds that the visual perception of fragrant sandal is not a simple psychosis but a psychic compound of a presentative element and a representative element. It is a mixed mode of consciousness made up of a perceptual consciousness and a non-perceptual consciousness. There is a presentation of the sandal (i.e. its visual qualities) through the visual organ; and there is a representation of fragrance, since it cannot be perceived by the visual organ, these two heterogeneous elements are mixed up together and produce the compound perception of fragrant sandal. This psychic compound is not of the nature of a chemical compound but of the nature of a mechanical mixture. The presentative element and the representative element do not lose their identity in the mixed mode.

The Naiyayika may urge that if we recognize a mixed mode of presentative and representative processes, then presentation and representation would not be regarded as natural kinds. There cannot be an intermixture of natural kinds. But the Samkarite contends that there is no contradiction in the intermixture of presentative and representative elements in perception. The Naiyayika prejudice against intermixture of natural kinds or genera (*samkarya*) does not find place in the Vedantic monism.

It may be asked : In the visual perception of fragrant sandal is the apprehension of fragrance presentative or non-presentative ? It may be said that it can be neither. It cannot be presentative because here the apprehending mental mode does not take in the form of fragrance and identify itself with it, which is a condition of perception, according to the Samkarite. Nor can it be non-presentative, because the conditions of non-presentative knowledge are absent. For example, the knowledge of invariable concomitance between sandal and fragrance being absent, there can be no inference of fragrance in the visual perception of fragrant sandal. But the Samkarite holds that the apprehension of fragrance must be non-presentative for if fragrance of this piece of sandal were already perceived, then the apprehension of fragrance in this case would be a recollection (*smrti*) and if it were not already perceived, then the apprehension of fragrance in this case would be inferential. It can never be presentative because fragrance is not an object of visual perception. Thus according to the Samkarite, the visual perception of fragrant sandal is a mixed mode of consciousness made up of a presentative element and a representative element. It is a compound perception or tied perception in which an idea is tied to a percept. It is a presentative-representative complex.

In this way the visual perception of sweet mangoes also may be explained.

The Samkarite does not hold that such an experience is not a kind of perception at all but a case of inference. According to him, even an act of inference involves an element of perception as a constituent factor; for instance, in the inferential cognition of fire in a mountain the apprehension of fire is inferential, but the apprehension of the mountain is perceptual. These two psychoses are the integral factors of inferential knowledge. So, here, an act of perception involves an element of recollection and sometimes an act of inference as an integral factor. Herein lies the difference between the Jaina and the Vedantist in their views of acquired perception.

### *The Nyaya-Vaisesika*

According to both the Jaina and the Samkarite, the visual perception of fragrant sandal is a mixed mode of consciousness or a psychic compound of presentative and representative processes. But the Nyaya-Vaisesika, like William James, does not admit the possibility of a mixed mode of consciousness. Every psychosis is simple. There cannot be a psychic compound of simultaneous psychoses owing to the atomic nature of the *manas*, without which there can be no psychosis at all. According to this view, the visual perception of fragrant sandal is a simple psychosis, though it is preceded by the visual perception of the sandal and the recollection of its fragrance. It is an integral pulse of consciousness in the language of William James.

Sridhara refutes the theory of psychic fusion in explaining an acquired perception in *Nyayakandali*. In the visual perception of fragrant sandal, fragrance is the qualification (*visesana*) and sandal is the qualified object (*visesya*). Some hold that both the qualification and the qualified object the fragrance and the sandal are apprehended by a single compound psychosis. They explain this perception in the following manner. The visual organ cannot apprehend odour (fragrance), and the olfactory organ cannot apprehend the sandal (i.e. the visual qualities of the sandal) ; and hence these two sense-organs cannot apprehend the relationship between fragrance and the sandal, since the perception of relationship would depend upon the perception of the two factors related. But just as the single psychosis of recognition, which is a kind of perception, is produced by a sense-organ in co-operation with the subconscious impressions of past experience, and thus apprehends both the past and the present, so the visual perception of fragrant sandal is produced jointly by the visual organ and the olfactory organ, and hence it apprehends both the sandal and its fragrance. This requires a word of explanation. According to this view, the visual perception of fragrant sandal is a compound perception involving two factors, viz. the visual perception of the sandal and the recollection of fragrance. Here the first psychosis depends upon the past experience of fragrance produced by the olfactory organ. Thus ultimately the visual perception of fragrant sandal is produced by both the visual organ and the olfactory organ.

But Sridhara contends that this explanation is not satisfactory. A cognition is not made up of parts; if it were so, then one part of it could be produced by the olfactory organ, and the other by the visual organ. But, in fact, there can be no composite consciousness or a psychic compound. A cognition is an impartible whole or a simple psychosis. And if such a simple psychosis produced by both the visual organ and the olfactory organ apprehends the sandal as well as its fragrance, then from this it would follow that the odour (fragrance) is apprehended by the visual organ, and the sandal (apart from fragrance) by the olfactory organ; because that thing is apprehended by an organ which is the object of the cognition produced by that organ. But since the internal organ or *manas* is atomic, it cannot operate upon the two sense-organs at one and the same time.

Hence it must be admitted by all that in the visual perception of fragrant sandal at first the fragrance of the sandal (*visesana*) is perceived by the olfactory organ, and then afterwards the visual organ produces the visual perception of the sandal alone (*visesya*) in co-operation with the previous olfactory perception of fragrance.

Jayanta Bhatta also gives a similar account of acquired perception in *Nyayamanjari*. He analyses the visual perception of a fragrant flower. In this perception there is a visual perception of the flower, but not of its fragrance, since odour is not an object of visual perception. So there cannot be a visual perception of the flower as qualified by fragrance, or the fragrant flower. What happens in this case is that the present visual perception of the flower is qualified by the previous cognition of the fragrance produced by the olfactory organ on a previous occasion, and the flower is perceived as fragrant not by the visual organ, because it cannot apprehend odour, but by the internal organ or *manas*. Thus, according to Jayanta Bhatta, though there is a visual perception of the flower, there is not a visual perception of the fragrant flower. The visual presentation of the flower is qualified by the idea of fragrance perceived in the past by the olfactory organ, and the single unitary perception of the fragrant flower is not produced by the visual organ but by the internal organ or *manas*, even as the single unitary process of recognition which is a kind of qualified perception or a perception produced by peripheral stimulation qualified by the recollection of a past experience is produced by the internal organ or *manas*. Thus Jayanta Bhatta regards an acquired perception as a new type of a synthetic unity of apperception.

It may be objected that the flower is qualified by present qualifications. But the fragrance that is manifested in consciousness in the perception of the fragrant flower does not exist at present, but existed in the past and was apprehended by the olfactory organ. How can a past qualification qualify a present object? Jayanta Bhatta replies that just as after eating ninety-nine fruits we come to the hundredth fruit and recognize it as such, only because the perception of this fruit is qualified by the previous perception of the ninety-nine fruits which no longer exist, so in the perception of a fragrant flower the present visual perception of the flower is qualified by the previous olfactory perception of fragrance.

Thus Jayanta Bhatta holds that there cannot be a visual perception of a fragrant flower, since odour can never be perceived by the visual organ. When the flower is perceived by the visual organ, and the idea of fragrance is revived from past experience, the fragrant flower is perceived by the central sensory or *manas*, which can apprehend all sensible objects, colour, odour, etc. But this is rather avoiding the difficulty. When we see a flower, or a piece of sandal-wood, we distinctly feel that it is fragrant. We distinctly feel that we have a visual perception of the fragrant flower or the fragrant sandal.

The neo-Naiyayikas, Gangesa and his followers hold that when we see a piece of sandal-wood and feel that it is fragrant, we have not an internal perception of fragrant sandal through the central sensory, as Jayanta Bhatta holds, but a distinctly visual perception of the fragrant sandal. But how can we have a visual perception of fragrant sandal, since fragrance can never be an object of visual perception? Gangesa replies that the visual perception of fragrant sandal is not an ordinary perception (*laukika-pratyaha*) due to an ordinary intercourse (*laukika-sannikarsa*), but it is an extraordinary perception (*alaukika pratyaksa*) due to an extraordinary intercourse (*alaukika sannikarsa*). There cannot be an ordinary intercourse of the visual organ with the fragrance of the sandal, since odour is not an object of visual perception. But the fragrance of the sandal revived in memory by association constitutes an extraordinary intercourse called *jnana-laksana-sannikarsa* and through it gives rise to the visual perception of the fragrant sandal. Here, though there is an ordinary intercourse of the visual organ with the sandal and thus there is a direct visual perception of the sandal. There is an extraordinary intercourse through the idea of fragrance revived in memory by association, and thus there arises a visual perception of the fragrant sandal. Thus the neo-Naiyayika differs from Jayanta Bhatta, who holds that though the sandal is perceived by the visual organ, the fragrant sandal is not perceived by it but by the central sensory or *manas,* when there is a visual perception of the sandal and a recollection of its fragrance perceived by the olfactory organ in the past.

Vardhamana distinguishes between the visual perception of fragrant sandal and the olfactory perception of the fragrance of sandal. Sometimes we see a piece of sandal and at once perceive that it is fragrant. And sometimes we smell an odour and at once perceive that it is the fragrance of sandal. The former perception is produced by the visual organ in co-operation with the recollection of fragrance perceived by the olfactory organ on a previous occasion. And the latter perception is produced by the olfactory organ in co-operation with the recollection of sandal perceived by the visual organ in the past.

Both the earlier and later Naiyayikas admit that the perception of fragrant sandal is a single unitary presentation; it is not a compound of presentative and representative elements but a presentation qualified by a representative process which is its immediate antecedent. The Naiyayika does not admit a psychic compound or a mixed mode of consciousness, which is admitted by the Samkarite. According to him, there is no simultaneity of psychoses owing to the atomic nature of the *manas*, and, moreover, there cannot be an intermixture of two heterogeneous psychoses, e.g. a presentative process and a representative process. This has been clearly pointed out by Udayana in *Nyayakusumanjali.*

# 6

# Recognition

## The Nature of Recognition

The process of recognition has been analysed by all the schools of Indian thinkers from both the standpoints of psychology and epistemology. Here, we shall attempt only a psychological analysis of recognition from the different standpoints of Indian thinkers. Recognition is a complex psychosis depending upon presentative and representative processes. It depends both upon peripheral stimulation and ideal reproduction of a past experience. A cognition produced by peripheral stimulation is admitted by all to be perception, and a cognition reproduced in imagination by the revival of the residua of past experience is admitted by all to be recollection. But recognition is a complex psychosis which depends both upon peripheral stimulation and reproduction of a past experience. Is it, then, to be regarded as a single psychosis or two psychoses ? If it is a single psychosis, is it a kind of perception, or quite a new psychosis? The Buddhist holds that recognition is not a single unitary psychosis but a mechanical composition of two psychoses, presentative and representative. The Nyaya-Vaisesika, the Mimamsaka, and the Vedantist hold that recognition is single psychosis of the nature of perception; according to them, it is a qualified perception. The Jaina holds that recognition is a single psychosis, but it is not a kind of perception; it is a unique psychosis; it is neither presentative nor representative, nor both, but *sui generis*; it is a chemical compound, as it were, of presentation and representation, different from both. Let us now consider the different views of recognition in detail.

### *The Buddhist*

When we perceive a pot and recognize it to be an object of our past experience, we have a recognitive consciousness such as "this is that pot". Is this recognition a single psychosis or a combination of two psychoses, presentative and representative ? If it is a single psychosis, the Buddhist asks, what is its cause?

1. The sense-organ cannot be the cause of recognition, since it requires a present object for its stimulation to produce a cognition; it can never come in contact with a past object and so cannot account for the consciousness of thatness or the past condition of the object involved in recognition.
2. The subconscious impressions (*samskara*) left by previous perceptions cannot be cause of recognition, because they refer to past perceptions of which they are residua, and therefore cannot account for the consciousness of thatness or the present condition of the object involved in recognition.
3. Nor can recognition be brought about by the co-operation of the sense-organ with sub-conscious impressions, because they are found to operate separately and produce different effects. The sense-organ always produces direct apprehension, and subconscious impressions always produce memory; so they can never bring about a single effect in the shape of recognition when they co-operate with each other.

Hence recognition is not a single psychosis produced either by the sense-organs or by subconscious impressions or by both together, but it involves two discrete psychoses, presentative and representative, mechanically associated with each other. It cannot be a single unitary process, for one and the same psychosis cannot apprehend the past as well as the present condition of an object, and thus can never apprehend its identity in the past and the present. It is a mechanical composition of presentative and representative processes, of which the former apprehends the present character of its object and the latter apprehends its past character. We have no psychosis to apprehend the identity of an object in the past and the present.

Even if we concede that recognition is a single psychosis, what is the nature of its object ? If it apprehends a past object, it does not differ from recollection; if it apprehends a future object, it does not differ from constructive or anticipatory imagination; if it apprehends only what exists at the present moment, then it does not recognize the identity of its object in the past and the present; and it is self-contradictory to hold that it can apprehend an object as existing in the past, the present, and the future.

For the same reason it cannot be held that recognition apprehends an object as qualified by a previous cognition, for a past cognition does not exist at present, and therefore cannot qualify the object of the present cognition; and if the past cognition, which is supposed to qualify the object of recognition, is not at all apprehended as past, an object cannot be perceived as qualified by the previous cognition in an act of recognition. Thus recognition cannot be regarded as a kind of qualified perception. It consists of two distinct psychoses, presentative and representative.

### *The Nyaya-Vaisesika*

The Nyaya-Vaisesika holds that recognition is a single unitary process. It apprehends both the past condition of its object and its present condition by a synthetic act of apperception. Jayanta Bhatta severely criticizes the Buddhist theory of recognition in *Nyayamanjari*.

The Buddhist argues that there is no recognition as a single psychosis because there is no cause of recognition. The effect cannot exist if there is no cause of it. But this is reversing the order of things. We may infer a cause of a given effect, but we cannot deny the existence of the effect, even if we cannot account for it. Though neither sense-organs nor subconscious impressions by themselves can account for the fact of recognition, still when they cooperate with each other, their co-operation can account for it. Though sense-organs can produce only perception, and subconscious impressions can produce only recollection, yet when they co-operate with each other, they can produce recognition, which is a kind of qualified perception.

What is the object of recognition, according to the Nyaya-Vaisesika ? The object of recognition is something existing at present but also qualified by the past time. Thus recognition apprehends both the past and present character of its object.

But the Buddhist asks : Is it not self-contradictory to suppose that one and the same mental process, viz. recognition, apprehends the past as well as the present character of its object, inasmuch as the past and the present cannot exist at the same time, and so cannot simultaneously qualify an object ? The past is past; it does not exist at present; how, then, can both the past and the present be apprehended by the same act of recognition, and qualify its object? The Naiyayika replies that the past is apprehended as past, and the present is apprehended as present by recognition; so that the object of recognition is one and the same, being qualified by the past and the present both. Hence there is no contradiction in holding that recognition apprehends an object qualified both by the past and the present.

But the Buddhist asks again : How is it that a presentative cognition produced by peripheral stimulation apprehends an object qualified by the past time ? The Naiyayika replies that the object which existed in the past exists at present also ; so in recognition the object is presented to consciousness as existing at present and also qualified by the past. And there is nothing incongruous in this. When we eat a number of fruits, say, one hundred, and after eating ninety-nine fruits come to the hundredth fruit, we have the consciousness of having eaten ninety-nine fruits, so that the cognition of the hundredth fruit is qualified by the fruits which existed in the past, many seconds before the hundredth fruit is eaten, and the number hundred recognized; and even though what is past is not present at the time, yet the relation which the object had with the past time is certainly present in the object, and the qualification of an object by its relation to the past time is all that is necessary for recognition apprehending an object as qualified by the past time.

Is, then, recognition presentative or representative? According to the Nyaya-Vaisesika, it is presentative or perceptual in character, though it is produced by the sense-organs with the help of subconscious impressions. For, according to the Nyaya-Vaisesika, whatever mental state is produced by peripheral stimulation is an immediate, presentative or perceptual cognition. Recognition is produced by peripheral stimulation, though with the help of subconscious impressions left by previous perceptions; hence it must be regarded as a kind of presentative cognition or perception. Though the sense-organs by themselves cannot produce the cognition of a past object, yet in co-operation with the subconscious impressions of past experience they can produce the cognition of an object as qualified by the past time. Hence recognition is defined by Jayanta Bhatta as the perception of a present object qualified by the past time, due to the contact of a sense-organ with the present object, or as the perception of a present object, as modified by its past cognition. Just as the visual perception of a flower is modified by the previous olfactory perception of its fragrance, which is not perceived by the visual organ at the present, and thus brings about the indirect visual perception of a fragrant flower through the central sensory or manas, so in recognition the perception of a present object is modified by a past cognition reproduced in imagination. Though pure perception is produced by the peripheral organs, and pure recollection is produced by subconscious impressions, recognition is produced by the cooperation of both, and the object of recognition is perceived through the manas, as qualified by the past cognition of the object. Sivaditya also defines recognition as the apprehension of aṇ object as qualified by the past time. Madhava Sarasvati regards recognition as the apprehension of an object as qualified by the present and the past time. Visvanatha refers to a doctrine which regards recollection as a cause of recognition, since a subconscious impression without being revived cannot bring about recognition, and it is better to hold that a recollection, rather than a revived impression, is the cause of recognition.

Thus recognition is not a mixed mode of consciousness made up of presentative and representative elements, for the Nyaya-Vaisesika does not admit the simultaneity of two or more cognitions owing to the atomic nature of the manas. According to this view, recognition is a single presentative cognition or perception, but qualified by the past time or by the past cognition of the object. Recognition, therefore, is a kind of qualified perception.

### *The Mimamsaka*

Kumarila agrees with the Naiyayika in regarding recognition as a presentative cognition. He puts forward the following reason. Whatever cognition is produced by peripheral stimulation is presentative or perceptual in nature. Recognition is present when there is peripheral stimulation. Though recognition is preceded by an act of recollection, it is not to be regarded as non-perceptual in character, inasmuch as it is produced by the contact of a senseorgan with a present object. There is no injunction that only such a cognition is to be regarded as a perception, as is prior to recollection. Nor is the operation of the sense-organs, after recollection, precluded by any valid reason. Thus the fact of following upon recollection cannot deprive a cognition of its perceptual character, if it is produced by peripheral stimulation. For these reasons, Kumarila regards every cognition as a perception, which is produced by peripheral stimulation, whether it appears before or after recollection. Hence he regards recognition as a kind of perception.

*The Samkara-Vedantist*

The Samkarite agrees with the Naiyayika and the Mimamsaka in holding that recognition is a perceptual cognition produced by peripheral stimulation and subconscious impressions co-operating together.

Akhandananda Muni, the author of *Tattvadipana* asks : What is the cause of recognition? Is it produced by the residua of past experience? Or is it produced by peripheral stimulation? Or is it produced by both together? The first alternative is false. Residua of past experience can apprehend only the past condition of an object; they cannot apprehend the distinctive character of the object as determined by the present time and space. The second alternative also is false. The sense-organs can apprehend only the present condition of the object. They cannot apprehend the distinctive character of the object as determined by the past time and space. And the Buddhist contends that the third alternative also is false for the following reason. If recognition were produced by peripheral stimulation and subconscious impressions together, it would be characterized by the dual nature of perception and recollection, and thus would not be able to apprehend the identity of the object in the past and the present. According to the Buddhist, one and the same cognition cannot be both immediate and mediate, presentative and representative. But the Vedantist believes in the fusion of psychoses, and thus regards recognition as a single complex psychosis apprehending the identity of an object in the past and the present, due to peripheral stimulation in co-operation with subconscious impressions. Akhandananda Muni points out that though recognition is produced by the co-operation of peripheral stimulation and subconscious impressions, it is perceptual in character and does not involve the twofold element of perception and recollection, for recollection is produced by subconscious impressions alone. But it may be objected that if recognition is perceptual in character, it cannot apprehend the past condition of the object, which is involved in recognition. The Vedantist replies that recognition apprehends the past condition of the object, because it is not produced by peripheral stimulation alone but by peripheral stimulation together with subconscious impressions.

Thus both the Vedantist and the Naiyayika regard recognition as a kind of perception. But there is a slight difference between the two views. According to the Vedantist, recognition is a single complex psychosis containing presentative and representative elements. It is a presentative-representative process. According to the Naiyayika, recognition is a single simple psychosis which is presentative in character; it does not contain both presentative and representative elements; it is a kind of perception which is produced by peripheral stimulation and subconscious impressions together. The Vedantist believes in the fusion of elementary psychoses into a composite psychosis. But the Naiyayika cannot believe in psychic fusion for two reasons. In the first place, two psychoses cannot be simultaneously present in the self, owing to the atomic nature of the mind. In the second place, perception and memory are entirely different kinds of psychoses, and there can be no intermixture of two distinct classes. But the Vedantist does not believe in the atomic nature of the mind, and he has no prejudice against the intermixture of distinct kinds of psychoses. So he believes in the simultaneous occurrence of two distinct kinds of psychoses and their fusion into a unitary composite psychosis. Herein lies the difference between the Naiyayika view of recognition and the Vedantist view.

### *The Jaina*

The Jaina regards recognition as a single unitary psychosis produced by perception and recollection both, which apprehends the identity of an object in the past and present. It is neither of the nature of perception nor of the nature of recollection, nor a mechanical association of perception and recollection both, nor a composite psychosis containing the twofold element of perception and recollection. It is a unique psychosis; it is *sul generis*; it Is a single unitary psychosis produced by perception and recollection both. Perception apprehends the present condition of an object. Recollection apprehends the past condition of an object. Recognition which is a quite new psychosis apprehends the identity of an object in the past and the present. So recognition is different from perception and recollection, and its object also is different from that of perception and recollection. Thus the Jaina differs from the Nyaya-Vaisesika, the Mimamsaka and the Vedantist, who regard recognition as a kind of perception, and from the Buddhist, who regards it as a mechanical association of two distinct psychoses, viz. perception and recollection.

### The Jaina Criticism of the Nyaya-Vaisesika View

The Nyaya-Vaisesika, the Mimamsaka and the Vedantist regard recognition as a kind of perception. But it cannot be regarded as a kind of perception. For wherever peripheral stimulation is present perception is present, and wherever peripheral stimulation is absent perception is absent. But wherever peripheral stimulation is present, recognition is not present, and wherever peripheral stimulation is absent, recognition is not absent. In other words, recognition does not directly follow upon peripheral stimulation. If it did, then we should have recognition even at the time of the perception of an individual object for the first time. Nor can it be said that recognition is produced by a sense-organ in co-operation with the recollection of the object owing to the revival of the residua left by the previous perceptions of the object, because perception is quite independent of memory. If perception did depend upon memory, it would never apprehend an object which was never perceived in the past it would never apprehend a new object.

It may be argued that recognition is different from recollection, since it apprehends an object existing here and now; and hence it is a kind of perception. The Jaina contends that perception is produced by peripheral stimulation; and peripheral stimulation is possible only when the stimulus is present; and hence perception apprehends only a present object. But as recognition apprehends the identity of an object in the past and the present, its object cannot be apprehended by perception which depends upon the stimulation of a sense-organ by a present object. It has been urged that the recollection of an object of past experience gives rise to a cognition in response to peripheral stimulation, which is called recognition. Thus recognition is a kind of perception, inasmuch as it is produced by peripheral stimulation not independently, but in co-operation with the recollection of a past experience. But this also is impossible. A perception can never apprehend the past condition of an object. How, then, can it incorporate into itself the recollection of past experience ? In fact, recognition is neither perception nor recollection, but a sui generis psychosis produced by both. It is not a kind of perception, since it is not direct and immediate knowledge.

## *The Jaina Criticism of the Buddhist View*

The Buddhist holds that recognition is not a single psychosis, but a mechanical association of two distinct psychoses, presentative and representative, there being no third kind of cognition different from perception and memory, which may be called recognition. The Jaina contends that recognition is distinctly felt as a single unitary process produced by perception and memory both, which apprehends the identity of an object in the midst of past and present modifications. Recollection cannot apprehend the identity of an object in the past and the present, since it can apprehend only the past condition of an object. Nor can perception apprehend the identity of an object in the past and the present, since it can apprehend only the present condition of an object. And if it is said that a determinate cognition arising out of the residua of both perception and recollection apprehends the identity of an object in the past and the present, then that is nothing but recognition which is quite a new psychosis.

The Buddhist himself admits the possibility of a psychic fusion in the consciousness of a motley colour (*citrajnand*) in which many cognitions of blue, yellow, etc., are fused together. Why, then, should he object to the possibility of a new psychosis of recognition produced by presentation and representation both? Even supposing that recognition consists of two discrete psychoses presentative and representative mechanically associated with each other, are they felt in consciousness as interpenetrating each other, or in mechanical juxtaposition with each other ? In the former case, recognition would be felt either as perception or as recollection. In the latter, it would be felt as a dual consciousness, both presentative and representative, distinct from each other. But, in fact, recognition is never felt either as perception or recollection or both together. Hence it must be regarded as a unique psychosis differing both from perception and recollection. And the object of recognition is neither a past object nor a present object, but the identity of an object in the past and the present, which can never be apprehended by perception and recollection.

The Jaina holds that there is a sort of mental chemistry in the production of the state of recognition; it is not a result of mechanical composition and association of presentative and representative processes, as the Buddhist supposes. Recognition is *sui generis*. It is a compound psychosis, no doubt, but like a chemical compound, it differs in quality from its constituent elements. It differs both from perception and recollection, and is yet a combination of the two psychoses.

Prabhacandra includes all kinds of presentative-representative cognition of relations in recognition. The perception of identity, similarity, dissimilarity, relation of sign and signate, etc., are involved in recognition. It implies the elaborative processes of comparison, assimilation, discrimination, spatial and temporal localization. Prabhacandra agrees with Herbert Spencer and William James in holding that not only the ultimate feelings and sensations are presentations, but the relations among them also are presentations. The relational processes do not imply the synthetic activity of the understanding, and consequently are not necessarily involved in the operations of conceptual thinking. Thus Prabhacandra differs from Bradley and Green who regard relational processes as the synthetic operations of the understanding.

But is it not self-contradictory to say that one and the same psychosis has two temporal marks ? The Jaina replies that if there is dual nature in the process of recognition, it is not self-contradictory, because the manifoldness of one and the same object of knowledge is usual, since contradiction is the very essence of the reality. The manifoldness of recognition is a datum, we cannot deny its existence or explain it away.

# 7

# Theories of Perception

## The Buddhist Theory of Perception

There are four schools of *Buddhists*. The Vaibhasikas hold that the external world is an object of perception. They maintain the independent existence of nature and mind; the nature is extramental and is immediately perceived by the mind. The Sautrantikas also hold that the external world exists. But according to them, it is not an object of direct perception. The external objects produce presentations in the mind through which we infer the existence of external objects. From the epistemological point of view, both the Vaibhasikas and the Sautrantikas are realists; but the former are advocates of naive realism, while the latter are hypothetical dualists or cosmothetic idealists, to use the expression of Hamilton. The Yogacaras do not believe in the existence of extra-mental objects. According to them, the immediate objects of our consciousness are the ideas of the mind; these ideas can never carry us beyond themselves to extra-mental objects. Thus the Yogacaras are subjective idealists. The Madhyamikas annul the existence of mind and matter, subject and object, and go beyond them to the void (*sunya*) which is beyond the scope of intellectual knowledge. Thus the Madhyamikas are nihilists. But here we are not concerned with the epistemological theories of perception. We shall deal here only with the psychological analysis of perception given by the *Buddhists*. The only *Buddhist* work in which we find a psychological analysis of perception is Nyayalindu of Dharmakirti with its commentaries, *Nyayabindutika* and *Nyayabindutikatippam*. Here the subject has been treated probably from the Sautrantika point of view.

Dinnaga defined perception in his *Pramana-samuccaya* as the cognition which is free from *kalpanas* or mental concepts, e.g. name, class, and the like. Dharmakirti defined perception as the non-erroneous cognition devoid of mental concepts or kalpanas? Perception must be non-erroneous. This is the logical condition of valid perception. But here we shall not discuss the conditions of valid perception. So far as its psychological nature is concerned, perceptual cognition must be free from mental constructs or kalpanas. Perception is direct or immediate knowledge. If perception is defined as the cognition produced by the sense-object-contact, as the Naiyayika does, mental perception will be excluded from the category of perception. Perception is direct presentation of an object (*saksatkarijnanam*).

Perception must be free from kalpanas. But what is kalpana ? Kalpana, according to Dharmakirti, is a name which denotes an object. Perception, therefore, must be free from all association of names. It must be inarticulate, nameless, or indeterminate perception. Names are artificial verbal signs which are assigned by the mind to the objects of perception, when it recognizes them as members of a particular class or as the same as perceived before. To associate an object of perception with a name, therefore, is to remember similar objects perceived in the past and recognize them. This is not produced by the object of perception. When the sense-organs come in contact with their appropriate objects, they produce direct presentations or perceptual cognitions. The objects are presented to the mind, when they come in contact with the proper sense-organs. But the act of recognition or assigning a name to the object of perception is not directly produced by the sense-object contact. Names of objects are never presented to the sense-organs. They are never presented to the senses by the objects of perception. The acts of recognition and naming involve the unification of the objects of present experience with the objects of past experience, so that they are not directly produced by objects coming in contact with the proper sense-organs, for past objects can never be presented to the senses.

Sometimes though the objects of perception are not associated with definite names, they are capable of being associated with names. For instance, though an infant does not know the names of objects, and as such his perception is not associated with any name, it may not be free from kalpana or mental construct. Even an infant does not begin to suck the breast of his mother, until he recognizes the breast to be the same as experienced before. Thus perception must be free from all association with names, and it must not involve any content of consciousness which may be represented by names; it must not involve naming and recognition; it must not contain any ideal factor or mental construct. It must be the direct and immediate presentation of an object, free from all elaborative or interpretative processes. It must represent only the given element in experience. It must not import anything new into the given order from within the mind from past experience.

The Naiyayikas and others hold that indeterminate perception apprehends the qualified object (*visesya*) and qualifications (*visesana*) but not their relations to each other. But the *Buddhi*st contends that indeterminate perception does not at all apprehend the qualifications of its object, viz. generality, substantiality, quality, action, and name, but it simply apprehends the mere object apart from its qualifications. It cannot apprehend both the qualified object and its qualifications. It merely apprehends the specific individuality of an object (*svalaksana*) devoid of all qualifications.

The specific individuality of an object is unique and *sui generis;* it is quite different from anything other than itself; it can never be expressed by words, it is apprehended only by perception. So perception is always indeterminate. There is no determinate perception. The so-called determinate perception is not perceptual in character because it is not produced by peripheral stimulation. It is produced by the recollection of the name of the object perceived. Between peripheral stimulation and the determinate cognition there is an intervening factor of the recollection of the name. So the determinate cognition is not purely presentative in character, but it is a presentative-representative process. But the *Buddhi*st regards perception as entirely free from factors of imagination. So he does not admit the possibility of determinate perception.

Dharmakirti recognizes four kinds of perception; sense-perception (*indriyajndna*) mental perception (*manovijnana*), self-consciousness (*svasamvedana*) and yogic perception (*yogipratyaksa*). Sense-perception is produced by the sense-organs. It is an "immediate feltness", a bare sensation. It gives rise to mental perception which immediately succeeds it, and belongs to the same series. Mental perception is due to four causes : the objective datum, e.g. external stimulus (*alambana-pratyaya*), the co-operative cause (*sahakaripratyaya*), e.g. light in visual perception, the dominant cause, e.g. the sense-organ (*adhipatipratyaya*), and the immediate cause, e.g. the immediately preceding cognition (*samanantarapratyaya*). Dharmottara distinguishes mental perception from sense-perception. When the visual organ has ceased to operate we have mental perception. So long as the visual organ continues to operate, the perception of colour is nothing but sense-perception. So mental perception is continuous with sense-perception, and immediately follows upon it. Self-consciousness is, the perception of the mind and mental states like pleasure and pain, The direct and immediate apprehension of mental states is of the nature of self-conscious awareness (*svasamvedana*). They are not perceived by other cognitions, as the Nyaya-Vaisesika holds. They are directly perceived by themselves. Self-consciousness is perception, since it directly intuits itself, is devoid of concepts, and free from error. Yogic perception is the direct intuition of the real, due to intense meditation on the four truths of *Buddhi*sm, We shall discuss the *Buddhi*st doctrine of yogic intuition later on.

**The Jaina Theory of Perception**

The Jaina recognizes only two kinds of valid knowledge : direct knowledge (*aparoksa*) and indirect knowledge (*paroksa*). Knowledge is direct when it is immediate or distinct. Knowledge is indirect when it is mediate. Perception is direct or immediate knowledge because it is directly derived from the senses and the mind, while mediate knowledge (e.g. inferential knowledge, verbal knowledge, etc.) is derived through the medium of some other knowledge.

Manikyanandi defines perception as distinct apprehension (*visadam pratyaham*). What is the meaning of distinctness ? That knowledge is distinct, which is not mediated by some other kind of knowledge. And that knowledgẹ is distinct, which apprehends an object in all its details.

Perception is of two kinds : *samvyavaharika pratyaksa* and *mukhya pratyaksa*. The former is the ordinary perception of everyday life. The latter is super-normal perception. *Samvyavaharika pratyaksay* again, is of two kinds : perception produced by the senses (*indriya-niwandhana*) and perception not produced by the senses (*anindriya-niwandhana*). The Jaina regards the eye, the ear, the nose, the tongue, and the skin only as sense-organs. He does not regard the mind (*manas*) as a sense-organ. The mind is called no-sense-organ (*anmdriya*). Hence the two varieties of ordinary perception are : sense-perception and mental perception. *Mukhya pratyaksa* is of three kinds: *avadhi* or clairvoyant perception of objects at a distance of time and space, *manahparyaya* or telepathic knowledge of thoughts in other minds, and *kevala* or infinite knowledge unlimited by time and space, or omniscience. All of them are perceptual in nature.

The Jaina distinguishes between *darsana* and *Jnana*. *Darsana* is the simple apprehension of an object. Just after peripheral stimulation there is the bare cognition of an object in a general way. It apprehends only its general features (*sattamatra*) and not its particular features. *Jnana* is the apprehension of the special features of an object. *Darsana* is the "knowledge of acquaintance", while *jnana* is the "knowledge about" an object. *Darsana* is called indeterminate perception (*nirvikalpa jnana*) in other systems of philosophy. But the Jaina does not recognize it as *jnana* or knowledge. *Jnana* is always determinate; it must have a definite form (*sakara*); it must apprehend the special features (*visesa*) of its object. So the Jaina does not regard *darsana* as indeterminate perception, because perception is always definite and determinate.

In our ordinary perception (*sarivuyavaharika pratyaksa*) there are four stages : (1) *Avagraha,* (2) *Iha,* (3) *Avaya,* and (4) *Dharana.*

Just after *darsana* there is *avagraha. Darsana* is the simple apprehension of an object in a general way. When a stimulus acts upon a sense-organ, there is an excitation in consciousness, and the person is barely conscious of the mere existence (*sattamatra*) of an object. This is *darsana.* It is indistinct and indefinite. Just after this simple apprehension, there is the cognition of an object together with its general and special features (e.g. white colour). This is *avagraha.* It grasps the details of an object. But it does not apprehend all the details of the object. It excites a desire in the person to know more about the object. This desire to know the particulars of the object is called *iha.* It is a desire to know whether the object is this or that. In the stage of *avagraha* we have the perception of white colour. But in the stage of *iha,* we desire to know whether the white object is a row of herons or a flag. Then there is *avaya*. It is the ascertainment of the true nature of the object. "In the third stage, *avaya,* there is a definite finding of the particulars which we desired to know in the second stage. The second stage (*avagraha*) is merely an attempt to know the particulars, while the third stage consists in the ascertainment of these particulars." When we observe the upward and downward movement of the birds and the fluttering of their wings we definitely know that there is a row of herons and not a flag. *Avaya* is the definite perception of an object as this and not that. It involves assimilation and discrimination. In it we clearly perceive the similarities of the object with other objects perceived in the past, and its differences from others. It involves the recognition of an object as belonging to a definite class. It is definite and determinate perception. Then it gives rise to *dharana* or retention. "*Dharana* consists of the lasting impression which results after the object, with its particulars, is definitely ascertained. It is this impression (*samskara*) which enables us to remember the object afterwards." Retention is the cause of recollection. Thus the Jaina recognizes four stages of ordinary perception : *avagraha* or the perception of some features of an object, *iha* or the desire to know more about it, *avaya* or the definite ascertainment of its real nature, and *dharana* or retention of the perception. Of these the last can hardly be regarded as a stage in perception. *Avaya* or definite and determinate perception should be regarded as the last stage of perception. The Jaina does not recognize *darsana* as a distinct stage in perception. It is quite different from *jnana* or knowledge. And perception is a kind of *jnana*. *Darsana* is presupposed by perception but not involved in it. Perception gives us knowledge of an object with its qualities and relations. Different accounts are given by different authors, of the four stages of perception given above.

Thus the Jaina theory of perception differs from the *Buddhi*st theory mainly in this that perception, according to the latter, is the direct presentation of an object, while, according to the former, perception is preservative-representative. According to the *Buddhi*sts perception is always indeterminate, while according to the Jaina perception is always determinate. According to the *Buddhi*sts, perception is the immediate knowledge of the specific individual (*svalaksana*) devoid of all association with names or facts of past experience. According to the Jaina, however, perception is the presentative-representative cognition of extra-mental objects and their relations to one another. According to the *Buddhists*, perception does not represent the relations of extra-mental objects; these are imported by thought or imagination from within the mind into the sense-data to bring about determinate cognitions, which are, therefore, not perceptual in character. According to the Jaina, on the other hand, the extra-mental objects and their relations to one another are facts of direct and immediate experience. The Jaina, therefore, agrees with James and Herbert Spencer in holding that relations are not imposed by the intellect upon the raw sense-materials to convert them into a system of intelligible experience, but they are embedded in direct and immediate experience as contents of consciousness.

**The Natyayika Theory of Perception**

Gautama defines perception as the non-erroneous cognition produced by the intercourse of the sense-organs with the objects, not associated with any name, and well-defined. In this definition the different kinds of perception, the condition of valid perception, and the genesis of perception have been described. Perception is of two kinds, viz. indeterminate (*avyapadesya*) and determinate (*vyavasayatmaka*). We have already discussed the nature of indeterminate (*nirvikalpa*) and determinate (*savikalpa*) perception in detail. Here we shall briefly discuss the nature and origin of perception, and not the conditions of valid perception. Perception is that cognition which is produced by the intercourse of the sense-organs with the objects. This definition is given in *Tarkasamgraha.*

In this definition only the specific condition of perception has been stated. In perception there is not only the contact of the sense-organs with the objects, but also the contact of the sense-organs with the mind, and the contact of the mind with the self. Thus there is a fourfold contact between the sense-organs and the objects, the sense-organs and the mind, and the mind and the self.

This definition, therefore, does not give us an exhaustive enumeration of all the factors that co-operate in producing perception. It points out only that condition which is the specific cause of perception, and which distinguishes it from all other forms of cognition. It does not mention the other conditions, viz. the contact of the mind with the sense-organs, and the contact of the mind with the self, because they are common to inference and other forms of cognition also.

But it may be contended that the contact of the mind with the sense-organs also is a specific condition of perception, which is not present in other forms of cognition. So this condition also should be distinctly mentioned. Vatsyayana rightly points out that the contact of the sense-organs with the objects is as good a distinctive feature of perception, as the contact of the mind with the sense-organs. So when one distinctive feature has been mentioned, there is no need of mentioning the other similar features, as the definition is not meant to be an exhaustive enumeration of all the conditions of perception.

Udyotkara offers other explanations too. Firstly, the sense-object-contact is the distinctive feature of every individual perception. In every individual perception, which is produced by the senseobject-contact, what differentiates it from every other perception is either the sense-organ concerned, or the object perceived; and each individual perception is called either after the sense-organ, or after the object. For example, the perception of colour is called either visual perception or color-perception; and no perception is ever called after the mind-sense-contact; the perception of colour, for instance, is never called mental perception.

Secondly, the mind-sense-contact is the common factor among all kinds of perception, which are otherwise different. In other words, the contact of the mind with the sense-organs does not differ in different kinds of perception; it remains the same in different kinds of perception.

Thirdly, the mind-sense-contact is not mentioned as the distinctive feature of perception, since with regard to perception the mind-sense-contact stands on the same footing as the mind-soul contact, firstly because individual perceptions are never called either after the mind or after the soul; and secondly because both these contacts subsist in a substratum which is imperceptible by the senses; thirdly because neither of these two contacts belongs to the perceived object; and lastly because both these contacts subsist in the mind. These are the reasons why the mind-sense-contact has not been mentioned in the definition of perception. An objection has been raised against this definition that it excludes cognition of the self and its qualities of pleasure, pain, etc., from the category of perception, because the mind is not a sense-organ. Gautama does not mention the mind as a sense-organ, when he enumerates the sense-organs. Thus the cognition of pleasure, pain, etc., which is produced through the instrumentality of the mind, cannot be regarded as perception, since the mind is not a sense-organ. But, as a matter of fact, the cognition of pleasure and pain is neither inferential nor verbal, since the conditions of inference and verbal cognition are absent. So it is absolutely necessary that the cognition of pleasure, pain, etc., should be included in perception, and yet the above definition excludes it.

Vatsyayana points out that the cognition of pleasure, pain, etc., is included in perception by Gautama, since perception is defined by him as that kind of cognition which is produced by the contact of the sense-organ and the object, and the mind is a sense-organ. Gautama has not mentioned the mind as a sense-organ when he has enumerated the sense-organs owing to the fact that the mind is different in character from the other sense-organs. What is the difference between the mind and the other sense-organs ? Vatsyayana mentions three points of difference. In the first place, the external sense-organs are material, while the mind is immaterial. In the second place, the external sense-organs operate upon only a limited number of objects, while the mind is effective on all objects. For instance, colours are apprehended by the visual organ; odours are apprehended by the olfactory organ; tastes are apprehended by the gustatory organ; sounds are apprehended by the auditory organ; and touch is apprehended by the tactual organ. But the mind apprehends all objects. In the third place, the external sense-organs are of the nature of sense-organs owing to the fact that they are endowed with the same qualities as are apprehended by them. The olfactory organ is endowed with the quality of odour and consequently it can apprehend odour. The visual organ is endowed with the quality of colour and consequently it can apprehend colour. The gustatory organ is endowed with the quality of taste; so it can apprehend taste. The auditory organ is endowed with the quality of sound; so it can apprehend sound. And the tactual organ is endowed with the quality of touch; so it can apprehend touch. But the mind is not endowed with the qualities of pleasure, pain, etc., which are apprehended by the mind.

Thus when perception is defined as the cognition produced by the contact of the sense-organs with the objects, the cognition of pleasure and pain also is included in perception, inasmuch as the mind is a sense-organ.

Though both the contact of the mind with the self and the contact of the sense-organs with the objects are necessary conditions of all external perceptions, the latter must be regarded as the principal cause. For sometimes a man goes to sleep with the determination that he will wake up at a certain time and by force of this determination he wakes up at that time; but sometimes when a man is awakened from deep sleep either by a very loud sound or by a rude shaking, his waking perceptions of the sound or the touch are primarily due to the contact of the sense-organs with the objects. So predominance must be given not to the mind-soul-contact, but to the sense-object-contact, because in such cases the soul has no desire to know and does not put forth an effort to direct the mind towards the object. Moreover, when a man with his mind entirely pre-occupied with one thing, desires to know another thing, he puts forth energy to direct his mind towards the object and perceives it. In such a case we cannot say that the sense-object-contact is the principal cause. But when a man with his mind entirely pre-occupied with one thing suddenly comes to have the cognition of another thing, brought about by the forcible impact of the object upon a sense-organ, without any desire or mental effort on his part, the contact of the sense-organ with the object must be regarded as the principal cause of perception, since in this case there is no desire or effort on the part of the self to know the object.

In the case of the man whose mind is pre-occupied, the cognition that suddenly appears is sometimes entirely due to the force of a particular object of sense-perception; its force stands for intensity (*tivrata*) and vigour (*patuta*); and this force of the object affects the sense-object-contact, and not the mind-soul-contact. This clearly shows that the sense-object-contact is the principal cause of perception. The different kinds of sense-object-contact have already been dealt with. Jayanarayana holds that the soul is the constituent cause, the mind-soul-contact is the non-constituent cause, and the sense-object-contact is the efficient cause of perception.

Thus the Naiyayika explains the origin of perception by a concatenation of conditions, viz. the sense-object-contact, the mind-sense-contact and the mind-soul-contact. It does not describe the specific functions of the different factors involved in perception, as the *Samkhya* does. It, indeed, overcomes the Samkhya dualism of *buddhi* (intellect) and *purusa* (self) by regarding the former as a quality of the self. But it does not explain the relation between the self and the object, and the correspondence between knowledge forms and object-forms. An unwarranted and uncritical assumption on which the Naiyayika theory of knowledge is based is that knowledge is produced, like any other physical effect, out of a collocation of causal conditions; psychic causation and physical causation are quite the same in nature. "The production of knowledge is no transcendental occurrence, but is one which is similar to the effects produced by the conglomeration and movements of physical causes." The self, the mind, the sense-organs, and the objects are the main factors which bring about perceptual knowledge by their contact with one another. They have no specific functions in the production of perceptual knowledge; they simply come into contact with one another, and by their mutual contact generate perception.

## The Neo-Naiyayika Theory of Perception

The older Naiyayika defined perception as the non-erroneous cognition produced by the contact of the sense-organs with the objects, not associated with any name, and well-defined. This definition describes the nature of perception as well as the conditions and kinds of perception. Perception is produced by the intercourse of the sense-organs with their appropriate objects. The logical condition of right perception consists in the want of contradiction or in its correspondence with reality. It is of two kinds, indeterminate (*avyapadesya*) and determinate (*vyavasayatmaka*). But this definition does not apply to the perception of God or to the perception of yogis. So Bhasarvajna defines perception as right and direct or immediate cognition.

This definition is peculiar to Bhasarvajna. Raghava points out in his commentary that if we adopt the definition of Gautama, we exclude from perception the direct cognition acquired by the yogi, which is undoubtedly a perceptual knowledge and yet it is not produced by the intercourse of the sense-organs with the objects. The word *aparoksa* in the definition is explained by Raghava as the cognition not produced by the word (*sabda*) or the mark or sign of inference (*linga*), for the former is the instrument of verbal knowledge or knowledge derived from authoritative statement (*sabdajnana*) and the latter is the instrument of inferential knowledge (*anumiti*). Visvanatha defines perception as the cognition which is not produced through the instrumentality of another cognition. It is direct or immediate knowledge. It is not derived through the medium of some other knowledge. This definition applies both to human perception and divine perception. It excludes inferential knowledge, analogical knowledge, memory and verbal knowledge, because inferential knowledge is produced through the instrumentality of the knowledge of universal concomitance; analogical knowledge is produced through the instrumentality of the knowledge of similarity; verbal knowledge is produced through the instrumentality of the knowledge of words and memory is produced through the instrumentality of previous apprehension (*anubhava*).

This is the neo-Naiyayika definition of perception. Gangesa, the founder of this school of Nyaya, defined perception in this way. Perception is direct or immediate knowledge. This is the characteristic of perception. It may be produced by the intercourse of the sense-organs with their proper objects. Or it may be produced directly by the contact of the mind with the objects owing to certain occult powers of the mind. So it is proper to define perception as direct immediate knowledge not derived through the medium of some other knowledge.

## The Mimamsaka Theory of Perception

Jaimini defines perception as the cognition produced in the self by the intercourse of the sense-organs with objects, and he points out that it cannot apprehend super-sensuous merit. This definition is practically the same as that of the Naiyayika. Gautama defines perception as the non-erroneous cognition produced by the sense-object-contact, inexpressible by words, and well-defined. This definition states the conditions and kinds of perception. It shows that perception is of two kinds, viz. indeterminate (*avyapadesya*) and determinate (*vyayasayatmaka*). It lays down the condition of valid perception. Perception must be non-erroneous, in order to be valid. Jaimini's definition does not describe the different kinds of perception. Nor does it lay down the condition of valid perception, Barring these, the two definitions are practically the same. Annam Bhatta defines perception as the cognition produced by the intercourse of the sense-organs with objects. This definition is almost identical with that of Jaimini. If we analyse Jaimini's definition, we find that perception requires the existence of (1) a present object of perception, (2) a sense-organ with which the object comes into contact, and (3) the self (*purusa*) in which the cognition is produced. In perception there must be an intercourse between the sense-organs and their objects. And there must be something more. The sense-organs must be connected with the mind, and the mind with the self. Thus there must be the sense-object-contact, the mind-sense-contact, and the mind-soul-contact in external perception.

The *Naiyayika* contends that this definition includes doubtful perception and illusion in perception Though perception is said to be produced by a real object, and as such excludes hallucinations which are not produced by external stimuli, it does not exclude doubtful perception and illusion which are produced by external stimuli.

Kumarila tries to avoid this objection by saying that *samprayoga* means the right application of the sense-organs to their objects, so that doubtful perception and illusion are excluded from perception.

Parthasarathimisra points out that Jaimini has not defined perception in the above *sutras*. He simply says that perception is not the condition of the apprehension of supersensuous merit. So the Naiyayika's objection is beside the mark. It cannot be urged that this definition does not include the perception of pleasure, pain, etc., since it does not depend upon the external sense-organs. For it depends upon the contact of pleasure, pain, etc., with the internal organ or mind.

Prabhakara defines perception as direct apprehension (*saksat pratitih*). In every act of perception there is a triple consciousness (*triputisamvit*)) viz. the perception of the knowing self, the known object, and knowledge itself. As regards the objects of perception, they are to be classified into substances, qualities, and classes. As regards the act of perception itself, it is of two kinds, viz. indeterminate perception and determinate perception. As regards the knowing self, it is manifested as the knower or subject of all kinds of knowledge, e.g. perceptual, inferential, verbal, etc., because all cognitions are appropriated by the self. And direct apprehension itself also is always self-cognized. It is not cognized by another cognition, as in that case there would be regresses ad infinitum). According to Prabhakara, consciousness is self-luminous; it manifests both the self and the not-self, the knowing subject and the known object. This is the peculiarity of the Prabhakara doctrine of perception as distinguished from the Bhatta doctrine of perception explained above.

## The Samkhya Theory of Perception

Kapila defines perception as a cognition which takes the form of an object, being related to it. Vijnanabhiksu elucidates the definition by saying that perception is the psychic function (*buddhivrtti*) which goes out to the object and is modified by the particular form of that object to which it is related. The psychic function itself is not produced by the proximity of the object, but only its particular mode is produced by it, which inheres in the psychic function. The psychic function goes out, like the flame of a lamp, through the gateways of the sense-organs, to the external object which is proximate to it, and is modified by the particular form of the object.

Thus the proximity of an external object to the buddhi (intellect) is the indispensable condition of perception in general. And the proximity of the sense-organs is a special condition of external sense-perception. But if the proximity of the object to the *buddhi* were the condition of perception in general, perception would be possible even when there was no contact of the sense-organs. But such perception is unknown. The Samkhya holds that *tamas* or inertia of the *buddhi* obstructs its functioning, and when it is overcome by the contact of the sense-organs with objects, or by certain intuitive powers of the yogis, we come to have mental modes. And it is for this inertia of the *buddhi* that there are no mental modes in dreamless sleep.

Isvarakrsna defines perception as determinate cognition of an object (produced by its proximity to the sense-organ).

Vacaspatimisra fully brings out the significance of this definition.

In the first place, there must be a real object of perception. This characteristic differentiates perception from illusion. The object transforms the mental mode into its own particular form, which is in itself formless. The objects of perception are both external and internal, external as the gross sensible objects, e.g. earth, water, etc., and internal, as pleasure, pain, and the like. Even the subtile *tanmatrasy* which are infra-sensible to us, are the objects of perception to the yogin.

In the second place, the perception of a particular kind of object (colour, sound, etc.) involves the operation of a particular sense-organ (eye, ear, etc.), which consists in its intercourse with its object. This characteristic differentiates perception from memory, inference, etc.

In the third place, perception not only involves the existence of an object, and the intercourse of a sense-organ with the object, but it also involves the operation of the intellect (*buddhi*) which produces a definite and determinate cognition of the object. When the sense-organs come in contact with the objects, the inertia (*tamas*) of the intellect is overcome, and the essence or intelligence-stuff (*sattva*) springs forth in it, in consequence of which a definite and determinate cognition of the object is produced. This characteristic of perception excludes doubtful cognitions.

## The Place and Function of the Sense-Organs

Vacaspatimisra illustrates the process of perception by an example. Just as the headman of a village collects the taxes from the villagers and gives them over to the governor of the province, and the local governor hands them over to the minister, and the minister, to the king, so the external sense-organs, having an immediate apprehension of external objects, communicate the immediate impressions to the mind (manas), and the mind reflects upon them and gives them over to the empirical ego (*ahamkara*) which appropriates them to itself by its unity of apperception and gives these self-appropriated apperceived impressions of the objects for the enjoyment of the self (*purusa*).

Thus perception involves the functioning of certain organs. It involves the operation of the external sense-organs, the central sensory or the mind (*manas*) empirical ego (*ahamkara*) and the intellect (*buddhi*).

## The Function of the External Sense-Organs

The sense-organs have only an immediate apprehension (*alocanamatra*) of objects. *Vacaspatimisra* explains this immediate apprehension (*alocanajnana*) as *sammugdha-vastu-darsana*, i.e. intuitive apprehension of an object as a homogeneous unit. The external sense-organs apprehend an object as an undifferentiated homogeneous unit, as merely this but not as like this or unlike this.

But while Vacaspatimisra interprets the *alocanajnana* as indeterminate perception *(nirvikalpajnana),* Vijnanabhiksu interprets it as both indeterminate (*nirvikalpa*) and determinate (*savikalpa*) apprehension. Some hold that the external sense-organs produce an immediate, indeterminate apprehension of objects, and regard the definite and determinate apprehension as the product of the manas. But Vijnanabhiksu cites the authority of Vyasa who says in his *Yoga-bhasya* that the sense-organs give us definite and determinate apprehension of objects. Vijnanabhiksu further says that there is nothing to contradict the determinate apprehension of the sense-organs.

## The Function of the Manas (Mind)

When the sense-organ has an immediate apprehension of the object, the mind (*manas*) reflects upon it, breaks up its object into its component factors, viz. the substance, and its adjuncts, its thatness and whatness and thus assimilates it to similar objects and discriminates it from disparate objects. Thus Isvarakrsna defines the function of the manas as reflection or discrimination. Vacaspatimisra explains it thus. The mind carefully reflects upon the object intuitively apprehended by a sense-organ, and determines it as like this and unlike this, and thus discriminates it by relating the object to its properties in the subject-predicate relation (*visesana-visesyabhava*). The first apprehension is simple and immediate, like the apprehension of a child, a dumb person, and the like; it is produced by the mere thing, but when after this, the thing as distinguished from its properties, by its genus and the like, is recognized, that process of determination is the operation of the mind. Vijnanabhiksu also describes the function of the mind as determination or ascertainment. Thus the function of the mind may be interpreted as the power of selective attention which, by its analytico-synthetic function of dissociation and association, breaks up the non-relational immediate intuition of the object, brings out all the relations involved in it, and thus renders it definite and determinate by assimilation and discrimination.

## The Function of Ahamkara (Empirical Ego or Egoism)

When the mind renders the immediate and indeterminate

apprehension of the sense-organs definite and determinate by assimilation and discrimination, the empirical ego (ahamkara) appropriates it to itself and thus transforms the impersonal apprehension of the object into a personal experience suffused with egoism.

Isvarakrsna identifies egoism (*ahamkara*) with self-appropriation (*abhimana*). Vacaspatimisra explains the function of *ahamkara* as follows:

"I alone preside over the object that is intuited by the sense-organ, and definitely perceived by the mind, and I have the power over all that is perceived and known, and all those objects are for my use. There is no other supreme except "I". I am. This self-appropriation is called *ahamkara* or egoism from its exclusive application". Vijnanabhiksu also regards self-appropriation as the function of *ahamkara*.

**The Function of *Buddhi* (Intellect)**

When the empirical ego (*ahamkara*) appropriates the determinate apprehension of the mind to itself by its empirical unity of apperception, the intellect (*buddhi*) assumes a conative attitude to react to it, and resolves what is to be done towards the object. The function of the intellect is the ascertainment of its duty towards the object known. This explanation has been offered by Vacaspatimisra, who observes : "Every one who deals with an object first intuits it, then reflects upon it, then appropriates it to himself, then resolves, this is to be done by me, and then he proceeds to act. This is familiar to every one."

Thus the act of ascertainment that such an act is to be done is the operation of the intellect. This is the specific function of the intellect, not differing from the intellect itself.

This will be clear from another example of Vacaspatimisra, which illustrates the successive operation of the internal and external organs in perception. "In dim light a person at first apprehends the mere object as an undifferentiated unit, then attentively reflects upon it, and determines it to be a terrible thief by his bow and arrow, then thinks him in reference to himself, e.g. 'he is running towards me', and then resolves or determines, 'I must fly from this place'."

Narayana Tirtha gives the same explanation of adhyavasaya in *Samkhya-Candrika*. *Adhyavasaya* is a modified condition of the intellect, as flame is that of a lamp; it is determination in such a form as "such an act is to be done by me".

But Gaudapada explains *adhyavasaya* as intellectual determination of the object of perception as belonging to a definite class, such as "this is a jar", "this is a cloth", etc. Vacaspatimisra also explains *adhyavasaya* elsewhere as ascertainment or determinate knowledge consequent upon the manifestation of the essence (*sattva*) of the intellect, when the inertia of the intellect is overcome by the operation of the sense-organs in apprehending their objects.

## The Unity of the Functions of the Internal Organs

According to the Samkhya, external perception involves the co-operation of the internal organs with the external sense-organs. But the internal organs are not to be regarded as three different and independent substances or faculties, but only as *antahkarana* in its three grades of functions. *Buddhi*, *ahamkara*, and *manas* are one in nature; they together constitute the one internal organ (*antahkarana*). The Samkhya does not believe in faculty psychology.

Vijnanabhiksu clearly brings out the organic unity of these three internal organs and their functions. Everyone has, at first, a definite knowledge (*niscayajnana*) of an object, and then thinks it in reference to himself in this way : "Here am I", "This is to be done by me". Thus self-apperception (*abhimana*) is an effect of determinate knowledge (*niscayajnana*). The function of the empirical ego (*ahamkara*) is self-appropriation (*abhimana*) and that of the intellect (*buddhi*) is determinate knowledge (*niscayajnana*); but self-appropriation is the effect of determinate knowledge, since it is invariably preceded by determinate knowledge. And if the functions of two substances are related to each other as cause and effect, the substrata of these functions too must be related to each other as cause and effect. So empirical ego (*ahamkara*), the substratum of self-appropriation (*abhimana*) must be the effect of the intellect (*buddhi*), the substratum of determinate knowledge (*niscaya-jnana*). Hence though the internal organ (*antahkarana*) is one and the same, it appears in its threefold character as it has three distinct functions. *Buddhi*, *ahamkara*, and manas are three successive functional modifications of one and the same *antahkarana*.

Vijnanabhiksu supposes that self-appropriation follows upon determinate knowledge. But Vacaspatimisra interprets *adhyavasaya* as the intention or volition of the agent to react to the object of perception in a definite way and holds that this intention follows upon self-appropriated knowledge.

**The Relation of the External Sense-Organs to the Internal Organs**

The relation of the external organs to the internal organs has been well defined by calling the former the gateways or doors of knowledge and the latter the gatekeepers.

The external organs receive immediate impressions from external objects, and communicate them to the internal objects, and communicate them to the internal organ (*antahkarana*) which, in its different functions of reflection (*manana*) self-apperception (*abhimana*), and determination (*adhyavasaya*), makes them definite and determinate, and receives them for the enjoyment of the self. The external sense-organs come in contact with external objects and thereby supply us with the "manifold of intuitions" in the language of Kant. The function of the particular senses is simple apprehension. What they apprehend is a mere manifold, a congeries of discrete impressions, though each apprehends only a manifold of a particular kind. The mind or central sensory operates on this "manifold of intuitions" and synthesizes the congeries of discrete impressions into distinct aggregates or groups. Until the discrete sensations given by sensibility (or the external senses) are formed into groups, there can be no perception of them as things. It is the function of the mind (manas) to form these groups and thereby to transform a certain number of sensations into one distinct percept. Then the fluctuating sensations are referred to the unity of the empirical ego, when the consciousness supervenes that the sensations are mine, that perceive. This self-apperception is the function of the empirical ego (*ahamkara*). The perception is not complete, till the object has been determined by a further process of thought, till it has been identified by reference to the category to which it belongs. It is the function of the intellect (*buddhi*) to define and ascertain objects by recognizing that they realize a certain type. And it is the intellect which imports the empirical relations of space and time, which are nothing but the constructions or categories of the understanding (*buddhi-nirmana*) into the spaceless and timeless continuum of discrete impressions synthesized by the mind into distinct groups and referred to the unity of the empirical ego. When the percept has been fully determined in this way, it is presented by the intellect to the self (*purusa*) in order that it may have an experience of it. According to Kant, sensibility supplies us with mere "manifold of intuitions"; the unity of the manifold is contributed entirely by the understanding. According to the Samkhya, synthesis proceeds from the three internal instruments, mind, empirical ego, and the intellect or understanding. According to Kant, time and space are the forms of sensibility. According to the *Samkhya-Yoga,* space and time are the categories of the understanding. But according to both, knowledge is the joint product of sensibility and reason (or the intellect). But the Samkhya does not oppose sensibility and reason to each other; sensibility, mind, self-apperception, and reason (or intellect) all are the channels of perception; all these are opposed to the self (*purusa*) which alone is conscious sensibility, mind, empirical ego, and intellect being but insentient evolutes of *prakrti* for the enjoyment of the self.

**The Purusa as the Transcendental Principle in Perception**

We have explained the function of the external and internal organs in the process of perception. But how is it that the external and internal organs, which are insentient principles, can have conscious apprehension of objects. It is the self (*purusa*) that makes them apprehend objects. According to the *Samkhya-Yoga,* perception depends upon two metaphysical conditions. In the first place, it implies the existence of an extra-mental object. In the second place, it implies the existence of the self (*purusa*).

Thus Vyasa observes that the object is independent of the mind, and common to all persons; and the minds, too, are independent of objects, which operate for the enjoyment of the self; the enjoyment of the self (in the form of the knowledge of an object) arises from the relation of the mind to the object.

The *Buddhi*sts, however, deny the existence of the self and hold that the mind is self-conscious and self-luminous. But the *Samkhya-Yoga* holds that the mind (*citta*) is not self-luminous, since it is object of consciousness. Just as the other sense-organs and sensible objects are not self-luminous, inasmuch as they are objects of consciousness, so the mind, too, is not self-luminous inasmuch as it is an object of consciousness. The mind cannot be self-conscious (*svabhasa*) as it is the effect of the unconscious *prakrti*. How, then, can it manifest the object? The *Samkhya-Yoga* admits the existence of the self (*purusa*) as the cognizer and enjoyer of the mind. The essence of the self is consciousness; it is not an attribute of the self. The self-luminous self is reflected upon the unconscious mind (*buddhi*) and mistakes the state of the mind for its own state. The self is neither entirely similar to the mind nor entirely different from the mind. It is different from the mind for the following reasons :

Firstly, the mind (*buddhi*) undergoes change or modification, since its objects are sometimes known and sometimes unknown; but the self is unchanging or immutable, since its object, the mind is always known.

Secondly, the self realizes its own end; but the mind (*buddhi*) realizes the end of the self, which is different from the mind, since it co-operates with the body and the sense-organs.

Thirdly, the mind (*buddhi*) takes the forms of all insentient objects which are the combinations of the three ultimate reals, viz. essence (*sattva*), energy (*rajas*) and enertia (*tamas*), and thus apprehends them. Hence the mind itself is made up of the three fundamental reals and is thus insentient; but the self is the witness of the unconscious *buddhi* and the ultimate reals.

But if the self is not quite similar to the mind (*buddhi*), it is not quite different from the mind (*buddhi*), since the self, though pure in itself, knows the state of the unconscious mind (*buddhi*) intelligized by the reflection of the self in it, and erroneously supposes it to be its own state. The *buddhi* though unconscious in its nature, becomes conscious or intelligized by the reflection of the self-luminous *purusa*. But on this point there are two slightly different views. Vacaspatimisra holds that the self-conscious *purusa* is reflected on the unconscious *buddhi* and thus intelligizes it or makes it conscious. Vijnanabhiksu, on the other hand, holds that not only is the self reflected on the *buddhi* in its particular state, but the illuminated condition of the *buddhi* too, is reflected back upon the self. Thus there is mutual reflection of the self upon the *buddhi* and of the *buddhi* upon the self. Thus the *Samkhya-Yoga* avoids the theory of interaction, but it does not commit itself to the theory of psychophysical parallelism, since there is a mutual reflection of the sentient self and the insentient *buddhi* upon each other. Here we take the word "mind" in the sense of *buddhi* (intellect).

The Samkhya doctrine of perception is based upon dualistic metaphysics. But the Samkhya does not advocate the Cartesian dualism of matter and mind because both these are made up of the same stuff, viz. the ultimate reals, e.g. mass-stuff, energy-stuff, and intelligence-stuff, and both are unconscious. The Samkhya dualism is the dualism of *purusa* (conscious self) and *prakrti* (unconscious primal nature) of which *buddhi* is an evolute or modification. The Samkhya dualism is not the uncompromising dualism of the Cartesians. The dualism of the Samkhya is modified by the admission that there are different grades of existence among the modifications of *prakrti*, the highest of which is *buddhi*. *Buddhi* is unconscious, no doubt, but it is not entirely foreign to the nature of faze *purusa*, it is so transparent and light owing to the predominance of intelligence-stuff (*sattva*) that it can catch the reflection of the *purusa*, whereas gross material objects cannot reflect the light of the purusa owing to the predominance of mass-stuff (*tamas*), the factor of obstruction. Thus, according to the Samkhya, *buddhi* is an intermediate reality between gross matter and the conscious *purusa*, which partakes of the nature of both, it is unconscious like gross material objects, but it is transparent like the self-luminous *purusa*. It is only in the *buddhi* that the conscious *purusa* and the unconscious material objects come into contact with each other. This supposition may be compared with the hypothesis of Descartes that it is only in the pineal gland of the brain that the body and the mind, which are entirely heterogeneous in nature, can interact upon each other. The Samkhya, however, does not believe in the theory of interaction. Nor does it believe in the theory of parallelism. It holds an intermediate theory which partakes of the nature of both. It advocates the theory of mutual reflection, of the conscious *purusa* upon the unconscious *buddhi*, and of the unconscious but intelligized *buddhi* on the conscious *purusa*. Thus the conscious *purusa* seems to act upon the unconscious *buddhi*, when it is reflected upon the unconscious *buddhi*; and the unconscious *buddhi* seems to act upon the conscious *purusa*, when the intelligized *buddhi* is reflected upon the conscious *purusa*. The Samkhya doctrine of mutual reflection of *purusa* and the *buddhi* on each other thus looks like the theory of interaction. And since corresponding to the consciousness of the self there is a modification of the unconscious *buddhi* and corresponding to the modification of the *buddhi* there is a consciousness of the self, the Samkhya theory looks like the theory of parallelism. But really it is neither of the two. The *buddhi* is unconscious but active; the *purusa* is conscious but inactive. But the *purusa* erroneously regards itself as active owing to the reflection of active *buddhi* on it, and the unconscious *buddhi* seems to be conscious owing to its proximity to the conscious *purusa*.

But how is contact or proximity possible between two objects which are entirely heterogeneous in nature and are thus independent of each other ? Though the *purusa* and the *buddhi* are heterogeneous, they stand in a definite relation to each other. They are related to each other as a means to an end ; the *buddhi* serves the purpose of the *purusa;* the activity of the *buddhi* is for the realization of an end of the *purusa*.

Thus though the self is changeless and inactive and consequently cannot act upon the unconscious *buddhi* to make it conscious, still it reflects itself upon the transparent essence of the *buddhi* (*buddhisattva*) when it is transformed into the form of its object, and appears to have the same function in itself, and the unconscious *buddhi* appears to be conscious by receiving the reflection of the *purusa*.

**The Relation of the Sense-Organs to the Purusa**

We have discussed at length the relation of the *purusa* to the *buddhi*. Let us consider the general relation of the organs of perception, both external and internal, to the *purusa* and to their appropriate objects. Why do the organs or instruments of perception act at all ? What induces them to perform their respective functions ? They are not guided by the *purusa* in performing their functions. The external and internal organs perform their respective functions for the accomplishment of the purpose of the *purusa*. They have a spontaneous disposition to realize the ends of the *purusa* and perform their respective functions by mutual incitements.

We may quote a few lines here from Professor Wilson's comment. "The organs of sense are said to act by mutual invitation or incitement. Their co-operation in the discharge of their respective functions is compared to that of different soldiers in an army, all engaged in a common assault, but of whom one agrees to take a spear, another a mace, another a bow. It is objected, that the organs being declared non-sentient, incapable of intelligence, cannot be supposed to feel, much less to know, any mutual design or wish, *akuta* or *abhipraya* and the terms are explained to signify the sensible influence which the activity of one exerts upon that of another, if there be no impediment in the way, a sort of sympathetic action. The motive for this sympathetic action is the purpose of soul, fruition, or liberation; which purpose they of their own accord, but unconsciously, operate to fulfil, in the same way as the unconscious breast spontaneously secretes milk for the nourishment of the infant. As the milk of the cow of its own accord exudes for the use of the calf, and awaits not the effort of another, so the organs of their own accord perform their office for the sake of their master, soul. They must act of their own nature; it is not in the power of anyone to compel them to act.... They are not compelled to action even by soul, as a divinity; but fulfil soul's purposes through an innate property, undirected by any external agent."

Thus there is an unconscious adaptation of the external and internal organs to their appropriate objects and there is also an unconscious adaptation between the organs of perception and the self. There is an unconscious teleology between them.

Vacaspatimisra explains the operation of the sense-organs by the thirst for enjoyment (*bhogatrsna*). So long as it persists in the mind, the sense-organs apprehend their proper objects for the enjoyment of the self; but when it is rooted out from the mind, the activity of the sense-organs ceases and consequently there is the cessation of the enjoyment of the *purusa* too.

Vyasa says that even as the inactive loadstone attracts a piece of iron to it by its own power, so the objects, though inactive in themselves, attract the active mind by their own influence, relate the mind to themselves, and transform it into their own forms. Hence that object which colours the mind in a particular state is known by the mind in that state, and all other objects are unknown.

**The Conditions of Perception**

We may summarize the conditions of perception as follows :

1. A real object of perception must exist. This characteristic distinguishes perception from illusion.

2. The external sense-organs yield an immediate apprehension of their objects.
3. The mind (*manas*) reflects upon this immediate apprehension of the external sense-organs, and makes it definite by assimilation and discrimination.
4. The *ahamkara* (empirical ego) appropriates to itself this determinate apprehension of the mind and refers it to the empirical unity of apperception.
5. The *buddhi* (*intellect*) resolves what is to be done towards the object perceived ; it is the will to react to the object perceived.
6. The *purusa* (self) enjoys the perception of the object. It is the transcendent principle of intelligence which intelligizes the unconscious *buddhi* and makes perceptive consciousness possible.

Perception, therefore, involves many processes from the mere sense-cognition to the conative attitude of the mind to react to, the object perceived, it involves immediate apprehension as well as many interpretative processes.

**The Vedanta Theory of Perception**

According to the Samkara Vedanta, there is one universal, eternal, ubiquitous, changeless light of consciousness, which is called Brahman. This eternal consciousness is modalized in three ways. It is modalized by different objects and called object-consciousness (*visaya-caitanya*). It is modalized by mental modes and called cognitive-consciousness (*pramana-caitanya*). And it is modalized by different minds and called cognizing-consciousness (*pramatrcaitanya*). Thus though there is only one universal consciousness, it is determined by the mind or internal organ (*antahkarana*), the activities of the mind or mental modes (*antahkaranavrtti*), and the objects cognized (*visaya*). These are the determinants of the universal light of consciousness.

Perception, according to the Samkarite, is only *caitanya* or consciousness. Though the universal and eternal consciousness (*Brahman*) can never be produced, the empirical modalities of this consciousness as determined by the mental modes may be said to be produced by the sense-organs; for the sense-organs produce the mental mode or activity of the internal organ, which serves to manifest and modalize the eternal light of consciousness. And the activity of the mind or internal organ is said to be cognition (*jnana*) inasmuch as it serves the purpose of qualifying or determining the consciousness.

**The Identification of Pramana-caitanya with Prarneya-caitanya**

Perception involves the function (*vrtti*) of the internal organ (*antahkarana*). The translucent *antahkarana* which is of the nature of light (*taijasa*), moves out to the object through the channel of the sense-organs, and is modified into its form. This modification of the internal organ into the form of the object cognized is called *vrtti*. *Vrtti*, therefore, is the mental mode which apprehends the object.

This out-going of the apprehending mental mode (*vrtti*) to the object is involved only in perception. In inference and other kinds of cognition the mental mode does not go out to the object. For instance, in the case of inference of fire from smoke, the mental mode (*vrtti*) does not go out to the fire, since the visual organ does not come in contact with the fire but with the smoke. But in the case of the perception of a jar, the mental mode which apprehends the jar goes out to the jar, is modified into its form, and occupies the same position in space with it. So the consciousness determined by the apprehending mental mode becomes identified with the consciousness determined by the jar, since the determinants of the two consciousnesses having an identity of locus cannot bring about any difference in the consciousnesses determined by them. Thus in the perception of the jar, the consciousness modalized by the jar (*ghatavacchinnacaitanya*) is identified with the consciousness modalized by the mental mode which is modified into the form of the jar (*ghatakaravrttyavacchinnacaitanya*). In other words, there is an identification of the apprehending mental mode (*pramana-caitanya*) with the object (*visaya-caitanya*) of the perceptive-consciousness with the percept.

**The Identification of Pramatr-caitanya with Pramana-caitanya**

There is a distinction between the bare perception of an object and the perception of the object as object. In the former there is only an identification of the cognitive-consciousness (*pramana-caitanya*) with the object-consciousness (*visaya-caitanya*). But in the latter there is not only an identification of the cognitive-consciousness with the object-consciousness but also an identification of the cognitive-consciousness (*pramana-caitanya*) with the cognizing-consciousness (*pramatr-caitanya*).

In it the apprehending mental mode is referred to the empirical self (*pramatr*) and identified with it.

But it may be objected that in the perception "I see this" the empirical self or consciousness (*aham*) is clearly distinguished from the empirical object or consciousness (*idam*). How, then, can the former be identified with the latter? The Samkarite points out that the perception of an object depends on the identification of the object-consciousness (*visaya-caitanya*) with the cognitive-consciousness (*pramana-caitanya*), and the cognitive-consciousness is not different from the cognizing-consciousness, or the consciousness determined by the activity of the internal organ (*antahkaranavrttyavacchinn-acaitanya*) is not different from the consciousness determined by the internal organ itself (*antahkaranavacchinnacaitanya*). Thus in the perception of an object as object, not only the object-consciousness is identified with the cognitive-consciousness, but also the cognitive-consciousness is identified with the cognizing-consciousness, so that the object-consciousness becomes identified with the cognizing consciousness or self-consciousness. Here the identification of the object-consciousness (*prarneya-caitanya*) with the self-consciousness (*pramatr-caitanya*) does not mean the absolute identity of the two. All that it intends to convey is that the being of the object is not independent of, and separate from, the being of the self. The object becomes—a percept, only when there is an identity of the knowing subject with the known object. When I see a jar, the jar becomes identified, in point of being, with my being; hence the jar becomes an object of my perception. In the perception "I see the jar", though there is a distinction between my self and the jar, the being of the jar (*ghatasatta*) is not independent of, and separate from, the being of my self (*pramatr-satta*). The object is not identical with the self, nor is it an evolute or modification of the self. But the object being super-imposed on the object-consciousness (*visaya-caitanya*) the being of the object is identical with the being of its substratum, viz. the object-consciousness, since the Samkarite does not admit that the being of a superimposed entity (*aropitasatta*) is separate from the being of its substratum (*adhisthana-satta*).

Thus the being of the substratum of the percept is identical with the being of the percept The substratum of the percept is the object-consciousness (*visaya-caitanya*). The object-consciousness is identical with the cognitive-consciousness (*pramana-caitanya*), because when the mental mode is modified into the form of the object, the consciousness determined by the mental mode (*pramana-caitanya*) is identified with the consciousness determined by the object (*visaya-caitanya*). The cognitive-consciousness (*pramana-caitanya*), again, is identical with the cognizing-consciousness or self-consciousness (*pramatr-caitanya*), because the former is the consciousness determined by the activity (*vrtti*) of the internal organ (*antahkarana*), while the latter is the consciousness determined by the internal organ itself and there is not a real difference between the internal organ and its activity. Thus the object-consciousness is identical with the self-consciousness, and hence the being of the object perceived is identical with the being of the percipient self. The self-consciousness (*pramatr-caitanya*) is the substratum of the percept, so that the being of the percept is identical with the being of the self. Thus the perception of an object as distinct from the self and yet related to it involves the identification of the object-consciousness (*visaya-caitanya*) with the cognitive-consciousness (*pramana-caitanya*) and the self-consciousness (*pramatr-caitanya*). In other words, it involves the identification of the perceived object with the apprehending mental mode and the percipient self.

## The Internal Perception

Just as in external perception the object-consciousness is identified with the cognitive-consciousness, so in the internal perception of pleasure the consciousness determined by pleasure is identified with the consciousness determined by the mental mode apprehending the pleasure. Here both the consciousness determined by the pleasure and the consciousness determined by the mental mode are determined by limitations which subsist in the same substratum. In other words, the pleasure and the apprehending mental mode, both of which are determinants of universal consciousness,, subsist in one and the same substratum, viz. the internal organ. Thus both in external perception and internal perception there is an identification of the object-consciousness with the cognitive-consciousness and the self-consciousness. According to the Samkarite, this is the most fundamental condition of perception.

Thus mental states of pleasure and pain are perceived by the self with the aid of their corresponding *vrttis* or mental modes. But though pleasure and pain are perceived with the aid of their corresponding *vrttis,* these *vrttis* themselves are directly perceived by the self without the intervention of other *vrttis*. If one *vrtti* requires another *vrtti* for its apprehension, then that will require a third *vrtti* and so on ad infinitum. So, according to the Samkarite, *vrttis* or mental modes are cognized by direct intellectual intuition (*kevalasaksivedya*)) in which the adventitious processes are not necessary. The mind and its qualities, viz. pleasure and pain, are directly perceived by the witness (*saksiri*) through the agency of the corresponding *vrttis* or mental modes, but the *vrttis* themselves are directly perceived by the witness (*saksin*) not through the medium of other intervening *vrttis*.

## The Identity of Locus of the Mental Mode and the Object

In the perception of an object the mind (*antahkarana*) streaming out of the sense-orifices of the organism reaches the object, and is determined into a mode or *vrtti* by taking the form of the object, which occupies the same position in space with the object. In this way there is a correspondence or harmony between the mental order and the given order. The apprehending mental mode (*vrtti*) and the object (*visaya*) are distinct from each other, but still they correspond with each other in occupying the same position in space, and the mental mode (*vrtti*) having the same form as that of the object. In fact, according to the Samkarite, there is not an ultimate distinction between the mind and the object, both of them being the products of nescience and determinants of the one universal, eternal. consciousness. It is by means of the *vrtti* or empirical mental mode that the mind comes to be related to the object. The *vrtti* therefore, relates the mind to the object. But it is not a tertium quid between two unrelated terms. The *vrtti* is an empirical mode of the mind, which takes the form of the object. The vrtti, therefore, is the meeting-place, as it were, of the two substances, the mind and the object. It is not different from the mind, because it is a mode of the mind. It is not different from the object, because it is the transformation of the mind into the form of the object, i.e. it incorporates the form of the object into itself. Thus the mental mode, being identified with the object, occupies the same position in space. In perception the mind and the object occupy the same space-position; they have an identity of locus. This distinguishes perception from inference. In inference the mind does not go out to the object inferred to take the form of the object. It merely thinks of the inferred object but does not go out to meet it. But in perception the mind goes out to the object and is transformed into its shape. Professor Bhattacharya rightly observes: "The distinction is practically that drawn in modern psychology, only viewed from the point of view of the self's spontaneity, that in perception the given element and its interpretation are welded together in a unity, while in inference they are kept distinct. In perception, the self as invested with the mental mode becomes further materialized into the particular function of the sense-organ excited by the particular stimulus."

### The Identity of the Time-position of the Mental Mode and the Object

In perception the apprehending mental mode (*vrtti*) and the object (*visaya*) should not only occupy the same position in space but also the same position in time. The mental mode in the form of a perceptive process occupies the present moment in time. So the object of perception also should occupy the present moment in time. The perceptive process and the perceived object should occupy the same time-position. Otherwise the perception of pleasure would be quite the same as the recollection of pleasure. In the perception of pleasure the pleasure (*visaya*) and the apprehending mental mode (*vrtti*) occupy the same space-position. In the recollection of pleasure also the pleasure remembered (*waya*) and the recollection of pleasure (*vrtti*) occupy the same space-position. How, then, can we distinguish the perception of pleasure from recollection of pleasure ? We can do so if we admit another condition of perception. In the act of perception, the perceptive process and the perceived object must occupy the same time-position. In the recollection of pleasure, the pleasure, which is the object of recollection, exists in the past, while the apprehending mental mode (*vrtti*) in the form of recollection exists at present, so that the two are not co-eval. Hence, in order to exclude the act of recollection from the act of perception, we must lay down another condition of perception, viz. the object of perception must exist in the present time.

### The Fitness (Togyata) of the Object

In order to exclude the *sabdajnana* (knowledge through

authoritative statement) by means of which we can apprehend supersensuous objects such as spiritual merit and demerit (*dharmadharama*), we must add another qualification to the object of perception. The object of perception must be *yogya* or capable of being perceived; it must not be by its very nature imperceptible (*yogya*). Spiritual merit and demerit are as much qualities of the mind as pleasure and pain. Why, then, are not the former perceived, while the latter are perceived ? The Samkarite replies that the former are, by their very nature, imperceptible. What is capable (*yogya*) of being perceived and what is incapable (*ayogya*) of being perceived can be known only by the result of our attempt to perceive them. Some objects are perceptible by their very nature, while others are imperceptible by their very nature.

Thus the direct perceptibility of an object consists in the fact that the subjective consciousness underlying the apprehending mental mode becomes united with the consciousness underlying the object, the object existing in the present time and capable of being perceived through a specific sense-organ, and the apprehending mental mode also having the same form as that of the object.

## The Different Kinds of Perception

The author of *Vedanta Paribhasa* divides perception into two kinds, viz. sensuous (*aindriyajanya*) perception and non-sensuous (*indriyajanya*) perception. The former is produced by the senseorgans, while the latter is not. Dharmaraja Dvarnidra regards the external senses only as sense-organs. He does not regard the mind as a sense-organ. So by sensuous perception he means external perception, and by non-sensuous perception he means internal perception. We have sensuous perception of external objects, and non-sensuous perception of pleasure, pain, and the like. But the Naiyayika may object that if the mind is not a sense-organ, we cannot speak of the perception of pleasure and pain, because perception is always produced by a sense-organ. The Samkarite replies that the perception of pleasure and pain does not necessarily imply that the mind is a sense-organ through which the self perceives pleasure and pain. The directness (*saksattva*) of a cognition does not consist in its being produced by a sense-organ. If it did so, then inferential cognition also would be regarded as direct perception, since it is produced by the mind which is regarded by the Naiyayika as a sense-organ. Moreover, God has no sense-organ but still He has perception. Hence the Naiyayika contention is absolutely, unfounded. According to the Samkarite, production by a sense-organ (*indriyajanyata*) is neither a sufficing condition nor a necessary condition of perception (*pratyaksajnana*); the directness of a cognition (*saksattva*) or its perceptual character (*pratyaksatva*) depends on the identification of the cognitive-consciousness with the object-consciousness, or, of the apprehending mental mode with the perceived object as we have already seen.

The Samkarite divides perception, again, into the perception of an object (*jneyapratyaksa*) and the perception of a cognition (*jnanapratyaksa*). The former is perceived through the medium of a mental mode (*vrtti*). The latter is perceived in itself without the intervention of a mental mode as we have already seen.

The Samkarite recognizes the distinction between indeterminate (*nirvikalpa*) perception and determinate (*sauikalpa*) perception. We have already dealt with them.

The Samkarite divides perception into two other kinds, viz. the perception of the witness self (*jivasaksipratyaksa*) and the perception of the divine witness (*Isvarasakstpratyasa*). We shall deal with them in the last chapter.

### The Function of Antahkarana and the Sense-organs in Perception

We have seen that *vrtti* or mental mode relates the percipient self to the perceived object. It reveals the consciousness underlying the object. Without it there can be no perception of an object, mental or extra-mental. Pleasure and pain are perceived through the corresponding mental modes, and external objects also are perceived through the corresponding mental modes or *vrttis*. And *vrtti* is the modification of the internal organ (*antahkarana*) into the form of the object. Therefore, without *antahkarana* there can be no perception.

But if the empirical self (*jiva*) perceives an object through the instrumentality of a *vrtti* or function of the internal organ (*antahkarana*) what is the use of the sense-organs ? The Samkarite holds that the intercourse of the sense-organs, with external objects is necessary for perceiving them, since it is the cause of the *vrtti* or mental mode which reveals the object-consciousness. If the consciousness underlying the object is not revealed, it cannot be perceived. And if a *vrtti* or mental mode does not move out to the object and remove the veil of nescience which conceals the consciousness underlying the object, the object-consciousness cannot be revealed. And a vrtti or mental mode is not possible, if there is no intercourse of the sense-organs with the objects of perception. It is the sense-object-intercourse that produces a mental mode or *vrtti* which is necessary for perception. This is the function of the sense-organs in perception. We have already discussed the different kinds of sense-object-intercourse recognized by the Samkarite.

## The Vedantist Doctrine of *Vrtti*

The Samkarite agrees with the Samkhya in holding that the mind (*antahkarana*) goes out to the object and assumes its form, so that the form of the object corresponds to the form of the apprehending mental mode. This account of the Samkhya-Vedanta runs counter to the account of western psychology, according to which, the object comes in contact with a sense-organ and produces an affection in it, which is carried to the brain, and this affection produces an impression in the mind. Western psychology gives priority to the object which acts upon the mind or subject. The Samkhya-Vedanta, on the other hand, gives priority to the mind or subject which goes out to the object, acts upon it, and assumes its form. The physiological account of the perceptual process is extremely vague. There is a yawning gulf between the cerebral process and the mental process. It cannot be bridged over. How the cortical vibration in the sensory centre in the brain produces a sensation in the mind is a mystery. The Samkhya-Vedanta mitigates the uncompromising dualism of matter and spirit by admitting that *buddhi* or *antahkarana* is an intermediate reality between unconscious matter and conscious spirit. It is material, no doubt, but it is made up of very subtile matter, and is, so to say, a hyper-physical entity. It is plastic and translucent in nature and reflects the light of consciousness, on the one hand, and takes in the form of the object, on the other. According to the Samkhya-Vedanta, the object does not break in upon the mind and imprint its form in it, but the mind goes out to the object and assumes its form. Thus, though both the object and the subject (mind) are necessary for perception, dominance is given to the subject, and the object is regarded as subordinate to the subject. The subject and the object, therefore, cannot be regarded as co-ordinate terms in knowledge, but the subject is always the dominant factor. The supreme importance of the *vrtti* of the mind in perception proves the dominance of the subject-element. The object can never have priority to the subject. But the subject (mind) can pour itself into the object and incorporate it into itself. This is what is intended by the Samkhya-Vedanta, when it holds that the mind goes out to the object and assumes its form. And it is much easier to conceive the out-going of the mind intelligized by the conscious self to the object than the in-coming of the unconscious object to the mind. Moreover, according to the Samkarite, both the object and the mind (*antahkarana*) have only an empirical existence, being modifications of nescience; but the mind has this advantage over the object that it has the power of reflecting the light of consciousness in itself and thus appearing to be conscious. So the mind is supposed to go out to the object and assume its form. Thus the hypothesis of *vrtti* is not entirely unreasonable.

## Objections to the Vedantist Doctrine of Vrtti Considered

Some object that all objects are capable of being illumined by the light (*prasada*) of the witness self (*saksin*). What, then, is the use of the *vrtti* or mental mode ? Even though it may be necessary to postulate the *vrtti* to assume the form of the object, there is no need of admitting that the *vrtti* moves outward to the object of cognition. Just as it is held that the witness (*saksin*) illumines an object of inference, which is not present to a sense-organ, through the agency of a *vrtti* which does not move out to the object, so it may be held that the witness illumines the object of direct perception, which is present to a sense-organ, with the aid of a *vrtti* which does not move out to the object perceived.

This theory does not obliterate the distinction between perceptual knowledge and non-perceptual knowledge. The difference between the two lies in the fact that the former is produced through the instrumentality of the sense-organs, while the latter is not produced through the instrumentality of the sense-organs.

This objection has been refuted in three ways by the Vedantists.

1. Some Vedantists hold that in perceptual knowledge the light of consciousness determined by the object of perception illumines the object, since the object-consciousness (*visaya-cattanya*) is the substratum of the object and hence this alone

can illumine it. The cognizing-consciousness (*pramatr-caitanya*) or the consciousness determined by the internal organ cannot illumine the object, because it does not constitute the essence of the object, and is not related to it by the relation of identity in essence (*tadatmya*). And it is the *vrtti* or apprehending mental mode that moves out to the object, removes the veil of nescience that conceals the object-consciousness, and reveals it. When the object-consciousness is thus revealed by the *vrtti* it illumines the object. But in non-perceptual knowledge there is no sense-object-intercourse which is the cause of the moving out of the *vrtti* of the mind; so the consciousness determined by the mental mode, which does not move out to the object, illumines the non-presented object.

2. Other Vedantists hold that just as the perception of pleasure, pain, etc., is due to these being in direct relation to the principle of consciousness underlying them, so the perception of external objects is due to these objects being in direct relation to the light of consciousness underlying them, and the outward movement of the *vrtti* of the internal organ is necessary for disclosing the consciousness that underlies these objects. Thus the direct cognition of external objects is due to the direct relation between these objects and the consciousness underlying them. But if the object-consciousness is not disclosed, it cannot be directly related to external objects of which it is the substratum. And the object-consciousness is disclosed by the *vrtti* of the internal organ which moves out to the external objects, removes the veil of nescience, and reveals the light of consciousness underlying them.
3. Other Vedantists hold that in the perceptual knowledge of an object we perceive a certain vividness (*spastata*) which is lacking in the object of non-perceptual knowledge. Thus though we might hear of the sweetness and fragrance of the mango from a trustworthy person even a hundred times, our knowledge of the sweetness and fragrance would lack in vividness. This vividness in the object of direct sensuous perception is due to the fact that the consciousness underlying the object, which is disclosed by the *vrtti* or mental mode moving out to the object, is identical in essence with the object itself. In other words, the vividness of the object perceived is

due to the disclosure of the object-consciousness which consists in the removal of the veil of nescience which conceals it; and this removal of the veil of nescience is due to the *vrtti* moving out to the object. The absence of vividness in the object of non-perceptual knowledge is due to the fact that no *vrtti* moves out to the object, and thus does not disclose the identity of the object with the consciousness underlying it. So the outward movement of the *vrtti* to an object is the necessary condition only of the direct knowledge of the object.

# 8

# Perception of Space and Movement

## Introduction

The Nyaya-Vaisesika holds that there is one, eternal, ubiquitous space, which is not an object of perception. It is inferred from the spatial characters of proximity (*aparatva*) and remoteness (*paratva*). But the spatial characters of position, direction, and distance can be perceived directly through vision and touch. The Mimamsakas also hold that these can be perceived directly through vision and touch. According to them, the spatial characters of direction and distance can be directly perceived through the auditory organ also.

The Samkhya-Patanjala, on the other hand, holds that space and time are the categories of the understanding or constructions of the intellect (*buddhinirmana*) according to which, it understands the phenomenal world. It is the understanding which imports the empirical relations of space, time, and causality into the world of reals, viz. intelligence-stuff (*sattva*) energy-stuff (*rajas*) and matter-stuff (*tamas*). When we have intellectual intuition (*nirvicharanirvikalpaprajna*) we apprehend the reals as they are in themselves without the imported empirical relations of space, time, and causality. According to Samkara also, space, time, and causality are categories of the understanding, according to which the world of phenomena is interpreted. According to the Buddhist idealists, space and time apart from concrete presentations are ideal constructions of the mind.

## The Mimamsaka: Direct Auditory Perception of Direction

Space must be distinguished as *desa* (locus) and *dik* (direction). According to the Mimamsaka, both locus and direction are directly perceived through the auditory organ, though they are perceived as qualifying adjuncts (*visesana*) of sounds. The Mimamsaka holds that the ear-drum or the auditory organ is *prapyakari* and hence produces the perception of a sound, only when it actually comes in contact with the sound. The ear does not go out to its object, viz. the sound which is at a distance, but the sound is produced in a certain point of space at a distance and propagated to the ear-drum through the air-waves. Thus the ear-drum never comes in contact with the locus of a sound, it comes in contact with the sound, when it is carried into it through the air-waves. Thus we perceive a sound, only when the sound is carried to the ear-drum through the air waves. But can there be a direct perception of the locus (*desa*) of the sound through the ear-drum ? The ear-drum produces the perception of a sound when it is in actual contact with the sound, which is propagated to the ear-drum through the air-waves from another point of space. So the audible sound may be said to have its locus in the ear-drum itself. But is a sound perceived to have its locus in the ear-drum ? Or, is it perceived to have its locus in another point of space ? We find in our actual experience that sound is never perceived without a local colouring and it is never perceived as having its locus in the ear-drum. It is always perceived as having its locus in another point of space. But if the ear-drum can never produce the auditory perception of a sound without coming in direct contact with the sound, and if it can never go out to the locus of the sound, where it is produced (*sabdotpattidesa*), it cannot produce the perception of a sound having its locus in a distant point of space. All that it can do is to produce the perception of a sound having its locus in the ear-drum, because the perception of the sound is produced only when the sound is not in its original locus, i.e. the point of space where it was produced, but when it is in the ear-drum. But, as a matter of fact, we never perceive a sound as having its locus in the ear-drum, but in another point of space outside the ear-drum. Sounds coming from different directions are perceived as having different local characters. Whenever sounds are perceived they are perceived as coming from particular directions; they are never perceived without their local characters. We have a distinct auditory perception in such a form as "the sound comes from this direction". Thus when sounds come into the ear-drum from different directions, they come into it not as mere sounds, but as coloured by the different directions from which they come. And the ear-drum, being in contact with these sounds, is in contact with their different local colourings too, and consequently, it produces the perception of different sounds with different local characters. Thus though the ear-drum cannot come in actual contact with the direction of a sound, yet it can produce the perception of the sound with the local character of its direction. This is the reason why we perceive audible sounds not as seated in the ear-drum but coming from different directions outside the ear-drum.

According to the Mimamsaka, therefore, just as sounds are directly perceived through the ear, so also the directions from which they come. We never perceive sounds, pure and simple, but sounds with their different local characters and hence through these local characters of sounds we directly perceive the different directions from which they come.

But though according to the Mimamsaka there is a direct auditory perception of direction, we must not suppose that, according to him, there can be a direct auditory perception of direction apart from, and independently of, the perception of sounds. Just as there can be no independent perception of time through the sense-organs apart from the perception of their appropriate objects, so there can be no independent perception of space in the form of direction through the ear apart from the perception of sounds. Thus we perceive space as direction through the auditory organ, not as an independent entity, but only as a qualifying adjunct of sounds, which are coloured by the directions from which they come. Hence, according to the Mimamsaka, we have a direct auditory perception of space in thick form of direction. The Naiyayika also holds that direction is perceived through the perceptions of east, west, and the like.

**Direct Auditory Perception of Distance and Position**

The local position of an object can be determined, if its direction and distance from us can be ascertained, because the local position of an object is nothing but its position in a point of space in a particular direction and at a particular distance from us. Thus the local position of an object in relation to us involves its direction and distance from us. We have already seen that according to the Mimamsaka, the direction of a sound can be directly perceived as the local character of the sound through the auditory organ. But how can distance be perceived through the ear? Sounds coming from a proximate point of space are perceived as most intense (*tivra*) is not perceived.

## Perception of Movement

### *The Prabhakara*

The Prabhakara holds that movement is not an object of perception. It is inferred from disjunction and conjunction which are its effects. Salikanatha says : "We do not perceive anything over and above disjunctions and conjunctions in a moving substance. The movement in a moving object is inferred from its disjunctions and conjunctions." When an object moves, what we actually perceive is not the movement of the object, but only its disjunctions and conjunctions with certain points in space, from which we infer the existence of movement. Movement is not the same thing as disjunctions and conjunctions, since the former subsists in the moving object, while the latter subsist in outside space.

### *The Bhatta Mimamsaka*

Parthasarthimisra disputes the view of Prabhakara and holds that movement is an object of perception. Prabhakara argues that we perceive only the disjunction of an object from one point of space and its conjunction with another point of space which did not exist in the object before so they must spring out of a cause which is inferred from the effect, and that cause is movement we never perceive movement but infer it from its effect. The substance itself cannot be regarded as the cause of its disjunctions and conjunctions, since it was there even before they came into being. Parthasarathimisra contends that movement can never be inferred, since it could be inferred only as the immaterial cause (*asamavayikarana*) of the conjunctions and disjunctions of a thing with points in space, and this would mean that movement would be cognized as subsisting in the thing as well as in space; but, as a matter of fact, we never cognize movement in space but only in the moving thing. So movement cannot be regarded as an object of inference. Prabhakara argues that we do not perceive anything over and above the conjunctions and disjunctions of a moving object. Parthasarathimisra contends that when a snake moves on the ground both the snake and the ground have conjunctions and disjunctions; but still we apprehend that the snake is moving, and not the ground. Hence the object of apprehension is the movement of the snake which is responsible for our cognition that the snake is moving, and not the ground. And this movement can never be an object of inference. It is an object of perception.

### *The Vaisesika*

Kanada holds that movement is an object of visual perception when it inheres in a coloured substance. Samkaramisra points out that it is an object of visual and tactual perception both. Movement cannot be perceived through vision and touch when it inheres in an uncoloured substance. According to the older Vaisesikas, colour or form (*rupa*) is a condition of both visual and tactual perception. But the later Vaisesikas discard this doctrine. They make manifest colour a condition of visual perception, and manifest touch a condition of tactual perception. But both the schools hold that movement is an object of visual and tactual perception under certain conditions. This doctrine finds favour also with the Western psychologists.

Sridhara quotes a passage from Prakaranapandka explaining the Prabhakara doctrine of inferrability of movement, and subjects it to severe criticism. His criticism is substantially the same as that of Parthasarthimisra. Prabhakara argues that we do not perceive anything apart from disjunctions and conjunctions in a moving object movement is not perceived, but inferred from disjunctions and conjunctions. This argument is unsubstantial. If movement of an object is said to be inferred from disjunctions and conjunctions, it should be inferred as subsisting both in the object and in what it moves, since disjunctions and conjunctions belong to both of them. For instance, when a monkey moves from the root of a tree to its top and again from the top to the root, we ought to infer that the tree is moving as well as the monkey, since the disjunctions and conjunctions inhere as much in the tree as in the monkey. But we never infer that the tree is moving. When we suddenly perceive a flash of lightning at night in the midst of dense darkness we perceive its movement, but not its conjunctions and disjunctions with points of space. Hence movement is an object of perception.

# 9

# Perception of Time

## Introduction

In this chapter we shall deal with perceptual time as distinguished from conceptual time, or with the time apprehended by perception as distinguished from the time of ideal construction. We shall not consider the nature of time as a reality. The Indian philosophers are of opinion that time is a coefficient of all consciousness including external perception and internal perception. But they do not recognize the perception of time as an independent entity. According to them, there is no sense for empty time apart from events or changes; succession and duration are the two important constituents of time. So some Naiyayikas and the Vedantists analyse the perception of time into the perception of succession and the perception of duration. They derive the perception of succession from the perception of changes, and the perception of duration from the perception of the "specious present". And they regard the perception of the "specious present" as the nucleus of all our time-consciousness. They derive the conception of the past and the future from the perception of the "specious present" in which there is an echo of the immediate past and a foretaste of the immediate future. In it there is a rudimentary consciousness of the past and the future which are clearly brought to consciousness by memory and expectation respectively. The Buddhists, however, do not believe in duration and the "specious present". They believe only in succession and the mathematical present. They recognize succession alone as the only constituent of time, and identify the perception of time with the perception of succession. And they regard the perception of succession as identical with the perception of changes. They do not believe in time apart from changes. They identify time with succession, and succession with changes. Thus they identify perception of time with the perception of changes. They do not believe in the perception of time as a qualifying adjunct of all events or changes. But the consciousness of change is not identical with change-consciousness. The consciousness of transition is not the same as transition-consciousness. So the Buddhists try their best to derive duration from succession, and explain away the unity and continuity of time. Let us now discuss the main problems of temporal perception.

**Is Time an Object of Perception ?**

The first question that arises in connection with temporal perception is whether time is an object of perception or not. According to the Vedantists, time is a coefficient of all perception. The Bhatta Mimamsakas and some Naiyayikas too hold that time is perceived by both the external and the internal sense-organs as a qualification of their objects of perception. Jayanta Bhatta has discussed the possibility of the visual perception of time. Can time be an object of visual perception? According to the Vaisesika, an object of visual perception must have extensity or appreciable magnitude (*mahattva*) and manifest or sensible colour (*udbhutarupavattva*). But time is colourless. How, then, can it be an object of visual perception ? The Naiyayika retorts : How is colour perceived though it is colourless ? Certainly an object has colour which inheres in it; but colour itself has no colour inhering in it. And if colour can be perceived, though it is colourless, then time also can be an object of visual perception, though it is colourless. Jayanta Bhatta says that time is perceived through the visual organ; it is a fact of experience, and so it cannot be denied, though we may not account for it; a fact of experience cannot be argued out of existence. As a matter of fact, that is visible which can be perceived through the visual organ, be it coloured or colourless; and time can be perceived through the visual organ, though it is colourless, hence none can deny the visual perception of time.

Ramakrsnadhvarin, the author of *Sikhamani*, rightly points out that if we deny the visual perception of time because it is colourless, we cannot account for our visual perception of an object as existing at present, e.g. "the jar exists now" (*idanirh ghato vartate*). If the present time were not an object of this perception, then there would be no certainty as to the time in which the jar is perceived to exist, but there would be a doubt whether the jar exists at present or not. But, in fact, the jar is definitely perceived as existing now; the actual perception of the jar is not vitiated by the least doubt whether the jar exists at present or not. Such an undoubted perception of an object as existing "now" clearly shows that besides the object, an element of time also, viz. the present time, enters into the visual perception of the object.

But if time is regarded as an object of visual perception, though it is colourless, because of our visual perception of an object as existing "now", then it may equally be argued that *akasa* (ether) also is an object of visual perception, because of our visual perception of a row of herons in *akasa* (*akase valaka*). But *akasa* is not admitted to be an object of perception, it is regarded as a supersensible object which is inferred from sound as its substrate. And if, in spite of our visual perception of a row of herons in *akasa* (*akase valaka*), *akasa* is not regarded as an object of visual perception, or of any kind of perception, whatsoever, then why should time be regarded as an object of visual perception, because of our visual perception of an object as existing "now"?

It may be argued that the visual perception of a row of herons in akasa is an acquired perception like the visual perception of fragrant sandal. Just as in the visual perception of fragrant sandal the visual presentation of the sandal (i.e. its visual qualities) is blended with the representation of its fragrance perceived by the olfactory organ on a previous occasion and revived in memory by the sight of the sandal, so in the visual perception of a row of herons in *akasa,* the visual perception of the row of herons (*valaka*) is blended with the idea of *akasa* which is represented to consciousness by another cognition by association, and so *akasa* is not an object of visual perception. But if this argument is valid, then it may as well be argued that the element of time which enters into every perceptive process is not an object of perception, but it is represented in consciousness by another cognition, with which it is associated in experience, and thus the element of time entering into every perception is not an object of direct perception.

The truth is that the visual perception of an object as existing "now" is not an acquired perception like the acquired perception of fragrant sandal, because in this perception the element of time (now) is felt as an object of direct visual perception, nor is it like the visual perception of a row of herons in *akasa*, because *akasa* does not enter into the perception as a qualification (*visesana*) of its object. The present time is perceived as à qualification of every object of perception. Whenever an object, event, or action is perceived, it is not perceived as timeless, but as existing or occurring in time, or qualified by the present time.

And time is not only an object of visual perception, but of all kinds of perception. It is perceived by all the sense-organs, external and internal, as a qualification of their objects. Here we are reminded of Kant's doctrine that time is the form of external and internal perception.

**No Perception of Time as an Independent Entity**

But though time is an object of perception, it is never perceived as an independent entity. One of the essential characteristics of time is succession, and succession is never perceived apart from changes. So we can never perceive time apart from actions or changes which occur in time. The temporal marks of before and after, sooner and later, etc., are never perceived apart from actions or changes. And if there is no distinct perception of time apart from that of changes, are we to say that there is no perception of time, but only a perception of changes? Is time nothing but change or action ? Some hold that time apart from action is a fiction of imagination; time is identical with action or change ; time and action are synonymous. Hence there is no perception of time at all, but only that of actions (*karyamatravalambana*). The Naiyayika admits that there is no perception of time apart from that of actions. But from this it does not follow that there is no perception of time at all; for an element of time always enters into the perception of actions as a constituent factor. Actions are never perceived without being qualified by time; actions unqualified by time or timeless actions are never perceived. The perception of time is inseparable from the perception of actions, but they are not identical with each other. Hence the legitimate conclusion is that time cannot be perceived as an independent entity, but only as a qualifying adjunct (*visesana*) of events or actions; there is no perception of empty time devoid of all sensible content, but only of filled time or time filled with some sensible matter. Just as there is no perception of mere actions unqualified by time, so there is no perception of empty time devoid of all sensible content. When we perceive succession or simultaneity, sooner or later, we do not perceive mere actions, but we perceive something else which qualifies these actions, and that is time. Time, therefore, is perceived not as an independent entity, but as a qualification of the objects of perception; there is no perception of empty time. But it may be urged, if time is an object of perception, why is it perceived not as an independent entity, but only as a qualification of perceptible objects? Jayanta Bhatta says that it is the very nature of time (*vastusvalhava*) that it can be perceived only as a qualification of perceptible objects, and not as an independent entity like a jar; and the nature of things (*vastusvalhava*) or the law of nature can never be called in question. This is the final limit of explanation. We can never account for the ultimate nature of things. So time is an object of perception. The Bhatta Mimamsaka also admits that time cannot be perceived by the sense-organs as an independent entity, but it is perceived by all the sense-organs as a qualification (*visesana*) of their own objects.

This psychological analysis of the perception of time is parallel to that of William James. "We have no sense", he says, "for empty time. . . . We can no more intuit a duration than we can intuit an extension devoid of all sensible content". Kant's notion of a pure intuition of time without any sensible matter is psychologically false.

## Perception of the Present

Some deny the existence of the present time and consequently of the perception of the present. When a fruit falls to the ground, it is detached from its stalk and comes gradually nearer and nearer to the ground, traversing a certain space and gradually passing from one position to another, say, from *a* to *b*, from *b* to *r*, and so on until it comes to the ground. When the fruit has passed from *a* to *b*, the space between *a* and *b* is the space traversed, and the time related to that traversed space is that which has been passed through (*patitakala* or the past); and when the fruit will pass from *b* to *r*, the space between *b* and *r* is the space to be traversed, and the time related to this space is that which is to be passed through (*patitavyakala* or the future), and apart from these two spaces, the traversed space and the space to be traversed, there is no third space left intervening between them which may be perceived as being traversed and give rise to the perception of the present time. So the present time does not exist. Here by the present time is meant the mathematical time-point which is the boundary line between the past and future. But such a timepoint is never an object of actual perception. Hence there is no present time at all.

This argument reminds us of Zeno's dialectic against the possibility of motion. But Vatsyayana rightly points out that time cannot be conceived in terms of space but only in terms of action. Thus Vatsyayana anticipates Bergson in holding that there can be no spatial representation of time. According to him, time is perceived as qualifying an action, an action is perceived as occurring in time. When, for instance, the action of falling has ceased, and is no more, it is perceived as past; and when the action of falling is going to happen and not yet commenced, it is perceived as future; and when the action of falling is going on, it is perceived as present. Thus time-consciousness is found in the perception of action. When an action is no more, it is perceived as past, when it is not yet begun, it is perceived as future; and when it is going on, it is perceived as present. If an action is never perceived as going on, how can it be perceived as no more or as not yet ? For instance, if the action of falling is not perceived as going on, how can it be perceived as having ceased, or as going to happen? As a matter of fact, what is meant by the past time or the time "that has been fallen through" (*pattakala*). In the present case, is that the action of falling is over or no more and what is meant by the future time or the time "to be fallen through" (*patitavyaksla*) is that the action of falling is going to happen and not yet begun, so that at both these points of time, past and future, the object is devoid of action; but when we perceive that the fruit is in the process of falling, we perceive the object in action. Thus time is perceived not in terms of space but in terms of actions, when they are perceived as going on or in the process of happening, they are perceived as present, when they are perceived as over or no more, they are perceived as past, and when they are perceived as going to happen and not yet begun, they are perceived as future. The consciousness of the present is the nucleus of the consciousness of the past and the future, the past and the future are; built upon the present. Time is perceived only through an action; the actual happening of an action is perceived as present; and unless an action is perceived as happening or present, it can never be perceived as past or future, inasmuch as the action does not really exist in the past or in the future but only in the present. Hence the perception of the present cannot be denied as all our time consciousness is centred in it.

The whole controversy hinges on the meaning of the present time. Vatsyayana takes it in the sense of the "specious present" or felt present which is a tract of time. His opponent takes it in the sense of the mathematical time-point or indivisible instant which is never a fact of actual experience. Vatsyayana is right in so far as he gives a psychological explanation of the specious present which is the basis of our conception of the past and future. He anticipates the most modern psychological analysis of our time-consciousness in Western psychology. A few quotations from books on modern Western psychology will not be out of place here.

"Let anyone try," says William James, "to notice or attend to, the present moment of time. One of the most baffling experiences occurs. Where is it, this present? It has melted in our grasp, fled are we could touch it, gone in the instant of becoming, ... It is only as entering into the living and moving organization of a much wider tract of time that the strict present is apprehended at all. It is, in fact, an altogether ideal abstraction, not only never realized in sense, but probably never even conceived of by those unaccustomed to philosophic meditation. Reflection leads us to the conclusion that it must exist, but that it does exist can never be a fact of our immediate experience. The only fact of our immediate experience is what E.R. Clay has well called 'the specious present'. "Elsewhere he says," The original paragon and prototype of all conceived times is the specious present, the short duration of which are immediately and incessantly sensible". J. M. Baldwin also bears out this view of James. He says, "Subjectively, each individual constructs his own time-order from the standpoint of the specious or felt present by means of images in which past and future, not actually present, are represented. It is only from this standpoint that the terms past and future have proper meaning. In this construction are included not only the times of the individuals private experiences, but all times which may be dated from the present "now".

Vatsyayana's account of the perception of the time-series closely resembles that of Volkmann and Stout. "No more and not yet, says Volkmann, are the proper time-feelings, and we are aware of time in no other way than through these feelings." This doctrine of Volkmann has been elaborated by Stout, who has beautifully expressed his view as follows :

"Actual sensation is the mark or stamp of present time. The present time as distinguished from the past or future, is the time which contains the moment of actual sensation.... Distinction between past, present, and future can only be apprehended in a rudimentary way at the perceptual level. But there is, even at this level, what we may call a not yet consciousness and a no more consciousness. The not yet consciousness is contained in the prospective attitude of attention, in the pre-adaptation for what is to come which it involves. This not yet consciousness is emphasized when conation is delayed or obstructed, as when the dog is kept waiting for its bone. The no more consciousness emerges most distinctly when conation is abruptly disappointed or frustrated. With the advent of ideal representation the no more and the not yet experiences become much more definite."

Ladd says, "It is by the combination of imaging and thinking, in which every conceptual process consists, that the vague consciousness of a 'still-there' is converted into the conception of 'the present'; the consciousness of the 'now-going' or 'just-gone', into the conception of 'the past'; and the consciousness of the 'not yet there', with its affective accompaniment of expectation or dread, into the conception of 'the future'".

**The Sensible Present is Instantaneous (The Buddhist View)**

Time has two essential characteristics, viz. succession and duration. But the Buddhists do not recognize the existence of duration or block of time. They identify time with mere succession of ideas. The Buddhists hold with Berkeley and Hume that there is no abstract time apart from presentations. Time is not a substantive reality, as the Naiyayikas hold, but it is a cluster of successive presentations an abstract time apart from momentary impressions is an artificial conceptual construction. And according to the Buddhists, there are no continuous and uniform impressions (*dharayahika-jnana*) but only a series of detached and discrete impressions, a perpetual flux of successive presentations (*ksanabhangura-jnana*). Continuity is only an illusory appearance due to our slurring over the landmarks of impressions owing to their similarity. Momentary sensations alone are real ; there is no continuity among discrete sensations. The seeming continuity of impressions is nothing more than the rapid succession of impressions owing to the rapidity and uniformity of stimulations. Thus the Buddhist doctrine is quite the same as that of David Hume.

Time may be viewed either as one-dimensional or as bi-dimensional. Either it may be regarded as having only linear extension or succession, or it may be regarded as having simultaneity and succession both. The Buddhists hold that there is no synchronousness or simultaneity; there is only succession or sequence among our presentations. So a momentary presentation can neither apprehend the past nor the future, but it apprehends only the present which has no duration. Thus according to the Buddhists, the sensible present has no duration; it is an instant or a "time-point".

The Vedantists and some Naiyayikas hold that the sensible present is not a mathematical point of time but has a certain duration; the sensible present is a tract of time extending over a few moments it is an extended present or the "specious present" (*vitata eva kalah*). According to them the "specious present" having a certain duration yields us one unitary presentation without flickering of attention.

But the Buddhists hold that there is no "specious present"; the present has no duration; it is instantaneous or momentary inasmuch as our impressions are momentary. Our presentations are not somewhat prolonged processes, but instantaneous or enduring events. And there are no continuous and uniform impressions, as the Vedantists and some Naiyayikas hold.

According to Prabhakara, in the consciousness "I know this" (*aham idam janami*) there is a simultaneity of three presentations, viz. the presentation of the knower (I), the presentation of the known object (this) and the presentation of knowledge (or the relation between the knower and the known). This is Prabhakara's doctrine of *Triputi Samvit* or triple consciousness.

The Buddhists hold that the three elements are not simultaneous; but they are discrete and detached from one another; there is no relation among them; there can be no relation between the knower and the known. They hold that at first there is a particularized presentation (*sakara-jnana*) of "I" (*aham*), then that of "this" (*idam*) and then that of "knowing" (*janami*). Thus these discrete and momentary impressions flow in succession. But when the first impression of "I" vanishes, it leaves a residuum (*vasana*) which colours and modifies the second impression of "this"; and when the second impression vanishes, it leaves a residuum which colours and modifies the third impression. Thus though these three impressions are discrete and isolated from one another, there is a cumulative presentation of these momentary impressions owing to the transference of residua from the preceding impressions to the succeeding ones (*vasana-samkrama*) and the residua of the former colouring or modifying the latter (*upaplava*). Thus the Buddhists have invented the hypotheses of residua (*vasana*) transference of residua (*vasana-samkrama*), and modification of impressions by residua (*upaplava*) to explain away the fact of continuity or the consciousness of transition; a succession of presentations is certainly not the consciousness of succession. The Buddhists do not explain, but explain away the fact of unity and continuity of consciousness. The Buddhists examine the perceptive process and show that perception cannot apprehend the "specious present". A perception is nothing but a presentation; and a presentation is the presentation of a single moment; it cannot apprehend the past and the future. If there is a series of presentations, *a, b, b*, etc., is it the antecedent presentation *b* (*uttaravijnana*), or is it the succeeding presentation *b* that takes hold of the preceding presentation by the hind part, as it were ? The Buddhists answer that *b* can neither take hold of *c*, nor can it take hold of *a*. The past as past is not present; and the future as future is not present. Hence the present presentation can neither apprehend the past nor the future presentation, and consequently, there can be no direct apprehension or perception of the past and future.

But the Buddhists hold that the past enters into the present at the time of passing away, and the future also enters into the present, though it is not yet come, so that the present presentation is an echo of the immediate past and a foretaste of the immediate future. Thus the Buddhists surreptitiously introduce an element of linking or transition between the past and the present, and between the present and the future to explain our consciousness of the continuity of time. But though they admit that the past and the future enter into the present, they insist that it is only the present that is perceived and not the past or the future which enters into the present. Such is the nature of our experience that it unfolds successively one presentation appearing and then disappearing. And in this series of presentations an antecedent state (*purvadasa*) cannot come in contact with a subsequent state (*aparadasa*), and a subsequent state cannot come in contact with an antecedent state. All sense-presentations apprehend the present alone which is instantaneous or momentary.

Some Naiyayikas hold that sometimes the present is perceived as extended or with a certain duration, for instance, when we perceive a continuous action, e.g. cooking, reading, etc. The sensible present is not momentary, but has a certain length of duration (*vartamanaksano dirghah*); it is not made up of a single moment, but composed of a number of moments (*nandksanaganatmaka*)

The Buddhists urge that time cannot be a composite whole made up of parts; it cannot be a cluster of simultaneous presentations because there is no simultaneity among presentations. Time is not bi-dimensional, as some Naiyayikas hold, but it is one-dimensional There is no simultaneity, but only succession among our presentations. It is foolish to hold that perception apprehends an extended present with a certain duration.

The Naiyayika and the Vedantist hold that a continuous and uniform impression bears clear testimony to the unbroken and uninterrupted existence of its object; and consequently, it apprehends an extended present with a certain duration.

The Buddhists object that there is no uniform impression (*avicchinna-drsti*). Every impression is momentary; there cannot be a continuous impression. When there is a rapid succession of momentary impressions, they appear to be continuous, though they are not really so. And because there is no continuous impression, there can be no perception of the "specious present" with a certain duration. Even if there were a continuous impression, it would not be able to apprehend the "specious present", because an object must be presented to consciousness in order that we may have a presentative knowledge of the object, and the object cannot be presented to consciousness for more than one moment, since all objects are momentary.

But, as a matter of fact, there can be no continuous and uniform impression; consciousness must always apprehend itself as momentary; and not only consciousness is momentary, but also the consciousness of the momentariness of consciousness is momentary. Here the Buddhists differ from the Nco-Hegelians, Green, and others, who suppose that the consciousness of the relation, of impressions must be enduring; momentary impressions are apprehended as momentary by a consciousness which must be permanent. Thus, according to the Buddhists, all presentations are momentary, and as such they can apprehend only the present which has not a length of duration, but is constituted by a single moment; the sensible present, therefore, is instantaneous or momentary.

### The Sensible Present has Duration (The Naiyayika and the Vedantist View)

The Buddhists recognize only one aspect of time, viz. succession. They try to explain away the other aspect of time, viz. duration. But some Naiyayikas and the Vedantists clearly recognize the importance of duration apart from which succession has no meaning. The Buddhists have argued that a presentation cannot apprehend the past and the future as they are not presented to consciousness; it can apprehend only the present which is constituted by a single moment. The Naiyayika urges that even a momentary glance (*nimesa-drsti*) can apprehend the continued existence of an object. Why should, then, perception be regarded as apprehending the instantaneous present? Even supposing that a momentary glance cannot apprehend the past and the future, but only the present, what is the span of the present time perceived by a continuous and uniform impression (*animesa-drsti*) ? Is it a time-point or a tract of time ? Is it an instant or a length of duration ? The sensible present continues as long as the continuous and uniform impression persists without an oscillation of attention, and as long as it is not interrupted by another impression; so that this single unitary presentation apprehends not an instantaneous present but a lengthened or extended present with a certain duration.

The Buddhists may urge that such an extended present is a tract of time made up of a number of moments; but the present is really a single moment; the immediately preceding moment is past and the immediately succeeding moment is future; so they cannot be perceived. The Naiyayika replies that in determining the span of the sensible present we must not assume at the outset that it is momentary, but we must determine it by an appeal to experience. A psychological investigation must not be guided by metaphysical speculation; but metaphysics must be based on psychology. Psychologically considered, there is no mathematical point of time, but only a tract of time. That time must be regarded as present which is grasped by a single continuous impression without a break or interruption. And such an unbroken and uninterrupted impression apprehends the present as an unbroken and uninterrupted block or duration of time. Hence the sensible present is not an instant, but has a length of duration.

The Buddhists may urge that even according to the Naiyayika there cannot be a stable consciousness (*sthirajnana*) but only a series of momentary impressions; how, then, can he hold that there can be a perception of the "specious present"? Though all Naiyayikas hold that a psychosis extends over three moments: the moment of production, the moment of existence, and the moment of destruction and there can be no simultaneity of psychoses owing to the atomic nature of the central sensory or manasy yet there are some Naiyayikas who hold that a continuous and uniform impression is not destroyed at the third moment.

Besides, the temporal mark of a consciousness need not necessarily correspond with the temporal mark of its object. An object is apprehended by consciousness as having a continued existence. A pulse of consciousness, though existing at present can apprehend the past as well as the future as past and future. The feeling of the past is not a past feeling and the feeling of the future is not a future feeling. For instance, a present recollection apprehends the past; a present flash of intuition (*pratibha jnana*) apprehends the future; and a present inference apprehends both the past and the future.

The Buddhists may urge that the operation of the sense-organs does not exist for more than a single moment; and in the absence of a continued peripheral action there cannot be a perception of an extended time or the "specious present".

The Naiyayika replies that peripheral action does not exist for a moment, but continues for some time. The perception of an object depends upon the intercourse of a sense-organ with an object, and this intercourse is not momentary, but persists for some time; peripheral stimulation is not a momentary act, but a somewhat prolonged process; and consequently perception does not apprehend an instant or a "time-point", but a tract of time with a certain duration,

Vatsyayana says that sometimes the present is perceived as unmixed with the past and the future, for instance, when we perceive that a substance exists. And sometimes the present is perceived as mixed up with the past and the future, for instance, when we perceive the continuity of an action, e.g. cooking, cutting, etc. Thus Vatsyayana admits that the present is sometimes perceived as having a certain duration.

According to the Vedantists, too, a continuous and uniform impression (*dharavahikabuddhi*) is a single unitary psychosis with a certain duration; it is not a series of momentary impressions in rapid succession, as the Buddhists hold. In the continuous impression of a jar the mental mode which assumes the form of the jar is one and undivided as long as the jar is presented to consciousness without any flickering of attention, and is not interrupted by another psychosis. It is not made up of many momentary psychoses, because according to the Vedantist, a psychosis continues in the field of consciousness as long as the mind does not assume the form of a different object. So the Vedantist also admits that a continuous and uniform presentation does not apprehend an instantaneous present, but an extended present with a certain duration. Thus the Vedantists and some Naiyayikas hold that the sensible present has duration, while the Buddhists hold that the sensible present is instantaneous or momentary. Certainly the former view is psychologically correct. The Buddhists deny the "specious present" because it contradicts their fundamental doctrine of impermanence or momentariness.

This psychological discussion of the "specious present" in the medieval philosophical literature of India anticipates the same kind of discussion in the modern psychology of the West. Professor William James borrowed the word "specious present" from E.R. Clay and gave currency to it. He expresses his view most beautifully as follows:

"The practically cognized present is no knife-edge, but a saddleback, with a certain breadth of its own on which we sit perched, and from which we look in two directions into time. The unit of composition of our perception of time is a duration with a bow and a stern, as it were, a rearward and a forward looking end."

# 10

# Perception of the Universal (Jati) Indian Nominalism, Conceptualism and Realism

## Introduction

The problem of the universal and the individual has been approached in the West from the psychological, logical, and metaphysical points of view. The Indian thinkers also have investigated the problem from these different standpoints, not in abstract isolation from one another, but in their synthetic unity. The psychological aspect of this question, as understood by the different schools of Indian philosophers, is incomprehensible without a metaphysical consideration of it. So we shall attempt here a psychological study of the problem with reference to its metaphysical basis.

In the Western thought, there are mainly three theories of the universal, viz. nominalism, conceptualism, and realism. According to nominalism, the individuals alone are real. There are only individual things in nature, and particular ideas in the mind; there is no universal at all in reality only the name is general. According to conceptualism, there are only individual things in nature without any universal class-essence in them, but the mind has the power of forming a concept or an abstract general idea of individual things. Thus, according to it, there is no universal in nature, but the universal exists in the mind in the form of a concept or general idea. According to realism, the universal exists both in nature and in the mind; there is a universal or class-essence among the individual things of nature, and there is a universal notion or concept in the mind corresponding to the class-essence in nature. Thus, according to nominalism, there is no universal at all either in nature or in the mind; according to conceptualism, the universal exists only in the mind; according to realism, the universal exists both in nature and in the mind. Besides these main theories there are certain intermediate positions.

Among the Indian thinkers also we find a perpetual conflict between realists and nominalists. The note of conceptualism is not prominent, though not altogether absent. The Buddhists are thoroughgoing nominalists. The Naiyayikas, the later Vaisesikas, and the Mimamsakas (Bhatta and Prabhakara) represent different schools of realism. Kanada, the father of the Vaisesika system, and the earlier Vaisesikas are conceptualists. The Jaina is a nominalist tending towards realism. Ramanuja also is a nominalist with a bent for realism.

The Buddhists hold that specific individuals (*svalaksana*) alone are real; they are apprehended by indeterminate perception; there is no universal or class-essence at all in the specific individuals; the universal notion is an unreal abstraction of the mind; it is a conceptual construction of the mind to carry on the practical purposes of our life. The Buddhists are the most uncompromising nominalists.

The earlier Vaisesikas hold that universality or community (*samanya*) is a mark by which the understanding assimilates a number of objects and forms a group or class; the universal is relative to the understanding. Kanada and his earlier exponents hold that the universal is a concept of the mind. They are conceptualists. The Naiyayikas, the later Vaisesikas, the Bhattas, and the Prabhakaras hold that there is a real universal or class-essence among the individual objects of nature. But there is a difference of opinion as to the relation of the universal to the individual.

The Nyaya-Vaisesika and the Prabhakara hold that the universal is different from the individual, and the relation between them is that of inherence, the latter being the substrate of the former. The Bhatta, on the other hand, holds that the universal is both different from, and identical with, the individual; the relation between the two is that of identity in difference.

The Jaina holds that there can be no universal notion in the mind, unless there is a real universal in nature. The universal notion is not an unreal fiction of the mind as the Buddhists suppose; It is real, and consequently it must be based on reality. Corresponding to a universal notion in the mind, there must be a real universal in nature. But what is the nature of the real universal ? It is not a class-essence. The Jaina does not recognize its existence. There can be no one, eternal, ubiquitous class-essence in the individuals belonging to the same class, as the realists suppose. So far the Jaina agrees with the Buddhist and supports nominalism. But he differs from the Buddhist in that he recognizes the real existence of similarity or likeness among the individual members of the same class. The likeness is the objective ground of a universal notion. To this extent, the Jaina tends towards realism.

Ramanuja also holds a similar doctrine. According to him, individuals alone are real; there is no class-essence in them; but there is a close likeness or resemblance (*sausadrsya*) among them in the shape of certain definite collocations or configurations (*samsthana*) of parts among the individuals. Thus, Ramanuja agrees with the Jaina in holding that there is a real likeness among the individual things belonging to the same class. Ramanuja only gives an interpretation of the likeness among the individual members of a class. Thus, both the Jaina and Ramanuja are not out-and-out nominalists like the Buddhists, though they deny the existence of a class-essence; they are nominalists with a leaning towards realism. They are advocates of modified nominalism.

All Indian realists agree in holding that the universal is an object of perception; it can be perceived through the sense-organs; it is not an ideal construction of the mind. The experience of the universal is not conceptual, but perceptual. This is seldom admitted by the Western realists. The Indian realists differ from one another only in their views as to the relation of the universal to the individuals.

### *The Buddhist doctrine of Nominalism*

The universal in the form of a class-essence (*jati*) can never be an object of perception. A perceptible object produces the perception of it in the mind. But the universal (*jati*) is eternal; so it cannot produce its cognition. If, in spite of being eternal, the universal does produce a cognition, it will never cease to do so and consequently the cognition of no other object will be possible.

Moreover, the universal can never be perceived, for perception has for its object only the momentary specific individuals (*svalaksana*) unconnected with other individuals preceding and succeeding them. By the universal we mean that feature which is common to a whole class of objects. If such a universal character does exist at all, it can be known only after collecting all the individual objects belonging to a class and ascertaining their common character. Thus, the knowledge of the universal presupposes that of all the individuals in which the universal exists. How, then, can such a universal be known by indeterminate perception (*nirvikalpa pratyaksa*), which arises just after the contact of an object with a sense-organ, and is quite independent of any other cognition, preceding or succeeding it ? If it is apprehended by determinate perception (*savikalpa pratyaksa*) it is unreal for that very reason. According to the Buddhist, indeterminate perception alone is valid as it is free from all forms and categories (*vikalpa*); determinate perception is invalid as it is not free from thought-determinations. Thus, the universal can be apprehended neither by indeterminate perception nor by determinate perception.

Nor can it be proved by inference (*anumana*) and verbal cognition (*sabda*) for these too have for their objects the unreal forms of ideal construction (*vikalpa*), and as such cannot apprehend the ontological reality.

Hence specific individuals alone are real, since they are apprehended by indeterminate perception. The universal is nothing but a mere form of determinate cognition having no real existence in the world.

**The Buddhist Criticism of the Nyaya-Vaisesika Realism**

According to the Nyaya-Vaisesika, the universal is different from the individual; it inheres in the latter which is its substratum; there is one, eternal, ubiquitous universal among the members of a class.

The Buddhist offers the following criticism of this view :

1. Firstly, things which are different from one another must occupy different portions of space. But the universal is never perceived to occupy a space different from that of the individual. So the universal must not be different from the individual. Moreover, things which are different from one another can be perceived apart from one another. For instance,

a cloth can be perceived apart from a jar as they are different from each other. But the universal can never be perceived apart from the individual. Hence the universal cannot be different from the individual.

2. Secondly, it may be said that though the universal is different from the individual, it cannot be perceived apart from the individual simply because the former exists in the latter. But this is impossible. The universal can never exist in the individual. If it does so, does it exist in each individual wholly or partly ? Both the alternatives are untenable. If the universal exists in its entirety in one individual, then it cannot exist in any other individual, and being one, it cannot exist entirely in many individuals. Evidently, if the universal exhausts itself in one particular, it cannot exist in another without being produced anew. But this is absurd. The universal is eternal; it cannot be produced at all. Nor can it exist partly in all the individuals, for it has no parts. Then, again, it is not possible for the same universal to exist partly in the past, present, and future individuals.
3. Thirdly, even supposing that the universal exists in the individual, does it exist everywhere in all the individuals, or only in its proper objectives ? For instance, does the universal cow (*gotva*) exist in all individuals belonging to different classes, e.g. cows, horses, etc. (*sarvasarvagata*)? Or does it exist only in all the individual cows (*tyindasarvagata*).

   If a universal (e.g. the genus of cow or *gotva*) exists in all the individuals belonging to different classes (e.g. horses, cows, buffaloes, etc.), then we should perceive the genus of cow (*gotva*) in horses, that of horse (*asvatva*) in cows, and so on, and thus there would be an utter confusion or intermixture of genera (*sankarya*).

   It may be said that though a universal exists in all the individuals belonging to different classes, the individuals belonging to a particular class have the power of manifesting a particular universal. For instance, only the individual cows can manifest the universal cow (*gotva*) which is ubiquitous (*sarvasarvagata*). But according to the Buddhist idealist, existence consists in its being perceived.

If the universal exists everywhere, it should be perceived everywhere. Even if a universal, though all-pervading, can be manifested only by certain individuals, it does not follow that this universal must be perceived only in those individuals. If certain individuals manifest a universal which is ubiquitous, they must manifest it as it truly is. A lamp manifests certain objects. It does not follow from this that these objects are perceived in the lamp. Likewise, certain individuals manifest a universal. It does not prove that the universal must be perceived in those individuals.

If, on the other hand, a universal exists only in all its objectives or proper subjects (*pindasarvagata* or *svavyaktisarvagata*), how can it be perceived in a newly born individual? For instance, if the genus of cow (*gotva*) exists only in ail individual cows, how can it be perceived in a newly born cow, if it did not exist in that place before the individual was born? The universal cannot be born along with the individual as it is eternal. Nor can it come from any other individual, because, firstly, it is without any form (*amurta*), and consequently incapable of movement, and, secondly, it is not perceived in the individual from which it comes. Nor can it be said that the universal exists partly in the individual from which it comes, and partly in the newly born individual to which it comes, because the universal is without any parts. And thus when an individual is destroyed, the universal does not remain in that place, because it is not perceived there. Nor is it destroyed along with the individual, because it is eternal. Nor does it go to some other individual because, firstly, it is without any form (*amurta*) and consequently incapable of movement, and secondly, the universal cannot enter into another individual in which it already exists.

4. Fourthly, the Nyaya-Vaisesika holds that the relation between the universal and the individual is one of inherence (*samavaya*); the universal inheres in the individual. The Buddhist denies the relation of inherence altogether, and identifies it with identity (*tadatmya*). Inherence, according to the Vaisesika, is the relation between two entities which can never be perceived apart from each other, e.g. the relation between a substance

and its qualities, the relation between the constituent parts and the composite whole, the relation between the universal and the individual, etc. The Buddhist holds that those entities, which are not perceived apart from each other, are not different from each other, but they are identical with each other. Simultaneity and inseparability of perceptions constitute a test of identity. The universal can never be perceived apart from the individual; hence they are not different from each other.

5. Lastly, if the universal inheres in the individual, we must have such a perception as "there is the universal cow in this individual cow" (*iha gavi gotvam*). But, as a matter of fact, every one perceives a cow as "this is a cow" (*iyam gauh*), and not as "there is the class 'cow' in this particular cow" (*Iha gavi gotvam*). This clearly shows that the individual is not the substratum of the universal, but identical with it. Nor can it be said that the universal is the inner essence of the individual, because the former is entirely different from the latter. How can one, eternal, and ubiquitous universal be the essence of many, non-eternal, and discrete and isolated individuals ? If even such contradictory things, as the universal and the individual, were identical with each other, then cows and horses also would be identical with each other, and thus there would be an utter confusion in the whole world. Thus, the Buddhist comes to the conclusion that the universal can never be different from the individual.

## The Buddhist Criticism of the Srotriya View

According to the Srotriyas, there is a *rupa-rupi-laksana-sambandha* between the universal and the individual. But this also cannot be proved. If the universal is the *rupa* of the individual which is the *rupin* in relation to the former, what is meant by *rupa*? Does it mean colour (*sukladi*), or form (*akara*) or essential nature (*svabhava*) ?

1. If it means colour, if the universal is the colour of the individual then colourless substances such as air, mind etc., qualities, and actions would have no universality in them. But, as a matter of fact, they are supposed to have universality in them.

2. If *rupa* means form (*akara*) and consequently, if the universal is the form of the individual, then the formless qualities would have no universality in them, though they are supposed to have it.
3. If *rupa* means the intrinsic or essential nature (*svabhava*) and consequently, if the universal is the essential nature of the individual, then they are not different from each other. An object is never perceived as different from its essential nature. Hence the universal is not different from the individual. If there is any difference between them, there is a difference in name, but not in substance. Then, again, is the *rupa* a different substance from the *rupin*? Or is it the same substance as the *rupin*? Or is it the property of the *rupin*?
4. The first alternative is untenable. The universal, which is the *rupa* of the individual (*rupin*) is never perceived as a substance different from the individual (*vastvantaram*).
5. The second alternative contradicts the position of the opponent. If the universal is the same substance as the individual (*vastveva*), then they are identical with each other, and it is useless to speak of the *rupa-rupi-laksana-sambandha* between them.
6. The third alternative also is untenable. If the universal is the property of the individual (*vastudharma*), it should be perceived as distinct from the individual. But, in fact, it is never perceived as distinct from the individual. And if the universal is inseparable from the individual, it is useless to speak of a relation called *rupa-rupi-laksana-sambandha* between them, for they are not different from each other. Still if it is insisted that there is a *rupa-rupi-laksana* relation between the universal and the individual, the Srotriyas cannot distinguish it from conjunction and inherence.

Hence the Buddhists come to the conclusion that there cannot be a *rupa-rupi-laksana* relation between the universal and the individual.

### The Buddhist Criticism of the Bhatta Realism

The Bhatta Mimamsaka holds that there is a relation of identity in difference between the universal and the individual. The universal is both different from the individual, and identical with it. The perception of an object involves two elements, viz. inclusion or assimilation (*anugama*) and exclusion or discrimination (*vyavrtti*). This dual character of perception must correspond to the dual character of its object. Universality or community is the objective ground of assimilation, and particularity or individuality is the objective ground of discrimination. So the object of perception must be both universal and particular.

The Buddhist urges that it is self-contradictory to assert that one and the same object can be both universal and particular, one and many, eternal and temporary, existent and non-existent. Such an object is never found in experience; it is a fiction of imagination.

One and the same object can never be multiform in character. There is only one form in an object, viz. particularity that is real. The universality of an object is merely an unreal form superimposed upon the object by determinate cognition. It is the specific individuality (*svalaksana*), pure and simple, unmixed with universality, that is perceived just after the contact of the object with a sense-organ. Hence specific individuality alone is real; and universality is unreal. It cannot be said that both the characters of an object, viz. universality and particularity are perceived, and, therefore, both of them are real. For, in that case, the double moon also would be real because it is perceived.

According to the Buddhist, perception is always indeterminate; and indeterminate perception can never apprehend an object with the dual character of universality and particularity. It can apprehend only the specific individuality of an object, and never its universality, because, like all things, it has a momentary existence, and, consequently, it cannot apprehend that feature of the object which it has in common with many other objects. Thus, specific individuals alone are real, since they are apprehended by indeterminate perception; the universal is an unreal form of imagination.

### The Buddhist's refutation of the Realist's Objections

1. Firstly, the realist urges that just as various specific individuals are admitted to account for a variety of indeterminate perceptions, so various universals or class-essences (e.g. *gotva, asvatva,* etc.) must be admitted to account for various determinate cognitions (e.g. of cows, horses, and the like).

The Buddhist argues that the variety of determinate cognitions, too, can be explained by the variety of specific individuals. According to him, specific individuals are the causes of indeterminate perceptions, and indeterminate perceptions, again, are the causes of determinate cognitions; so that a variety of specific individuals produces a variety of indeterminate cognitions, which, in its turn, produces a variety of determinate cognitions. Thus, it is needless to suppose a variety of universals to account for a variety of determinate cognitions as the realist supposes.

2. Secondly, the realist may ask : If universals are nothing but unreal forms of imagination how can they serve the practical purposes of our life? According to the Buddhist, every thing is momentary, and so the specific individuals (*svalaksana*) are momentary. Hence the specific individual, which is apprehended by indeterminate perception, is destroyed at that very moment, and no action is possible with regard to that object; and that individual with regard to which there is an action is destroyed at that very moment, and so it cannot be attained. Hence one individual is perceived, while there is action on another individual, and thus practical actions are not in keeping with the real nature of things. How, then, can unreal forms of determinate cognitions serve the practical purposes of our life?

   The Buddhist argues that even the unreal forms (*vikalpa*) of determinate cognitions can serve the practical purposes of our life. Just as the cognition of a gem produced by the ray of a gem leads to the actual attainment of the gem, and thus serves a practical purpose of our life, so determinate cognitions produced by indeterminate perceptions of specific individuals and, consequently, having a semblance of specific individuals which are capable of evoking effective actions, lead those who are desirous of effective actions to the attainment of those specific individuals. Thus, determinate cognitions, though not in keeping with the real nature of specific individuals, indirectly lead to the actual attainment of them, and in this way serve the practical purposes of our life. Hence it cannot be said that determinate cognitions, having no real things for their objects, but having unreal forms (*vikalpa*) superimposed on them, cannot serve the practical purposes of our life. Thus, in spite of the non-existence of universals, practical actions can follow from unreal determinate cognitions.

3. Thirdly, the realist may contend that discrete specific individuals can never produce a universal notion in the mind. How can specific individuals, which are absolutely different from one another, produce one and the same universal notion, if the universal does not really exist ? If they can produce a universal notion, in spite of their absolute difference, the realist asks : How is it that certain individuals produce the universal notion of cow, while certain other individuals produce the universal notion of horse, and all individuals do not produce all universal notions?

The Buddhist retorts : How can the individuals of the realist, which are different from one another, have an identical essence in the form of the universal, and how can they be the substrates of the same universal, and how can they manifest the same universal? And, moreover, how is it that certain individuals are related to a certain universal, and not all individuals are related to all universals? If the realist argues that certain individuals, by their very nature (*svabhavat*), are related to a certain universal, and not all individuals are related to all universals, then it may equally be argued that certain individuals, by their very nature, produce the same universal notion in the form "this is a cow", "this is a cow", and so on, in spite of the non-existence of the universal. Thus the Buddhist does not believe in the existence of the universal.

## The Modified Nominalism of the Jaina

The Buddhist believes only in specific individuals which are like themselves. He does not believe in the universal. He is an uncompromising nominalist. According to him, particulars or individuals alone are real; there is no universal or class-essence among them; they are characterized by themselves; there is not even likeness or similarity among them. The Jaina agrees with the Buddhist in denying the existence of a class-essence in the individuals belonging to the same class; but he differs from the latter in recognizing the existence of common characters or resemblances among them, which he regards as the real universal. The Jaina does not go so far as to say that specific individuals alone are real and there is no likeness or similarity among them. According to him, there is likeness or similarity among the individuals belonging to the same class, and this likeness is the real universal; there is no universal class-essence among them. This doctrine may be compared with J. S. Mill's nominalism. According to Mill, though there is not a universal class-essence among the individuals belonging to the same class, still there are certain fundamental qualities common to them all; and in thinking of general terms, though we have concrete images before the mind, we concentrate our attention on the fundamental attributes common to them, and recognize them as common to the whole class.

Thus the Jaina is neither an uncompromising nominalist nor an uncompromising realist. The Buddhists are out-and-out nominalists. They recognize the existence of specific individuals only. They entirely deny the existence of the universal The Nyaya-Vaisesika and the Mimamsaka, on the other hand, recognize the existence of one, eternal, and ubiquitous universal in the individuals. They are out-and-out realists. The Jaina holds an intermediate position. He also recognizes the reality of the universal, but according to him, the universal is not one, eternal, and ubiquitous, as the realists hold, but is multiform, non-eternal, and non-pervading or limited; and this universal is nothing but the common character or similarity among the different individuals belonging to the same class. The Jaina does not recognize the existence of any other universal than this common character or similarity which is perceived through the sense-organs like colours and the like. And this common character, according to him, is the cause of the universal notion which has no other object than this.

The difference between the Nyaya-Vaisesika and the Mimamsaka, on the one hand, and the Jaina, on the other, is that according to the former, the universal notion has its objective counterpart in the real universal or class-essence in the individuals, which is different from them, and is one, eternal, and ubiquitous, while according to the latter, the universal notion has its objective counterpart in the common character or similarity of many individuals, which is not one, but many, existing in many individuals not eternal, but temporary, being produced and destroyed along with the individual in which it exists and not all-pervading, but confined only to the individual in which it exists. Thus the Jaina is neither an uncompromising nominalist like the Buddhist nor an uncompromising realist like the Nyaya-Vaisesika and the Mimamsaka, He is an advocate of modified nominalism.

According to the Jaina, an object of knowledge is both universal and particular (*samanya-vuesatma*). It is not merely universal like the Being or Brahman of Samkara; nor is it merely particular like the specific individuals (*svalaksma*) of the Buddhist. It is characterized both by common characters (*samanya*) and by uncommon or distinctive characters (*visesa*). Our consciousness of similarity (*anuvrttapratyaya*) has for its object common characters (*samanya*) and our consciousness of difference (*uyavrttapratyaya*) has for its object uncommon or distinctive characters (*visesa*). The consciousness of an object involves assimilation and discrimination both. Assimilation is due to common characters, and discrimination is due to uncommon characters. Hence an object of knowledge is both universal and particular, since it is characterized by common and uncommon characters both. The common characters again, which constitute the real universal (*samanya*), according to the Jaina, are of two kinds, viz. *tiryak samanya* and urddhvata samanya. By tiryak samanya he means similar *modifications* (*sadrsaparinamastiryak*) e.g. dewlap and the like in cows. By *urddhvata samanya* he means the permanent substance which abides in the midst of past, present, and future modifications (*paraparavivartavyapi-dravyamurddhvata*), e.g. earth in its various modifications. So the common characters of an object are constituted by its permanent substance which persists in the midst of all its modifications, and its modifications which are similar to those of other like objects. And these are the real universal; there is no other universal than these common characters.

**The Jaina Criticism of the Buddhist Nominalism**

Prabhacandra criticizes the Buddhist doctrine of nominalism in the following manner :

1. Firstly, the Buddhist argues that the universal is not perceived apart from the individual; hence it does not exist.

   But the Jaina urges that the universal is as much an object of perception as the individual; it is an object of uncontradicted experience in the form of "inclusive" or assimilative perception, just as the individual is an object of uncontradicted experience in the form of "exclusive" or discriminative perception. Just as the exclusive perception of particularity cannot be denied, so the inclusive perception of universality also cannot be denied. Both these experiences are uncontradicted. And the verdict of uncontradicted experience can never be called in question. Hence, uncontradicted assimilative perception establishes the real existence of the universal (*samanya*) common to many individuals, which cannot be apprehended by discriminative perception.

2. Secondly, the Buddhist argues that there is no universal apart from the individual, for there are not two distinct cognitions of the universal and the individual.

But the Jaina urges that there is a difference between the cognition of universality and that of individuality, for all of us perceive the difference. There are two distinct cognitions of the universal and the individual. It is true that both of them are perceived at the same time and in the same object. But that does not prove that they are apprehended by one and the same cognition. For, in that case, the colour and the taste of a cake perceived at the same time would be apprehended by a single cognition. But, as a matter of fact, the cognitions of the colour and the taste, though simultaneous, are different from each other. Nor can it be argued that the universal is identical with the individual, since both of them are perceived at the same time through the same sense-organ. For, in that case, the wind would be identical with the sun, since sometimes both of them are perceived at the same time through the tactual organ. In fact, the difference between two objects is proved by the difference in their cognitions. And there is a difference between the cognition of the universal and that of the individual : the former is inclusive, while the latter is exclusive in nature. Hence the universal is different from the individual. Moreover, sometimes we perceive only the common character (e.g. tallness) of two objects (e.g. a post and a man) but cannot perceive their distinctive characters as in doubtful perception. This conclusively proves that the cognition of the universal is different from the cognition of the individual. And this difference in cognitions proves the real difference in their objects. Thus the universal must be different from the individual.

3. Thirdly, the Buddhist contends that the experience of universality (*anugatapratibhasa*) does not necessarily imply the real existence of the universal, for it can be produced by different individuals.

   But the Jaina urges that the experience of universality is never possible without the real existence of the universal; for otherwise it would not be experienced in the same form in all times and places. Moreover, individuals are different from one another; difference constitutes the essential nature of individuals. How, then, can they produce the experience of universality? Still, if the Buddhist insists that different individuals can produce the experience of universality, then for the same reason, different horses would produce the universal notion of "cow", which is absurd.

4. Fourthly, the Buddhist contends that though individuals are absolutely different from one another, and devoid of common characters, still the preclusion of certain individuals (e.g. cows) from those individuals which are neither their causes nor effects (e.g. horses, buffaloes, etc.) is the cause of the experience of universality (e.g. "cow") and the consequent action.

   But the Jaina replies that the negation of contradictories is not at all possible in those individuals which are devoid of common characters; hence it cannot be the cause of the experience of universality. Moreover, the negative conception of the "negation of contradictories" can never lead to practical action, which always follows from positive cognitions. Besides, if the experience of universality is possible without the real existence of the universal in nature then, for the same reason, the experience of individuality also would be possible without the real existence of the individual in nature, which is not admitted by the Buddhist. Hence, if discriminative perceptions have for their objects discrete individuals in the world, then assimilative perceptions too must have for their objects real universals in the world. Thus the universal has a real existence in nature.

5. Fifthly, the Buddhist contends that though there is no real universal in the individuals, the experience of universality is due to the illusory identification of different individuals owing to the similarity of the actions produced by them. For instance, though different cows have no real identity among them, yet they seem to be identical in nature, since all of them produce similar actions, e.g. milking, carrying, etc.

   But the Jaina urges that different individuals produce different actions. If it is said that the identity of the actions produced by different individuals is due to the similarity of other actions, then it would lead to regressus ad infinitum. Even the cognitions produced by different individuals are different from one another; so they cannot account for the experience of universality.

6. Lastly, the Buddhist contends that the illusory identity of different indeterminate perceptions is due to their producing one and the same universal notion; and the illusory identity of different individuals is due to the illusory identity of the indeterminate perceptions which are produced by different individuals. Thus, according to him, an illusory identity is superimposed on the different indeterminate perceptions produced by different individuals, because of the identity of the universal notion produced by them; and an illusory identity is superimposed on the different individuals on account of the illusory identity of their effects, viz. indeterminate perceptions. Thus an identity is superimposed on indeterminate perceptions, though they are absolutely different from one another, and this superimposed identity, again, is superimposed on specific individuals which are absolutely different from one another.

The Jaina urges that this theory of the superimposition of a superimposition is, indeed, a nice hypothesis, which does not appeal to reason but to blind faith! As a matter of fact, indeterminate perceptions, which are absolutely different from one another, can never produce one and the same universal notion. Had it been so, the indeterminate perceptions of horses and other animals too would have produced the universal notion of "cow". So, it is wrong to argue that the illusory identity of different individuals is due to the illusory identity of the indeterminate perceptions of these individuals, and the illusory identity of the indeterminate perceptions is due to their producing one and the same universal notion.

Hence the Jaina concludes that the universal really exists in the world in the form of common characters or similarity (*sadrsa-parinama*), since it is an object of uncontradicted experience.

## The Jaina Criticism of the Nyaya-Vaisesika Realism

The Nyaya-Vaisesika holds that there is a real universal in the individuals, and it is one, eternal, and ubiquitous. But this doctrine is refuted by the Jaina almost by the same arguments which have been advanced by the Buddhist to prove the non-existence of the universal. The Jaina does not believe in any other universal than likeness, since likeness alone is an object of perception, and nothing beyond likeness is perceived. And this universal in the form of likeness is not one but many, since it exists in many individuals; it is not eternal but temporary, since it is produced and destroyed along with the individual in which it exists; it is not ubiquitous but limited, since it is confined to the individual in which it exists.

It cannot be argued that the cognition of the universal notion itself proves the existence of one, eternal, and ubiquitous universal. For, what does it mean? Does it mean that wherever there is a universal notion, there is such a universal? Or does it mean that wherever there is such a universal, there is a universal notion?

The first meaning is not possible. It cannot be held that whereever we have a universal notion, there is a real universal corresponding to it. For, we have a universal notion of universals such as the generic character of cows (*gotva*), the general character of horses (*asvatva*), etc.; but is there a universal of universals corresponding to the universal notion? The Nyaya-Vaisesika does not admit the existence of a universal of universals. Then, again, we have the universal notion of the different kinds of negation or non-existence, antecedent non-existence, subsequent non-existence, mutual non-existence, and absolute non-existence. But is there a universal of negation among these different kinds of negation? The Nyaya-Vaisesika does not admit the existence of the universal of negation. But these universals of universals and negations can be explained by the common characters in the different universals and the different kinds of negation respectively. Hence there is no other universal than common character or similarity.

The second meaning also is impossible. It cannot be held that wherever there is a real universal in the world, there is a corresponding universal notion in the mind. For, though there is not a real universal in the cooks in the form of their generic character (*pacakatva*) according to the Nyaya-Vaisesika, still there is the universal notion of "cook" (*pacakah pacaka ityadi*). Such a universal notion is not produced by the function (*karma*) of the cooks, for functions differ with each cook; and different causes can never produce the same effect. Nor can it be produced by the community of functions (*karmasamanya*), for, if it is possible at all, it can produce the universal notion of cooking but not of the cook.

Hence the Jaina concludes that the universal notion cannot have for its object one, eternal, and ubiquitous universal existing in different individuals. There is no other universal than the common character or similarity, which is not one in many individuals, but differs with each individual in which it exists. And such a universal in the form of a common character differs in each individual like the uncommon or distinctive characters. Just as an individual is distinguished from other individuals by virtue of its distinctive characters, so it is assimilated to other individuals by virtue of those characters which it has in common with them; and these common characters are perceived in the form "this is similar to that", "that is similar to this", and so on. Just as the distinctive characters of individuals lead to effective actions by producing discriminative perceptions in the mind, so the common characters of individuals lead to effective actions by producing assimilative perceptions in the mind.

**The Jaina Refutation of the Mimamsaka Objections**

1. Firstly, the Bhatta Mimamsaka urges that if the common character or similarity constitutes universality, why do we perceive an individual cow as "this is a cow", and not as "this is like a cow"? The Jaina replies that we have such a perception because of the superimposition of identity or similarity (*abhedopacarat*).

   The Jaina further retorts : How can the Bhatta explain such a perception as "this is like that", "the white cow is like the black cow?" If the Bhatta argues that we have such a perception, because of their relation to the same universal, then, the Jaina says, we should have such a perception as "these two individuals are possessed of the same universal". The Jaina holds that we have such a perception as "this is a cow", and not as "this is like a cow", because of the superimposed identity between the two individuals on account of their common characters.

2. Secondly, the Bhatta asks : If an individual is perceived to be like another individual on account of their common characters, how can these common characters, again, be perceived as like one another? Is it because of other common characters among these common characters? If so, then it would lead to infinite regress.

The Jaina replies that just as distinctive characters can be perceived as distinct from one another without supposing other distinctive characters among them, so the common characters among individuals can be perceived as like one another without supposing any other common character among them. The hypothesis of any other universal than the common characters among individuals is unwarranted by the facts of experience.

## The Modified Nominalism of Ramanuja

Ramanuja holds almost the same view as the Jaina, as regards the universal. According to him, there is no other universal (*jati*) than a configuration or arrangement of parts (*samsthana*) among the individuals; but there is a likeness in the configurations of individuals. In individual objects there are points of likeness, but not a universal class-essence (*jati*). Ramanuja entirely denies the existence of a class-essence, but he admits the existence of fundamental likeness or close resemblance. What is fundamental likeness (*sausadrsya*)? That property of the object, which is the unconditional and invariable condition of the use of the word "much alike" (*susadrsa*) is fundamental likeness (*sausadrsya*). If likeness is not a property of an object, it is no likeness at all. If it exists as a property in another object, then it leads to infinite regress. Therefore, there is no class-essence in individuals, but only a likeness or similarity among certain individuals. And even among these individuals not a single quality is found to belong to all the individuals of a class (e.g. cows). How, then, can we define fundamental likeness (*sausadrsya*) among them ? Ramanuja holds that the individual members of a class are not found to possess a definite quality in common, but they resemble one another in the greatest number of qualities (*pauskalya*). This doctrine reminds us of Mill's doctrine of natural kinds, according to which the members of the same class have the greatest number of resemblances among them, and differ from the members of a different class in the largest number of points. Ramanuja further urges that there is not only no identity of classessence among the different individuals of a class, but there is not even an identity of name among them. Thus Ramanuja goes further than Hume and Mill, when he holds that even the name is not general among the individuals of a class. When we say "cow", we mean different cows in different times and spaces. A is like B, B is like C, C is like D. Thus there is not a single likeness among A, B, C, and D; but there are different likenesses because the correlative terms differ in each case. Ramanuja, thus, is an advocate of thorough-going nominalism. But he does not go the length of saying that there is no likeness at all among the specific individuals, which are absolutely different from one another. Thus the Buddhists are the most uncompromising nominalists. Ramanuja is a bit less uncompromising, and the Jaina is still less so. If the Buddhists be regarded as typical exponents of thorough-going nominalism, the Jaina and Ramanuja both may be regarded as advocates of modified nominalism.

Ramanuja holds that at the stage of indeterminate perception, i.e. the perception of the first individual of a class, we perceive a particular arrangement of parts (*samsthana*) which is the distinctive character of the whole class, but we do not recognize it to be the common character of all the individuals belonging to the class, for at that time we have not yet perceived any other individual. Thus, even in indeterminate perception the universal character of an object is known, but not as universal, for, according to Ramanuja, there is no other universal than a particular collocation of parts, which is common to all the individuals of a class, and this class-character in the form of a particular collocation of parts (*samsthana-rupajatyadi*) is as much an object of sense-perception as the individual object (*pinda*) itself; and, moreover, the individual which has a particular collocation of parts can never be perceived apart from the particular arrangement of parts. Hence, according to Ramanuja, both universality and individuality enter into the indeterminate perception of an object, but the universality or common character is not recognized to be the common character of all the individuals belonging to the class. The common character is known to be, common only at the stage of determinate perception or the perception of the second, the third, and the subsequent individuals.

**The Modified Conceptualism of Kanada**

Kanada defines universality and particularity as mental concepts; they are relative to the understanding (*samanyam visesa iti buddhyapeksam*). He lays stress on the activity of thought in relation to universality and particularity. By universality he means a mark or quality by which the understanding assimilates a number of objects and forms a group or class. By particularity he means a mark or quality by which the understanding differentiates one object from others. Thus universality and particularity are mental concepts. Hence Kanada seems to advocate the doctrine of conceptualism. But he is not an extreme conceptualist, since he admits that universality (*samanya*) has a real existence in the form of common qualities in individual objects. Thus Kanada advocates a modified form of conceptualism with a tinge of realism. But the later Vaisesikas agree with the Naiyayikas and advocate realism.

**The Nyaya-Vaisesika Realism**

The Buddhist holds with Hobbes that universality lies only in name; it is an unreal fiction of imagination (*vikalpa*). He is a nominalist. The Jaina and Ramanuja hold that the universal is real; it exists in the individuals in the form of common characters; there is no other universal besides these. They are modified nominalists. Kanada holds that universality and particularity are relative to the understanding, though corresponding to them there are common qualities and individual peculiarities respectively in individual objects. He is a modified conceptualist. The later Vaisesikas, however, are realists. They lay stress on the reality of the class-essence in the individuals.

The Naiyayikas also recognize the existence of the universal as distinct from the individual. The universal is related to the individual by the relation of inherence. There is one universal in all the individuals belonging to the same class. Though it exists in them, it is independent of them. It is not born with them; nor does it perish with them. It is eternal; it is unborn and imperishable. This doctrine of eternal universals resembles the realism of Plato. The universals of the Naiyayika are eternal types like the ideas of Plato; the individuals are born and destroyed, but the universals subsist for ever. But still the Naiyayika does not support the Platonic doctrine of *universalia ante rem*. Plato's ideas exist in the transcendental world as eternal archetypes while his individuals exist in the sensible world; his Ideas are truly real, but his individuals are mere shadows of the ideas, and as such unreal. The Naiyayikas individuals are as real as his universals; both of them have ontological reality. Moreover, Plato's ideas are not immanent in the individuals so long as they exist; but the Naiyayika's universals exist in the individuals as their formative principles; they are immanent in them so long as they exist; there is an intimate and inseparable relation between them, called inherence (*samavaya*). Thus the Naiyayika supports the Aristotelian view of *universalia in re*. But his universal is one and eternal, while his individuals are many and non-eternal; the universal subsists before the individuals are born and after the individuals are destroyed. So far the Naiyayika supports the Platonic doctrine of *universal ante rem*. Thus his realism is a peculiar blend of Platonic and Aristotelian realism.

### The Psychological Basis of Realism Perception of the Universal (Jati)

Jayanta Bhatta shows that the universal is as much an object of perception as the individual. The Buddhists hold that the specific individual (*svalaksana*) alone is an object of perception; the universal is never perceived; it is an unreal fiction of imagination (*vikalpa*). The Naiyayika argues that the universal cannot be said to be unreal, since, like the individual, it is an object of uncontradicted and undoubted perception produced by the peripheral contact of an object with a sense-organ. The universal is as much an object of indeterminate perception as the individual. If the individual alone were the object of indeterminate perception, how could the universal suddenly enter into distinct consciousness at the stage of determinate perception? If it is urged that the universal is simply a name, and as such only a *vikalpa* or an unreal form of imagination, then the Naiyayika replies that the universality of an object can be apprehended, even when the name of the object is not yet known. For instance, when a man coming from the Deccan, where there are no camels, suddenly sees a number of camels, he perceives the universality of the camels, though he does not know their names. Though a man does not know the name of a number of objects belonging to the same class when he perceives them for the first time, he can perceive both their common and distinctive features, universality and particularity. At the first sight of four fingers we perceive them both as similar to, and different from, one another. So it cannot be held that through perception we can apprehend only the particularity of an object, and not its universality. Moreover, if at the time of perceiving the first individual belonging to a class only its distinctive feature is perceived, we cannot recognize the second individual perceived at some other time as belonging to the same class. The Buddhist may argue that the recollection of the first individual at the time of perceiving the second individual is the cause of recognition; the recognition of the second individual is a complex presentative-representative process involving the perception of this individual and the recollection of the first individual. But the Naiyayika points out that the second individual, according to the Buddhist, is quite different from the first, and has no similarity with it. Then, what is the use of remembering it at the time of perceiving the second individual? How can it help us in recognizing the second individual? If it has anything to do with the recognition of the second individual as belonging to the same class, then, at first, there must be a perception of both the common and distinctive features of the first individual. Thus at the first stage of indeterminate perception just after peripheral stimulation the universality of an object is as much perceived as its particularity, and hence universality can never be denied. Universality is as much real as particularity, since both of them are objects of indeterminate perception, which is purely immediate and unsophisticated experience.

If it is urged that at the stage of indeterminate perception we cannot distinctly point out the common feature of an object, then it may equally be argued that at this stage we cannot also point out the distinctive feature of the object. If it is urged that community cannot be perceived at the stage of indeterminate perception, because the perception of community depends upon the perception of those objects which have common qualities, then it may equally be argued that particularity of an object too cannot be perceived at this stage, because the perception of its particularity too depends upon the perception of those objects from which it is distinguished. If the community of an object cannot be perceived, because it depends upon the assimilation of this object to other like objects, its particularity also cannot be perceived, because it depends upon the discrimination of this object from other disparate objects. If the particularity of specific individuality (*svalaksana*) of an object is perceived at the stage of indeterminate perception, its universality too must be perceived at the same time.

But can we not apprehend an object, pure and simple, in its bare nakedness, stripped both of its common and distinctive features at the stage of indeterminate perception ? If so, what is the exact nature of its object? Evidently it cannot be determined at the stage of indeterminate perception, which is purely an immediate experience. It can be determined only at the stage of determinate perception, which clearly shows that both universality and particularity are objects of indeterminate perception. In fact, indeterminate perception is the immediate experience of the common and distinctive features of an object as mere *thats*, and not as *whats*; these are apprehended as unrelated to one another. In determinate perception we apprehend these common and distinctive features as whats or as related to one another. Indeterminate perception is the pure immediate apprehension of objects and their qualities (both common and particular) per se. Determinate perception is the clear apprehension of the objects and their qualities inter se.

It has been argued that it is self-contradictory to assert that one and the same object is characterized by contradictory qualities such as universality and particularity. But, in fact, there is no contradiction here, because we do not perceive the contradiction. Neither the perception of community contradicts that of particularity, nor does the perception of particularity contradict that of universality; hence both the perceptions are real, and none of them is illusory.

## The Nyaya-Vaisesika Criticism of Buddhist Nominalism

Jayanta Bhatta offers the following criticism of the Buddhist doctrine :

1. Firstly, the Buddhists argue that the universal is not different from the individual, because they are not perceived to occupy different portions of space, like a jar and a cloth. But this is false. The universal is not perceived to occupy a space different from, that of the individual, not because it does not exist, but because it exists only in the individual, which is its substratum.
2. Secondly, the Buddhists argue that the universal cannot exist in the individual, because it cannot be conceived to exist in the individual either wholly or partly. Jayanta Bhatta replies that the universal does exist in each individual wholly or entirely. It cannot be said that if the universal exists wholly in a particular individual, it cannot exist in any other individual because it has already exhausted itself in the former individual; for we do perceive the universal in each individual, and the fact of our uncontradicted experience can never be challenged; and the universal can never exist partly in each individual, because it has no parts.
3. Thirdly, the Buddhists argue that a universal can neither be all-pervading nor limited to certain individuals belonging to the same class; it can neither exist in all individuals to whatever class they may belong, nor can it exist in all its proper objectives.

   Jayanta Bhatta replies that a universal exists everywhere, not only in its proper subjects, but in all the particulars. But it cannot be perceived in all the individuals, because it is not manifested by all of them; a particular universal (e.g. the genus of cow or *gotva*) is manifested by a number of particular individuals (e.g. cows); and in the absence of these manifesting individuals, the universal is not perceived. And an individual can manifest a universal, only when it is perceived; unperceived individuals can never manifest a universal. Thus, though a universal exists everywhere, it cannot be perceived everywhere because the manifesting agents are not present everywhere. A universal is perceived wherever its manifesting agents or individuals are perceived, because individuals can manifest a universal only in that particular space and at that particular time, where and when those individuals are perceived. So we are not to suppose that the universal "cow" did not exist in the particular cow just born before its birth, but it comes into it when it is born; since the universal is incapable of movement.

And there is no harm in admitting that a universal exists only in its proper subjects. Whenever a particular individual cornes to cxist, it comes to be related to the universal. Though the universal is eternal, its relation to a particular individual comes into existence only at that moment when the individual comes into being.

4. Fourthly, the Buddhists argue that the universal cannot inhere in the individual, as the Nyaya-Vaisiesika holds, since there is no relation of inherence, inherence (*samavaya*) is nothing but identity (*tadstmya*). The Buddhists deny the possibility of any other relation than identity between two entities which are inseparable from each other, e.g. substance and quality, universal and particular, and so on.

   Jayanta Bhatta replies that inseparability of two things does not prove their identity. Though a substance and its quality are inseparable, being never perceived apart from each other, one is perceived as distinct from the other. Likewise, though the universal is never perceived apart from the individual, they cannot be regarded as identical with each other, since they are perceived as distinct from each other. Therefore, the difference of the universal from the individual is proved by the difference in their perceptions.

5. Fifthly, the Buddhists argue that only specific individuality is real, since it is the object of indeterminate perception; universality is the product of conceptual construction (*vikalpa*), and consequently unreal. To this Jayanta Bhatta replies that universality and individuality both are real, inasmuch as both of them are objects of uncontradicted experience. The Buddhists cannot deny the reality of universality. What is his complaint against the perception of universality? He does not deny the universal notion (*anuvrttijnana*). What, then, is the power (*sakti*) in the individual, which produces such a universal notion? And if there is such a power in the individual, is it different from the individual, or identical with it? Is it eternal or non-eternal? Is it perceptible or inferable? If it is

different from the individual, it must be universal; if not, the individual can never produce the universal notion. If it is eternal, it is universal, since the individuals are born and destroyed; and if it is non-eternal, and as such identical with the individual, it can never produce the universal notion. If it is perceptible, the universal is real, and if it is inferrable, then also the universal is real.

6. Sixthly, the Buddhists may argue that just as the Nyaya-Vaisesika holds that a particular universal (e.g. the class-essence of cows or gotva) can exist only in some particular individuals (e.g. cows), so it may be said that some particular individuals (e.g. cows) can produce a universal notion (e.g. of the class "cow"), though in reality there is no universality in them, Jayanta Bhatta urges that this argument is absurd. If there is a peculiarity (*atuaya*) in a cognition, there must be a corresponding peculiarity (*atisaya*) in its object. If you admit that a peculiarity in the effect is produced by a corresponding peculiarity in its cause, then you must admit that the universality of a notion must be produced by a corresponding peculiarity in its object, viz. universality. Hence the universal is real.

7. Lastly, the Buddhists may argue that the unity in the individuals is not the unity of their universality, but it is the unity of the individuals themselves. Sridhara replies that this is not possible. For, if there were no universality, there could be no unity among the individuals, or their causes, or their effects or actions. If the unity in the individuals were due to the unity of their causes, then there would be no unity among the individuals which are produced by different causes, e.g. fire produced by the friction of wood, fire produced by electricity, etc. So, also, if the unity among the individuals were due to the unity or sameness of their effects, then there would be a unity even among heterogeneous individuals; for instance, both cows and buffaloes give us milk , hence cows would be regarded as the same as the buffaloes. Hence the unity in the individuals must be due to the universal in them. The universal can never be denied. It is a fact of uncontradicted experience. So the Nyaya-Vaisesika affirms the reality of the universal.

**The Prabhakara Realism**

The Prabhakara holds that the universal (*jati*) is real, since we recognize an essential identity among a number of individuals which are perceived as different from one another the sameness in the midst of differences proves the existence of the universal in them. It exists in each individual entirely, since we recognize the same class-character in every individual. It is distinct from the individuals in which it subsists. It is eternal. It is an object of sense-perception. It is never perceived apart from the individual. So far the Prabhakara agrees with the Nyaya-Vaisesika. But he differs from the latter in holding that the relation of inherence (*samavaya*) between the universal and the individual is not eternal. When a new individual of a class is born, a new relation of inherence is generated, by which the individual is brought into relation with the universal (*jati*) that exists in other individuals. And when an individual is destroyed, the relation of inherence between this individual and the universal is destroyed. Moreover, according to the Vaisesika, there is the *summum genus* (*para jati*) viz. Being or existence which is supposed to be the common character of all entities. The Prabhakara does not recognize the existence of the highest genus, viz. Being (*satta*), since we have no consciousness of it. We have to admit that there is such a *jati* as substance, because we perceive a number of individual substances as having certain characters in common. But we have no such consciousness of *satta* or pure being; we do not perceive a number of things as merely "existing"; and so we cannot admit that there can be such *jati* as pure being or *satta*. When we speak of an individual object as existing (*sat*) we do not mean that it has any class-character as being (*sat*); but we mean simply that the individual has its specific existence (*svarupasatta*) or individuality. "That all things are said to be *sat* (existing) is more or less a word or a name without the corresponding apprehension of a common quality. Our experience always gives us concrete existing individuals, but we can never experience such a highest genus as pure existence or being, as it has no concrete form which may be perceived. When we speak of a thing as *sat* we do not mean that it is possessed of any such class-characters as satta (being); what we mean is simply that the individual has its specific existence or *svarupa-satta*".

Prabhakara agrees with Kumarila in holding that the universal (*jati*) is real and is an object of sense-perception. But he differs from Kumarila in his view of the relation between the universal and the individual. According to Prabhakara, the universal is different from the individual. But according to Kumarila, the universal is both different from, and identical with, the individual. According to the former, there is a relation of difference between the universal and the individual, while according to the latter, there is a relation of identity-in-difference.

Prabhakara objects to the Bhatta theory of identity-in-difference between the universal and the individual for the following reason. If both the universal and the individual were perceived by one and the same act of cognition without contradicting each other, then the theory would be regarded as valid. But they cannot be perceived as such. One and the same act of cognition cannot apprehend both the difference and the identity between the universal and the individual. Just as when we perceive the difference between the universal and the individual, we also perceive both the members of the relation (i.e. the universal and the individual) as distinct, so when we perceive the identity between the two, we should perceive only one of them, either the universal or the individual because of their identity. In such a case, a single object, viz. either the universal or the individual would give rise to two cognitions of both the universal and the individual and their identity with each other. But it is not possible either for the universal to produce a cognition of its identity with the individual, nor is it possible for the individual to produce a cognition of its identity with the universal. So it cannot be said that both difference and identity are apprehended by one and the same act of cognition. Hence the universal must be regarded as different from the individual.

**The Bhatta Realism**

We have already seen that Kumarila agrees with Prabhakara in holding that the universal (*jati*) is real. Its existence can never be denied, because it is an object of sense-perception. Whenever we perceive an object, we perceive it as belonging to a particular class. The act of perception involves assimilation as well as discrimination. It is inclusive (*anuvrtta*) as well as exclusive (*vyavrtta*). The element of assimilation or inclusion in perception clearly shows that in the object of perception there must be a class-character or universality. The reality of the universal in the object of perception is the ground of assimilation. The reality of the universal is also proved by inference and other sources of valid knowledge which are based upon it. The ground of inference and other kinds of knowledge is universality (*jati*). So they confirm the reality of the universal far from contradicting it. If they contradict the existence of universality on which they are based, they would contradict their own existence.

Kumarila does not hold with the Buddhist that the universal is non-different from, or identical with, the individual. Nor does he hold with the Nyaya-Vaisesika and Prabhakara that the universal is different from the individual. According to him, the universal is both different from, and identical with, the individual. He does not hold with the Nyaya-Vaisesika that there is a relation of inherence between the universal and the individual. He rejects the relation of inherence altogether. A relationship, according to him, can exist only between things which are distinct entities, but inherence is regarded as a relation between things which are inseparable, and hence it is impossible, Kumarila rejects the Jaina view of the universal as similarity, because similarity cannot exist without universality. He rejects also the view of the universal as a particular arrangement of parts, because configurations of parts are destructible, but the class-character is indestructible.

### The Bhatta Criticism of the Buddhist Doctrine

The Buddhists argue that if the universal is different from the individual, it must be perceived as different from it. But, as a matter of fact, the universal is never perceived as different from the individual. And if the universal is non-different from the individual, then the individual alone is real, and there is no universal apart from the individual. The Buddhists set forth their argument in the following way : "What is real must be either different or non-different (*yadvastu tadbhinnamabhinnam va bhavati*); the universal is neither different nor non-different from the individual; therefore the universal must be unreal."

Parthasarathimisra points out that there can be no inference, if there is not an apprehension of universal concomitance (*vyaptigraha*) between the major term (*vyapya*) and the middle term (*vyapaka*); so, in the above argument the universal concomitance between the major term and the middle term has already been apprehended; otherwise there would be no such inference. The major term here is "the genus of reality" (*vastutva*) and the middle term is "difference and non-difference" (*bhedabhedau*). And the apprehension of uniform connection between the genus of reality (*vastutva*) and difference and non-difference (*bhedabhedau*) establishes the existence of community (*jati*), for *vastutva* is of the nature of *jati*. Otherwise, how can the Buddhist argue that the reality (*vastutva*) of the universal is not possible because of the non-apprehension of its difference and non-difference from the individual? When he argues that there is a universal concomitance between "*vastutva*" (major term) and "difference and non-difference" (middle term), he admits the reality of *vastutva*, and consequently of community (*samanya*), because *vastutva* is of the nature of a universal. Thus the very act of inference by which the Buddhists prove the unreality of the universal presupposes its existence.

But the Buddhists may urge that the term *vastu* (reality) has not for its object *vastutva* (the genus of *vastu* or reality), but it is due to a phenomenal condition (*aupadhika*). Why, then, does the Bhatta say that the term *vastu* (reality) has *vastutva* (the genus of reality) for its object, which is of the nature of a universal?

Parthasarathimisra replies that the above argument of the Buddhists is not admissible; if there is no *vastutva*, call it a *jati* or *upadhi*, it must presuppose the existence of the universal; for the inference depends upon the existence of *vastutva* and this is called *jati* by the realist. Otherwise, even the non-existence of *vastutva* (reality) in a *samanya* (universality) cannot be proved. How can the negation of *samanya* be proved without assuming the *samanya* (community) itself? If words are only *aupadhika*, i.e. due to accidental conditions, they cannot have the power of denoting objects. According to the Buddhists, everything in the world is individual in nature, therefore, the individuals which are absolutely different from one another cannot constitute the denotation of words. The Buddhists hold that there is one condition or mark (*upadhi*) which is one and the same in different individuals, viz. apprehensibility. But that which remains identical in the midst of different individuals is nothing but the universal. Hence the reality of the universal is established both by perception and inference.

## The Bhatta Criticism of the Jaina Doctrine

The Jaina holds that there is no need of assuming a separate existence of the universal; it consists in the similarity of individuals. Parthasarathimisra urges that the universality cannot consist in similarity (*na ca sadrsyameva samanyam*). Because, in the first place, if universality consists merely in the similarity of individuals, then we should perceive an individual cow in the form "this is like a cow", and not in the form "this is a cow". But, as a matter of fact, we never perceive a cow as "this is like a cow". Hence universality cannot be identified with similarity, as the Jaina supposes. And, in the second place, even similarity among different individuals is not possible, if there is no real universal among them, for similarity means common qualities. Similarity is not possible apart from universality. Those things are similar to one another, which possess properties in common. Thus similarity does not constitute universality (*samanya*), but follows from it. For instance, a cow is similar to a *gavaya* (wild ox) , their parts are different from one another, so that the parts of the cow cannot exist in the parts of the *gavaya;* therefore, a certain property (*dharma*) must be supposed to exist in the different parts of the cow and the *gavaya*, so that their similarity may be perceived in spite of their difference; and that common property is called universality. Hence it cannot be held, with the Jaina, that mere similarity among things constitutes their universality or community (*sdmanya*).

## The Bhatta Criticism of the Nyaya-Vaisesika Doctrine

Is the universal different or non-different from the individual? According to the Buddhists, the universal is non-different from the individual which alone is real. The Buddhist doctrine has already been refuted. The Nyaya-Vaisesika, on the other hand, holds that the universal is different from the individual; but it is not perceived apart from the individual, because it is inseparably related to it. What is the relation between the universal and the individual ? It is inherence. What is inherence? It is a relation between two objects which are inseparably connected with each other, and which gives rise to such a cognition as "here it is".

Parthasarathimisra offers the following criticism of the Nyaya-Vaisesika doctrine :

1. The universal is said to inhere in the individual; inherence is the relation between two entities inseparably connected with each other, which gives rise to such a cognition as "here it is". But when we perceive a cow, we have such a perception as "this is a cow" (*iyam gauh*) and not as "here is the class-essence of cow (*gotva*) in the individual cow" (*iha gavi gotvam*). This clearly shows that the universal is identical with the individual it is not entirely different from the individual.
2. Then, again, what is meant by inseparable connection (*ayutasiddhi*)? It is the negation or absence of separable connection (*yutasiddhi*). What, again, is separable connection (*yuttasiddhi*)? Does it mean the capacity for separate or independent movements (*prthaggatimattva*)? Or does it mean subsistence in different substrates (*prthagasrayasrayitva*)? In either case, argues Parthasarathimisra, there would be no relation between the composite whole (*avayavi*) and its component parts (*avayava*), because there can be a movement in the parts without a movement in the whole, and because the whole and its parts inhere in different substrates the whole inheres in its parts and the parts inhere in their component atoms. Likewise, the universal and the individual too have different substrates, because the substrate of the universal is the individual, and the substrates of the individual are the parts of the individual

   Hence Parthasarathimisra concludes that inherence is such a relation between the container and the contained that the latter produces a corresponding cognition in the former. The universal inheres in the individual. This means that the universal (e.g. class-essence of cow, or *gotva*) produces an apprehension of it in the individual (e.g. an individual cow or *govyakti*). But if the universal produces an apprehension of it in the individual, for instance, if an individual cow is perceived as belonging to the class "cow", then we cannot admit a difference between the individual and the universal. We must admit a non-difference or identity between the two on the basis of perception.
3. The Nyaya-Vaisesika may urge that the universal is "inclusive" (*anuvrtta*), while the individual is "exclusive" (*vyavrtta*). The

universal is common to many individuals, but the individuals are different from one another. For instance, the class-essence of cow (*gotva*) is one and the same in all the individual cows, but the individual cows are different from one another. How? then, can the universal be identical with the individual ? If the two are identical with each other, they must be of the same nature; either the universal must be "exclusive" like the individual or the individual must be "inclusive" like the universal. In other words, if the universal is identical with the individual, either the universal will differ in different individuals, or the individual will be common to many individuals.

Parthasarathimisra retorts : If the universal is absolutely different from the individual, how can the individual be perceived as universal? How can an individual cow be perceived as belonging to the class "cow" when we perceive a cow as "this is a cow"? This can never be explained by the Nyaya-Vaisesika, according to whom, the universal is absolutely different from the individual, though the former inheres in the latter. But the Bhatta Mimamsaka has no difficulty in explaining it. If the different characters of the universal and the individual, viz. "inclusiveness" and "exclusiveness" prove the difference between the two, the "likeness" (*tadrupya*) between the universal and the individual as shown by the perception of an individual as belonging to a particular class proves their identity. Thus the Bhatta Mimamsaka concludes that there is a relation of identity-in-difference between the universal and the individual; the universal is both different from, and identical with, the individual.

4. The Nyaya-Vaisesika may urge : How can identity and difference both subsist in one and the same object? Is it not self-contradictory to assert that the universal is both different from the individual, and identical with it? The Bhatta Mimamsaka argues that there is no contradiction here; for both difference and identity are perceived together by a single act of perception; if difference and identity were perceived by two cognitions, one contradicting the other, like the two

cognitions "this is silver" and "this is not silver", then there would be a contradiction. But neither the perception of difference contradicts the perception of identity, nor does the perception of identity contradict the perception of difference. Hence both of them are valid. In the perception "this is a cow", there are two cognitions, viz. the cognition of "this" (*iyam buddhi*) and the cognition of "cow" (*gobuddhi*); these two cognitions have two different objects; the former has an "individual" (an individual cow or *govyakti*) for its object, while the latter has a universal (the class-essence of cow or *gotva*) for its object. Thus the twofold perception of an object such as "this is a cow" proves the dual character of the object, viz. both its individuality and universality. Hence the universal cannot be different from the individual.

**The Bhatta Criticism of Prabhakara's Objections**

Prabhakara has argued that one and the same act of cognition cannot apprehend both the difference and the identity between the universal and the individual. His argument has already been given in detail.

Parthasarathimisra contends that this argument is baseless. The cognition of two objects does not necessarily involve the cognition of their difference. For sometimes two objects are perceived, but not the difference between the two; for instance, when two trees are perceived from a distance, the difference between the two is not perceived. When an individual member of a class is perceived for the first time, both the individual and the universal are perceived, but not the difference between the two. When another individual belonging to the same class is perceived, it is assimilated to the first individual as belonging to the same class, and differentiated from it as being a different individual , and it is then alone that the difference between the individual and the universal is perceived. Hence it is unreasonable to hold that the cognition of two objects necessarily involves the cognition of their difference. Similarly, it is unreasonable to hold that the cognition of a single object necessarily involves the cognition of its identity. For instance, when a person is perceived from a distance, we have a doubtful cognition such as "Is he Devadatta or Yaniadatta"? Thus a single object gives rise to two cognitions. Hence it cannot be held that the cognition of two objects necessarily involves the cognition of their difference, or the cognition of a single object necessarily involves the cognition of its identity.

But the cognition in the form "this is another" apprehends difference; and the cognition in the form "this is no other" apprehends identity. A person who perceives both a white cow and a piebald cow has a cognition in such a form as "this is a cow and this also is a cow", and so he perceives the identity between the two; and he has also a cognition in such a form as "the white cow is different from the piebald cow" and thus apprehends their difference. Hence we conclude that the universal is both different from the individual, and identical with it.

Prabhakara may urge that the universal is eternal, while the individual is non-eternal the universal is common to many individuals, while the individuals are different from one another. How, then, can the universal be identical with the individual? If they were identical with each other, in spite of their opposite characters, the universal would be non-eternal and different in different individuals, and the individual would be eternal and common to many individuals, and thus there would be an utter confusion in the whole world.

Parthasarathimisra replies that there is no contradiction here. A multiform object may be eternal in some, and non-eternal in other, respects; it may be identical with other objects in some respects, and different from them in others. The universal considered as an individual is non-eternal; and the individual considered as a universal is eternal. So there is no contradiction here.

Thus, according to the Bhatta, the universal is not identical with the individual, as the Buddhists hold, nor is it different from the individual, as the Nyaya-Vaisesika holds, but it is different from the individual in some respects, and identical with it in others. The relation between the two is identity-in-difference. The Bhatta realism closely resembles the realism of Aristotle and Hegel, according to whom, the universal cannot exist apart from the individuals, and the individuals cannot exist apart from the universal; the universal is the inner essence of the individuals, and the individuals are the outer expressions of the universal; the universal and the individual are abstractions apart from each other; the universal is neither wholly identical with the individuals, nor wholly different from them; in fact, they together constitute the concrete reality.

## The Bhatta Doctrine of Identity-in-Difference

Parthasarathimisra sets forth two reasons for the Bhatta doctrine of identtty-in-difference between the universal and the individual.

1. In the first place, in the cognition "this is a cow" the co-inherence (*samanadhikaranya*) of the two elements, viz. "this" (an individual cow) and "cow" (the class-essence of cow) in the same object proves the identity between the individual and the universal. And the fact that the two cognitions of "this" and "cow" are not synonymous with each other proves the difference between the individual and the universal. Hence there is no contradiction in holding that the universal is both different from, and identical with, the individual
2. In the second place, the universal is different from the individual in some respects, and identical with it in others. If the universal were both different and non-different from the individual in respect of the same qualities, there would be a contradiction. But just as one and the same object can be both long and short in comparison with different objects, so one and the same universal can be both different and non-different from the individual in different respects. For instance, when we have such a perception as "this piebald cow is a cow", we perceive the individual cow as identical with the universal "cow". But when we have such a perception as "that white cow is not a piebald cow", the universal "cow" is perceived as different from the individual cow. The universal "cow" (*gotva*) differs from a white cow in respect of a black cow, but not in its essential nature. An individual cow differs from the universal "cow" (*gotva*) in respect of certain qualities, actions, and other universals, but not in its essential nature. And one individual cow differs from another individual cow in its specific nature, but not in its generic nature. Hence there is no contradiction in holding that the universal is both different from, and identical with, the individual.

### The Modified Realism of Samkara

According to Samkara, Brahman alone is ultimately real, which is one, universal, eternal, and ubiquitous Being. He admits no other real universal than Being which is Brahman. But he admits the existence of other universals in the phenomenal world. There are the universals of cows and other substances, qualities, and actions; these universals are not born. Only individual substances, individual qualities, and individual actions are generated; but their universal essences are not born. They are the archetypal forms, as it were, of the individual substances, qualities, and actions. But these archetypal forms or universals are not eternal in the sense in which Brahman is eternal. Brahman is beyond time, space, and causation; it is beyond all change and becoming. But the universals of individual substances, qualities, and actions have an empirical existence in the phenomenal world. They are the evolutes of nescience and as such phenomenal appearances from the standpoint of Brahman. Their reality is inferior to that of Brahman but superior to that of individual objects. They are, like the ideas of Plato, the types which are progressively realized in individual objects of the sensible world. The individuals are born and perish, but the universals are unborn. They are the models according to which God moulds the sensible world.

The later Samkarites, however, do not recognize the existence of the universal, because it can neither be perceived nor inferred. The perception of one and the same form (e.g. "cow") in different individuals (e.g. cows) cannot be regarded as a proof of the existence of the universal ("cow"). If it is regarded so, does it mean that we have the apprehension of "cow" in one individual cow as much as in another individual cow? Or does it mean that we have the apprehension of one and the same nature of cow in all individual cows? Or does it mean that we apprehend that the different individuals possess one and the same property? The first alternative is not tenable. Just as we apprehend the same form of the moon in different pots of water in which it is reflected though there is no universal moon, so we may apprehend the same form of cow in different cows though there is no universal cow (*gotva*) in them. The second alternative also is not tenable. It is not possible for us to determine the nature that is common to all individuals of the same kind. Even if we were able to ascertain the common quality it would be useless to postulate *jati* or class-essence which is different from the common quality. The third alternative also is untenable. When we perceive a man with a stick we perceive the man as possessing a stick. But when we perceive an individual cow, in which the class-essence is supposed to exist, we never perceive the cow as possessing the class-essence (*gotva*). It may be urged that we perceive at least the same configuration or arrangement of parts (e.g. dew lap, etc.) in different cows. But this resemblance in configuration of parts is not the universal or class-essence of the realist. Hence the universal can never be perceived. Nor can it be inferred. Citsukha sets forth the same arguments as the Buddhists have advanced against the existence of the universal (*jati*).

# 11

# Perception of Cognition

## Introduction

According to Rumania, an act of cognition cannot be directly perceived; it is inferred from cognizedness (*jnatata*) or manifestness (*prakatya*) produced by the cognition in the object. According to some Mimamsakas, the act of cognition is inferred from the consciousness of its object; it is not an object of perception. According to Prabhakara, a cognition is directly perceived by itself; every cognition perceives itself, the cognizing self and the cognized object. According to the Nyaya-Vaisesika, a cognition is an object of perception; but it is not perceived by itself but by another cognition through the internal organ or mind; we perceive a cognition by internal perception through the mind, just as we perceive an external object by external perception through the external senses. According to the Jaina, a cognition is perceived by itself in apprehending its object; it is not perceived by any other cognition. According to the Buddhist idealist, a cognition is self-luminous; it apprehends itself but not an external object as there is no such object; a cognition is not apprehended by the self because there is no self at all. According to the Sarhkhya-Patanjala, a cognition is not perceived by another cognition but by the self because a cognition is unconscious. According to Samkara, a cognition is not perceived by another cognition but by itself; it is self-luminous.

## The Bhatta Mimamsaka

Parthasarathimisra gives an exposition of Rumania's doctrine of inferrability of cognition. According to the Bhatta Mimamsaka, a cognition cannot be perceived, but it is inferred from the result of cognition, viz., cognizedness (*jnatata*) or manifestness (*prakatya*) in the object. For instance, when we know a jar we have an apprehension that the jar is cognized by us; and from this cognizedness of the object we infer the existence of the cognition; a cognition is inferred from the cognizedness of its object. Parthasarathi gives three arguments for the existence of cognition. In the first place, an action involves four factors, viz. an agent of action (*kartr*) an object of action (*karma*), an instrument of action (*karana*) and a result of action (*phala*) which inheres in the object. An act of knowledge, therefore, has an agent or subject of knowledge or knower (*jnatr*), an object of knowledge (*jneya*), an instrumental cognition (*karanajnana*) and a result of knowledge, viz. cognizedness (*jnatata*) in the object. Just as the act of cooking produces cookedness in the object cooked, so the act of cognition (*jnanakriya*) produces cognizedness (*jnatata*) in its object, and from this cognizedness as an effect we infer the existence of its cause, viz. cognition. Thus a cognition cannot be perceived either by itself or by any other cognition, but is inferred from the cognizedness in its object

In the second place, a cognition is inferred from the relation between the knowing subject (*atman*) and the known object (*artha*) which is apprehended by internal perception. If there is not an adventitious condition intervening between the self and the object, how is it possible for the self to be related to the object? Therefore, from the specific relation between the subject and the object involved in knowledge we infer the existence of cognition. Here, cognition or consciousness is hypostatized as a third term between the self and the not-self, which relates the two to each other. Even those who hold that all cognitions are self-luminous (*svaprakasa*) must admit that this relation between the self and the not-self, which is involved in knowledge, is an object of internal perception. Otherwise, it cannot be said "the jar is cognized by me". This self-appropriated cognition is not possible unless we know the relation between the cognizing self and the cognized object and the relation between the cognition and its object. No other object can be spoken of than what is manifested to consciousness. If it is urged that a cognition is self-luminous, and its object is manifested by the cognition, by what is the relation between the cognition and its object manifested? It may be urged that this relation too is manifested by the same cognition. But Parthasarathi points out that when the cognition is produced, the relation between the cognition and its object does not yet come into existence. The relation of a cognition to its object consists in its manifesting the object, it is no other than this. So when a cognition is produced and its object is manifested, the relation that is produced between the two cannot be the object of that cognition as it has ceased to operate. It cannot be argued that at first the cognition manifests its object, and then it manifests its relation to the object, since the cognition is momentary. Nor can it be argued that the relation between the cognition and its object is self-luminous, because there is no proof of its self-luminosity. Hence, Parthasarathi concludes that the relation between the self and the object, which is an object of internal perception, proves the existence of a cognition, and this relation cannot be denied by any one.

In the third place, the existence of a cognition is inferred from the peculiarity (*atisaya*) produced by the cognition in its object. This peculiarity must be admitted even by those who hold that the cognizer, the cognized object, and the cognition are manifested by consciousness. From this peculiarity (*atisaya*) produced in the object by a cognition we infer the existence of the cognition itself. Hence a cognition can be perceived neither by itself nor by any other cognition.

Kesavamisra gives an exposition of the Bhatta doctrine and criticizes it. He puts the Bhatta argument in a slightly different form. When I know a jar the cognition of the jar produces in it a peculiar property, viz. cognizedness (*jnatata*). After the cognition of the jar is produced, the cognizedness of the jar is recognized in such a form as "the jar is cognized by me". The peculiar property of cognizedness is produced in the jar when the cognition of the jar is already produced, and cognizedness is not produced in the jar when the cognition of the jar is not produced. So the existence of cognizedness is proved by the method of double agreement. Cognizedness is not possible without cognition; the effect cannot be produced without the cause. Thus cognizedness proves the existence of cognition as its cause by means of presumption (*arthapatti*).

## The Nyaya-Vaisesika Criticism of the Bhatta Doctrine

1. Sridhara urges that the Bhatta Mimamsaka commits the fallacy

of hysteron proteron when he argues that a cognition is inferred from cognizedness in its object. An object is cognized when it is related to a cognition. Its cognizedness (*jnatata*) consists in its relationship with the cognition (*jnanasambandha*). We cannot apprehend cognizedness unless we apprehend the cognition itself. The apprehension of a relation presupposes the apprehension of the terms of the relation. In order to apprehend cognizedness, which consists in the relation of an object to a cognition, we must already apprehend the object and the cognition which are related to each other. Cognizedness presupposes cognition, and apprehension of cognizedness presupposes the apprehension of cognition. So cognition can never be inferred from cognizedness.

The Bhatta may argue that we must admit a peculiar property called cognizedness (*jnatata*) in an object in order to account for the regularity in the relations of cognitions to their objects. A particular cognition apprehends a particular object and not any other. The cognition of a jar apprehends the jar, and not a cloth. What is the reason of this? The Bhatta answers that the cognition of a jar produces cognizedness in the jar, and not in a cloth. So it apprehends a jar, and not a cloth. It is cognizedness (*jnatata*) that relates particular cognitions to particular objects. An object is apprehended by that cognition which produces cognizedness in it. So we must admit cognizedness in an object of cognition, which relates the cognition to the object.

2. Udayana contends that even cognizedness is not possible without some regularity in the natural relation between cognitions and their objects. The Bhatta argues that a particular cognition apprehends a particular object because it produces cognizedness in it, and not in any other object. Udayana asks: Why should a particular cognition produce cognizedness in a particular object and not in any other? It may be argued that a particular cognition produces cognizedness in that object which is apprehended by it. Udayana says that the argument involves circular reasoning. A cognition apprehends a particular object because it produces cognizedness in it, and a cognition produces cognizedness in a particular object because

it apprehends it. Thus the objectivity (*visayata*) of an object depends upon its cognizedness (*jnatata*) and its cognizedness depends upon its objectivity. Udayana argues that it is needless to assume the existence of cognizedness. The so-called cognizedness of an object is nothing but its objectivity or the character of being an object of cognition. There is a natural relation between a cognition and its object so that the former apprehends the latter.

Vacaspatimisra also offers a similar criticism. The Bhatta holds that an object is apprehended by that cognition which produces cognizedness in it. Vacaspatimisra contends that there is no need of cognizedness in the object. The so-called cognizedness is held to be related to the object neither by conjunction nor by inherence but by natural relation. And if cognizedness is related to the object by natural relation, the cognition also may be related to it by natural relation, and there is no need of assuming the intervening factor of cognizedness between the cognition and its object.

Sivaditya also holds that cognizedness is nothing but the relation between a cognition and its object, and there is no proof of its existence apart from this relation.

Kesavamisra also argues that cognizedness is nothing but the character of being the object of cognition. When we apprehend a jar we do not apprehend its cognizedness; but we simply apprehend that the jar is the object of cognition. There is no cognizedness apart from its objectivity.

The Bhatta may urge that the jar is said to be the object of cognition because it is the substratum of cognizedness produced by the cognition. The objectivity of the jar cannot be of the nature of identity. The jar cannot be said to be an object of cognition because there is an identity between the jar and its cognition. There can be no identity between an object and its cognition because the former is the object (*visaya*) and the latter is the subject (*visayin*). If by the objectivity of a thing we mean that a cognition is produced by it, then objectivity would belong to the sense-organs and other conditions which produce a cognition. This leads us to conclude that something is produced in the jar by the cognition, by virtue of which the jar alone, and nothing else, becomes the object of consciousness, and this is called cognizedness. Thus cognizedness is not only perceived through the sense-organs but is also inferred from the possibility of the objectivity (*visayata*) of an object.

Kesavamisra disputes this view. He argues that subjectivity and objectivity follow from the very nature of things. There is such a natural peculiarity in a cognition and its object that the former is the subject (*visayin*) and the latter is the object (*visaya*) in relation to the other. An object does not require cognizedness in it to be apprehended by a cognition.

3. Otherwise, argues Kesavamisra, past and future objects could never be the objects of cognition, since it is not possible for any cognition to produce cognizedness in them. It is not possible for a property to be produced in an object at a time when the object does not exist; a property cannot exist with out a substratum. Cognizedness is a property of the object; hence it can never be produced in past and future objects, though they can be apprehended. Udayana also urges that a cognition can produce cognizedness in present objects but not in past and future ones, though they are apprehended. We have recollection of the past and expectation of the future at present. But the present recollection or expectation can never produce cognizedness in past or future objects, since they do not exist at present. This clearly shows that an object is apprehended by a cognition though it does not produce cognizedness in it. So we must admit that there is a natural relation of subject (*visayin*) and object (*visaya*) between a cognition and its object.

   The Bhatta argues that the act of cognition produces in its object a peculiar condition known as cognizedness, just as the act of cooking produces in rice the condition of cookedness. "And this cognizedness being a property of the object is known along with the object itself."

4. But Sridhara urges that this is a false analogy. In the case of rice we distinctly perceive cookedness in the rice in its being changed from *tandula* (uncooked rice) to *odana* (cooked rice); but in the case of the object in question we do not perceive any such cognizedness. As for the direct perceptibility

(*aparoksarupats*) of an object and its capability of being accepted or rejected, these also consist in its relationship to cognition; they are not properties of some other property of the object, viz. cognizedness.

5. Sridhara further argues that just as when an object is known, there is produced in it a peculiar property called cognizedness, so when this cognizedness is known, another cognizedness must be produced in that cognizedness, and so on ad infinitum: If cognizedness be regarded as self-luminous, in order to avoid this infinite regress, then we may as well admit that the cognition itself is self-luminous.

   It may be argued that an object has an existence extending over the past, the present, and the future; but when it is cognized it is cognized as belonging to the present. And cognizedness is nothing but the condition of the object determined by the present time, and this being an effect of the cognition is the mark for the inference of the cognition.

6. But Sridhara contends that by "the condition of the object determined by the present time" (*vartamanavacchmnata*) we mean its condition qualified by that time (*vartamanakalavtsistata*); and this belongs to the object by its very nature; and this condition is not produced, but only known by cognition.

   The Bhatta may argue that cognition is of the nature of an action, and an action always produces a result in its object; so the act of cognition must produce a result in its object in the shape of cognizedness.

7. Udayana contends that all actions do not produce results in their objects. For instance, an arrow penetrates the ether, but its motion cannot produce a result in it. So here the reason is overwide. Moreover, an action is always of the nature of motion (*spanda*) but cognition is not of the nature of motion. So here the reason is non-existent. If an action means the operation of an instrument, then the sense-organs, marks of inference, words, etc., do not produce a peculiar result in an object but in the self, Varadaraja also argues that cognition is not of the nature of an action; it is of the nature of a quality produced by the operation of the sense-organs and the like,

which inheres in an all-pervading substance, the self, like pleasure. Thus it cannot be argued that cognizedness in an object is inferred from its cognition because it is of the nature of an action.

The Bhatta may argue that determinate cognition (*visistabuddhi*) is determinate because it apprehends the relation between the qualified object (*visesya*) and its qualification (*visesana*). So the determinate perception of a jar as cognized (*jnato ghatah*) apprehends the relation between the jar (*visesya*) and the cognition of it (*visesana*) and this relation is cognizedness. Thus determinate perception proves the existence of cognizedness which constitutes the relation between a cognition and its object.

8. Udayana contends that determinate perception apprehends the natural relation between a cognition and its object, which may be called objectivity (*visayata*), it apprehends an object as apprehended by a cognition. It is needless to assume the existence of cognizedness to account for determinate perception. If determinate perception of a cognized object requires cognizedness in the object, then determinate perception of a finished (*krta*) jar or a desired (*ista*) jar would require finishedness or desiredness in the jar. If such a peculiar property is thought to be needless the peculiar property of cognizedness also is equally needless. Determinate perception of an object as cognized apprehends the natural relation between itself and its object, which is called *vtsayata* or objectivity. There is a *svarupasambandha* between a cognition and its object by virtue of which the former is the subject (*visayin*) and the latter is the object (*visaya*). There is no tertium quid in the form of cognizedness between a cognition and its object. The natural relation between a cognition and its object by virtue of which the former apprehends the latter is called *visayata*. It is needless to assume cognizedness (*jnatata*) apart from objectivity (*visayata*).

The so-called cognizedness (*jnatata*) is nothing but objectivity (*visayata*) which constitutes the *svarupasambandha* between a cognition and its object.

## The Jaina Criticism of the Bhatta Doctrine

The Bhatta Mimamsaka argues that if cognition is regarded as perceptible it would be regarded as an object (*karma*); and as an object of cognition it would require another instrumental cognition (*karanajnana*) because every action on an object requires an instrument; and if that instrumental cognition is regarded as an object of perception it would require another instrumental cognition, and so on ad infinitum. If this instrumental cognition through which a cognition is cognized is imperceptible, then the first cognition of an object also may be regarded as imperceptible, but yet capable of manifesting its object. One and the same act of cognition cannot be the object (*karma*) of cognition and the instrument (*karana*) of cognition. Hence a cognition cannot be regarded as an object of perception; it is imperceptible.

Prabhacandra, a Jaina philosopher, offers the following criticism of this argument :

1. The cognizer (*pramatr*), and the cognition or cognitive act (*pramana*), and the resultant cognition (*pramiti*) are as perceptible as the object of cognition (*prameya*), for we distinctly perceive these factors of knowledge in our experience. In the cognition "I know the jar through myself", the cognizer "I", the instrument "myself", and the result "knowing" are as much objects of perception as the cognized object, viz. "the jar". There is no hard and fast rule that whatever is perceived must be perceived as an object (*karma*) of perception. For, in that case, there would be no perception of the self which is never perceived as a cognized object (*karma*) but always as a cognizer (*kartr*). And if the self can be perceived as a cognizer, and not as an object of cognition, the cognition also may be perceived not as an object of perception, but as an instrument of perception.

2. It may be argued that the cognition through which an object is manifested to consciousness is simply an instrument (*karana*) of the manifestation of the object, but it is not perceptible. Then it may as well be argued that the self which is manifested as the cognizer is simply the agent (*kartr*) of cognition, but it is not perceptible. But the Bhatta recognizes the perceptibility

of the self. So he should as well admit the perceptibility of cognition. The self is perceived as a cognizer or the agent (*kartr*) of the act of cognition. And the cognition is perceived as the instrument (*karana*) of cognizing an object. Moreover, if the self is perceptible it can cognize an external object by itself. What, then, is the use of postulating an imperceptible cognition between the cognizing self and the cognized object? It may be urged that an agent can never produce an action without an instrument, and so the self as the agent of the act of cognition requires the instrumentality of a cognition to apprehend an object. In that case, the instruments of internal and external organs would be quite adequate to bring about the consciousness of an object. So there is no use of assuming an imperceptible cognition to serve the purpose of an instrument here.

3. If no action is possible without an instrument what is the instrument in the cognition of the self by itself? If the self itself is the instrument of self-cognition, then let it be the instrument of object-cognition too. There is no use of assuming an imperceptible cognition. Hence the cognition through which an object is known must be regarded as perceptible.
4. If the Bhatta admits that both the self and the resultant cognition (*phalajnana*) of the object can be perceived, though they do not appear in consciousness as the object (*karma*) of cognition, but as the agent and the result of cognition respectively, he must also admit that the instrumental cognition or cognitive act (*karanajnana*) too can be perceived, not as an object of cognition but as an instrument of cognition.
5. Again, according to the Bhatta, the instrumental cognition (*karanajnana*) is not entirely different from the cognizer (*kartr*) and the resultant cognition (*phalajndna*); so if the latter are perceptible the former also must be regarded as perceptible. If the instrumental cognition differs from the cognizer and the resultant cognition not as a form of cognition, but only as an instrument, then the instrumental cognition cannot be said to be imperceptible for as cognition it does not differ from the cognizer and the resultant cognition; and so if the latter are regarded as perceptible the former also must be regarded so.

6. Moreover, the self and the cognition (*karanajnana*) through which it knows an object are directly revealed in our experience. So they cannot but be regarded as objects of consciousness; for whatever is revealed in our experience is cognized, and whatever is cognized is an object of consciousness. It is self-contradictory to suppose that the self and its cognition are not objects of perception though they are directly revealed in our experience. If the cognitive act cannot be perceived as an object (*karma*) of consciousness though it is directly revealed in our experience, it cannot be an object of consciousness through another instrumental cognition. Hence the cognitive act must be regarded as an object of perception.
7. In the cognition "I know the jar", I am directly conscious of myself as qualified by the cognition of the jar. So my cognition of the jar is as much an object of perception as myself and the jar. Just as we cannot deny the perception of the object, so we cannot deny the perception of its cognition. If there is no perception of the cognition of the jar there can be no perception of the jar itself. An unperceived cognition can never manifest an object.
8. Then, what is the nature of cognizedness from which the cognitive act is said to be inferred? Is it a property of the object (*arthadharma*)? Or is it a property of the cognition (*jnanadharma*)?

   It cannot be a property of the object, for, in that case, it would persist in the object like its other properties (e.g. blueness) even when it is not cognized by a particular person. But, as a matter of fact, cognizedness does not persist in the object at any other time than when it is cognized. And when the object is cognized by a person, its cognizedness appears at that time as the private property of the particular person (*svasadharanavisaya*). It is never found to exist in the object as the public property of many cognizers (*anekapramfitr-sadharanavisaya*). Hence cognizedness cannot be a property of the object.

   Nor can cognizedness be a property of the cognition, since the cognitive act of which it is supposed to be a property is imperceptible according to the Bhatta, and what is imperceptible can never be the substrate of cognizedness.

9. Is cognizedness, then, of the nature of consciousness (*infinasvabhava*)) or of the nature of an object (*arthasvabhava*)? Is it subjective or objective ? If the former, then as consciousness it must be imperceptible like the act of cognition; and so it cannot serve as the mark (lingo) of inferring the cognitive act. Moreover, it is foolish to argue that though the act of cognition (*karanajnana*) is imperceptible, cognizedness is an object of perception in spite of its being of the nature of consciousness. If the act of cognition cannot be an object of perception because it is of the nature of consciousness, cognizedness too cannot be an object of perception for the same reason. If, then, cognizedness is of the nature of an object (*arthasvabhava*) it is nothing but the ramifestness (*arthaprakatya*) of the object. But an object cannot be manifested if the cognition by which it is manifested is itself unmanifested. If the cognition itself is unperceived, it can never manifest its object.

Hence the Jaina concludes that a cognition must cognize itself in order to cognize an object; it manifests itself and its object (*svaparaprakasaka*).

**The Ramanujists Criticism of the Bhatta Doctrine**

The Bhatta holds that cognition is inferred from cognizedness (*jnatata*) or manifestation (*prakatya*) of an object. Venkatanatha, a follower of Ramanuja, urges that a cognition is nothing but the manifestation of an object; so the former cannot be inferred from the latter. It may be argued that the cognition or manifestation in the self is inferred from manifestation in the object. The former is the object of inference and the latter is the mark of inference. But, if in spite of the presence of cognition or manifestation in the self, manifestation in the object (*prakatya*) is thought to be necessary in order to make it an object of speech and action, then let all the conditions which are said to produce cognition be regarded as the immediate cause of manifestation in the object. What, then, is the use of cognition? It is neither necessary for the use of an object nor for its manifestation. Thus the Bhatta doctrine leads to the negation of cognition, which is absurd. So cognition is not inferred from manifestation of an object.

## Another School of Mimamsa

Sridhara considers another doctrine which is kindred to the Bhatta doctrine. Some hold that the act of cognition is inferred from the consciousness of objects. We are conscious of objects; and this consciousness is not possible without an act of cognition. The cognitive act, therefore, is inferred from the consciousness of objects. Bhaskara refers to this doctrine in his commentary on the Brahmasutras. He says that this doctrine is held by some Mimamsakas. According to them, the act of cognition (*jnanakriya*) is the cause of the consciousness of objects (*visayasamvedana*).

This doctrine slightly differs from the Bhatta theory. The Bhatta holds that the act of cognition is inferred from cognizedness (*jnatata*) which is a peculiar property of the object produced by the cognition. But according to this theory, the act of cognition is inferred from the consciousness of an object (*visayasamvedana*) which is a property of the self.

## Criticism of the Doctrine

1. Sridhara rightly points out that there is nothing to choose between the two doctrines. They are of a piece with each other. Where does the so-called consciousness of an object (*visayasamvedana*) reside? It abides either in the object or in the self. It cannot inhere in the object because it is unconscious. Nor can it inhere in the self, for in that case there would be no difference between the cognitive act and the consciousness of an object both inhering in the self. Hence it cannot be argued that the former is inferred from the latter.

   It may be urged that there is some difference between the two so that the former can be inferred from the latter. The act of cognition is the activity of the cognizing self (*jnatrvyapara*) by which it apprehends an object. Cognitive activity is the cause, and consciousness of an object is the effect. The cause is inferred from the effect.
2. Sridhara contends that if such an activity of the cognizing self (*jnatrvyapara*) exists it is either non-eternal or eternal. If it is non-eternal it must have a cause. The Mimamsaka argues that the intercourse of an object with the sense-organ aided by the

contact of manas with the self is the cause of cognitive activity (*jnanakriya*) which, in its turn, is the cause of object-consciousness (*visayasamvedana*). Sridhara urges that the sense-object-contact aided by the mind-soul-contact may as well be regarded as the cause of object consciousness. It is needless to assume another intermediate cause in the shape of cognitive activity (*jnatruyapara*) to produce object consciousness. If, on the other hand, the cognitive act is held to be eternal, then also it is a needless hypothesis. Consciousness of an object is not eternal. Sometimes it appears and sometimes it does not appear. So it is non-eternal. Its occasional appearance is due to certain accessory conditions, viz. the occasional contact of objects with the sense-organs and the like. And as these conditions can adequately account for the consciousness of objects it is needless to assume any eternal cognitive act as its cause. In fact, the apprehension of the object (*arthavabodha*) and all subsequent activity (*vyavahara*) bearing on the object can be accomplished by the consciousness of the object itself. Hence, the existence of cognitive activity which is said to be inferred from consciousness of an object is a gratuitous assumption.

It may be argued that consciousness of an object cannot inhere in the self because consciousness does not constitute the essential nature of the self. Consciousness of an object is produced by the object, the sense-organs, *manas* and the self. If the self is essentially unconscious it is on a par with the other conditions of consciousness, viz. the object, the sense-organs, and *manas*, which are unconscious. The self has no special efficacy in the production of consciousness. So there is no special reason why consciousness should inhere in the self, and not in the sense-organs, and the like.

3. Sridhara contends that everything cannot be proved. Reason has ultimate limits. It cannot get over the Law of Nature (*svabhavaniyama*). Though consciousness is produced by the self, *manas*, the sense-organs, and the object it is the Law of Nature that consciousness inheres in the self and not in others, even as a cloth produced by threads and the shuttle inheres in the threads and not in the shuttle. Threads are not the cloth,

but still the cloth inheres in the threads. Likewise, the self is not of the nature of consciousness, but still consciousness inheres in the self. Thus it cannot be argued that consciousness cannot inhere in the self. Hence Sridhara concludes that cognition is not inferred from consciousness of an object.

4. Bhaskara also repeats substantially the same arguments against the above Mimamsaka doctrine. It is needless to assume the cognitive act (*jnanakriya*). There is nothing to prove its existence. What is the cause of the cognitive act? These Mimamsakas hold that the sense-organs produce the cognitive act which, again, produces consciousness of objects (*visayasamvedana*). Bhaskara urges that there is no use assuming the production of the cognitive act by the sense-organs. They may as well directly produce consciousness of objects. What is the use of the intermediate process of the act of cognition ? When there is the action of objects on the senseorgans there is consciousness of the objects, and when there is no action of objects on the sense-organs there is no consciousness of the objects. So the method of double agreement proves that the sense-organs are the cause of consciousness of objects. If they require an intermediate process of cognitive act to produce consciousness of objects, then this cognitive act will require another cognitive act, and so on ad infinitum. To avoid this infinite regress we must admit that the sense-organs directly produce consciousness of objects.

5. The advocates of the doctrine hold that the act of cognition (*jnanakriya*) is inferred from consciousness of objects (*visayasamvedana*). Bhaskara asks : What is the mark of inference here? It cannot be consciousness, since the relation between consciousness and the act of cognition is not apprehended because the latter is imperceptible. If the act of cognition is perceived there is no need of assuming that it is inferred from consciousness of objects. Thus Bhaskara concludes that consciousness of objects is itself cognition; there is no act of cognition different from it; and the subsequent action on objects in the form of their acceptance or rejection is the result of consciousness of objects. Hence the hypothesis of the act of cognition is entirely useless.

## Prabhakara

Prabhakara holds that in every act of cognition three things are apprehended. Every object-cognition reveals the object, itself, and the subject (*triputipratyaksa*). The object is apprehended when it is related to a cognition; the cognition reveals the object. And the cognition reveals itself; it is self-luminous. It not only reveals itself and its object but also the self which is its substrate. Cognition may be compared to light. Light reveals an object to which it is related. So cognition reveals an object to which it is related. Light does not require any other object to reveal it; it is self-luminous; it reveals itself. Likewise, cognition does not require any other cognition to apprehend it; it is self-luminous; it apprehends itself. Light not only reveals itself and its object but also the wick of a lamp which is its substrate. Similarly, cognition not only reveals itself and its object but also the self which is its substrate. Thus a cognition apprehends itself, its object, and its subject. Every act of cognition involves object-consciousness, subject-consciousness, and cognition-consciousness or self-conscious awareness. But cognition does not cognize itself as an object of cognition but as cognition.

## Criticism of Prabhakara's Doctrine

Sridhara argues that every cognition does not reveal the self and itself. For instance, in the visual perception "this is a jar" the self and the cognition are not apprehended; there is simply the apprehension of the jar. This is the primary cognition of an object. But sometimes this cognition is appropriated by the self and apprehended in the form "I know the jar". This is the secondary cognition of an object. It reveals the object, the subject, and itself. In the primary cognition of the jar only the jar is apprehended through the visual organ. But in the secondary cognition of the jar there is the mental perception of the jar as qualified by the cognition and the self. In the visual perception of the jar, the self and the cognition are not apprehended. If they were apprehended along with the jar they would become objects of visual perception, which is not possible. They are perceived by the mind as qualifying the object of perception when it is appropriated by the self. A cognition is not necessarily self-cognition. Consciousness does not necessarily involve self-consciousness.

## The Nyaya-Vaisesika

The Nyaya-Vaisesika holds that a cognition is not inferred from the cognizedness of its object, as the Bhatta holds. Nor is It cognized by itself, as the Buddhist idealist, the Jaina, and the Vedantist hold. A cognition is perceived by another cognition which is called *anuvyavasaya*. A cognition is directly apprehended by internal perception. According to the Nyaya-Vaisesika, therefore, a cognition can never turn upon itself to make itself the object of cognition. Though a cognition manifests another object (*paraprakasaka*), it can never manifest itself (*svaprakasaka*); it is other manifesting but never self-manifesting. But though a cognition is not manifested by itself, it can be manifested by another cognition. A cognition is perceived by another cognition through the mind.

## The Jaina Criticism of the Nyaya-Vaisesika Doctrine

Prabhacandra criticizes the Nyaya-Vaisesika doctrine as follows :

1. The Nyaya-Vaisesika holds that a cognition is perceived by another cognition, as it is an object of valid knowledge like a cloth. Just as an external object is known by a cognition, so a cognition is known by another cognition. According to the Bhatta, the act of cognition can never turn upon itself and make it an object of apprehension; it is inferred from the result of the cognitive act in the object, viz. apprehendedness; there is a cognitive act between the self and the object of cognition, which is not perceptible. The Nyaya-Vaisesika holds that a cognition cannot, indeed, turn upon itself and make it an object of its own apprehension, but it can be apprehended by another cognition.

   The Jaina argues that just as pleasure is not cognized by another cognition but by itself, and the divine cognition is not cognized by another cognition but by itself, so a cognition too in the self must be regarded as self-cognized, and not cognized by any other cognition. If a cognition in us is cognized by another cognition, then this cognition must be cognized by another cognition and so on ad infinitum.

2. The Naiyayika may argue that there is no infinite regress here. For in God there are two cognitions, one of which apprehends

the entire universe, and the other apprehends that cognition; there is no need of postulating any other cognition in God.

The Jaina asks : If there are only two cognitions in God, is the second cognition in God, which apprehends His first cognition of the entire universe, perceived or not ? If it is not perceived, then how is it possible for it to perceive the first cognition? If the second cognition of God can perceive His first cognition, though it is not itself perceived, then the first cognition of God too may perceive the entire universe, though this cognition is not itself perceived. If the second cognition in God also is perceived, is it perceived by itself or by some other cognition? If it is perceived by itself, then the first cognition too may be perceived by itself. If the second cognition in God is perceived by another cognition, then this third cognition too would be perceived by another cognition and so on ad infinitum. If the second cognition of God is perceived by the first cognition, then there would be a circular reasoning; for, in that case, the first cognition would be perceived by the second cognition, and the second cognition would be perceived by the first cognition. Hence the divine cognition must be regarded as self-luminous or self-cognizing; it must apprehend itself in apprehending the entire universe.

3. The Naiyayika may argue that there is a difference between the divine cognition and the human cognition, and consequently, an attribute of the former cannot be ascribed to the latter; if the divine cognition is self-luminous, and thus both manifests itself and other objects (*svaparaprakasaka*), the human cognition cannot be regarded as self-luminous. For if you ascribe a divine attribute to a human being, then you might as well argue that because God is omniscient, man must be so.

The Jaina contends that this argument is fallacious. Consciousness, by its very essential nature, both manifests itself and other objects (*svaparaprakasaka*); this is the common and essential characteristic of all consciousness; this is not a special characteristic of the divine consciousness.

If the self-and-object-manifesting character (*svaparaprakasa-katva*) is regarded as a special characteristic of the divine consciousness because it is simply found in God, then it may equally be argued that because *svaparaprakasakatva* is found in the sun, it cannot be an attribute of a lamp.

4. It may be argued that if the human cognitions are of the nature of the divine cognition, then the former would be as omniscient as the latter.

   But this argument is unsound. Omniscience is not a general characteristic of all cognitions, like *svaparaprakasakatva*, but it is the special characteristic of the divine cognition. The above argument is as unsound as that because a lamp illumines both itself and other objects like the sun, it should as well illumine the whole world like the sun. If it be argued that though both the lamp and the sun manifest themselves as well as other objects, the former manifests only a few objects owing to its limited capacity (*yogyatabasat*) then it should equally be argued that though both the human consciousness and the divine consciousness manifest themselves as well as other objects, the former manifests only a few objects owing to its limited capacity.

   Hence the Jaina concludes that the human cognition is as self-manifesting and other-manifesting (*svaparaprakasaka*) as the divine cognition, for both of them are of the nature of consciousness, which by its very essential nature both manifests itself and its object.

5. The Nyaya-Vaisesika holds that the cognition of an object is cognized by another cognition (*anuvyavasaya*). But the existence of the second cognition (*anuvyavasaya*) can never be proved by valid knowledge. If it does exist, is it known by perception or by inference?

   It can never be known by perception. For perception always depends upon the contact of the object of perception with a sense-organ. But *anuvyavasaya* can never come in contact with the external sense-organs; nor can it come in contact with the internal organ of mind, which is supposed to be the organ of its perception. The Nyaya-Vaisesika argues that the mind is in contact with the self; and the cognition inheres in the self, hence there is a relation of *samyukta-samavaya* or united-inherence between the cognition and the self; and the perception of the cognition is produced by this relation.

The Jaina replies that this argument is not right, for the existence of the mind cannot be proved. It may be argued that the existence, of the mind can be proved by the following inference : The cognition of the cognition of a jar is produced by its contact with the internal organ or mind, for it is a perceptible cognition, like the cognition of colour produced by its contact with the visual organ.

The Jaina urges that this argument is fallacious, for the "mark" of inference or the middle term is not proved to exist. The "mark" of inference here is the "perceptibility of the cognition of the cognition of a jar". If it is proved by the existence of the mind, then there would be a circle in reasoning; the perceptibility of the cognition of the cognition of an object would be inferred from the existence of the mind, and the existence of the mind, in its turn, would be inferred from the perceptibility of that cognition.

Moreover, not only the perceptibility of the cognition of the cognition of an object is unproved, but that cognition (*anuvyavasaya*) itself is not proved. We never perceive that the cognition of a jar is perceived by some other cognition; it is always perceived by itself.

External objects, indeed, first come in contact with the sense-organs, and then produce their cognitions. But we do not perceive that the mental states of pleasure, etc., are first produced in the self when they are quite unknown; then they come in contact with the mind, and then they are perceived through the mind. Pleasure and pain are perceived just after the perception of their external causes, viz. desirable and undesirable objects respectively; they are not perceived by another cognition different from them; they are cognized by themselves. Likewise the cognition of an external object is not perceived by another cognition, but by itself; it cognizes itself as well as its object.

6. Even supposing that a cognition is perceived by another cognition, does the second cognition arise when the first cognition continues to exist or when it is destroyed ? The first

alternative is impossible, for, according to the Nyaya-Vaisesika, cognitions are always successive; they are never simultaneous. The second alternative also is impossible; for if the second cognition arises when the first cognition is no longer in existence, what will be cognized by the second cognition? If it cognizes the non-existent first cognition, then it is illusory like the cognition of the double moon.

7. Then, again, is the second cognition perceived or not? If it is perceived, is it perceived by itself or by some other cognition? If it is perceived by itself, the first cognition, i.e. the cognition of an external object, too may be perceived by itself and there is no use of postulating the second cognition. If the second cognition is perceived by another cognition, then that cognition also would be perceived by another and so on ad infinitum; thus there would be a regressus ad infinitum. If the second cognition is not perceived, then how can this unperceived cognition perceive the first cognition ? If a cognition can be perceived by another cognition which is not perceived, then my cognition can be perceived by another's cognition unknown to me. But this is absurd.

8. The Nyaya-Vaisesika may argue that just as the sense-organs, which are not themselves perceived, can produce the apprehension of an object, so the second cognition can produce the apprehension of the first cognition, though it is not itself perceived, and in this sense it apprehends the first cognition.

   But this is a childish argument. For, in that case, it may as well be argued that the first cognition of an external object apprehends its object, though it is not itself perceived. But this is not admitted by the Nyaya-Vaisesika. This is the doctrine of the Bhatta Mimamsaka, according to whom an unperceived cognition can apprehend an object.

Hence the Jaina concludes that a cognition cognizes itself and its object. It illuminates both itself and its object (*svaparaprakasaka*).

### The Samkhya-Patanjala

A cognition is a psychic function or a function of the *buddhi*. The *buddhi* is unconscious, and as such it cannot be an object of its own consciousness. Just as the other sense-organs and sensible objects are unconscious and as such are manifested by the self which alone is conscious, so the unconscious *buddhi* also must be regarded as an object of the apprehension of the self; it is not manifested by itself but can only be manifested by the self. A cognition, therefore, which is nothing but an unconscious psychic function or mental mode cannot apprehend itself; nor can it apprehend an object. It is apprehended by the self.

The Nyaya-Vaisesika holds that a cognition is apprehended by another cognition. But by what is this second cognition cognized? If it is cognized by another cognition then the third cognition would require another cognition to apprehend it, and so on ad infinitum. Thus the Nyaya-Vaisesika hypothesis of *anuvyavasaya* leads to infinite regress. Moreover, it leads to the confusion of memory. If a cognition is cognized by another cognition, then there are as many psychic traces or residua (*samskara*) as there are cognitions of cognitions, and there are as many reminiscences as there are residua; thus the doctrine of *anuvyavasaya* leads to the confusion of memory.

According to the Samkhya-Patanjala, it is the self that apprehends an object, and apprehends the cognition of the object. But how can the self, which is inactive according to the Samkhya-Patanjala, know a cognition? According to Vacaspatimisra, the self is reflected on the unconscious mental mode owing to the proximity of the mind to the self and its transparency, its inertia (*tamas*) and energy (*rajas*) being completely overpowered by its essence (*sattva*), and thus some sort of relation is established between the self and the mental mode, by virtue of which the self apprehends the mental mode, though it is inactive. According to Vijnanabhiksu, on the other hand, the self is reflected on the mental mode, and this reflection in the mental mode is reflected back on the self, so that there is a double reflection of the self on the mental mode and of the mental mode on the self, and thus some sort of direct relationship is established between the self and the mental mode. Thus, according to the Samkhya-Patanjala, a cognition or mental mode is apprehended only by the self; it cannot be apprehended by another cognition or by itself as it is unconscious.

### The Samkara-Vedantist

According to the Samkara-Vedanta, a mental mode (*vrtti*) must have an object (*visaya*); but the object may be either itself or other than itself. A mental mode may either apprehend an external object, when it is modified into the object, or it may apprehend itself (*svavisayavrtti*). The Samkarite does not admit that there is a cognition of a cognition; a cognition, according to him, is self-luminous; it is not manifested by any other cognition. There is no intervening mental mode (*vrtti*) between a cognitive process and the cognition of this cognitive process. There is a direct and immediate consciousness of a cognition; a cognition is directly apprehended by itself. If we represent the object as O and the cognition of the object as S, then, according to the Samkarite, we do not go beyond SO to SO nor do we go to SO simply; the cognition of a mental mode may be represented as SO. In the apprehension of a mental mode there is a direct intellectual intuition (*kevalasaksivedyatva*). There is an elaborate discussion of the self-luminosity of consciousness (*svaprakasatva*) in *Tattva-pradipika* of Citsukha.

The Samkarite holds that a cognition which is itself unperceived can never apprehend an object, as the Bhatta Mimamsaka holds. A cognition cannot also be the object of another cognition (*anuvyavasaya*) as a cognition is not of the nature of an unconscious object; a cognition is conscious, while an object is unconscious; a cognition, therefore, cannot be regarded as an object of another cognition. Besides, the Nyaya-Vaisesika doctrine of *anuvyavasaya* leads to infinite regress. A cognition is self-luminous.

The Buddhist idealist also holds that cognitions are self-luminous. But his view is not the same as that of the Samkarite. According to the former, a cognition cognizes itself, it manifests itself. According to the latter, a cognition is not apprehended or manifested by any other cognition. If a cognition can make itself an object of cognition, then it can as well be an object of another cognition. Hence the Samkarite holds that a cognition is self-luminous (*svaprakasa*), not in the sense that it is an object of its own apprehension, as the Buddhist holds, but in the sense that it is not manifested by any other cognition. The conception of self-luminosity is positive, according to the Buddhist, it is negative, according to the Samkarite. The Samkarite doctrine closely resembles the doctrine of Prabhakara, according to whom cognitions are self-luminous. By this Prabhakara means that a cognition is not an object of another cognition; it is not cognized as an object of its own cognition, a cognition is cognized, no doubt, but it is cognized as a cognition not as something cognized.

**Ramanuja's Criticism of Samkara's Doctrine**

Samkara holds that consciousness alone is ultimately real and it is self-luminous. There is no self apart from consciousness and there is no object apart from consciousness. Consciousness is above the distinction of subject and object, which have only an empirical reality. And this consciousness is self-luminous; it manifests or apprehends itself.

Ramanuja disputes this view, and urges that consciousness is not possible without the knowing self and the known object, both of which are real. There is no objectless consciousness (*nirvisayasamvit*). Consciousness and its object are perceived as different from each other; one apprehends and the other is apprehended; they are correlative to each other. So to annul the object altogether contradicts the clear testimony of consciousness.

Samkara holds that consciousness is self-luminous; it apprehends itself; it is never an object of any other consciousness. This is true under certain conditions. Consciousness manifests itself to the cognizing self when it apprehends an object. It does not manifest itself to all selves at all times. The consciousness of one person is inferred by another from his behaviour; so it becomes an object of inferential cognition. And our own past states of consciousness too become the objects of our present recollection. So consciousness is not necessarily self-luminous. Consciousness does not lose its nature simply because it becomes an object of consciousness. The essential nature of consciousness consists in its manifesting itself at the present moment through its own being to its substrate, or in being instrumental in proving its own object by its own being.

# 12

# Perception of the Self

## Introduction

Can the *Atman* or self be perceived ? This question has been answered in different ways by different schools of Indian philosophers. The Carvaka holds that there is no self at all, and it can neither be perceived nor inferred. The Buddhist idealist recognizes the distinction of subject and object only within consciousness. He does not recognize any permanent self apart from the ever-changing stream of consciousness. The Naiyayika recognizes the self as a substance endowed with the qualities of cognition, pleasure, pain, desire, aversion, and effort. Some earlier Naiyayikas hold that the self can never be an object of perception; it is known by an act of inference from its qualities. The Vaisesika, too, is of the same opinion. But he admits that the self can be object of yogic intuition. The Samkhya holds that the self is an object of inference, it is inferred as an original (*timba*) from its reflection (*pratibimba*) in *buddhi*. The Patanjala holds that the self can be an object of higher intuition (*pratibha-jnana*). The neo-Naiyayika holds that the self is an object of internal perception (*manasapratyaksa*); it can be perceived only through the mind in relation to its distinctive qualities. The Bhatta Mimamsaka also holds that the self is an object of internal perception or self-consciousness (*ahampratyaya*).

The Prabhakara Mimamsaka holds that the self is revealed in every act of knowledge as the knowing subject or ego; it is known as the subject of perception and not as the object of perception; and it is known not as the subject of internal perception or self-consciousness, but of external perception, since there can be no self-consciousness apart from object-consciousness. The Jaina holds that the self is an object of internal perception; it is perceived as the subject which has pleasure, pain, and the like. In external perception also the self knows itself through itself as having the cognition of an object. The *Upanisads* regard the self as an object of higher intuition. Amkara holds that the self is pure consciousness above the distinction of ego and non-ego, and it is known by an immediate, intuitive consciousness. Ramanuja holds that the self is nothing but the knower or the ego and it is known as such by perception.

### The Carvaka

The Carvakas do not recognize the existence of the self as an independent entity. Sadananda speaks of four schools of Carvakas. Some Carvakas identify the self with the gross body. Some Carvakas identify the self with the external sense-organs. Some Carvakas identify the self with the vital force. And other Carvakas identify the self with the mind. Thus the Carvakas do not regard the self as an independent entity. Jayanta Bhatta says that the Carvakas regard consciousness as a by-product of unconscious elements, e.g. earth, water, fire, and air. Just as intoxicating liquor is produced by unintoxicating rice, molasses, etc., so consciousness is produced by unconscious, material elements. There is no self endowed with consciousness, since there is no proof of its existence. It cannot be perceived through the external sense-organs, like jars, etc.; nor can it be perceived through the mind. And inference is not recognized by the Carvakas as a means of valid knowledge. Moreover, there is no mark of inference. Hence the self can neither be perceived nor inferred.

### The Buddhist Idealist

The Buddhist idealists (*Yogacaras*) regard the self as a series of cognitions or ideas. Cognitions alone are ultimately real. They are polarized into the subject and the object, which are not ultimately real. There is no self apart from cognitions; and there are no objects apart from cognitions; cognitions apprehend themselves as their own objects. Cognitions are self-luminous. They reveal neither the self nor the not-self apart from them. There is no self apart from the ever-changing stream of cognitions. And there are no extra-mental objects apart from cognitions. The distinction between subject and object is a creation of individual consciousness within itself; it is not a relation between two independent entities. Hence the problem of perception of the self as a permanent intelligent principle does not puzzle the Buddhist idealists though they cannot explain, as Samkara points out, how momentary cognitions can become subjects and objects of each other.

### The Naiyayika

According to the Naiyayikas, the self is a permanent substance in which cognition, pleasure, pain, desire, aversion, and effort inhere. It is not a series of cognitions but a permanent principle in which these cognitions exist. It is not a stream of consciousness but an abiding substance which becomes conscious at times.

All Naiyayikas admit that the self is an object of inference. But some of the earlier Naiyayikas hold that the self is an object of perception as well. Others deny it. Gautama makes the self an object of inference. It is inferred from its qualities such as pleasure, pain, cognition, desire, aversion, and effort. Gautama nowhere mentions in the sutras whether the self is an object of perception or not.

Vatsyayana makes apparently conflicting statements about this question. In one place he says, "The self is not apprehended by perception." In another place he says, "The self is perceived by the yogin through a particular kind of conjunction between the self and the *manas* owing to the ecstasy of meditation. The self is an object of yogic perception."

These two statements apparently conflict with each other. But they can be easily harmonized. The self is not an object of normal perception. It cannot be perceived br ordinary persons through the internal organ. It can be perceived only by the yogin in a state of ecstasy. So the self is not an object of normal internal perception but of supernormal perception. Here by the self Vatsyayana means the pure self free from its connection with the organism. Udayana has made it clear in *Nyayavartikatatparyaparisuddhi*. He raises the question why Vatsyayana should deny the normal perception of the self when, as a matter of fact, it is always an object of mental perception, being always perceived as "I" along with every cognition; and answers that we have indeed the notion of "I" along with every cognition through mental perception; but it may be taken as referring to the body. The empirical self or the self as connected with the organism is the object of mental perception. The pure self apart from the body cannot be apprehended by mental perception.

Mental perception is not a sufficient proof of the existence of the pure self apart from the body, so long as it is not strengthened by other means of knowledge, inference, etc. This is the answer from the standpoint of those Naiyayikas who do not regard the self as an object of normal perception. But some Naiyayikas hold that one's own self is always an object of mental perception. From their standpoint the self of any other person is not an object of perception.

Udyotkara, however, holds that the self is an object of perception. It is directly perceived through the internal organ. This direct knowledge of the self is perceptual in character inasmuch as it is independent of the recollection of the relation between a major term and a minor term, and it varies with the variations in the character of its object. Inferential knowledge depends on the recollection of the invariable concomitance of major and minor terms. The internal perception of the self is independent of any such recollection. Besides, the perception of an object varies with the variation in the character of its object. The perception of a blue object will vary if the object becomes yellow. Likewise, the internal perception of the self varies according as the character of the self varies. The perception of the self as "I am happy" is different from the perception of the self as "I am unhappy". So the self is an object of self-consciousness (*ahampratyaya*) which is of the nature of direct perception. Udyotkara does not draw a distinction between the self apart from the body and the self connected with the body, between the pure self and the empirical self.

Jayanta Bhatta says that according to some Naiyayikas and the Aupavarsas, the self is an object of internal perception or self-consciousness (*ahampratyaya*). But Jayanta himself holds that the self cannot be established by perception. It is not an object of self-consciousness. Our self-consciousness has the body for its object. The self is established by inference. Thus Jayanta's view is opposed to that of Udyotkara.

Udayana, however, agrees with Udyotkara, and holds that the

self is perceived through the *manas* just as colour is perceived through the visual organ, both of them being of the nature of direct and immediate knowledge.

The later Naiyayikas also hold that the self is an object of mental perception. Laugaksi Bhaskara holds, the self is perceived as "I" owing to its ordinary conjunction with the manas. Kesavamisra also holds the same view. But in case of diversity of opinion as to the perceptibility of the self, the self is inferred from its qualities. Visvanatha also makes the self an object of mental perception. But he lays down a condition. The self apart from its specific qualities cannot be perceived through the manas. It is perceived through the manas only as endued with its specific qualities such as pleasure, pain, and the like. The self is always perceived as "I know", "I will", etc. It is never perceived apart from its qualities. The self is the object of self-consciousness. The body is not the object of self-consciousness. Thus Visvanatha's view is opposed to that of Jayanta Bhatta. Jagadisa Bhattacharya holds 'the same view as Visvanatha. He also holds that the self is perceived through the *manas* as "I am happy" and the like.

### The Naiyayika's Criticism of the Bhatta Mimamsaka View

We have seen that according to Jayanta Bhatta and some earlier Naiyayikas, the self is not an object of perception but an object of inference. The self is the substance in which cognition, pleasure, pain, desire, aversion, and effort inhere; it is the substratum of these qualities. We cannot perceive the self. But we can infer it from its qualities. The qualities of the self are the marks of inference.

Jayanta offers the following criticism of the Bhatta Mimamsaka doctrine, that the self is an object of internal perception:

Firstly, how can the self be the subject as well as the object of one and the same act of cognition? If one and the same act of cognition cannot be polarized into the subject and the object, as the Buddhist idealist holds, then, for the same reason, one and the same self also cannot be bifurcated into the subject and the object of the same act of knowledge.

Secondly, the Bhatta urges that the same self is the subject in one condition and the object in a different condition. The self is the subject, in so far as it is conscious; and it is the object, in so far as it is a substance. The self is a conscious substance; as conscious it is the subject or cognizer; as a substance it is the object cognized. But this is unreasonable. If substantiality constitutes the object of consciousness, then the self can never be the subject or knower for the self is as much a substance as a jar is, and if the jar as a substance is simply the object of consciousness, but never its subject, then, on the same ground, the self also as a substance is simply the object of consciousness, but it can never be the subject or knower.

Thirdly, it may be urged by Kumarila that the pure form of transcendental consciousness is the subject or knower, and when it is empirically modified, qualified, or determined in various ways, it becomes the object of consciousness. The pure transcendental consciousness is the subject, and its empirical modification is the object. Elsewhere, there is simply the consciousness of an object apart from the subject. Thus we may distinguish three factors : (i) a pure subject (*suddha inatrta*) (ii) a pure object (*suddha-visayagrahanam*), and (iii) the subject as modified by the object, which is a mixed mode (*ghatavacchinna inatrta*).

But this argument also is unsubstantial. In the consciousness "this is a jar" there is simply a consciousness of an object. Then, when this consciousness is appropriated by the self, there arises a consciousness "I know the jar". Here, there is merely a self-appropriation of the consciousness of the jar, or there is simply a consciousness of the consciousness of the jar; it does not refer to the noumenal substrate or the self.

Fourthly, Kumarila may urge that in the consciousness "I know the jar" there are three elements : (i) the consciousness of the "jar", (ii) the consciousness of "knowing the jar"; and (iii) the consciousness of "I" or the "self". In one and the same unitary act of consciousness, one part cannot be valid, and the other invalid. In the same consciousness "I know the jar", the consciousness of "jar", and the consciousness of "knowing the jar" cannot be said to be valid, and the consciousness of "I" or the self to be invalid. If the first and second parts are valid, the third part also must be regarded as valid. In other words, we must admit that there is a consciousness of the self as an object of "I" consciousness or self-consciousness (*ahamvitti*).

The Naiyayika contends that the self can never be both the subject and the object of one and the same act of consciousness. In the consciousness "I know the jar" there are three parts : (i) "I", (ii) "know", and (iii) "the jar". The second and third parts evidently refer to the object (*visayanisthameva*); if the first part viz. "I" refers to the self, then the self remains in its pure, indeterminate form both as the knowcr and the known, the subject and the object in the same condition. Hence it cannot be maintained that the self becomes the subject in one condition and the object in a different condition. If really there is no difference in the essential nature of the self, how can it be both subject and object ? If it is insisted that the pure, unmodalized self assumes the forms of the subject and the object under different conditions, then this doctrine does not differ from Buddhist subjectivism, according to which one and the same cognition is the subject as well as the object of itself. Hence the Naiyayika says that the self can never be known as an object of self-consciousness; it is known only by inference; the subject can never enter into the object-stream; it always stands apart. This reminds us of the doctrine of Kant, according to whom the category of substantiality cannot be applied to the self. But the Naiyayika himself regards the self as a substance endowed with qualities, though he does not admit that it is an object of perception.

### The Naiyayika's Criticism of Samkara's Fiew

According to Samkara, the self is essentially conscious; it is one, eternal, ubiquitous, undifferenced consciousness. The self is not manifested by fleeting states of consciousness, as a jar is manifested by some transient state of consciousness. But it manifests itself, or it is self-luminous. Consciousness constitutes the essential nature of the self; it is natural or essential to the self, and not an adventitious or accidental property of the self. The self is not conscious owing to its connection with consciousness produced by the internal organ or the external organs; the self is not inert in itself like matter, which is endued with consciousness, as the Nyaya-Vaisesika holds. If the self were conscious owing to its connection with the consciousness produced by the sense-organs, then an external object, too, e.g, a jar, would be conscious owing to its connection with the consciousness produced by it. The self is the light of consciousness; it lights up everything; but it does not depend upon anything to manifest itself. Other objects depend upon many factors for their manifestation, but the self is self-luminous or self-manifesting; it is not caused or conditioned by anything else; it is unconditioned, uncaused, and independent. The self can never be the object of consciousness, it is the pure, unmodalized, or transcendental consciousness above the phenomenal distinction of the subject and the object, the knower and the known. Consciousness is here hypostatized as a third term existing independently of the subject and the object. Consciousness alone is ultimately real in its pure, unmodalized, or transcendental form; the distinction of subject and object within this ultimate reality has only empirical reality.

Jayanta Bhatta criticizes it as follows :

Firstly, the Samkarite holds that the self is of the nature of unconditioned consciousness. But has anybody ever experienced unconditioned or transcendental consciousness ? Our consciousness is produced by an external organ or by the internal organ. Hence we can never conceive of a self whose essence is transcendental consciousness.

Secondly, the Samkarite holds that the self, the essence of which is transcendental consciousness, is self-luminous. But if the self is self-luminous, why is it that I am conscious only of my own self, and not of other selves ? What is the reason for it ? Then, again, if I am conscious of my own self, it is apprehended by me, and if it is apprehended, it must be apprehended as the object of apprehension (*anubhava-karma*).

Thirdly, the Samkarite may urge that the self is not the object of perception; it cannot be presented to consciousness as an object, but it can be known by immediate intuitive consciousness (*aparoksajnana*). But this is self-contradictory. Perception means the same thing as direct and immediate consciousness. If it is said that the self cannot be the object of perceptual or preservative consciousness, then it cannot be an object of immediate and intuitive consciousness for the same reason. It is self-contradictory to say that the self is not an object of perception but it is an object of immediate intuition.

Fourthly, the Samkarite may urge that the self is luminous, and hence it is known by an immediate intuition. If so, then a luminous lamp too would manifest itself to a blind man, though unperceived by him. If the lamp manifests itself only to him by whom it is apprehended, then the self too must be regarded as manifesting itself, only when it is apprehended. If the self manifests itself, it must also be apprehended; and as apprehended it must be regarded as an object of apprehension. Thus the self becomes both the subject and the object of consciousness; it cannot, therefore, be regarded as the pure, unmodalized, or transcendental consciousness above the distinction of subject and object.

Fifthly, the Samkarite holds that the self is of the nature of consciousness which is self-luminous; it manifests itself and is not manifested by any other thing. Thus both the self and consciousness which constitutes its essence are self-luminous. If it were self-luminous, it would become both the subject and the object of consciousness, which is impossible. And, in fact, nobody is ever conscious of two self-luminous entities, viz. the self-luminous self and the self-luminous consciousness.

Lastly, the Samkarite holds that consciousness constitutes the essence of the self; it is natural or essential to the self, not accidental to it. But this does not stand to reason. That is to be regarded as conscious (*cetana*), which has consciousness of an object (*cita yogat*) and that is to be regarded as unconscious (*jada*), which has no consciousness of an object. And there is no other consciousness than the consciousness of an object, If it is held that an object too is self-luminous, then every object in the world would manifest itself to everyone, and thus everyone would be omniscient. Hence, we must admit that consciousness is not essential to the self, but an adventitious property of the self; the self is not conscious in itself and by itself, but it is endowed with consciousness which is produced by various causes and inheres in the self. But why should consciousness inhere in the self and not in the object which produces it ? Jayanta replies that this is the nature of consciousness that it inheres in the self and not in the object. There are certain acts which inhere only in their agents or subjects and never in their objects, e.g. the act of going. So the act of consciousness, by its very nature, inheres in its subject, viz. the self, and not in its object. And the inexorable law of nature (*vastusvabhava*) cannot be called in question.

Jayanta, therefore, concludes that consciousness does not constitute the essential nature of the self, nor is the self an object of internal perception (*manasa pratyaksa*) or immediate intuition (*aparoksa-*

*jnana*). The self is an object of inference, and the qualities of the self, e.g. cognition, pleasure, pain, desire, aversion, and effort constitute the mark of inference,

**The Vaisesika**

Kanada holds that the self is not an object of normal perception but of supernormal perception. It cannot be perceived through the internal organ or manas owing to its ordinary conjunction with the self. My own self is as imperceptible as any other self. But Kanada admits that the self can be perceived by the yogis through a particular kind of conjunction between the self and the manas. This conjunction is due to a peculiar power (*dharma*) born of meditation. Thus the self, according to Kanada, is an object of higher intuition.

Śamkaramisra holds that the self in its essential nature is an object of higher intuition. But the self as modified by its own specific qualities is an object of internal perception. I directly perceive through the manas "I am sorry", "I am happy", "I know", "I will", "I desire". I cannot perceive the self as modified by these specific qualities through the external senses; I perceive it through the internal organ when the external organs do not operate. So there is a direct perception of the self as modified by its specific qualities through the internal organ. This knowledge of the self is perceptual in character, since it is directly produced by the internal organ. It is neither inferential nor verbal. It is not inferential knowledge, since it is not produced by a mark of inference. It is not verbal knowledge, since it is not produced by any verbal authority. It is of the nature of direct internal perception derived through the internal organ.

But Samkaramisra does not make the pure self an object of normal internal perception. He also, like Kanada, makes it an object of yogic perception. But he admits that sometimes ordinary men like us also have flashes of intuition of the pure self; but it is so much obscured by nescience (*avidya*) that it is as good as non-existent. It is especially to be found in yogis who have a direct perception of the pure self owing to a particular conjunction of the self with the internal organ brought about by a peculiar power born of meditation.

Sridhara also holds that the pure self free from all attributes is not an object of normal internal perception. His conception of the self approaches that of Samkara. The self is known to us as "I" and "mine", as the doer and the possessor. But these are not the essential attributes of the self; they are rather accidents of the self due to its connection with the limitations of the body. The notions of "I" and "mine", subject and ego are false conceptions of the self. The self in itself is not an ego. The ego or subject is the empirical self. It is the self limited by the organism. The empirical self is an object of normal perception through the manas. But the pure self is not an object of normal perception. It is perceived by the yogis alone. It is an object of higher intuition. The real nature of the self free from all impositions of "I" and "mine" is perceived by the yogis when he withdraws his mind from the external organs, concentrates it on an aspect of the self, and constantly meditates upon the self with undivided attention.

**The Samkhya-Patanjala**

According to the Samkhya-Patanjala, consciousness is the essence of the self which is self-luminous. But the self cannot know its essential nature, so long as it illusorily identifies itself with the unconscious *buddhi* on which it casts its reflection and gives it an appearance of a conscious self. The self knows an external object in the following manner. The transparent *buddhi* goes out to the object through the channel of a sense-organ and assumes the form of the object, but it cannot manifest the object as it is unconscious; it manifests the object to the self only when a reflection of the self is cast upon the function of the unconscious *buddhi* modified into the form of the object. Thus the self knows an external object only through the mental modification on which it casts its reflection. This is the view of Vacaspatimisra. Vijnanabhiksu assumes that the self casts its reflection on the unconscious *buddhi* functioning in a particular way, and the mental function which takes in the reflection of the self and assumes its form is reflected back on the self, and it is through this reflection that the self knows an external object.

Now, the question is: Can the self know itself? Though the self is self-luminous, it cannot know itself directly so long as it is connected with the organism. Ordinarily, the self infers its existence through its reflection in *buddhi*. Just as we cannot see our own faces but infer their existence from their reflection in a mirror, so we cannot perceive the self but infer its existence from its reflection in *buddhi* inasmuch as a reflection (*pratibimba*) must have an original (*bimba*).

But Patanjali says that when we develop the power of concentration, we may have supernormal intuition (*pratibha jnana*) of the self through its reflection in *buddhi*. But how can the self know itself through an unconscious mental modification though it takes in the reflection of the self ? Vacaspati holds that the self can know itself only when attention is entirely withdrawn from the mental function in which the self is reflected, and is wholly concentrated on the reflection of the self in the pure intelligence-stuff (*sattva*) of *buddhi*, its matter-stuff (*tamas*) and energy-stuff (*rajas*) being completely overpowered. Thus the self knows itself only through its reflection in the pure intelligence-stuff of *buddhi*, viewed apart from the unconscious mental mode which takes in the reflection of the self. The self is always the knower, the witness (*saksin*), the seer or spectator (*drastr*); so it can never turn back upon itself and make itself an object of knowledge (*drsya*).

Then, what is the knowing subject and what is the known object in the supernormal intuition of the self? Vyasa says that the self cannot be manifested or known by the intelligence-stuff (*sattva*) of *buddhi* as *buddhi* is unconscious; it is the self which knows itself through its reflection in the pure intelligence-stuff of *buddhi*? If we call the self in its pure essence the pure or transcendental self, and the mental mode in which the self is reflected the empirical self, then the pure self can know the empirical self, but the empirical self can never know the pure self.

Vacaspatimisra says that the self is reflected in the unconscious intelligence-stuff of *buddhi* so that the mental mode may be said to have the self for its object in the sense in which a mirror in which a face is reflected is said to have the face for its object; the mental mode cannot be said to have the self for its object in the sense that it manifests or apprehends the self, inasmuch as the unconscious mental mode can never manifest the conscious self. Vacaspati says, "The notion of self-knowledge consists in making the object of knowledge, the reflection of the *purusa* into the *buddhi*". Again, he says, "In the trance cognition the object of knowledge is the self reflected into the *buddhi*. It is different from the real self, because it becomes the support of that self (*atma*)". The self, in its pure essence, is the subject of self-apprehension, and the pure intelligence-stuff of *buddhi* which takes in the reflection of the self and is modified into its form is the object of self-apprehension, so that the subject and the object of self-apprehension are not the same. In other words, the transcendental self is the subject of self-apprehension, and the empirical self is the object of self-apprehension. Thus Vacaspati avoids self-contradiction in the view that the self can be both subject and object of knowledge.

Nagesa also corroborates the view of Vacaspatimisra. He asks : In the apprehension of the self is it *buddhi* which knows the self, or is it the self which knows itself ? In the first alternative, *buddhi* would be conscious, which is not admitted by the Samkhya-Patanjala. In the second alternative, the self would be both subject and object of knowledge, which is self-contradictory. Nagesa says that the second alternative does not involve self-contradiction. The self cannot be known by the mental mode in which the self is reflected because it is unconscious. But it is the self itself which knows the mental mode which is modified into the form of the self and is reflected in the self. Thus the self has knowledge of itself in the form of the reflection in itself, of the mental mode which takes in the reflection of the self and which is modified into the form of the self. Here, in the apprehension of the self by the self there is no self-contradiction, for there is a difference between the self as the subject and the self as the object. The self as it is determined by the empirical mental mode modified into its form, or the empirical self is the object, and the self as it is in itself undetermined by any mental mode, or the transcendental self is the subject. The self in itself can never be an object of knowledge. The transcendental self is always a knower; it can never be an object known. Thus Nagesa substantially agrees with Vacaspatimisra's view that the pure self is the subject of self-apprehension, and the empirical self is the object of self-apprehension. But he differs from the latter in holding that the mental mode in which the self is reflected is reflected back in the self. On this point he agrees with Vijnanabhiksu.

According to Vacaspatimisra, the self is reflected in the intelligence-stuff of *buddhi* which is modified into the form of the self. But, according to Vijnanabhiksu, the self is reflected in the intelligence-stuff of *buddhi* functioning in a particular manner, and the mental function too, in which the self is reflected, is reflected back in the self. Thus, according to Vijnanabhiksu, the self knows itself through the reflection, in itself, of the mental mode, which takes in the reflection of the self and is modified into its form, just as it knows an external object (e.g. a jar) through the reflection, in itself, of the mental mode which assumes the form of the object. He says, "We must admit that just as there is a reflection of *buddhi* in the self, so there is a reflection of the self in *buddhi* also; otherwise the self's experience would not be possible.

But how does he avoid self-contradiction, if the self knows itself through the reflection, in itself, of the mental mode which assumes the form of the self ? He says that there is no contradiction in the cognition of the self by the self, inasmuch as the self is essentially self-luminous, and hence it can be both the illuminating agent and the illumined object, the knowing subject as well as the known object. There is no inconsistency in the relation between the self as a knowing subject and the self as a known object, because the self is essentially self-luminous, and that which is of the nature of light or illumination (*prakasa*) is itself illumined; there is no contradiction in it. But a relation always implies two terms; how can there be relation of the self to itself of the self as the subject to the self as the known object? Vijnanabhiksu holds that though there is no real difference in the nature of the self, yet we may distinguish the self in its pure essence, as the original (*bimba*) from the reflection of the mental mode in the self, as an image of the self (*pratibimba*). Of these two aspects of the self, which is the knowing subject and which is the known object? Vijnanabhiksu holds that the self as determined by the mental mode which is modified into the form of the self is the knowing subject, and the self, in its pure essence, free from all determinations, is the known object. Thus Vijnanabhiksu goes against the views of Vyasa, Vacaspati, and Nagesa who regard the pure self as the subject of self-apprehension, and the empirical self as the object of self-apprehension. He says that the self is self-luminous, because it illumines itself, or knows itself as an object of knowledge. The self is not, indeed, an object of an ordinary mental function, but it is an object of supernormal yogic intuition. But still Vijnanabhiksu's interpretation does not seem to be in keeping with the spirit of the Samkhya-Patanjala distinction between the knower (*drastr*) and the known (*drsya*), the self (*purusa*) and the not-self (*prakrti*).

**The Bhatta Mimamsaka**

There seems to be a difference between Kumarila and his followers on this question. Kumarila holds that the self is of the nature of pure consciousness and is illumined by itself. It is self-luminous; it is manifested by itself. But Parthasarathimisra, a follower of Kumarila, holds that the self is an object of mental perception. This distinction is not recognized by all. Dr. Ganganatha Jha, and Dr. S. N. Das Gupta represent Kumarila as holding that the self is an object of mental perception. "Kumarila holds," says Dr. Jha, "that the Soul is not self-luminous, but known by mental perception." Dr. Das Gupta states, "Kumarila thinks that the soul which is distinct from the body is perceived by a mental perception (*manasa-pratyaksa*), . . . Kumarila agrees with Prabhakara in holding that soul is not self-illuminating (*syayamprakasa*)".

Dr. P. Sastri, however, rightly points out that according to Kumarila, the self is self-illumined. Kumarila clearly says, "The self is a light which illumines itself. When it is said to be imperceptible (*agrahya*) the epithet apparently means that the self is imperceptible to all; but as the Sruti says that it is self-illumined (*atmajyoti*), we conclude that it is imperceptible only to others and not to itself." Again he says, "The notion of "I" (which is all the notion that we have of the soul) always points to the mere existence of the Soul, which is of the nature of pure consciousness." Kumarila seems to accept the doctrine of self-illumination of the self from *Savarabhasya*. Savara says, "The Atman is known by itself (*svasamvedya*); it is incapable of being seen or shown by others."

But Parthasarathi says, "The self or the knower, which is distinct from the body, is an object of self-consciousness in the form of mental perception." This distinction between Kumarila's view and that of his followers is not generally recognized. The author of *Sarvasiddhantasamgraha* credits Kumarila with the view that the self is an object of mental perception. So we shall take Parthasarathi as the typical exponent of the Bhatta Mimamsaka view. The Bhatta holds that the self is not an object of inference as some Naiyayikas hold; nor is it an object of immediate intuition as Samkara holds; nor is it perceived as the subject of object-cognitions as Prabhakara holds. According to him, the self is an object of mental perception (*manasapratyaksa*) or self-consciousness (*ahampratyaya*).

**The Bhatta's Criticism of the Naiyayika Doctrine**

Firstly, some Naiyayikas hold that the self cannot be an object of perception, because it cannot be the subject and the object of the same act of knowledge. The Bhatta asks : How, then, can the self be an object of inference? Here, the self knows itself by inference through itself. The self is the subject of inference, the object of inference, and the instrument of inference. Thus it cannot be held that the self is always the subject and never the object of knowledge. If in inference the self can be both the subject (*anumatr*) and the object of inference (*anumeya*) at the same time, it may also be regarded as an object of perception, when it is both the knower and the known. If the self can be known by inference, it may as well be known by perception.

Secondly, if it is argued that the self cannot be perceived because it has no form (*rupa*) then it may equally be argued that the mental states of pleasure and the like cannot be perceived because they are without any form. And if the latter can be perceived, though without any form, then the former also can be perceived, though devoid of any form. And as a matter of fact, pleasure, etc., are never perceived apart from the self to which they belong. Pleasure is perceived as pleasure of the self, we have no consciousness of mere pleasure such as "this is pleasure"; but we have a consciousness of pleasure always in such a form as "I have pleasure". Thus the mental states of pleasure and the like are not perceived apart from the self, but they are perceived as belonging to the self, and thus manifest themselves as well as the self to which they belong.

Thirdly, sometimes an external object is known together with its knowledge; the consciousness of the object is appropriated by the self. In this self-appropriation of the consciousness of the object, there is not only a consciousness of the object, but also a consciousness of the self which has consciousness. In this act of cognition there is the apprehension of an object as qualified by the consciousness of the self (*jnatr-jnanavisistartha-grahana*). There cannot be a consciousness of a qualified object, without apprehending the qualifications which qualify the object. In the cognition "I know the object", the qualified object cannot be known unless its qualifications, viz. the consciousness and the self are already known. Thus the self must be regarded as an object of consciousness.

Fourthly, if the self is not perceived already, it can never be remembered afterwards; and if it cannot be remembered it cannot be an object of inference. Thus the self must be regarded as an object of perception.

**The Bhatta's Criticism of Prabhakara's Doctrine**

According to the Bhatta Mimamsaka, the self is the object of internal perception or "I" consciousness. But Prabhakara urges that the self cannot be the subject as well as the object of consciousness; it is self-contradictory to suppose that the self is the object of perception, inasmuch as the self cannot be both the percipient and the perceived. Prabhakara holds that there is no consciousness (*ahamvitti*) apart from the consciousness of objects (*ghatadivitti*). So the self cannot be regarded as the object of "I" consciousness, which is different from object-consciousness. According to him, in every act of consciousness there are three factors : (i) the consciousness of an object or object-consciousness (*visayavittt*), (ii) the consciousness of the subject or the self (*ahamvitti*) and (iii) the self-conscious awareness or consciousness of consciousness (*svasamvitti*), There is a triple consciousness (*triputt-samvit*) in every act of consciousness. There is no consciousness of an object, pure and simple, apart from the consciousness of the self. There can be no consciousness of an object which is not appropriated by the self. There is no consciousness of an object which does not reveal the self. In every act of cognition the self is revealed not as the object of knowledge, but as the subject of knowledge or the knower (*jnatr*). It is self-contradictory to suppose that the self can be perceived as an object of consciousness, the self is always the knower so it can never be a known object.

Parthasarathimisra, a Bhatta Mimamsaka asks : What do you mean by self-contradiction in the self, if it is both the subject and the object of perception? Prabhakara evidently means that the self is simply the agent (*kartr*) of the act of cognition, it is not the object (*karma*) of the act of cognition; in other words, the act of cognition cannot produce its result (*svaphala*) in the self. Parthasarthi asks : What is the result of the act of cognition? It is manifestation or illumination (*bhasana*). And it exists in the self which is the agent of the act of cognition. The self is manifested by the act of cognition. And since it is manifested by the act of cognition, it is the object of consciousness. If it is not manifested by the act of cognition, it cannot be said to be revealed by it. Thus if the self is revealed by an act of consciousness, as Prabhakara holds, then it is both subject and object of consciousness, and so Prabhakara also cannot avoid self-contradiction.

According to the Bhatta Mimamsaka, the self is not manifested in every consciousness of an object; the object-consciousness (*insayavttti*) is not always appropriated by the self. For instance, sometimes I know that "this is a jar", but I do not know that "I know the jar". So, the Bhatta holds that though the self is manifested when an object is known, it is not manifested either as the subject (*kartr*) or as the object (*karma*) of this object-consciousness (*visayavitti*), but along with this object-consciousness there is sometimes another distinct consciousness, viz. self-consciousness (*manasahampratyaya*) of which the self is the object.

Prabhakara is right in so far as the self is always implicitly involved in the consciousness of the not-self or object; and the Bhatta Mimamsaka is right in so far as the self is not always explicitly manifested in the consciousness of the not-self, but it is explicitly manifested only in self-consciousness or "I" consciousness which cannot be identified with mere object-consciousness. Self-consciousness is certainly a higher degree of conscious life than the mere consciousness of an object; it involves an additional factor of self-appropriation. Hence the self may be regarded as the object of the self-consciousness, as the Bhatta holds, rather than the subject of object-consciousness, as Prabhakara holds.

Prabhakara tries to avoid self-contradiction in the nature of the self by supposing that the self cannot be both the subject and the object of knowledge, but it is only the subject of knowledge or the knower. If so, then there can be neither recollection nor recognition of the self. Both in recollection and in recognition it is the object of recollection and recognition that appears in consciousness, and not their subject. In these representative processes it is the object presented to consciousness in our past experience that is represented to consciousness. Hence, in the recollection and recognition of the self it is the self apprehended as an object of previous perception that is represented to consciousness as the object of present recollection and recognition. If, in the recognition of the self, the self is not known as the object of recognition, then the act of recognition would be without an objective basis; it would be objectless. But there can be no consciousness without an object. Hence the Bhatta concludes that the self must be regarded as an object of self-consciousness. But how can the self be the subject and the object, the knower and the known at the same time? Is it not self-contradictory? The Bhatta holds that the self as a conscious entity is the subject, and as a substance it is the object, and thus tries to avoid self-contradiction. This view may be contrasted with that of Kant, according to whom the self is the subject or knower, but not an object or substance.

### The Bhatta's Criticism of Samkara's Doctrine

Samkara holds that consciousness constitutes the essence of the self which is self-luminous or self-manifesting; it does not depend for its manifestation on any other condition. How, then, can it be the object of consciousness? How can the self which is self-luminous be manifested by consciousness? The Bhatta retorts : If the self is self-luminous because it is of the nature of consciousness, then why should the mental states of pleasure and the like be not regarded as self-luminous ? Besides, if the self were self-luminous by its very nature, then it would never cease to be so, and it would manifest itself even in dreamless sleep. But, in fact, the self is not manifested in deep sleep. How, then, can it be regarded as self-luminous?

It may be urged that the self is manifested even in dreamless sleep, the self with its natural bliss. Otherwise, on waking from sleep we cannot have the recollection that we slept well. What, then, is the difference between dreamless sleep and waking consciousness? The Vedantist urges that in dreamless sleep the self alone is manifested, neither the organism, nor the sense-organs, nor external objects, but in waking consciousness all these are manifested, while in dream-consciousness only the self and the mind are manifested.

But the Bhatta points out that this is contradicted by our experience. On waking from sleep we have a consciousness that we apprehended nothing during deep sleep. So it cannot be held that the self is manifested in dreamless sleep. On waking from sleep we have a consciousness that we slept well, not because the self is manifested with its essential bliss in dreamless sleep, but because of the absence of pain at the time. Hence the self cannot be regarded as self-luminous, as Samkara holds, but it must be regarded as the object of internal perception or self-consciousness (*manasapratyaksagamya evayam*).

**The Prabhakara Mimamsaka**

According to Prabhakara, consciousness is self-luminous; it manifests itself; and in manifesting itself it manifests both the self and the not-self. Neither the self nor external objects are self-luminous; both of them are manifested by consciousness which is self-luminous. The self is directly manifested by every act of cognition, presentative or representative. There can be no consciousness of an object apart from the consciousness of the self; every act of cognition is appropriated by the self; all experience is the self's experience. In every act of cognition there is a triple consciousness, a consciousness of the self (*ahamvitti*), a consciousness of an object (*visayavitti*), and self-conscious awareness (*svasamvitti*). Thus in every act of cognition there is a direct and immediate knowledge of the self, not as an object of knowledge, but as the knowing subject; the self can never be known as an object of knowledge. But though there is always a direct and immediate knowledge of the self in every act of cognition, there is not always a direct and immediate knowledge of the not-self or an external object. An object is not directly presented to consciousness in recollection and inference.

But though an object is indirectly revealed to consciousness in representative and inferential cognitions, all experience, be it presentative or representative, perceptual or inferential, is directly and immediately presented to consciousness. In other words, though in indirect knowledge its object is not directly presented to consciousness, yet the indirect knowledge itself is directly presented to consciousness. And because there is a direct and immediate knowledge of every act of cognition, be it immediate or mediate, there is also a direct and immediate knowledge of the self in every act of cognition, immediate or mediate. Thus every act of cognition directly reveals the self in directly revealing itself. But we must not suppose that this cognition requires another cognition for its direct and immediate presentation to consciousness; it is self-luminous; it directly reveals itself. There is no regressus ad infinitum in the consciousness of experience. According to Prabhakara, consciousness is self-luminous; it manifests itself; there is no consciousness of consciousness as the Naiyayika supposes; consciousness is self-aware or self-manifesting; consciousness itself is self-consciousness. If there were a consciousness of consciousness, there would be a consciousness of that consciousness and so on ad infinitum.

Thus there is a difference between the apprehension of the self and that of an object. There is always a direct and immediate knowledge of the self in every act of cognition, preservative, representative, or inferential; but there is not always a direct and immediate knowledge of an object, e.g. in recollection and inference. But both the self and the not-self or an object are non-luminous, and are manifested by consciousness. Thus Prabhakara regards consciousness as an external relation between the self and the not-self.

There is also a difference between the apprehension of an object and that of a cognition; an object is sometimes directly presented to consciousness, and sometimes indirectly revealed to consciousness, but a cognition is always directly and immediately presented to consciousness.

And there is also a difference between the apprehension of the self and that of a cognition. There is a direct and immediate knowledge both of the self and the cognition. But the self is apprehended by a cognition as its knowing subject, but the cognition is not apprehended by any other cognition, it apprehends itself. Thus both the self and the not-self are non-luminous as they are manifested by consciousness. But consciousness itself is self-luminous as it manifests itself. Without consciousness neither the object nor the self can be manifested. In dreamless sleep there is no consciousness; so neither the self nor any object is manifested in deep sleep. It cannot be said that the self does not exist in deep sleep, for, in that case, there would be no recognition of personal identity on waking from sleep. If the self were self-luminous, as the Vedantist holds, then it would be manifested in deep sleep. But since it is not manifested in deep sleep, it must be regarded as non-luminous. But consciousness is self-luminous, it is not manifested in deep sleep because it does not exist at that time.

**Prabhakara's Criticism of Samkara's View**

Prabhakara rejects the Vedantist doctrine of the self-luminous self for the following reasons : Firstly, the self is not manifested in deep sleep, though it exists as pure ease at that time. Secondly, all the phenomena of our experience can be explained by the theory of self-luminous consciousness and, therefore, it is needless to assume that self-luminosity of the self. Thirdly, the self is not of the nature of consciousness.

**Prabhakara's Criticism of Kumarila's View**

According to Kumarila, the self is as much an object of perception as an external object. An external object is perceived by external perception, but the self is perceived by internal perception. There is no contradiction in the self being both the subject of knowledge and the object of knowledge; for the self is a conscious substance, and as conscious it is the subject of consciousness, and as a substance it is the object of consciousness, the element of substance in the self is the known object and the element of consciousness in the self is the knowing subject.

Prabhakara urges that this view is untenable. What Kumarila calls the substantial element in the self is unconscious, and so cannot be a self at all. Thus there remains only the conscious element; and if this conscious element is the object of knowledge, then the self becomes the knowing subject and the known object at the same time, and thus Kumarila cannot avoid self-contradiction. Nor can it be said that the conscious element in the self is capable of undergoing a change so as to have simultaneously the character of the knowing subject and the known object, because the self is not made up of parts and so cannot undergo any change. Therefore, it must be held that the self is immediately known not as the object of consciousness as Kumarila holds, but as the knowing subject or substrate of consciousness.

Prabhakara rejects Kumarila's theory on the following grounds:

Firstly, the self is always the knower; it can never be an object of knowledge. It is self-contradictory to suppose that the self can be both the subject and the object of the same act of knowledge.

Secondly, as the self is directly revealed in every cognition of an object as its cognizer, it is needless to assume another cognition, viz. internal perception which should directly reveal the self as its object.

Prabhakara's view may briefly be compared with that of the Buddhist idealist According to both of them, consciousness is self-luminous. But according to the Buddhist idealist, consciousness alone is real, which is polarized into the subject and the object, though in reality there is neither the subject nor the object. But according to Prabhakara, both the subject and the object are real and are manifested by consciousness which is self-luminous.

**The Jaina**

The Jaina holds with Prabhakara that a cognition is always appropriated by the self, and it reveals itself, the self, and its object; every act of cognition cognizes itself, the cognizing subject and the cognized object. But he differs from Prabhakara's view that consciousness alone is self-luminous, which reveals the cognizing subject and the cognized object, which are equally non-luminous. The Jaina does not regard the self as non-luminous. According to him, in the cognition "I know the jar through my self" it is not the cognition of the jar that reveals the self and the jar, as Prabhakara holds, but it is the self which reveals itself through itself, the jar, and the cognition of the jar. In this cognition the cognizer, "I" or the self, the instrument "myself" and the result "knowing" are as much objects of perception as the cognized object, e.g. the jar. In this cognition I am directly conscious of myself as qualified by the cognition of the jar , hence myself is as much an object of perception as the jar and the cognition of the jar. Just as we cannot deny the perception of the cognition and the object so we cannot deny the perception of the cognizing subject. The cognition and the cognizing self are directly revealed in our experience. Hence they cannot but be regarded as objects of consciousness. For whatever is revealed in our experience is cognized, and whatever is cognized is an object of consciousness. It is self-contradictory to suppose that the self and its cognition are not objects of perception, though they are directly revealed in our experience.

The Jaina holds that the self is an object of internal perception. When I feel that "I am happy", or "I am unhappy", I have a distinct and immediate apprehension of the self as an object of internal perception. But how can it be an object of direct and immediate apprehension or perception, though it nas no form at all? The Jaina replies that just as pleasure can be perceived though it is without any form, so the self also can be perceived though it is without any form. When pleasure is perceived it is not perceived apart from the self. It is perceived always as belonging to the self. Pleasure is never perceived as "this is pleasure" just as a jar is perceived as "this is a jar". Pleasure is always perceived as "I am pleased", or "I have pleasure". Hence the perception of pleasure in the form "I am pleased" not only reveals pleasure but also the self. Thus the self is an object of internal perception. This is another point of difference between the Jaina and Prabhakara. Prabhakara holds that the self is always perceived as the subject of external perception or object-cognition; it can never be perceived as an object of internal perception. The Jaina holds that the self is manifested both by external perception and by internal perception.

**The Upanisads**

The *Upanisads* identify the self with the Absolute, the Atman with Brahman. The *Atman* is not an object of knowledge. In the *Upanisads* we do not find clear-cut arguments for this doctrine. But we find certain passages in them, which may be regarded as symbolical expressions of the following arguments.

Firstly, the Atman is absolutely unconditioned. It has no qualities or attributes. It is devoid of sound, devoid of touch, devoid of colour, devoid of taste, and devoid of smell. It is devoid of all sensible qualities, So it cannot be perceived through the external sense-organs. It is devoid of pleasure, pain, and the like. So it cannot be perceived through the internal organ or manas. It is undefinable by speech, and unattainable by the outer or inner senses.

Secondly, the Atman is beyond the categories of space, time, and causality. It contains space but is not spatial; it contains time but is not temporal; it contains causality, but is not subject to the law of causality. It is spaceless, timeless, and causeless. It is the ultimate reality. It is the phenomenon. It is beyond the categories of the phenomenal world. So it cannot be comprehended by the intellect which can know only phenomena bound by space, time, and causality.

The intellect can give only categorized knowledge. The Atman is beyond all categories. So it is beyond the grasp of the intellect.

Thirdly, the Atman is the knower of all things and as such cannot be known by anything. How can the knower be known? How can you see the seer of seeing? How can you hear the hearer of hearing? How can you know him through the mind, which impels the mind to know? How can you comprehend him through the intellect, which makes the intellect comprehend? The Atman is the seer but is not seen; it is the hearer but is not heard, it is the comprehender but is not comprehended; it is the thinker but is not thought. The Atman is the witness (*saksin*) the seer (*paridrastr*), the knower (*vijnatr*)? And the knower can never be known. The subject can never be an object of knowledge, Deussen says : "The Atman as the knowing subject can never become an object for us, and is therefore itself unknowable." Ranade says : "The Atman is unknowable because He is the Eternal Subject who knows. How could the Eternal Knower been object of knowledge?"

Fourthly, the Atman is all-comprehending. It comprehends all relations. It can never be a term of any relation. It embraces the distinction of subject and object, knower and known. How, then, can it be an object of knowledge? The distinction of subject and object is within it, it is not subject to the distinction. It is non-dual. It is one. It is infinite (*bhuma*). In it one cannot see any other thing, one cannot hear any other thing, one cannot comprehend any other thing. Where there is duality in appearance, there one smells the other, one sees the other, one hears the other, one addresses the other, one comprehends the other, and one knows the other. But where there is no duality, where everything is realized as the Atman, how should one smell, see, hear, address, comprehend, and know the other? The Atman is the one, infinite reality. It is beyond duality. It is beyond distinction. So it cannot be an object of knowledge. "The supreme Atman," says Deussen, "is unknowable, because it is the all-comprehending unity, whereas all knowledge presupposes a duality of subject and object." This conception of the Atman as beyond the distinction of subject and object is higher than the conception of the Atman as the Eternal Knower or Subject. And this conception we find in Samkara's system.

Lastly, though the *Upanisads* make the Atman absolutely

unknowable as the unconditional Brahman, they do not make it so as the inner self (*pratyagatmari*) of man. The Atman which is hidden in the heart of man (*gahvarestha*) as the inner self is apprehended by ecstatic intuition (*adhyatmayoga*)? God created the sense-organs in such a way that they always turn outwards to external objects : they can never turn inwards to apprehend the inner self. So we cannot perceive the inner self through the sense-organs. But some men can perceive it by withdrawing their senses from the external objects and concentrating their minds on the inner self (*prulyagatman*) The inner self hidden in all creatures cannot be comprehended by the gross or unrefined intellect. It can be perceived only by yogis or subtle seers (*Suksmadarsibhih*) through their subtle one-pointed intellect or intuition. The Atman can be realized by one in meditation through the pure, enlightened heart, where there is the illumination of spiritual vision. The Atman can be realized only by supra-intellectual Intuition (*frajnana*). Thus the inner self of man is inaccessible to the outer and inner senses, the manas and the *buddhi*. It is only an object of higher intuition which is above intellect.

**The Samkara-fedantist: The Self and Consciousness**

Samkara develops the Upanisadic conception of the Atman and regards it as the universal light of consciousness. Ramanuja holds that consciousness is a substance (*dravya*), and still it may be regarded as a property of the self even as a ray of light, though a substance, is regarded as a property of the lamp. The Naiyayika, Vaisesika, and Prabhakara hold that consciousness is a quality (*guna*) of the self. Kumarila holds that consciousness is an action (*karma*) of the self because it is the result of its cognitive activity (*jnanakarma*) and the cognitive activity and its result, viz. consciousness, should be regarded as one. The Samkhya, on the other hand, holds that consciousness constitutes the very essence (*svarupa*) of the self and is not its quality or action.

Samkara also holds with the Samkhya that consciousness is neither a substance, nor a quality, nor an action of the self : it is the very nature of the self. The self is mere consciousness. It is not a substance to which consciousness belongs either as a quality or an action. Though there is no difference between the self and consciousness, yet we draw a distinction between the two, and speak of "consciousness" when we wish to emphasize the relation of the self to objects, and we speak of the "self" simply when we do not want to emphasize that relation. In fact, the self and consciousness are one. The self is of the nature of eternal consciousness.

**Samkara and Prabhakara**

Prabhakara holds that consciousness is self-luminous, but the self which is the substrate of consciousness is not self-luminous. Samkara, on the other hand, holds that the self is nothing but consciousness, and as such it is self-luminous. Prabhakara holds that the self is always known as an ego or a knower; it is identical with the ego. But Samkara holds that the self is the eternal light of consciousness beyond the distinction of ego and non-ego. The self cannot be identical with the ego. It it were so, it would be known as an ego even in dreamless sleep. But, as a matter of fact, there is no such consciousness in dreamless sleep, though all admit that the self persists at that time.

Prabhakara argues that there is no "I"—consciousness in dreamless sleep, because, at that time, there is no consciousness of objects, and there can be no "I"—consciousness apart from object consciousness. But the Samkarite asks : In dreamless sleep is there the absence of pure consciousness ? Or is there the absence of empirical consciousness which depends on the affection of the self by objects ? The first alternative is impossible since pure consciousness is eternal and so can never be suspended. The second alternative also is excluded, since the consciousness of the self does not depend on the affection of the self by objects. So the Samkarite holds that the self is not identical with the ego, and it is not manifested as an ego in dreamless sleep because it remains in that state as pure self-luminous consciousness above the distinction of ego and non-ego. "When a man, on waking from dreamless sleep, reflects 'I slept well', he transfers the character which belongs to all waking cognition to the state of deep sleep in which the self, freed for the time from all shackles of egoity was abiding in its own blissful nature and associated only with general non-particularized nescience, not with any of its special modifications." In dreamless sleep egoism (*ahamtara*) is resolved into general nescience (*avidya*); at the time of waking it is formed again out of nescience. So in waking life there is ego-consciousness, but in dreamless sleep there is none. Thus amkara differs from Prabhakara in his conception of the self. According to

Prabhakara, the self is identical with the ego; egoism constitutes the essence of the self-consciousness is a permanent characteristic of the self; in all cognitions of objects the self is revealed as the subject of knowledge or ego. According to Samkara, on the other hand, the self is consciousness, pure and simple; it is neither the substrate of consciousness nor the subject of consciousness; it is neither a conscious substance nor a conscious subject or ego. The self is the pure light of consciousness which is self-luminous; it is above the distinction of ego and non-ego, subject and object. But though the self is pure self-luminous consciousness, it appears as an ego when it is determined by the limiting condition of the internal organ (*antahkarana*) modified into egoism (*ahamkara*) and cannot distinguish its pure essence from its phenomenal appearance as an ego.

Thus egoism does not constitute the essence of the self, as Prabhakara holds, but it is a modification of the internal organ (*antahkarana*) which is an evolute of nescience. Egoism is an adventitious mark of the self, which is superimposed on it by nescience. The self which is one, eternal, changeless consciousness can neither be a knower (*jnatr*) nor an agent (*kartr*), nor an enjoyer (*bhoktr*), since these imply agency, activity, and change which cannot belong to the changeless and eternal self. These are phenomenal appearances of the self superimposed on it by nescience.

**Jiva and Atman**

Samkara draws a distinction between the Jiva and the Atman. The *Atman* is the eternal light of consciousness. The Jiva is the eternal consciousness as limited by the organism, sense-organs, manas, and *ahamkara*. The Atman is the pure consciousness which is the presupposition of all experience; it is presupposed by experience of all objects, and as such is entirely non-objective. But the Jiva is both subject and object, knower and known, ego and non-ego. It is both the and the me. The Atman is never an object of consciousness. The Jiva is an object of self-consciousness (*asmatpratyaya*). The Atman becomes an object of self-consciousness when it loses its purity and is determined by the limiting conditions of body, sense-organs and the like. When it is freed from all these fetters it is not an object of self-consciousness. The Atman as the inner self (*pratyagatman*) is apprehended by immediate intuition.

## Samkara's View of Atmapratyaksa

Samkara says that even as fire cannot burn itself so the Atman cannot know itself. The Atman is not of the nature of an object; so it can never be an object of knowledge. The Atman cannot be perceived through the sense-organs, since it is the witness of all perceptible objects. It is not an object of mental perception or intellectual comprehension. The Atman cannot be an object of its own apprehension, since being without parts it cannot be split up into the knowing subject (*jnattr*) and the known object (*jneya*) at the same time. But though it can never be an object of empirical knowledge, it can be apprehended by higher intuition. The yogis have a vision of the Atman, which is undefinable and beyond all phenomenal appearances by meditation (*samradhana*). Meditation consists in devotion, concentration of mind and ecstatic intuition. Govindananda says, " The Atman can be realized by intuition."

## The Later Samkarites' View of Atmapratyaksa

Vacaspati discusses this question in *Bhamati*. He holds that the inner self (*pratyagatman*) is an object of higher intuition, but the Jiva or the individual soul, which is its phenomenal appearance, is an object of self-consciousness (*ahampratyaya*). The inner self (*pratyagatman*) is self-luminous, non-objective, and partless; still when it is determined by the gross body, subtle body, sense-organs, manas, and (*buddhi*) which are the products of beginningless undefinable *avidya* though unlimited, it appears as limited, though single, it appears as multiple, though inactive, it appears as active, though not an enjoyer, it appears as an enjoyer, though not an object of consciousness, it appears as an object of self-consciousness, and is manifested to us in the condition of a jiva. The Atman is unlimited. But when it is limited by *buddhi* and other conditions, and cannot distinguish itself from these limiting conditions, it appears as a jiva. And this jiva is a knower (*jndtr*) a doer (*kartr*) and enjoyer (*bhoktr*). It is of a composite character. It is the self and the not-self, the subject and the object, the knower and the known. As pure consciousness (*cidatma*) it is self-luminous, and not an object of self-consciousness. But as conditioned by the limiting adjuncts of buddhi and the like, it is an object of self-consciousness. Though the jiva is non-different from the Atman, it is entangled in empirical life as limited by certain conditions.

The active agent, which is the object of self-consciousness, is the *jivatman*, which is determined by the aggregate of limiting conditions. The *paramatman*, which is the witness of this empirical self, is not an object of self-consciousness. Self-consciousness (*ahampratyaya*) is a mental mode which is unconscious. And this unconscious mental mode can never manifest the Atman. It is the Atman that manifests the mental mode of self-consciousness. It is the presupposition of all experience, and so can never be an object of experience. It is the presupposition of self-consciousness, and so can never be an object of self-consciousness.

Vacaspati holds that the inner self is of the nature of pure consciousness and as such manifests all things, but is not manifested by any other thing. Still we must admit that it is apprehended by immediate intuition. Otherwise all things would be unmanifested to us, since they are manifested by the inner self, and this would lead to utter ignorance of the whole universe. Anandagiri holds that the Atman is self-luminous, and the not-self (*anatman*) is the object of its consciousness. The Atman, which is of the nature of consciousness, is manifested as the witness (*saksin*). It cannot be said that the Atman is not at all an object of consciousness like the void. Though it is not an object of self-consciousness (*asmatpratyaya*), it is apprehended by immediate intuition.

Govindananda holds that what is apprehended by self-consciousness is the active agent or Jiva. But how can the Jiva be the knowing subject and the known object at the same time ? Apyayadiksita holds that the Jiva as determined by the mental modes of pleasure, pain, and the like is the object of self-consciousness, and as determined by *antahkarana* is the knowing subject. So there is no contradiction here.

Padmapada raises the question of contradiction in the apprehension of the Atman by itself. The Atman is the self (*visayin*); the object is the not-self (*visaya*). There is an essential difference between the two. The Atman is of the nature of consciousness. The object is unconscious. The Atman is internal (*pratyak*) but the object is external (*parak*). Consciousness is directed inward to the self, but it is directed outward to the object. The object is of the nature of this (*idam*), but the Atman is of the nature of not-this (*anidam*). The object is the common property of everybody's experience. The Atman is not a property of anyone's experience. How can the single, impartible Atman break up into two such contradictory parts as the knowing subject and the known object ? Padmapada answers that the Atman is not an object of self-consciousness; egoism (*ahamkara*) which is of a dual character of subject and object is the object of self-consciousness.

Prakasatman elaborates the view of Padmapada. He says that the Atman cannot be the knowing subject and the known object because they are of contradictory characters. The light of the sun is self-luminous; it illumines all things, but is not illumined by any other thing. But its reflection in the mirror is illumined by the light of the sun. Likewise, the Atman is the universal light of consciousness. It is self-luminous. It manifests all objects, but is not manifested by any other object. But its reflection in *ahamkara* is manifested by the *Atman* through the mental mode of selfconsciousness. So the Atman is not the object of self-consciousness. It is *ahamkara* (egoism) or the *antahkarana* superimposed on the Atman that is the object of self-consciousness.

Vidyaranya also holds that the Atman cannot be apprehended by itself because it does not possess the dual character of subject and object. But *ahamkara* is of a dual character. Even as a piece of iron modified by contact with fire appears to have the dual character of iron and fire, so the *antahkarana* being superimposed on the *Atman* which is reflected in it in the form of *ahamkara* appears to have the dual character of subject and object. *Ahamkara* is of a composite character. It is, as it were, a mixture of the self and the not-self. It is the *antahkarana* superimposed on the Atman, or the *Atman* as reflected in, and determined by, the *antahkarana*. The Atman which is the presupposition of all experience of objects is the conscious and non-objective element, and the *antahkarana* which is superimposed on the self and is impregnated with the reflection of the self is the unconscious and objective element in *ahamkara*. So *ahamkara* is the object of self-consciousness.

Anantakrsna Sastri gives a similar account of the Samkarite view of *Atma-pratyaksa* in his lucid and elaborate introduction to *Vedantaparibhasa*, In the cognition "I am conscious", "I" does not stand for the Atman but for egoism (*ahamkara*) with which it is erroneously identified. In self-consciousness (*ahampratyaya*) the Atman as reflected in egoism (*ahamkara*) is manifested. Ramanuja objects that if the Atman is not the ego (*aham*) or "I", it cannot be the inner self or the seer. The Samkarite urges that the object of self-consciousness is the Atman as determined by egoism, and the subject of self-consciousness is the universal consciousness as conditioned by egoism. Egoism enters as a constituent element into the object-self, but not into the subject-self, of which it is only a limiting adjunct.

Universal consciousness is the ultimate reality. It is subject-objectless. It is beyond the distinction of subject and object. It has really neither subject (*nirasraya*) nor object (*nirvisaya*). The pure light of universal consciousness appears as the knowing subject owing to nescience when it is determined by egoism (*ahamkara*). *Ahamkara* is material; it can never be the knower, since it is unconscious. The Jiva is the knower, and the jiva is the Atman as conditioned by ahamkara. Though *ahamkara* is material and unconscious, it can be the knower when the Atman is reflected in it owing to its proximity to the Atman. The universal consciousness as reflected in *ahamkara* is the Jiva which is the knower and the doer. Neither *ahamkara* in itself nor the Atman in itself is the knower. But the Atman as reflected in *ahamkara* and conditioned by it is the knower. Owing to the reflection of the Atman in *ahamkara* there is an erroneous identification of it with *ahamkara*. The Atman which is above the distinction of ego and non-ego appears as the ego. In itself it is not the ego. In deep sleep the Atman persists as the seer or witness, not as the knower because *ahamkara* is resolved at that time.

The author of *Pancadasi* holds that the Atman is neither perceptible nor imperceptible. It is the subject (*visayin*); so it can never be the object of perception (*visaya*). But though it is not an object of sense-perception, it is apprehended by immediate intuition. Ramakrsna holds that the Atman is self-luminous without being an object of cognition like cognition, since it is realized by higher intuition. It cannot be the subject and the object at the same time. So it can never be an object (*karma*) of cognition. If it is argued that the Atman, in its pure essence, is the subject (*kartr*) and as determined by a mental mode is the object (*karma*), it may as well be argued that a person in his essential nature is the subject of going, and as determined by the act of going is the object of going, which is absurd. So Ramakrsna concludes that the Atman can never be an object (*karma*) of cognition.

Citsukha also holds a similar view. The Atman cannot be an object of cognition. If it were so, it would be the subject and the object of the same act of cognition, which is self-contradictory. It cannot be argued that the Atman in itself is the subject and as determined by the mental modes of pleasure, pain, and the like is the object. In that case, the same person would be the subject as well as the object of going, which is absurd. So Citsukha holds that the Atman is self-luminous without being an object of cognition.

The Samkarite position may be thus briefly summed up. The self cannot be an object of introspection (*manasa-pratyaksa*) or self-consciousness (*aham-pratyaya*) as Kumarila holds, for, in that case, it would become a not-self as unconscious as an external object; nor can it be perceived as the ego as opposed to the non-ego, or the subject of all knowledge of objects, as Prabhakara holds, because the ego is the phenomenal appearance of the self, being really a modification of the internal organ (*antahkarana*) which is an evolute of nescience. The self which is the one, eternal light of consciousness, above the distinction of ego and non-ego subject and object can be known only by an immediate and intuitive consciousness.

Though the knower (*drastr*), the known (*drsya*) and knowledge or consciousness (*drsi*) are apprehended by all as undoubted, still the subject of consciousness or the knower (*drastr*) and the object of consciousness or the known (*drsya*) depend upon consciousness (*drsi*) for their reality. Hence, consciousness alone has ultimate reality, and the knower and the known, the ego and the non-ego, have empirical reality only. Consciousness, again, is of two kinds : unconditional (*nirupadhika*) and conditional (*sopadhika*). Unconditional consciousness is both subjectless (*nirasraya*) and objectless (*nirvisaya*) : it is identical with Being (*sanmatrarupa*) : it does not depend upon anything else to realize its existence. It is called Brahman. Conditional consciousness, on the other hand, has a subject (*sasraya*) as well as an object (*savisaya*) and depends on perception, inference, and the like. As it depends upon the subject and the object it has only an empirical reality. It is manifested by the *antahkarana* (internal organ). It consists in the function (*vrtti*) of the *antahkarana*. Hence, subjecthood or egoity (*jnatrtva*) must belong to the *antahkarana* or the Jiva (the individual self) which is conditioned by the *antahkarana*. It cannot belong to the pure self. The pure self is of the essence of consciousness. It cannot be the knower, subject, or ego. Egoity belongs to *ahamkara* which is a modification of *avidya*. Selfhood (*atmatva*) is falsely attributed to *ahamkara*, which is entirely different from the self. So, unconditional consciousness, which is above the distinction of ego and non-ego, constitutes the essence of the self. It can be known only by an immediate intuition.

Ramanuja holds with Samkara that consciousness constitutes the essence of the self. But he differs from Samkara in holding that the self is not mere consciousness but also the subject of consciousness : even as a lamp itself is of the nature of light, and still light is its property, so the self itself is of the nature of consciousness, and still consciousness is a property of the self. According to Ramanuja, there can be no consciousness without a self, just as there can be no light without a lamp; just as the lamp is nothing but light, but still light is referred to the lamp, so the self is nothing but consciousness, but still consciousness is referred to the unity of the self. Thus the self, according to Ramanuja, is not mere consciousness, but the subject of consciousness or the ego; the ego is not a phenomenal appearance of the self when it is determined by the limiting condition of *ahamkara* (egoism), a modification of *antahkarana* (internal organ) which is a particular form of nescience (*avidya*); but the ego is identical with the self and constitutes its very essence.

Samkara holds that just as the idea of silver is illusorily superimposed upon a nacre, so egoity is illusorily superimposed upon the self which is really beyond the distinction of ego and non-ego. But if egoity is nothing but an illusory superimposition of nescience upon the self, then there would be a non-discrimination of the ego from pure consciousness or the self, and there would be such a consciousness as "I am consciousness", and not as "I am conscious". But, as a matter of fact, we always have such an experience as "I am conscious"; this undeniable fact of experience clearly shows that the self is the subject of consciousness. You cannot divide this single indivisible consciousness into two parts and hold that the element of "I" is illusory and the element of consciousness is real "I"ness or egoity is an illusory superimposition of nescience, and consciousness alone is a real ontological verity.

Samkara has argued that by the ego we mean the agent (*kartr*) of cognition (*jnana*) and this agency of knowledge cannot be regarded as an attribute of the self which is changeless and eternal. Hence, egoity or the character of a knower which involves an action and consequently change, is not a property of the unchanging and eternal self, but of the unconscious *antahkarana* (internal organ) which is modified into egoism (*ahamkara*). Ramanuja contends that egoity or the character of a knower cannot be the property of an unconscious object, viz. the *antahkarana* (internal organ), but it is the distinctive character of a conscious being, viz. the self. Moreover, the ego or a knower does not involve any change; the ego is the subject of knowledge; a knower is not necessarily an active, energizing, and changing principle. According to Ramanuja, the self is eternal, and the natural consciousness of the self is eternal; but though the consciousness of the self is eternal, it is subject to contraction and expansion, which are not natural properties of the self, but its mere accidents due to the *karma* of the person in the cycle of his mundane existence. The self, in its pure essence, is unchanging. But though changeless, it is a knower or an ego. The agency of knowledge cannot belong to the unconscious organ of egoity (*ahamkara*). How can the unconscious *ahamkara,* which is a modification of the antahkarana become a conscious knower?

It may be argued that the unconscious organ of egoity (*ahamkara*) may appear as a conscious knower (*jnatr*) because of the reflection of consciousness in it owing to its proximity to consciousness or the self. But this argument is quite unsound. What is the meaning of the "reflection of consciousness"? Does it mean the reflection of *ahamkara* on consciousness ? Or does it mean the reflection of consciousness on the unconscious *ahamkara* ? The first alternative is impossible, since Samkara does not admit at all that consciousness in itself, or the self, is a knower. Nor can consciousness be reflected upon the unconscious *ahamkara* since that which is unconscious can never be a knower.

Samkara holds that the self exists in deep sleep as the witness (*saksin*) of the general non-particularized nescience (*avidya*) when the organ of egoity (*ahamkara*) is dissolved. But Ramanuja asks : What is the meaning of a *saksin*? By a *saksin* we mean that which directly and immediately knows an object; and hence that which does not know an object cannot be called a *saksin;* mere consciousness is never regarded as a *saksin;* a *saksin* is nothing but a knower or an ego. Egoity is not an adventitious property of the self, so that when this property is destroyed, the self may remain in its own essential condition as the pure light of consciousness which is above the distinction of ego and non-ego; but egoity constitutes the essence of the self; the ego is identical with the self and the self is identical with the ego. And this egoity of the self persists even in dreamless sleep, but there is no clear and distinct consciousness of this egoity at that time, as it is overpowered by *tamas* (ignorance), and as there is no consciousness of external objects at that time. If it did not persist in deep sleep, we could never remember that we slept well on waking from sleep. And even when the self is released from the fetters of mundane existence, it does not realize itself as pure consciousness but as an ego. The self is always manifested as an ego, and never as mere consciousness above the distinction of ego and non ego. Ramanuja's conception of the self as an ego agrees, to a great extent, with Prabhakara's view of the self, the only difference being that according to the latter, consciousness does not constitute the essence of the self, as Ramanuja holds with Samkara, but it is a quality of the self which is its substrate. Venkatanatha holds that the self is an object of self-consciousness but the self, in its pure essence, is clearly apprehended by yogic intuition.

**Comparison of the Different Views**

The Carvaka identifies the self either with the gross body, or with the sense-organs, or with the life-force, or with the mind. He cannot proceed any further. His conception of the self is that of "the material self" of James, since even mind is material, and thought is a function of matter. He cannot rise above "the sensitive and appetitive self" of Ward. Sadananda speaks of some philosophers who identify the self with the sons, i.e. near and dear ones. Their conception of the self is that of "the social self" of James. The Buddhist idealist, like James, identifies the self with the stream of consciousness without any core of substantiality. He regards the self as a psychic continuum. He cannot rise above the psychological *Me.* His conception of the self is purely empirical. Like James, he does not recognize the transcendental or pure self.

The Naiyayika, however, recognizes the self as a permanent substance endowed with the qualities of cognition, pleasure, pain, desire, aversion, and effort. Some older Naiyayikas hold that the self is an object of inference. It is inferred from its qualities as their substratum. It cannot be perceived because it cannot be the subject and the object of the same act of knowledge. It cannot be the percipient and the perceived at the same time. The Naiyayika rises above the psychological *Me* or the empirical self to the conception of the pure self or *I*. He conceives the pure self as the substratum of the empirical self or the stream of cognitions, affections, and conations. These psychoses are the qualities of the pure self. They inhere in it. They have no existence apart from it. There is an inseparable relation between the two. But they cannot be identified with each other. A substance cannot be identified with its qualities. "To identify *I* and *Me*" says Dr. Ward, "is logically impossible., for, example termmorum, it is to identify subject and object." Again he says, "the *I* cannot be the *Me* nor the *Me* the *I*. At the same time the objective *Me* is impossible without the subjective *I*." Some earlier Naiyayikas hold that the self cannot be perceived because the subject can never become the object. But this position is not satisfactory. We cannot be deprived all together of the perception of the self, which thinks, feels, and wills. Hence, the Vaisesika holds that the self is not an object of ordinary perception, but it is an object of yogic perception or higher intuition.

The Samkhya also holds with some Naiyayikas that the self is an object of inference. But, according to him, the self can be inferred from its reflection (*pratibimba*) in *buddhi* as its original (*bimbo*). The Samkhya dualism of *Purusa* and *Prakrti, Drastr* (the seer) and *Drsya* (seen), the self and the not-self makes the perception of the self impossible. The self is only the seer; it can never be seen; it can never turn back upon itself and perceive it. If it is ever perceived as the object, it will cease to be the subject. But the Patanjala, like the Vaisesika, holds that the self can be perceived by higher intuition (*pratibha jnana*). But how can the same self be subject and object at the same time ? The Patanjala holds that the self in its essence, or the pure self, is the subject, and the self as reflected in *buddhi*, or the empirical self, is the object. The pure self intuits itself through its reflection in *buddhi* or the empirical self; it cannot make itself an object of direct intuition. Thus the Patanjala agrees with the Vaisesika's view that the self can be perceived only by the yogis. But there is a difference between them. The Patanjala holds that even in yogic intuition the pure self is the subject, and the empirical self, or the self as reflected in *buddhi*, is the object. The Vaisesika, on the other hand, holds that the self in itself, or the pure self, apart from its cognitions, feelings, and conations, which constitute the empirical self, is the object of yogic intuition. For, unlike the Patanjala, the Vaisesika does not set up an antagonism between the pure self and the empirical self and consider the former as a conscious subject and the latter as an unconscious object.

But if the self can be an object of yogic perception, why should it not be an object of ordinary perception ? Can we not distinguish between the minimal perception of the self and the maximal perception of the self, and hold that we have the former in ordinary perception, and the latter in yogic perception? Can we not have even a glimpse of the self in ordinary perception? The Neo-Naiyayika holds that the self is an object of ordinary perception. It is perceived only through the mind in relation to its qualities. The older Naiyayika holds that the self is inferred from its qualities, while the neo-Naiyayika holds that the self is perceived together with its qualities.

The Bhatta agrees with the neo-Naiyayika that the self is an object of introspection or internal perception (*manasapratyaksa*). He does not hold with Prabhakara that every act of cognition is appropriated by the self and all consciousness involves self-consciousness. There is a distinction between consciousness and self-consciousness. The Bhatta holds that only when an object is known and appropriated by the self the self is known as an object of internal perception or self-consciousness. Prabhakara, on the other hand, holds that every act of cognition apprehends itself, the cognizing subject and the cognized object. Self-consciousness is not a higher degree of consciousness. All consciousness is self-consciousness. Object-consciousness and self-consciousness always go together. There is no self-consciousness apart from object consciousness. The self is always perceived as the subject of object-consciousness. Psychologically it is more reasonable to hold that the self is an object of self-consciousness than to hold that it is always the subject of object-consciousness.

The Jaina agrees with Prabhakara in holding that in every cognition of an object there is the cognition of the self, the object, and itself; every cognition is appropriated by the self. But he differs from Prabhakara in holding that it is the self that perceives itself through itself together with the object and the cognition of the object, and also that the self is an object of internal perception such as "I am happy", "I am unhappy" etc. But how can the subject be perceived as an object? The Jaina replies that whatever is directly and immediately experienced is the object of perception. But still the difficulty remains. How can the subject become an object? How can the knower become the known? "The whole difficulty," says Kant, "lies in this, how a subject can internally intuit itself." Dr. Ward holds that the pure self is always immanent in experience in the sense that experience without an experient is unintelligible. But it is transcendent in the sense that it can never be a direct object of its own experience. So there is no difficulty in maintaining that the pure subject is immanent in experience and yet it is never a direct object of experience. In this sense, Prabhakara's view is right.

Samkara avoids all these difficulties by conceiving the self as pure consciousness above the distinction of subject and object. He puts pure consciousness above the distinction of subject and object, while the Buddhist idealist puts the distinction of subject and object within consciousness. Hence, both of them have not to face the difficulty how the subject can become an object. But at least from the psychological point of view, this is cutting the Gordian knot. The pure self or Atman of Samkara is the Brahman or Absolute. The individual self (Jiva) of Samkara is the knower, the doer, and the enjoyer. Thus it is the subject from the individual point of view. The Jiva is an object of self-consciousness (*ahampratyaya*) but the Atman is apprehended by immediate intuition. According to the *Upanisads*, the Atman is beyond the grasp of the senses, the mind, and the intellect; it is known only by higher intuition (*adhyatmayoga*).

Ramanuja holds that the self is essentially an ego or subject; egoity is not an accidental quality of the self; it constitutes the very essence of the self, and the self is always perceived as an ego or subject. It is an object of self-consciousness and is clearly apprehended by higher intuition.

# 13

# Indefinite Perceptions

## Different Kinds of Indefinite Perceptions

We have dealt with the nature and conditions of various kinds of perception. But our treatment of Indian Psychology of Perception would be inadequate without reference to the analysis of the various kinds of erroneous perceptions. Prasastapada divides knowledge into two kinds : (1) True knowledge (*vidya*) and (2) erroneous knowledge (*avidya*). He subdivides the former into four kinds : (1) perception, (2) inference, (3) recollection, and (4) higher intuition of an ascetic. He subdivides the latter also into four kinds : (i) doubt (*samsaya*), (ii) error (*viparyaya*), (iii) indefinite and indeterminate perception due to lapse of memory (*anadhyavasdya*), and (iv) dream (*svapna*). Sivadtya recognizes another kind of indefinite perception called Uha. In this chapter we shall discuss the nature of doubtful and uncertain or indefinite perceptions. In subsequent chapters of this book we shall deal with illusory perceptions, dreams, and abnormal perceptions. Three kinds of indefinite perceptions have been analysed in the Nyaya-Vaisesika literature : (1) *Samsaya* or doubtful perception; (2) *Uha* or conjecture; and (3) *Anadhyavasaya* or indefinite and indeterminate perception due to lapse of memory. Let us consider the psychological nature of these indefinite perceptions apart from their epistemological value.

**Samsaya (Doubtful Perception)**

We may have doubt with regard to perceptible objects or with regard to inferrable objects. But here we are concerned only with doubtful perception. Bhasarvajna defines doubt as uncertain knowledge (*anavadharana-jnana*). But this definition is too wide. It includes two other kinds of indefinite perception, e.g. *Uha* and *Anadhyavasaya*, Prasastapada defines doubt as uncertain knowledge of the mind wavering between two alternatives, which arises from the perception of the common qualities of two objects, the peculiar qualities of which were perceived in the past, the recollection of the peculiar qualities of both the objects, and demerit (*adharma*). Sridhara explains it in the following manner. When we perceive a tall object from a distance but do not perceive the peculiar qualities of the object, we have a doubtful perception such as, "is it a post or a man?" Here, we perceive the tallness of the object, which is common to a post and a man, but we do not perceive their distinctive features such as crookedness and cavities which are the peculiar characteristics of a post, and hands and feet which are the peculiar features of a man; but the perception of the common quality (e.g. tallness). Simultaneously revives in memory the subconscious impressions of the peculiar characters of both the objects (e.g. a post and a man) left by previous perceptions; and our minds oscillate between these two objects revived in memory, and cannot come to a definite decision whether the object of perception is a post or man, because when we are inclined to think that the object is a post we are met by the opposite characters of a man revived in memory by the perception of the common quality; and thus our minds are drawn from the one to the other by conflicting trains of ideas, and consequently come to have a doubtful perception such as "is it a post or a man?"

Thus the perception of the common quality of two objects in the same substance is the cause of a doubtful perception. But how can it be so ? Is it not destroyed when there is a reproduction of the peculiar qualities of the two objects? Sridhara contends that the perception of the common quality simultaneously revives the residua of the peculiar qualities of both the objects with which it was associated in our past experience, but it does not vanish after reinstating the ideas of the peculiar features of both the objects, it lingers in the mind, and together with the conflicting trains of ideas constitutes a complex psychosis called doubtful perception. Udayana points out that a doubtful perception arises from the perception of an object endowed with the common qualities of two objects along with the non-perception of their peculiar qualities, which brings about the recollection of the peculiar qualities of both the objects.

Thus a doubtful perception is a complex presentative representative process in which there is the perception of the common quality of two objects in the same substance together with two conflicting trains of ideas revived by the perceptions. But these conflicting trains of ideas are not integrated with the percept, they hover round the percept; sometimes the one train of ideas suggested by the percept gives rise to the apprehension of one object, and sometimes the other train of ideas suggested by the percept gives rise to the apprehension of the other object. Thus the mind oscillates between two alternatives in a doubtful perception.

Udayana points out that the state of doubt has always an unpleasant feeling tone, and we always try to avoid it. Otherwise, it would never bring about the desire to know the object of doubtful cognition more definitely. Jayanta Bhatta says that a doubtful cognition arrests all activity for the time being.

Samkaramisra defines a doubtful cognition as the knowledge of many contrary qualities in one and the same object. Annam Bhatta also defines it in the same way. Thus doubt has three characteristics: (1) There must be knowledge of several qualities, (2) the qualities must be contrary to one another; and (3) they must be apprehended in one and the same object. The definition, however, is not quite satisfactory, since it is difficult to define what is meant by contrary (*viruddha*) qualities. "There is no certain test," says Mr. Athalye, "to determine what properties are contrary to one another and what not. Roughly we may say that those which are never observed together as existing in one object are irreconcilable." Laugaksi Bhaskara defines a doubtful cognition more precisely as knowledge consisting in an alternation between various contrary qualities with regard to one and the same object. Sri Vadi Devasuri also defines it as uncertain knowledge consisting in an alternation between various extremes owing to the absence of proof or disproof. According to all these definitions, in the state of doubt the mind oscillates between more than two alternatives, while according to Prasastapada, Sridhara, Udayana, and others, the mind oscillates only between two alternatives in the state of doubt. Visvanatha distinguishes between definite knowledge (*niscaya*) and doubtful knowledge (*samsaya*). Definite knowledge (*niscaya*) consists in knowledge of the presence of an attribute in an object, which it possesses, and of the absence of an attribute in an object, which it does not possess. Doubtful knowledge (*samsaya*) consists in knowledge which has for its characteristic the presence or absence of contrary qualities in one and the same object. When we have a doubtful perception such as, "Is this a post or a man?" we have four alternatives (*koti*) : (1) "This is a post"; (2) "This is not a post", (3) "This is a man"; and (4) "This is not a man". Thus the doubtful perception has four alternatives (*catuskotika*).

In the Nyaya and Vaisesika literature the various kinds of doubt and the various causes of doubt have been discussed elaborately. But these are not so much concerned with the psychological nature of doubtful perception. So we cannot consider them here.

**Uha (Conjecture)**

Generally in a doubtful perception (*samsaya*) we have a distinct consciousness of two alternatives reproduced in memory by the perception of the common quality of two objects. But sometimes one of these alternatives is suppressed and the other is manifest, and sometimes both the alternatives are indistinct and unmanifested. Thus we have two other kinds of indefinite perceptions : Uha and Anadhyavasaya.

*Uha* or conjecture is an indefinite perception in which the mind does not oscillate between two equally distinct alternatives as in samsaya or doubtful perception described above. In *Uha* the mind is conscious of one of the alternatives, the other being suppressed. Sivaditya defines *Uha* as a doubtful or indefinite perception in which only one of the suggested alternatives is manifest to consciousness (the other being suppressed). When we perceive a tall object from a distance, in a field of corn in which posts are not generally found, but only men, we have an indefinite perception such as "That may be a tall man in the field".

Here, we perceive only the tallness of an object, but do not perceive its peculiar features; the perception of tallness which is common to a post and a man tends to reinstate in memory the two conflicting trains of ideas, e.g. those of the peculiar qualities of a post and a man. But one of these conflicting trains of ideas is suppressed by the other owing to the greater strength of its associative connection. Generally we do not find posts in fields of corn; but we very often meet with men working in fields. So when we perceive a tall object in a field from a distance, though the perception of tallness tends to revive the ideas both of a post and a man, it actually revives the idea of a man owing to the greater strength of its associative connection which suppresses the idea of a post suggested by the perception of tallness. One alternative is suppressed by the strength of the other. But though the idea of a post is suppressed by the idea of a man, it tends to come to the margin of consciousness, and colours the whole mental process and invests it with indefmiteness. Herein lies the difference between Uha or conjecture and definite perception. Thus the suppressed alternative also has a function in such an indefinite perception.

Venkatanatha gives a similar account of Uha in *Nyayaparisuddhi.* Uha is a kind of perception in which only one alternative is distinctly present to consciousness owing to repeated perception of this object in the past, the other being suppressed. In it the mind does not oscillate between two alternatives because they are not equally distinct to consciousness. Only one of them is manifest to consciousness and the other is unmanifest so that the mind tentatively accepts the former alternative. Srinivasa urges that Uha should not be regarded as having only one alternative. It has two alternatives, one of which comes up to the level of consciousness, and the other still remains below the threshold of consciousness so that one is manifest and the other is unmanifested. "Uha is not quite an indefinite cognition. It is almost definite".

**Samsaya and Uha**

In *Samsaya* both the alternatives suggested by the perception of their common quality are manifest to consciousness, both of them are above the threshold of consciousness; but the mind oscillates between these two alternatives, since it cannot perceive the peculiar qualities of the object present to a sense-organ. But in Uha only one alternative suggested by the perception of the common quality is manifest to consciousness, only one alternative is above the threshold of consciousness, it is revived by the perception of the common quality owing to its stronger association with the object and suppresses the other alternative. This alternative was very often perceived together with the object in the past; so a strong bond of association has been established between their subconscious impressions; hence, this alternative is revived in memory, which suppresses the other alternative, because it was seldom perceived together with the object in the past. Thus in Samsaya both the alternatives are manifest to consciousness, while in Uha only one alternative is manifest to consciousness, and the other is suppressed. This distinction is brought out by Venkatanatha.

Thus though Uha is an indefinite perception like Samsaya, it is more definite than the latter as here the mind tentatively accepts one alternative which is manifest to consciousness, the other being suppressed,, while in Samsaya the mind wavers between two alternatives equally manifest to consciousness and cannot accept one and reject the other.

**Anadhyavasaya (Indefinite and Indeterminate Perception)**

Sometimes an indefinite perception takes the form of which is defined by Sivaditya as an uncertain or indefinite perception of an object in which both the alternatives are unmanifested to consciousness. It is an indefinite and indeterminate perception due to lapse of memory. For example, when we perceive a tree but do not remember its name, we have an indefinite perception of the tree in the form : "What may be the name of the tree ?".

According to Sivaditya, in this perception also there are two conflicting trains of ideas suggested by the perception of a common quality, but these trains of ideas are not distinct and manifest to consciousness, as in the doubtful perception : "Is it a post or a man?" but they are indistinct or unmanifested (*analingita, aspasta*), occupying only the margin of consciousness, or the level of the subconscious; and when these marginal or subconscious ideas are brought back to the field of distinct consciousness by an effort of the mind afterwards, the mind oscillates between the two distinct trains of ideas and comes to have a doubtful perception : "Is it a mango-tree or a jack-fruit tree?" But when the conflicting trains of ideas suggested by the perception of a common quality occupy the margin of consciousness or the subconscious region, the mind is in an aching void, groping in the dark, as it were, for one of these marginal or subconscious ideas. This kind of indefinite perception is different from a doubtful perception in which both the alternatives are manifested to consciousness.

But Prasastapada and his exponents, Sridhara and Udayana, give us a slightly different account of the nature of Anadhyavasaya. Prasastapada defines Anadhyavasaya as an indefinite perception of an object, either familiar or unfamiliar, due to absent-mindedness or desire for further knowledge. For instance, when a well-known king has passed by a road, one who has not been able to observe him through inattention or absent-mindedness, has only an indefinite perception that "somebody has passed by the road" without definitely recognizing the object of perception. As regards unfamiliar objects an indefinite perception appears on account of ignorance. For instance, a Bahika, an inhabitant of the Daksa country, has an indefinite perception of a jack-fruit tree, which is unfamiliar to him. Sridhara explains it in the following manner. When a Bahika perceives a jack-fruit tree, he has many definite perceptions with regard to it, such as (1) "this exists", (2) "this is a substance", (3) "this is a modification of earth", (4) "this is a tree", (5) "this has a colour", and (6) "this has branches". He has also an indistinct perception of the generic character of the jack-fruit tree, which is common to all jack-fruit trees, and which distinguishes these from other kinds of trees. What he does not know is the only fact that this tree bears the particular name, viz. "jack-fruit tree", since he has not yet heard this name from any other person, but he has an idea that it must have a name. And such an indefinite perception devoid of the definite idea of the particular name is called Anadhyavasaya.

Venkatanatha's account of Anadhyavasaya is similar to those of Prasastapada and Sridhara. He holds that it is the apprehension of an object, the name of which is forgotten. In it the mind has a definite perception of an object but has no definite recollection of its name, though it feels that it must have a name. After definitely perceiving a tree, for instance, we are in doubt whether its name is "mango-tree", or "jack-fruit tree", and want to know its name definitely. So in Anadhyavasaya there is a doubt as to the name of an object due to lapse of memory.

Udayana differs from Prasastapada and Sridhara in his conception of Anadhyavasaya. According to him, Anadhyavasaya is an indefinite perception due to the perception of a common quality of two alternatives both of which are not distinctly apprehended. There is a distinct apprehension of one alternative, but no apprehension of the other. So Anadhyavasaya is different from Samsaya. Samsaya, or doubt, arises from the perception of the common quality of two alternatives, both of which are distinctly apprehended. In it the mind oscillates between two alternatives, both of which are distinctly present to consciousness. But in Anadhyavasaya there is no oscillation of the mind, since the two alternatives are not distinctly present to consciousness.

Udayana's conception of Anadhyavasaya resembles Sivaditya's conception of Uha. Samkaramisra defines Anadhyavasaya as the apprehension of an object as something. When a person who has never seen a camel sees it suddenly for the first time he apprehends it as something. He perceives the distinctive qualities of the camel, e.g. long neck, wide lips, etc., and so distinguishes it from a horse or an elephant. But he cannot refer it to the class of camels nor does he know its name. So Anadhyavasaya is different from Samsaya. In Samsaya the mind wavers between two conflicting alternatives such as, "Is it a post or a man?" But in Anadhyavasaya the mind does not waver between two alternatives, since they are not present to consciousness. It does not arise from the perception of the common quality of two objects, and the recollection of their distinctive qualities. It apprehends the distinctive qualities of an object. Samsaya and anadhyavasaya both are indefinite knowledge. They give rise to a desire for further knowledge. In Samsaya the alternatives are distinct (*udbhidyamanakotika*) while in anadhyavasaya they are unmanifested. Thus Anadhyavasaya differs from Samsaya for three reasons. First, they are different kinds of indefinite knowledge. Secondly, they apprehend different objects. Thirdly, they are produced by different causes.

Vallabhacarya, the author of *Nyayalilavati*, gives us a slightly different account of Anadhyavasaya. According to him, Anadhyavasaya is the indefinite perception of an object as something in a general way, the particular features of which are not perceived. In it there is a bare apprehension of an object as something, but no apprehension of its distinctive character. Still there is a desire to know its nature.

Sri Vadi Devasuri gives us a similar account of Anadhyavasaya. He defines it as an indefinite perception of an object in the form "What is it"? He gives an example. When a passer-by treads on grass with an inattentive mind he has an indefinite perception of something in the form of *anadhyavasaya*.

Ratnaprabhacarya further explains the nature of Anadhyavasaya as defined by Sri Vadi Devasuri. He says that Anadhyavasaya is the bare apprehension of an object in the form "What is it"? In it the particular features of the object are not distinctly presented to consciousness. For instance, when a person with his mind engrossed in some other thing treads on grass he has an indefinite perception that he has touched something, but owing to inattention he cannot recognize what class it belongs to and what its name is. Such a bare apprehension of an object with no knowledge of its particular features is called Anadhyavasaya. Thus it is an indistinct impression in the field of inattention surrounding the focal point of clear and distinct consciousness.

**Samsaya and Anadhyavasaya**

Sridhara points out that Anadhyavasaya must not be identified with Samsaya, because it differs from the latter both in its origin and nature. Firstly, Samsaya arises from the recollection of the peculiar features of two objects; while in Anadhyavasaya there is no such recollection of the peculiar features of two objects, which often arises from mere absence of a distinct cognition of peculiarities. Secondly, in Samsaya the mind wavers between two distinct alternatives, sometimes touching the one and sometimes touching the other. In Anadhyavasaya, on the other hand, the mind does not oscillate between two alternatives.

Udayana distinguishes Samsaya from Anadhyavasaya in the

following manner : Samsaya arises from the perception of the common quality of two extremes which are revived in memory; in it the mind oscillates between two alternatives which are distinctly present to consciousness. Anadhyavasaya on the other hand, arises from the perception of the common quality of two extremes both of which are not distinctly revived in memory; it is indefinite knowledge consisting in an alternation between two extremes one of which is distinctly present to consciousness, while the other is suppressed. Here, evidently, Udayana means by Anadhyavasaya what has already been explained as Uha.

# 14
# Illusions

## Introduction

In this chapter we shall confine our attention to illusory perceptions. The treatment of Indian philosophers is more psychological than physiological. And their psychological analysis of illusory perception is closely allied with the determination of its epistemological value and ontological basis. Indian philosophers treat psychology always as the basis of epistemology and ontology; and their psychological analysis is sometimes coloured by their metaphysical presuppositions. They do not give an exhaustive classification of the different kinds of illusions with reference to all the sense-organs. But still they give a psychological classification of the principal types of illusions. Their enumeration of the different sources of illusions is almost complete. The different schools of Indian philosophers have tackled the problem of illusion in different ways. They give us slightly different accounts about its psychological nature. There is a hot controversy among them about its ontological basis. Different schools of Indian philosophers have advanced different theories of illusion, and their polemics against one another exhibit their wonderful power of psychological analysis and rare metaphysical acumen. Western psychologists are more concerned with the physiological conditions of illusions than with their psychological nature. Their treatment is more physiological than psychological, and their treatment of illusions from the epistemological and ontological points of view is extremely meagre in comparison with the Indian treatment.

## Different kinds of Illusions

### *Anubhuyamanaropa viparyaya and smaryamanaropa viparyaya*

Samkara Misra divides illusions into two kinds : (1) those which consist in false ascription of an actually perceived object to another object present to a sense-organ (*anubhuyamanaropa*); and (2) those which consist in false ascription of an object revived in memory to another object present to a sense-organ (*smaryamanaropa*). The illusory perceptions of bitter molasses and yellow conch-shell are examples of the first kind. And the illusory perception of silver in a nacre is an example of the second kind. In the illusory perceptions of bitter molasses and yellow conch-shell., bitterness of the bile in the gustatory organ and yellowness of the bile in the visual organ, which are actually perceived, are falsely ascribed to molasses and conch-shell respectively. These illusions are not due to subconscious impressions. In them both the object which is superimposed and the object on which the former is superimposed are actually perceived. The illusions of the second kind are produced by the sense-organs in co-operation with subconscious impressions, like recognition. They cannot be produced by the sense-organs alone; nor can they be produced by subconscious impressions alone; they are produced by both taken together. For instance, the illusory perception of silver in a nacre is produced by the visual organ in contact with the nacre, in co-operation with the subconscious impression of silver revived by the perception of brightness of the nacre, which it has in common with silver.

Jayasimhasuri also divides illusions into the above two kinds. He illustrates the first kind of illusion by the illusory perception of the double moon. He explains it in the following manner. When we press the eye-ball with a finger, the moon appears to be double, but before the eye-ball was pressed the moon appeared to be single, and after the pressing has ceased the moon appears to be single. And sometimes the illusion of the double moon is due to the excess of darkness (*timira*) within the eye-ball, which bifurcates the ray of light issuing out of the eye-ball. In this illusion an object revived in memory is not falsely ascribed to an object present to a sense-organ. He illustrates the second kind of illusion by the illusory perception of elephants, etc., during sleep. In dreams the objects which were perceived in the past are revived in memory and appear to be actually perceived here and now. Thus centrally initiated illusions or hallucinations fall within the second category.

***Indriyaja Bhranti (Illusion) and Manasi Bhranti (Hallucination)***

Jayanta Bhatta divides illusory perceptions into two kinds : (1) those which are produced by the peripheral organs (*indriyaja*) and (2) those which are produced by the central organ or mind (*manasa*). The former are peripherally excited, while the latter are centrally excited. The former are produced by some defects in the external stimuli, or by some defects in the peripheral organs. The latter are produced by some defects in the central organ or mind. The former are never without objective substrates; they are always produced by external stimuli (*salambana*). The latter are always without objective substrates, they are never produced by external stimuli (*niralambana*). The former are called illusions and the latter hallucinations in Western psychology.

Jayanta Bhatta illustrates these different kinds of illusory perceptions. The illusory perceptions of silver in a nacre, and of a sheet of water in the rays of the sun reflected on sands in a desert are illusions due to defects in the external stimuli (*visaya-dosa*). The illusory perceptions of bitter sugar, double moon and a mass of hair are illusions due to defects in the peripheral organs (*indriya-dosa*). All these are illusions. Hallucinations have no external stimuli; they are independent of the peripheral organs; they are solely of mental origin; they are due to some defects in the mind (*manodosa, antahkarana-dosa*). For example, when a lover is overpowered by stormy passion awakened by pangs of separation, he perceives the semblance of his beloved lady near him, though she is far away. Hallucinations are due to the recollection of objects distant in time and space owing to the revival of their subconscious impressions. Dreams also are hallucinations due to revival of subconscious impressions left by previous perceptions; they are excited by the mind overcome by drowsiness. Thus in hallucinations the forms which appear in consciousness are mostly memory-images owing to the revival of their subconscious impressions. But what is the cause of the resuscitation of these subconscious impressions? Sometimes they are awakened by similar cognitions (*sadrsa vijnana*), sometimes by strong passions, e.g. lust, grief, etc. (*kamasokadi*), sometimes by the habitual perception of these objects (*taddarsanabhyasa*), sometimes by drowsiness (*nidra*), sometimes by constant thinking (*cinta*), sometimes by perversion of the bodily humours (*dhatunam vikrti*) and sometimes by *adrsta* (i.e. merit or demerit) where there are no other causes.

Sridhara also divides illusory perceptions into peripherally excited illusions and centrally excited illusions or hallucinations. He divides the former again into indeterminate (*nirvikalpaka*) illusions and determinate (*savikalpaka*) illusions. Indeterminate illusions contain only presentative elements; they are due to pathological disorders of the peripheral organs alone. For example, when we perceive a white conch-shell as yellow, the illusion is purely presentative in character, and is produced by the visual organ perverted by preponderance of the bilious humour. Determinate illusions contain both presentative and representative elements; they are produced by the peripheral organs in co-operation with subconscious impressions. For example, when we mistake a nacre for a piece of silver, the illusion is produced by the perverted visual organ in contact with the nacre in co-operation with the subconscious impression of silver. Here the illusory perception contains both presentative and representative elements, the presentative element (*idam*) is produced by the perverted visual organ, and the representative element (*rajatam*) by the subconscious impression. But the illusion is perceptual in character, though it contains presentative and representative elements, hence it is produced by the perverted visual organ in co-operation with the subconscious impression of silver. Sridhara points out that these illusions are produced by external stimuli which have certain features in common with those objects which are manifested in illusory perceptions; this similarity between the real objects or external stimuli (e.g. nacre) and the illusory objects (e.g. silver) appearing in consciousness is the cause of these illusions. But hallucinations are not peripherally excited; they arise solely from some derangement of the mind or the central sensory. Hallucinations never arise out of the perception of similarity which is not possible in these cases, since there are no external stimuli to excite them. For instance, when a man is infatuated with love for a woman he perceives the semblance of his beloved, here, there, and everywhere, though there is no objective stimulus. Hallucinations are illusory perceptions because in them absent objects appear in consciousness as present.

Jayanta Bhatta also says that in the illusory perception of silver in a nacre we perceive only the common feature of the nacre (e.g. brightness); the perception of this similarity between the nacre and silver reminds us of the peculiar features of silver, and so we have an illusory perception of silver in a nacre. But this is possible only in peripherally excited illusions. In centrally excited illusions or hallucinations there are no external stimuli; so they cannot be produced by the perception of the common features of two objects and the recollection of the peculiar features of one of the two. In hallucinations there is no perception of external objects, but only a perception of those objects which are reproduced in memory and projected into the external world. Recollection alone is the cause of hallucinations, while perception and recollection both are the causes of those peripherally excited illusions which contain representative elements. Thus both these kinds of illusions consist in false ascription of memory-images (*smaryamanaropa*). The former consist in the projection of memory-images into the external world. The latter consist in the superimposition of memory-images on external objects actually perceived. Thus the above two divisions of illusions are not mutually exclusive. But they are based on two different principles.

**Different Causes of Illusions**

Illusory perceptions are due to some defects (*dosa*) in the conditions of perception, or to wrong operation of the sense-organs with regard to their objects (*asamprayoga*) or to subconscious impressions (*samskara*).

(1) In the first place, illusory perceptions are produced by defects in any condition of perception. Ordinarily, sense-perception is produced by several conditions taken together. It requires an external object of perception and sometimes an external medium of perception, e.g. light in the case of visual perception. Then it requires an external sense-organ through which the object is perceived, and also the central organ or mind without the help of which the peripheral organs cannot operate on their objects. And in internal perception the mind alone is the channel of perception. Besides these, the self is involved in every act of perception; it is the self which perceives an object through the senses. These are the conditions of sense-perception. Jayanta Bhatta holds that if any of these conditions is vitiated by defects it gives rise to illusory perceptions.

(i) Some illusions are due to defects in the external stimuli or objects (*visaya-dosa*) e.g. similarity (*sadrsya*) movement (*calatva*), distance (*duratva*), etc. For instance, we perceive a nacre as a piece of silver (*sukttka-rajata*), a rope as a snake (*raju-sarpa*), a cow as a horse (*gavasua*), clouds coloured by fading light as a town of ethereal beings (*jalada-gandharva-nagard*) owing to similarity between the two in each case. Again, the rapid movement of a firebrand in a circle produces the illusion of a circle (*alatacakra*). But when it is moved slowly it cannot produce the illusion of a circle. Then, again, the moon appears to be small because it is at a great distance from us.

(ii) Some illusions are due to the movement of the conveyance (*bahyasraya-dosa*) in which we travel. For instance, when we sail in a boat the boat moves and we also move along with it, but the trees and other objects around us appear to be moving. This illusion is known as "parallax" in Western psychology.

(iii) Some illusions are due to defects in the external medium of perception (e.g. *alokamalimasatva*). For instance, when the light is dim or dirty, we sometimes mistake one object for another.

(iv) Some illusions are due to pathological disorders of the peripheral organs (*bahyendriya-dosa*). For instance, when the visual organ is affected by jaundice or preponderance of bile, we perceive a white conch-shell as yellow (*pita-sankha*). When the gustatory organ is affected by provocation of bile, we taste molasses or sugar as bitter (*tiktaguda* or *tiktasarkara*). When the rays of light issuing out of the visual organ are bifurcated by darkness (*timira*), we perceive the moon as double. Or when the eye-ball is pressed with a finger, the moon appears to be double (*dvicandra*). The illusion of a mass of hair (*kesa-kurcaka* or *kesondraka*) also is due to some defect in the visual organ. Jayanta Bhatta explains it in the following manner. There are particles of darkness within the cavities of the eye-ball here and there; the rays of light issuing out of the visual organ are intercepted by these particles of darkness so that they become thinly distributed; these thinly distributed fine rays of light issuing out of the eye-ball are obstructed by the rays of the sun and appear as a mass of hair. Before sunrise or after sunset we do not get this illusory perception. All these illusions are due to some defects in the peripheral organs. Thus when the peripheral organs are overpowered by predominance of flatulent, bilious, and phlegmatic humours, we have illusory perceptions.

(v) Some illusions are due to pathological disorders of the bodily humours (*adhyatmagatadosa*), e.g. the flatulent humour, the bilious humour, and the phlegmatic humour. For instance, pillars of fire are seen owing to provocation of the bodily humours.

(vi) Some illusions are due to defects in the central sensory or mind (*antahkarana-dosa, mano-dosa*). For instance, when the mind is overpowered by the predominance of *rajas* or *tamas*, we have illusory perceptions. When the mind is overpowered by strong emotion or passion we have illusory perceptions. A man infatuated with love for a woman, sees the semblance of his beloved here, there, and everywhere. When the mind is overpowered by drowsiness, we have illusory perceptions in the form of dreams. All these illusions which are due to some disorder of the mind only are called hallucinations.

(vii) Some illusions are due to defects in the self (*pramatr-dosa*). For instance, when the self is affected by strong desire, aversion, hunger, rage, etc., we have illusory perceptions.

Dharmottara describes four sources of illusions, e.g. disorders of the peripheral organs, disturbances in the external stimuli, movement of the conveyance in which we travel, and disorders of the bodily humours. According to him, all these different causes of illusions must involve a derangement of the sense-organs. There can be no "sense-illusions" unless there are "sense-disorders". Thus some illusions are due to some defects in the various conditions of perception. This condition of illusions is emphasized by the Nyaya-Vaisesika.

(2) In the second place, illusory perceptions are produced by wrong operation of the sense-organs with regard to their objects (*asamprayoga*). This condition of illusions is mentioned by the Bhatta Mimamsakas. Right perception depends upon right intercourse between the sense-organs and their objects (*satsamprayoga*). It requires a real object (*sat*), and right intercourse between this object and the proper sense-organ (*samprayoga*). If there is no real object and still we have perceptual experience, the perception is illusory. In dreams there are no real objects or external stimuli, but still we have illusory perceptions of various objects. So dreams should be regarded as hallucinations. If, in spite of the presence of a real object, there is wrong intercourse between it and the proper sense-organ, we have

illusory perception. For instance, when we mistake a nacre for a piece of silver, there is wrong intercourse between the visual organ and the nacre. Right perception depends upon the intercourse of that object with the proper sense-organ, which is manifested in consciousness. When one object is in contact with a sense-organ, but another object appears in consciousness, the perception is illusory. For instance, when a nacre is in contact with a visual organ, but a piece of silver appears in consciousness the perception is illusory. Thus right perception depends upon right operation of the sense-organs with regard to their objects, and illusory perception depends upon wrong operation of the sense-organs with regard to their objects. This condition of illusions, viz. *asamprayogay* emphasized by the Mimamsakas, is included in *visaya-dosa* and *indriya-dosa* mentioned by the Nyaya-Vaisesika.

(3) In the third place, illusory perceptions are produced by subconscious impressions (*samskara*). We have already found that subconscious impressions are the causes of those peripherally excited illusions which contain representative elements. For example, when a nacre is in contact with the visual organ, we sometimes perceive only its brightness which is common to both nacre and silver, and the perception of this brightness revives the subconscious impression of silver, and the visual organ in co-operation with this subconscious impression produces the illusory perception of silver. Thus subconscious impressions in co-operation with the peripheral organs produce those peripherally excited illusions which contain representative elements. We have also found that centrally excited illusions or hallucinations are due to subconscious impressions alone. For example, a lover infatuated with love for a woman sees his beloved near him, though she is far away. Here the subconscious impression of the woman is revived by the strong passion of love and invades the field of consciousness; the memory-image of the woman distant in time and space appears like a woman actually perceived here and now. Thus subconscious impressions alone are the causes of hallucinations.

Prasastapada says that an illusory perception consists in the misapprehension of one object as another object, both of which were perceived in the past with their peculiar characters, and it is due to three causes : (1) wrong apprehension by a peripheral organ perverted by provocation of the bilious, phlegmatic, and flatulent humours; (2) the mind-soul-contact depending upon the subconscious impression left by the previous cognition of an absent object; and (3) demerit (*adharma*); as, for example, the illusory perception of a horse in a cow. Here Prasastapada refers to peripherally excited illusions which contain representative elements.

Sridhara explains the functions of the peripheral organs and subconscious impressions in producing these kinds of illusions. He asks : When we mistake a cow for a horse, what is the cause of non-apprehension of the distinctive character of a cow; and what is the cause of apprehension of the distinctive character of a horse which is not present to the visual organ? He says that the visual organ cannot apprehend the distinctive character of a cow, though it is in contact with a cow, because it is perverted by the disorders of the bilious phlegmatic, and flatulent humours. But how can the perverted sense-organ produce apprehension of the distinctive character of a horse which is not present to the visual organ? Can it produce apprehension of absent objects? If so, then it can produce apprehension of any absent object whatsoever at any time, and thus there will be nothing to determine the appearance of particular objects in consciousness in illusory perceptions. Sridhara points out that the perverted sense-organ brings about apprehension of an absent object only in co-operation with the mind-soul-contact which depends upon the subconscious impression of an absent object. Though the visual organ is in contact with a cow, it cannot apprehend the object as a cow because it is perverted by disorders of the bodily humours. But still it apprehends the individual as endowed with those features which are common to cows and horses. The perception of similarity revives the subconscious impression of a horse; and this subconscious impression being revived brings about the recollection of a horse; and this recollection of a horse, owing to some perversion of the mind, produces the perceptual experience of a horse, in contact with the visual organ because of the similarity between a cow and a horse. Thus any absent object cannot appear in consciousness at any time in the presence of any object in contact with a perverted sense-organ. Similarity between a present object and an absent object, and the subconscious impression of the latter revived by the perception of similarity determine the appearance of a particular absent object in an illusory perception. Hence, the perverted sense-organs in co-operation with subconscious impressions produce certain illusory perceptions.

## Psychological Analysis of an Illusion

A centrally excited illusion or hallucination is solely due to revival of subconscious impressions. A peripherally excited illusion which contains only presentative elements is due to pathological disorders of the peripheral organs. So these two kinds of illusions are simple psychoses. But a peripherally excited illusion which contains both presentative and representative elements is complex in character. It is due to the peripheral organs and subconscious impressions. This kind of illusion has been analysed by different schools of Indian thinkers in slightly different ways. Let us consider the illusory perception of silver in a nacre. Is it a single psychosis? Or is it a combination of two psychoses? If it is a single psychosis, what is its nature? Prabhakara holds that an illusion is a complex psychosis, made up of a presentative element or perception (*anubhava*) and a representative element or recollection (*smarana*) and as long as the illusion lasts we do not discriminate these two factors from each other. The Nyaya-Vaisesika and the Vedantist hold that an illusion is a single psychosis of a presentative or perceptual character.

### *Prabhakara's Analysis*

Prabhakara holds that in an illusion there are two elements, an element of perception or presentation and an element of recollection or representation. When we perceive a nacre as silver, we perceive only the common qualities of nacre and silver, viz. brightness and the like, and the common qualities which are perceived in the nacre revive the idea of silver in memory by association. Thus in the illusion of silver in a nacre there is the perception of brightness and the like, and the recollection of silver. But so long as the illusion lasts we do not distinguish the presentative element from the representative element. Thus an illusion is made up of a presentative element and a representative element, in which there is no discrimination of the two factors from each other. This non-discrimination (*vivekakhyati*) of the presentative element from the representative element is the cause of exertion for the appropriation or avoidance of the object of illusion.

A sublating cognition (*badhaka-jnana*) does not contradict an illusion, but simply recognizes the distinction between the presentative element and the representative element. But why are not the two elements discriminated from each other before the so-called sublative cognition? Prabhakara holds that we cannot discriminate the representative element from the presentative element, because the former does not appear in consciousness as representation or memory owing to *smrtipramosa* or obscuration of memory.

### *The Nyaya-Vaisesika Analysis*

According to the Nyaya-Vaisesika, an illusion is a single psychosis of a presentative or perceptual character. In the illusion of silver in a nacre at first we perceive those qualities of the nacre which are common to both silver and nacre, e.g. brightness, etc., but we do not perceive the peculiar qualities of the nacre owing to the perversion of the visual organ; then the perception of these common qualities reminds us of the peculiar qualities of silver by association. So far the Nyaya-Vaisesika agrees with Prabhakara. But according to the Nyaya-Vaisesika, the recollection of silver, owing to some perversion of the mind, produces the perception of silver, in contact with the visual organ; the illusion of silver is perceptual in character, it is experienced as a direct perception, and not as a recollection. If we regard an illusion as a mere reproduction of past experience, then we miss its distinctive psychological character.

According to the neo-Naiyayika, the visual perception of silver in a nacre depends upon the extraordinary intercourse through the idea of silver revived in memory by association as we have already seen. Here there is no contact of the visual organ with actual silver; there is no ordinary intercourse (*laukika sannikarsa*) between the sense-organ and its object. But there is an extraordinary intercourse (*alaukika sannikarsa*), by means of which the idea of silver reproduced in memory by association produces the visual perception of silver. This is called the extraordinary intercourse whose character is knowledge (*jnana-laksana-sannikarsa*).

### *The Samkara-Vedantist's Analysis*

According to the Vedantist, an illusion is a presentative process. The Samkara-Vedantist explains the illusion of silver in a nacre in the following manner. At first the visual organ perverted by certain pathological disorders comes in contact with the nacre which is present to the sense-organ, and brings about a mental mode in the form of "this" or "brightness". Then the object-consciousness determined by "this" is reflected in the mental mode, so that the mental mode streaming out of the sense-orifice, the object-consciousness (*visaya-caitanya*) determined by "this", the mental consciousness (or consciousness determined by the mental mode) in the form of "this" (*vrtti-caitanya*) and the logical subject-consciousness (*pramatr-caitanya*) are identified with one another. Then there is produced *avidya* or nescience in the form of nacre, this *avidya* exists in the object-consciousness which has been identified with the subject-consciousness. This *avidya* in co-operation with the subconscious impression of silver revived by the perception of the common features, e.g. brightness and the like, and with the help of the peripheral disorders, is transformed into illusory silver (*pratibhasika rajata*) on the one hand, and the illusory perception of silver (*rajata-jnanabhasa*), on the other. Stripped of all epistemological and metaphysical implications, the Samkarite's analysis of an illusion is exactly the same as that of the Nyaya-Vaisesika from the psychological point of view. According to both, an illusion is a simple psychosis of a presentative character. According to both, an illusion is produced by a sense-organ vitiated by a certain derangement in co-operation with a subconscious impression revived by the perception of similarity. They do not differ in their psychological analysis of an illusion, though they differ in their epistemological and metaphysical doctrines of illusion, which we shall consider later on.

### Illusion (*viparyaya*) and Doubtful Perception (*samsaya*)

Udayana says that both an illusion (*viparyaya*) and a doubtful perception (*samsaya*) are not produced by the corresponding objects (*anarthaja*); but the former is definite (*niskayatmaka*), while the latter is indefinite (*aniscayatmaka*). An illusion is a false perception of a definite character in the waking condition. Jayanta Bhatta points out that an illusion differs from a doubtful perception both in its nature and in its origin. Firstly, in an illusion one object is definitely perceived as another object, e.g. a post as a man, or a man as a post; while in a doubtful perception the rnind wavers between two alternatives, sometimes touching the one, and sometimes touching the other. Thus an illusion is a definite, false perception, while a doubtful perception is an indefinite, or uncertain, false perception. Secondly, an illusion springs from the recollection of the peculiar qualities of one object (e.g. silver, or water) which is suggested by the perception of the common quality in another object (e.g. nacre, or the rays of the sun), while a doubtful perception springs from the recollection of the peculiar qualities of two objects (e.g. a post and a man) which are suggested by the perception of their common quality (e.g. tallness).

**Different Theories of Illusions**

Different schools of Indian philosophers have advanced different theories of illusions. These theories are not only based on the purely psychological analysis of illusions, but also on their epistemological significance and ontological basis, Prabhacandra refers to seven different theories of illusions in *Prameyakamalamartanda*, viz. *Akhyati* (non-apprehension), *Asatkhyati* (apprehension of a nonexistent object), *Prasiddharthakhyati* (apprehension of a real object established by knowledge), *Atmakhyati* (apprehension of a subjective cognition projected into the external world), *Anirvacaniyarthakhyati* (apprehension of an undefinable object), *Anyathakhyati* or *Viparitakhyati* (apprehension of an object as otherwise, i.e. as a different object), and *Smrtipramosa* (obscuration of memory) or *Vivekakhyati* (non-apprehension of discrimination or non-discrimination). It is not known who is the advocate of the first doctrine. The second doctrine is held by the Madhyamika. It is not known who is the advocate of the third doctrine. The fourth doctrine is held by the Yogacara; the fifth, by the Samkara School of Vedantists; the sixth, by the Patanjala, the Naiyayika, the Vaisesika, the Bhatta Mimamsaka, and the Jaina; and the seventh, by the Prabhakara Mimamsaka.

In *Nyayatatparyadipika* Jayasimhasuri mentions eight different theories of illusions, adding to the above list *Alaukikakhyati* (apprehension of an extraordinary object, different from the ordinary objects of experience). Jayanta Bhatta also discusses the theory of *Alaukikakhyati* in *Nyayamanjari* and says that this doctrine is held by a certain Mimamsaka. The Samkhya advocates the doctrine of *Sadasatkhyati*. Ramanuja advocates the doctrine of *Satkhyati* (apprehension of a real object). We shall consider these theories one by one.

## The Doctrine of Akhyati

### *Exposition of Akhyati*

According to this doctrine, an illusion has no objective substratum; it is objectless (*niralambana*); it does not apprehend any object at all; it is a pure hallucination. Let us consider the illusion of a mirage, or the illusory perception of water in the rays of the sun. What is the object of this illusion? Is it water, absence of water, or the rays of the sun, or something else? Water cannot be the object of the illusory cognition, for, in that case, the cognition would be valid and not illusory. The absence of water cannot be the object of the illusion, because it is the cognition of water that induces the person under illusion to exert himself to get water. The rays of the sun, too, cannot be the object of the illusion, for, in that case, the cognition would not be illusory but valid, representing the real nature of the external stimulus. It cannot be argued that the rays of the sun are perceived as water, inasmuch as one thing cannot be perceived as something different; a cloth is never perceived as a jar. Hence an illusion is objectless or without any objective substratum (*niralambanam-viparyaya-jnanam*). This account of the doctrine of *Akhyati* is given by Prabhacandra, a Jaina philosopher, in *Prameyakamalamartanda*).

### *Criticism of Akhyati*

Prabhacandra offers the following criticism of the doctrine of *Akhyati* : If illusions have no objective substrates (*alambana*), if they are not excited by external stimuli, by what peculiar mark are we to distinguish one illusion from another? For instance, how can we distinguish the illusory cognition of water (in the rays of the sun) from the illusory cognition of silver (in a nacre)? If, again, illusions are not produced by external objects, what is the difference between an illusion and a state of dreamless sleep ? It may be urged that there is no difference between the two, except that in an illusion there is consciousness, while in dreamless sleep there is no consciousness at all; they agree in having no external stimulus. But Prabhacandra contends that at least the object that appears in consciousness in an illusion must be regarded as the object of that illusion. Thus an illusion can never be held to be a non-apprehension of an object.

## The Doctrine of Asatkhyati

### *Exposition of Asatkhyati*

The Madhyamika holds that in the illusory cognition of silver, there is a cognition of silver as real, though really there is no silver at all. Hence he concludes that in an illusion something non-existent is cognized as existent. This is the doctrine of *Asatkhyati.*

### *Criticism of Asatkhyati*

Jayanta Bhatta offers the following criticism of the doctrine of *Asatkhyati* on behalf of Prabhakara :

What is the meaning of *Asatkhyati,* or apprehension of a non-existent object ? What is the object of an illusion according to this doctrine ? Is it an absolutely non-existent object like a sky-flower ? Or is it an object existing in some other time and place ? If the latter, then *Asatkhyati* is nothing but *Vipantakhyati,* according to which, silver existing in some other time and place appears in the illusory cognition of silver, but not existing in that time and place. If the former, then there would be a cognition of a sky-flower also; but because such an absolutely non-existent object never appears in consciousness, it cannot be the object of an illusion.

It may be argued that non-existent things appear in consciousness through the intensity of residua or subconscious impressions (*vasanabhyasa*). But a residuum (*vasana*) is not possible without a real object; it is nothing but a vestige left by the previous perception of an object; why should such a residuum be the cause of the cognition of an absolutely non-existent object ? If we admit that some other kind of residuum (*vasana*) produces the cognition of a non-existent object, why should such a residuum produce the cognition of silver and not that of a sky-flower? What regulates the operation of such a residuum? An absolutely non-existent object can never appear in consciousness, nor can it induce a person to exert himself to get hold of it. Thus the doctrine of *Asatkhyati* is untenable.

Prabhacandra points out that according to the Madhyamika, there is neither an external or objective reality, nor an internal or subjective cognition; so there is neither any variety in external objects nor any variety in cognitions. Hence there cannot be a variety of illusions. Thus the doctrine of Asatkhyati cannot be maintained.

## The Doctrine of Atmakhyati

### *Exposition of Atmakhyati*

Vidyaranya Muni, a Samkarite, gives the following exposition of the doctrine of *Atmakhyati* held by the Yogacara in *Vivaranaprameya-samgraha.*

According to the Buddhists, mind (*citta*) and mental states (*caitta*) are produced by four different causes : (1) co-operating cause (*sahakari-pratyaya*), (2) dominant cause (*adhipati-pratyaya*), (3) immediate cause (*samanantara-pratyaya*), and (4) objective datum or external cause (*alambana-pratyaya*). Now, in the first place, the illusion of silver cannot be produced by the co-operating cause (*sahakari-pratyaya*) which, in the present case, is light; for light is the cause of the distinctness of the perception. In the second place, it cannot be produced by the dominant cause (*adhipati-pratyaya*) which, in the present case, is the visual organ, for the visual organ is the cause only of the visual character of the perception, it cannot account for the particular nature of the visual perception, viz. that of silver. In the third place, it cannot be produced by the immediate cause (*samanantara-pratyaya*) which is the immediately preceding cognition, for the illusory cognition of silver may arise immediately after a cognition of an entirely different kind, e.g. that of a jar. In the fourth place, it cannot be produced by an external cause (*alambana-pratyaya*) for, according to the Buddhist idealist (Yogacara), there is no external reality at all. How, then, can the Buddhist idealist account for the illusory cognition of silver ? The Yogacara holds that it is produced by a *vasana* or residuum of silver which, at some time or other, arose in the beginningless series of nescience (*avidya*) which, again, had been produced by a yet earlier idea of silver, and so on. Thus the idea of silver is the result of a beginningless series of residua; and owing to error this subjective idea appears to consciousness as something external. An illusion, therefore, is not produced by an external object in contact with a sense-organ; but it is simply an eccentric projection of a subjective idea into the external world; it is a purely subjective hallucination.

Prabhacandra gives the following gist of the doctrine of *Atmakhyati* in *Prameyakamalamartanda*. In the illusory perception of silver, the object of consciousness, e.g. silver, is a subjective form of consciousness itself; it appears as an extra-mental object owing to the potency of erroneous cognitions arising out of beginningless nescience. The beginningless series of various residua or subconscious impressions are gradually awakened in persons on account of this, various cognitions (e.g. pots, cloths, etc.) arise, which cognize their own forms. There are no external objects corresponding to these cognitions. This is the doctrine of *Atmakhyati*.

### *Criticism of Atmakhyati*

Jayanta Bhatta offers the following criticism of the doctrine of *Atmakhyati*, on behalf of Prabhakara :

According to this doctrine, a mere idea appears as the cognizer, the cognized object, and the cognition; there is neither a subject apart from ideas, nor an object apart from ideas, there is simply a series of ideas or cognitions. Thus, if in an illusion a mere idea is manifested in consciousness, and not an external object, then we would have such a cognition as "I am silver", and not as "this is silver". Moreover, this doctrine implies *Viparitakhyati*, inasmuch as, according to this view, an internal or subjective idea is cognized as something different, viz. an external or objective reality. And this doctrine implies *Asatkhyati* too, since the cognition of externality has no real objective basis, there being no extra-mental reality according to the Yogacara.

Prabhacandra gives the following criticism of the doctrine of *Atniakhyati* :

If all cognitions apprehend only their own forms, and not those of external objects, as the Yogacara holds, there would be no distinction between an illusory cognition and a valid cognition, and consequently, there would be neither any sublating cognition nor any sublated cognition. If, again, the forms of illusory cognitions such as silver and the like are not those of external objects, but mere forms of consciousness, then they would be apprehended as such, like the forms of pleasure and pain, and not as something external. And also a person under illusion would exert himself to get the object of illusion, as if it were a subjective momentary cognition, and not an extra-mental reality. If it is urged that an internal momentary cognition is mistaken for an external permanent object owing to the potency of nescience (*avidya*), then the doctrine of *Ātmakhyati* leads to *Viparitakhyati,* since the internal form of a momentary cognition appears as an external permanent object. Thus the doctrine of *Atmakhyati* is untenable.

The Samkara-Vedantist (Vidyaraṇya) offers the following criticism of the doctrine of *Atmakhyati.* In the illusion of silver, is the illusory silver devoid of origination, on account of its extraordinary nature? Or does it originate like an ordinary silver ? On the first alternative, it would not be of the nature of an emergent cognition as it really is; it comes into being, and so it cannot be without an origin. On the second alternative, it must be produced either by a cognition or by an object. It cannot be produced by an object, as the Yogacara does not admit the existence of an extramental object. If it is produced by a cognition, is it produced by a pure cognition or a cognition which is due to a vitiated cause? It cannot be produced by a pure (*visuddha*) cognition, as pure cognition constitutes liberation. If it is produced by a cognition which is due to a vitiated cause, is it the same originating cognition which apprehends the silver ? Or is it some other cognition? The first alternative is not possible, because the originating cognition and the originated cognition both being momentary, and hence occupying different points of time, there would be no presentation of silver at all. The second alternative also is impossible. If it is another cognition that apprehends the silver, it cannot be a cognition produced by a non-vitiated cause, as in that case there would be no reason why such a cognition should specially apprehend silver. If, on the other hand, the cognition apprehending the illusory silver is produced by a vitiated cause, then that cause is either silver or it is not silver. It cannot be silver, for, in that case, silver would have causal efficiency and consequently it would have a real existence, which is not admitted by the Yogacara. If silver is not the cause, then it cannot be manifested in the illusory cognition. Thus on the doctrine of *Atmakhyati* the illusory cognition of silver would never come into being.

### The Doctrine of Alaukikakhyati

#### *Exposition of Alaukikakhyati*

Jayanta Bhatta gives the following exposition of the doctrine of

*Alaukikakhyati* in *Nyayamanjari* and says that it is held by a certain Mimamsaka. According to this doctrine, in the illusory cognition of silver it is not a nacre that is the object of the illusory cognition, but it is silver; but this silver is different from ordinary or *laukika* silver, it is *alaukika* or extraordinary silver. Just as the valid cognition of silver has for its object ordinary or *laukika* silver, so the illusory cognition of silver has for its object extraordinary or *alaukika* silver. What is the difference between *laukika* silver and *alaukika* silver? Whatever is manifested to consciousness as silver must be regarded as silver; but some silver known as an object of consciousness serves our practical purposes (*vyavahara-pravartaka*), while some other silver does not; the former is called ordinary or *laukika* silver, while the latter is called extraordinary or *alaukika* silver. In the illusory cognition of silver it is an extraordinary or *alaukika* silver that is the object of the illusion; it is silver because there is a cognition of silver; and it is *alaukika* or extraordinary silver because it does not serve any practical purpose.

### *Criticism of Alaukikakhyati*

Jayanta Bhatta offers the following criticism of the doctrine of *Alaukikakhyati* :

How do you know that there is extraordinary or *alaukika* silver corresponding to the illusory cognition of silver ? It is an absolutely new and unperceived object. The contradicting perception "this is not silver" clearly establishes the *alaukikatva* or extraordinariness of the silver which existed at the time of the illusory cognition. Hence there is neither silver corresponding to the illusion of silver, nor is it *alaukika* or extraordinary. So it is not right to hold that whatever is manifested to consciousness as silver must be silver; silver is manifested to consciousness in the illusory cognition of silver, though really there is no silver at all at that time and place. Real silver can be known only through the cognition of silver which is not contradicted by any other cognition ? Moreover, what differentiates an ordinary or *laukika* object from an extraordinary or *alaukika* object ? On what does the distinction depend ? Does it depend upon the distinction of our cognitions (*pratibhasa-nibandhana*) ? Or does it depend upon the fulfilment or non-fulfilment of our practical purposes (*vyavahara-sadasadbhava-nibandhana*)? The first alternative is not tenable; for sometimes we are conscious of the existence of silver, and sometimes of the non-existence of silver; but we are never conscious of the *laukikatva* (ordinariness) and *alaukikatva* (extraordinariness) of silver. The second alternative also cannot be maintained, for what is the meaning of practical use (*vyavahara*) ? Does it mean the capacity of being an object of thought and speech (*jnanabhidhanasvabhava*)? Or does it mean the capacity of producing an effect or action (*arthakriya-nirvartana*)? The first view is untenable, because there is no consciousness of *laukikatva* (ordinariness) or *alaukikatva* (extraordinariness) of an object. The second view also is not tenable, for, in that case, the woman embraced in a dream would be *laukika*, and a jar which is destroyed as soon as it is produced, and as such cannot serve any practical purpose, would be alaukika. Further, he who does not make an effort to pick up silver at the sight of a nacre does so, not because he recognizes the *alaukikatva* (extraordinariness) of the existing silver, but because he understands that there is no silver in reality. If there is *alaukika* silver as the object of the illusion of silver, why should a person under illusion make an effort to pick it up ? If it is urged that he perceived the *alaukika* silver as *laukika*, then at last the advocate of the doctrine of *Alaukikakhyati* comes to adopt the view of *Anyathakhyati*, according to which, one object appears as a different one in an illusion.

## The Doctrine of Anirvacaniyakhyati

### *Exposition of Anirvacaniyakhyati*

The Samkara-Vedantist holds that the object of an illusion is neither real, nor unreal, nor both, but undefinable (*anirvacantya*). This is called the doctrine of *Anirvacanlyakhyati*. According to this doctrine, whatever is manifested in a cognition is the object of that cognition. In the illusory perception of silver, it is silver that appears in consciousness; so silver must be the object of this illusion. If something else is regarded as the object of this illusion, as the doctrine of *Anyathakhyati* holds, why should we call this illusion an illusion of silver and not of something else ? So it is silver that is the object of the illusion of silver. But this silver is neither real (*sat*) nor unreal (*asat*), nor both real and unreal (*sadasat*) but it is undefmable (*anirvacantya*). It cannot be real, for, in that case, the cognition of silver would be valid, and not illusory, and as such would not be contradicted by any sublating cognition. Nor can it be unreal, for, in that case, it would not produce the cognition of silver, and, consequently, it would not lead the person under illusion to exert himself to get hold of silver. Nor can it be both real and unreal, as this supposition would involve both the above difficulties, and further, two contradictory qualities like reality and unreality cannot inhere in one and the same object. Hence the silver which is the object of the illusory cognition of silver must be regarded as undefinable (*anirvacamya*).

The Samkarite, therefore, holds that undefinable silver is produced at that time and place and continues as long as the illusion of silver persists. This kind of existence is called by him *pratibhasika-satta*, or apparent existence, which is different from *vyavahartka-satta*, or empirical existence.

But what is the use of admitting an undefinable reality to account for an illusion ? An illusory cognition may very well be explained by the doctrine of *Anyathakhyati*, according to which, an illusion is the misapprehension of one thing as a different thing, for example, the illusion of silver is the misapprehension of a nacre as silver which exists in some other time and place. The Samkarite urges that silver existing in some other time and place cannot be an object of perception, since it is not present to the sense-organ and there can be no presentation without a present object. The neo-Naiyayika argues that the silver existing in some other time and place is brought to consciousness by association, and produces the perception of silver by means of an extraordinary intercourse whose character is knowledge (*jnanalaksana-sannikarsa*). The Samkarite urges that in that case, in the inference of fire from smoke, fire which is not present to the sense-organ might be brought to consciousness by association, and produce the perception of fire by means of an extraordinary intercourse whose character is knowledge (*jnana-laksana-sannikarsa*) and thus there would be no inference at all.

Besides, what is the meaning of *Anyathakhyati*? If it means a cognition of one thing as otherwise, to what does the otherwiseness actually belong? Does it belong to the cognitive activity (the act of cognizing), or to the result of cognitive activity, i.e. the resulting cognition, or to the object of cognition? The first alternative is impossible. If the act of cognizing the shell is in the form of silver, then the shell cannot be called the objective substrate of the illusory cognition of silver; because an object can impart its own form to that cognition by which it is apprehended, and hence the shell cannot impart its own form to a cognition which apprehends silver. The second alternative also is not tenable. The otherwiseness (*anyathatva*) cannot belong to the result of cognitive activity or the cognition itself, for the cognition does not essentially differ, whether it is true or illusory; the cognition does not appear as something different or otherwise. Nor can the third alternative be maintained. In what sense, can the otherwiseness belong to the object, viz. the shell? Does it mean that the shell identifies itself with silver ? Or does it mean that the shell transforms itself into the form of silver? In the first alternative, is the shell absolutely different from silver? Or are they different and non-different at the same time? The first view is untenable, since things absolutely different from each other can never identify themselves with each other. The second view also is untenable, for, in that case, such judgements as "the cow is short-horned" would be illusory. In the second alternative, if the shell actually transforms itself into the form of silver, then the cognition of silver cannot be sublated as it is the cognition of a real change. If it is urged that the shell actually transforms itself into silver for the time being, i.e. so long as the illusion lasts, then silver would be perceived in the shell also by those who do not suffer from any defect of the sense-organs and the like. Thus the doctrine of *Anyathakhyati* cannot be stated in an intelligible form. It does not offer a better explanation of an illusion than the doctrine of *Anirvacamyakhyati*, according to which an undefinable object is produced at the time of an illusory cognition.

But it may be urged that the object of the illusory cognition of silver cannot be illusory or undefinable silver, inasmuch as the cause of silver (e.g. its different parts) is absent at the time. The Samkarite urges that it is produced by *amdya* in co-operation with the subconscious impression of silver perceived in the past, and revived by the perception of its similarity with a nacre which is in contact with the visual organ impaired by a certain derangement. Hence it cannot be said that illusory silver (*pratibhasika rajata*) cannot be produced at the time, which is the object of the illusory cognition of silver.

Thus the Samkarite argues that an illusion is a presentative cognition, and as such it must be produced by a present object; and the object of a cognition must be that which appears in consciousness; it cannot be some other object which does not appear in consciousness. In the illusory cognition of silver, it is silver that is the object of the cognition as it appears in consciousness; and that silver must be present at that time and place, when and where the illusion is produced; otherwise the illusion would not be a presentative cognition. Thus the illusion of silver has silver for its object which is produced then and there and continues as long as the illusion lasts. But this silver cannot be real, as in that case the cognition of silver would not be illusory. It cannot be unreal, as in that case there would be no cognition of silver and consequently no activity for the appropriation of silver. Nor can it be real and unreal both, as it involves self-contradiction. Hence it must be undefmable.

### *Criticism of Anirvacamyakhyati*

Ramanuja contends that even the doctrine of Anirvacamyakhyati cannot avoid Anyathakhyati, which it seeks to refute. The very assumption of an undefinable existence to account for an illusion implies that one thing appears as another, since an undefinable object appears to consciousness as real. If an undefinable object were apprehended as undefinable at the time of the illusory cognition, then the cognition would not be illusory, and hence it would not be contradicted by a subsequent cognition. If it is urged that the undefinable object of an illusion does not appear as undefinable so long as the illusion lasts, but subsequently it is known to be undefinable by rational reflection, then also the doctrine of Anirvacamyakhyati leads to *Anyathakhyati*, as an undefinable object appears to consciousness as real. Moreover, the doctrine of *Anyathakhyati* can adequately explain all the facts connected with an illusion, viz. illusory cognition, activity consequent upon an illusion, and the subsequent sublating cognition. What, then, is the use of supposing an undefinable object which is absolutely unperceived and groundless?

Even if we admit that an undefinable object is produced at the time of the corresponding illusion, what is its cause ? In the illusory cognition of silver what is the cause of the undefinable silver which is the object of the illusion? The cognition of silver cannot originate the undefinable silver, for there cannot be the cognition of silver before origination of the silver. It is absurd to argue that at first a cognition arises without any object, and then this objectless cognition produces the undefinable silver and makes it an object of apprehension. Nor can it be argued that a certain defect in the sense-organs is the cause of the illusory silver; for a defect abiding in the knowing person cannot produce an effect in an outward object. Nor can the sense-organs, apart from defects, give rise to the illusory silver, for the sense-organs are the causes of cognitions only, and not of the objects of cognitions. Nor can the sense-organs deranged by a certain defect originate the illusory silver; for they also can produce peculiar modifications only in the cognitions produced by them, but not in the objects of those cognitions. Nor can a beginningless nescience (*avidya*) be the cause of the illusory silver, for the doctrine of nescience does not stand to reason. Ramanuja has brought seven charges against the Samkarite doctrine of nescience (*avidya*).

**The Doctrine of Satkhyati**

***Exposition of Satkhyati***

The Ramanujist holds that an illusory perception has a real object (*sat*) for its objective substrate. In the illusory perception of silver in a nacre the silver that is manifested to consciousness is a real object, for an unreal object can never be apprehended. Otherwise, why is it that only silver is apprehended in a nacre, and not a jar, or a cloth, or some other thing? It cannot be argued that silver is apprehended owing to its similarity with the nacre, inasmuch as the similarity of the nacre with silver would revive the subconscious impression of silver, and thus produce the recollection of silver, but would never produce the perception of silver. It is real silver that is the object of the illusory perception of silver. But how is it real ? All objects of the world are produced by triplication or quintuplication (*pancikarana*) of the five elements of earth, water, fire, air, and ether, so that everything exists everywhere in the form of its elements. Hence silver in which the element of fire predominates exists in part in the nacre in which the element of earth predominates. Moreover, there is a law that an object is similar to that object which contains the parts of the latter. According to this law, a nacre which is similar to silver must contain the parts of silver. Thus in the illusory perception of silver in a nacre, silver must exist in part in the nacre. But, then, why is the perception of silver in a nacre called illusory ? It is called illusory, not because silver does not exist even in part in the nacre, but because in the nacre the parts of silver are much less than those of the nacre, and they do not serve our practical purposes. Thus every illusory perception has a real object for its objective substrate. This is the doctrine of Satkhyati.

### *Criticism of Satkhyati*

A Samkarite offers the following criticism of the doctrine of Satkhyati in *Advaitamoda* :

According to the Ramanujist, all cognitions are real; even an illusory cognition has a real object for its objective substrate. Thus the illusory perception of silver has real silver for its object. The Samkarite also holds that the illusory perception of silver has real silver for its object. But, according to the Samkarite, the silver which is the object of the illusory cognition of silver has only apparent or illusory existence (*pratibhasika-satta*), while according to the Ramanujist, it has real or ontological existence (*paramarthikasatta*).

But if the object of an illusion has real existence, how can we perceive water in a desert ? It is true that a part of water does exist in earth on account of triplication or quintuplication of the subtle elements. But the distinctive character of water does not exist in a particular earthy substance produced by triplication or quintuplication of the elements. Even if the distinctive character of water exists in the part of water which constitutes a part of that substance, it is not capable of being perceived. Triplication or quintuplication is such a combination of the elements that they cannot be separated. Before triplication or quintuplication the elements are subtle and imperceptible, after triplication or quintuplication also the part of water alone cannot be perceived in the earthy substance. Moreover, it does not stand to reason that the elements of water in the earthy substance, though subtle, are perceived from a distance, but they cannot be perceived by those who are near it. The Ramanujist says that fire and earth are not perceived owing to a certain defect of the peripheral organ, and water is perceived owing to demerit (*adrsta*). But this is no argument.

For the same reason it is wrong to hold that we have an illusory perception of silver in a nacre because silver really exists in the nacre in the form of the elements of fire, which enter into three-fold or five-fold combination to constitute the nacre. Moreover, why are the elements of fire in the nacre perceived as silver alone ? They might as well be perceived as lightning, the sun, and other fiery objects, because the elements of fire are common to all these objects before combination. It cannot be said that certain particles of the fire (*tejas*) which, by triplication or quintuplication, are transformed into silver, are combined and are perceived in the nacre, for there is no proof of their existence. It cannot be said that the cognition of silver is the proof of their existence, for it would involve a vicious circle. The existence of silver in the nacre would depend upon the cognition of silver being an apprehension of a real object; and the cognition of silver being an apprehension of a real object would depend upon the existence of a part of silver in the nacre. It cannot be said that the existence of a part of silver in the nacre is proved by the perception of similarity of the nacre with silver. The nacre is similar to silver because it is endowed with those qualities which are common to itself and silver, viz. brightness and the like, and not because it contains a part of silver; there is no law of nature that an object must contain a part of another object with which it has similarity. If the clothes and ornaments of Caitra are similar to those of Devadatta, Devadatta may mistake the clothes and ornaments of Caitra for his own. But the parts of the clothes and ornaments of Devadatta do not interpenetrate into the clothes and ornaments of Caitra. Hence the doctrine of Satkhyati is groundless.

**The Doctrine of Sadasatkhyati**

This doctrine is held by the Samkhya. Kapila criticizes all the rival doctrines of illusion and establishes his own doctrine. And Aniruddha explains his arguments. The Madhyamika holds that something non-existent, e.g. the identity of a nacre with a piece of silver, appears in consciousness in the illusory perception "this is silver". This is wrong, for a non-existent object can neither lead to action nor produce a cognition, e.g. the horns of a man. Prabhakara holds that in the illusory perception "this is silver" there are two cognitions : (1) the perception of "this" present to the visual organ, and (2) the recollection of "silver"; and non-discrimination of these two cognitions from each other leads to action. This also is wrong, for apprehension of non-difference or identity is found to lead to action, and the illusory perception "this is silver" is contradicted by the sublating cognition "this is not silver", while a valid cognition can never be contradicted. The Samkarite holds that the objective substrate of the illusory perception "this is silver" is neither real nor unreal nor both; if it were unreal, there would be no immediate or presentative cognition; if it were real, there would be no sublating cognition; and it cannot be both as it is self-contradictory; hence the object of the illusion is neither real nor unreal nor both, but it is undefmable. This also is wrong, for the illusory perception, in the present case, is defined as "this is silver". The Naiyayika holds that in the illusory perception "this is silver" it is a nacre that appears in consciousness as a piece of silver This also is wrong, because it is against experience that one object should appear in consciousness as another object.

Hence the Samkhya concludes that in the illusory perception "this is silver" the cognition of "this" is real (*sat*) and the cognition of "silver" is unreal (*asat*). The cognition of "this" has for its object an object present to the visual organ; so it is real. The cognition of "silver" has for its object "silver" which is not present to the visual organ, and it is contradicted by a sublating cognition; so it is unreal. So an illusion apprehends both a real object (*sat*) and an unreal object (*asat*). This is Aniruddha's interpretation of the doctrine of Sadasatkhyati. Vijnanabhiksu says that in the illusory perception "this is silver" the silver that appears in consciousness is real (*sat*), since it exists in the shop of a silver-merchant, and it is unreal (*asat*), since it is falsely ascribed to a nacre.

## The Doctrine of Prasiddharthakhyati

### *Exposition of Prasiddharthakhyati*

According to this doctrine, a non-existent thing is not the object of an illusory cognition, but a really existent object established by knowledge; for example, water is the object of the illusion of water, and when the illusory cognition is contradicted by the cognition of the rays of the sun, then the latter cognition has for its object the rays of the sun.

*Criticism of Prasiddharthakhyati*

This theory, too, is untenable. If all cognitions were true representations of their objects, there would be no difference between a valid cognition and an illusion, all cognitions would be equally valid. And a person having an illusory cognition of water and acting upon it would feel the wetness of the ground, etc., which are the effects of water though water itself may be absent, because the effect of water is not momentary like the flash of lightning. And if all cognitions are equally valid, no cognition can be contradicted by another cognition. But it is a fact of experience that some cognitions are contradicted by other cognitions. Hence the doctrine of Prasiddharthakhyati is untenable.

## The Doctrine of Vivekakhyati or Smritipramosa

*Exposition of Vivekakhyati*

Prabhakara's doctrine of *Vivekakhyati* (non-discrimination) is sometimes called *Akhyati* (non-apprehension). But in order to distinguish this doctrine from that of Akhyati described above we prefer to call it by the name of Vivekakhyati. According to Prabhakara, whatever is manifested to consciousness must be the object of that consciousness; and hence there can be no apprehension of an object as a different thing; there can be no Anyathakhyati or misapprehension.

What is the object of the illusion of silver, according to the doctrine of Anyathakhyati ? Is it silver existing in some other time and place? Or is it a nacre which conceals its own form and assumes the form of silver ? Or is it the nacre itself in its own true form?

The first alternative implies Asatkhyati. If silver existing in some other time and place is the object of the illusion of silver, then silver which does not exist at present becomes the object of the illusory cognition, and thus something non-existent is apprehended as existent. Hence Anyathakhyati implies Asatkhyati.

The second alternative is unintelligible. If a nacre, which conceals its own form and assumes the form of silver, is the objective substrate of the illusion of silver, then is there an apprehension of a nacre or an apprehension of silver? If the former, then there is no illusion, as a nacre is perceived as a nacre. If the latter, then there is no proof of the existence of the nacre there, which is manifested as silver in consciousness. It cannot be said that the nacre is known by the sublating cognition "this is not silver"; because the object of the illusion of silver cannot be established by some other cognition. A sublating cognition merely establishes the non-existence of the object of the sublated illusion, it does not ascertain the object of the illusory cognition.

The third alternative also cannot be maintained. It cannot be held that a nacre is the object of the illusion of silver. For, in that case, everything present at the time of the cognition, e.g. the proximate piece of land, etc., would be regarded as the object of the illusory cognition. Hence Prabhakara concludes that whatever is manifested in a cognition must be regarded as the object of that cognition. In the illusory cognition of silver, it is silver that is manifested in consciousness; so silver must be regarded as the object of the illusory cognition of silver. It is foolish to regard a nacre as the object of the illusion of silver.

We have already found that according to Prabhakara, there are two elements in an illusory cognition. It is made up of a presentative element and a representative element which are not discriminated from each other as long as the illusion lasts. This lack of discrimination between the two elements is the cause of exertion for the appropriation or avoidance of the object of illusion. A sublating cognition does not contradict an illusion, but simply recognizes the distinction between the presentative element and the representative element involved in an illusion. In the illusory cognition "this is silver", "this" is not identical with "silver", as the doctrine of Anyathakhyati holds, "this" is nothing but "this" which is perceived, and "silver" is nothing but "silver" which is remembered; "this" is one thing (e.g. brightness, etc.), and "silver" is quite a different thing. The distinction between these two is recognized when there is the so-called sublative cognition "this is not silver". But why are not the two elements discriminated from each other before the so-called sublative cognition ? Prabhakara holds that the representative element does not appear in consciousness as representation owing to *smritipramosa* or obscuration of memory.

### *Criticism of Vivekakhyati*

Jayanta Bhatta offers the following criticism of the doctrine of Vivekakhyati :

Prabhakara holds that an illusion is a complex psychosis made up of presentative and representative elements which cannot be discriminated from each other owing to obscuration of memory. But when the illusion is contradicted by a sublative cognition, the presentative element is discriminated from the representative element. In the illusory perception of silver in a nacre in the form "this is silver", there is a presentation of "this" and there is a representation or reproduction of silver in memory, which are not distinguished from each other. But the Naiyayika urges that in the illusion of silver there is an actual perception or presentation of silver. In this process we do actually feel that we are perceiving silver. But Prabhakara tries to explain away this fact of experience. He cannot account for the fact that as long as the illusion of silver lasts, there is an actual presentation or perception of silver, and not a mere representation of silver. He cannot give a satisfactory account of the so-called non-discrimination of the presentative element from the representative element in an illusion. He cannot also explain the nature of the so-called smritipramosa or obscuration of memory. Let us consider these in detail.

In the first place, Prabhakara holds that when we have the illusion of silver in a nacre the sense-organ does not come in contact with real silver; so there is no presentation of silver, but only a representation of silver. In the illusion "this is silver" there are two elements, a presentation of "this" and a representation of "silver", which are not discriminated from each other at the time. But the Naiyayika and the Vedantist contend that we are conscious of silver as something presented to consciousness "here and now" and not as something perceived in the past and remembered now. Nor can it be said that there is only a presentation of "this" and not of "silver", for we have a direct and immediate knowledge of both "this" and "silver" at the same time; so both of them are directly presented to consciousness or perceived at present. Gangesa and his followers hold that in the illusion "this is silver" both the elements "this" and "silver" are perceived, the first through the ordinary intercourse between the visual organ and its object, and the second through the extraordinary intercourse whose character is knowledge.

In the second place, what does Prabhakara mean by non-discrimination ? So long as an illusion lasts there is no apprehension of non-discrimination of its presentative factor from its representative factor. It is apprehended, if at all, when it is sublated. But as a matter of fact, the subsequent sublative cognition testifies to the immediate consciousness of "this is silver" at the time of the illusory perception, rather than non-discrimination of the presentative element from the representative element. Moreover, non-discrimination at the time of an illusion cannot induce exertion in the person under illusion to appropriate or avoid the illusory object. In the illusion "this is silver" what moves a person to action ? Is it the actual perception and the recollection together or either of the two ? If the former, then do the two psychoses operate together or in succession? The first of these latter alternatives is inadmissible, since presentation and representation being distinct psychoses cannot occur at the same time. If the two cognitions are successive, the former can have no casual efficiency with regard to the person's action, since the latter intervenes between the two. Nor can it be said that either psychosis by itself moves the person to action; for the particular action follows neither from the perception of "this" nor from the recollection of "silver", but from the direct and immediate apprehension of "this is silver". Thus mere non-discrimination cannot account for exertion induced by an illusion.

In the third place, what is the meaning of smritipramosa or obscuration of memory? If it means the absence of memory, then there cannot be a reproduction of silver perceived in the past, and it cannot differ from swoon in which there is no memory. If it means the consciousness of memory not as memory, but as something opposed to it, viz., perception, then the doctrine of smritipramosa would imply Anyathakhyati. If it means the apprehension of a past object as present, then also it would imply Anyathakhyati. If it means the blending of perception with recollection in such a way that the two psychoses cannot be distinguished from each other, then what is the meaning of blending ? Does it mean the apprehension of the two different psychoses as non-different or identical ? Or does it mean the actual blending of the two different psychoses ? The first alternative leads to Anyathakhyati. The second alternative is impossible, for two physical things can blend with each other as milk and water, but two psychoses cannot blend with each other. Thus the doctrine of smritipramosa is unintelligible.

**The Doctrine of Anyathakhyati**

According to the doctrine of Anyathakhyati, an object is apprehended as a different object in an illusion which is not a sum of two psychical processes—perception and recollection—but a single psychosis of a perceptual character. When we perceive silver in a nacre, we perceive in the nacre only the common qualities of nacre and silver, and not the peculiar qualities of the nacre; the perception of similarity revives the idea of the peculiar qualities of silver in memory; and the reproduction of silver in memory produces the perception of silver, and so we have an illusory perception "this is silver".

Jayanta Bhatta refutes Prabhakara's objections to the doctrine of Anyathakhyatı in the following manner :

First, Prabhakara has urged : What is the objective substrate of the illusion of silver ? Is it silver existing in some other time and place? Or is it a nacre that conceals its own form and assumes the form of silver? Or is it a nacre in itself? He has urged that the first alternative implies Asatkhyati or apprehension of a non-existent object as existent. The Naiyayika replies that silver is not non-existent; but it does exist in some other time and place. There is a difference between an absolutely non-existent thing (e.g. a skyflower, etc.) and an object not existing "here and now", but in some other time and place. The former is never an object of consciousness, while the latter is an object of consciousness.

Secondly, Prabhakara has urged that the second alternative is absurd and unintelligible. The Naiyayika replies that the nacre is said to conceal its own form, since we do not perceive its peculiar features (e.g. triangularity, etc.), and it is said to assume the form of silver, since we remember the distinctive features of silver.

Thirdly, Prabhakara has urged that the third alternative also is unreasonable. One object can never be apprehended as a different one; for, in that case, whatever is present to the sense-organ at the time of the illusory perception of silver would be regarded as the substrate of that illusion. The Naiyayika replies that he does not mean that whatever is present to the sense-organ is the object of consciousness, so that the piece of land before the eyes may be regarded as the object of consciousness. What he means is that the nacre is the cause of the illusion of silver; it is not an object of the illusory perception of silver. So all the charges of Prabhakara against Anyathakhyati are groundless.

**Different Theories of Illusions Compared**

According to the doctrine of Akhyati, an illusion consists in non-apprehension of an object (*akhyati*). An illusion has no external stimulus at all; it is objectless (*niralambana*). This doctrine is right in so far as the object that is manifested in consciousness in an illusory cognition does not exist at that time and place. For example, silver does not exist at that time and place when and where there is the illusory cognition of silver. But it is wrong for two reasons. In the first place, an illusory perception is not mere non-apprehension of an object, it is apprehension of something; in the illusory perception of silver there is apprehension of silver though the object does not exist at that time and place; there is not mere non-apprehension of a nacre. In the second place, an illusory perception is not always objectless, in most cases it has an external stimulus (*alambana*). But sometimes an illusion is not produced by an external stimulus; it is produced directly by the mind affected by a certain derangement. It is called a hallucination. But all illusions are not hallucinations.

The Madhyamika holds that an illusion consists in the apprehension of a non-existent object (*asatkhyati*). The Madhyamika agrees with the above view that an illusion has no external stimulus at all. But according to the former, an illusory cognition consists in non-apprehension of an object (*akhyati*), while according to the latter, it consists in apprehension of a non-existent object (*asatkhyati*). The doctrine of Asatkhyati is right in so far as the object of an illusion does not exist then and there. But it is wrong in so far as the object of an illusion is not absolutely non-existent, but exists in some other time and place. But this doctrine is in keeping with the spirit of nihilism of the Madhyamika. According to him, the ultimate reality is Void (*sunyarn*); neither the external world nor the inner world of ideas is real.

The Yogacara holds that an illusion consists in apprehension of a subjective cognition (*atmakhyati*). He agrees with the above two views that an illusion has. no external stimulus at all; it is absolutely objectless. But, according to him, an illusory cognition consists neither in non-apprehension of an object nor in apprehension of a non-existent object, but in apprehension of a purely subjective cognition as an external object; an illusion consists in projection of an idea into the external world. But only hallucinations are illusions of this kind. Other illusions are produced by external stimuli; they are not pure creations of fancy. They cannot be explained by the doctrine of Atmakhyati. But this doctrine is in keeping with the spirit of subjective idealism of the Yogacara. According to him, there is no external world at all; there is only the inner world of ideas which appear to us as external objects.

The Samkarite holds that an illusion consists in apprehension of an undefinable object (*anirvacaniyakhyati*). According to him, an illusion has an objective basis; it has an external stimulus, it has an illusory object corresponding to it. The Samkarite believes in three degrees of reality : (1) ontological reality (*paramarthikasatta*); (2) empirical reality (*vyavaharikasatta*), and (3) illusory reality (*pratibhasika-satta*). Brahman has ontological reality; the world of external objects conditioned by space, time, and causality has empirical reality, and objects falsely ascribed to empirical objects, like silver ascribed to a nacre, have illusory reality : these also have an extra-mental existence. The illusory perception of silver has for its object extra-mental illusory silver (*pratibhasika rajata*) which is neither real, nor unreal, nor both, but undefinable.

The doctrine of Alaukikakhyati is substantially the same as that of Anirvacaniyakhyati. According to Alaukikakhyati, the illusory perception of silver has extraordinary silver (*alaukika rajata*) for its object, which has no practical efficiency. These doctrines go beyond the province of psychology and seek to define the ontological nature of the object of an illusion. They recognize the distinctive character of an illusory cognition. According to them, it is presentative or perceptual in character. But a presentative cognition always requires a present object which is an illusory reality (*pratibhasika*) according to Anirvacaniyakhyati, and an extraordinary reality (*alaukika*), according to Alaukikakhyati.

The Ramanujist holds that an illusion consists in apprehension of a real object (*satkhyati*). The illusory perception of silver in a nacre has real silver for its object. The Samkarite believes in the illusory existence (*pratibhasika-satta*) of silver at the time of the illusory perception. But the Ramanujist believes in its ontological existence (*paramarthika-satta*) at the time of the illusory perception. According to him, silver really exists in the nacre in the form of its elements; and the nacre is similar to silver only because silver does exist in part in the nacre. But this is going too far. Similarity means similarity in qualities. It does not necessarily mean partial co-existence of two things in each other. The doctrine of Satkhyati is based on the cosmological doctrine of triplication or quintuplication of the elements.

The Samkhya holds that an illusion consists in apprehension of a real object and an unreal object both (*sadasatkhyati*). In the illusory cognition of silver in the form "this is silver" the cognition of "this" is the apprehension of an object present to the sense-organ, and the cognition of "silver" is the apprehension of silver which is not present to the sense organ. Prabhakara makes it more clear. According to him, an illusory cognition is a complex psychosis made up of a presentative element and a representative element. The illusory cognition in the form "this is silver" is made up of the perception of "this" and the recollection of "silver" which are not discriminated from each other until the illusion is contradicted. But Prabhakara misses the distinctive psychological character of an illusory cognition; it is a perceptual process, though it depends upon perception and recollection both. Prabhakara contends that the representative process in an illusory cognition appears to be a presentative process owing to smritipramosa or lapse of memory. But why should he explain away a fact of experience by an unintelligible theory. An illusory cognition is experienced as a direct and immediate perception.

The Naiyayika holds that an illusion consists in misapprehension of one object as another or apprehension of an object in that in which it does not exist. According to him, an illusory cognition is a single psychosis of a perceptual character which is produced by a sense-organ impaired by a certain defect in contact with an external object in co-operation with the subconscious impression of another object with which it has similarity. In the illusory perception of silver in a nacre, the nacre is wrongly perceived as silver owing to the perversion of the sense-organ and the subconscious impression of another object awakened by the perception of similarity. This theory is not based on metaphysical grounds. It is based on the evidence of our experience.

# 15

# Dreams

## The Psychological Character of Dream-consciousness

### *The Presentative Theory of Dreams*

Kanada defines a dream-cognition as the consciousness produced by a particular conjunction of the self with the central sensory or manas in co-operation with the subconscious impressions of past experience, like recollection.

Prasastapada defines a dream-cognition as an internal perception through the central sensory or mind, when all the functions of the external sense-organs have ceased and the mind has retired within a trans-organic region of the organism. When the internal organ (*manas*) retires within itself, the peripheral organs cease to operate and consequently cannot apprehend their objects as they are no longer guided by the mind. During this retired state of the mind, when the automatic vital functions of in-breathings and out-breathings profusely go on in the organism, dream-cognitions arise through the central sensory from such causes as sleep, which is the name of a particular conjunction of the self with the mind, and subconscious impressions of past experience; these dream-cognitions are internal perceptions of unreal objects.

Udayana says that in the dream-state, though the external sense-organs cease to operate, we distinctly feel that we see objects with our very eyes, hear sounds with our very ears, and so on. Samkaramisra also holds that though a dream-cognition is produced by the mind when it has retired, and the external sense-organs have ceased to operate, it is apprehended as if it were produced by the external sense-organs (*indriyadvareneva*) .

Sridhara also regards cognitions as presentative in character. He says that dream-cognitions are independent of previous cognitions, and as such are not mere reproductions of past experience; they are produced through the retired central sensory or mind when the functions of all the peripheral organs have ceased; they are direct and immediate presentations of a definite and determinate character. These dream-cognitions arising from sleep and subconscious impressions are direct and immediate presentations (*aparoksasamwedena*) of objects which have no real existence at that time and place. Thus Sridhara clearly points out that dream-cognitions are presentative in character; they are not mere reproductions of past experience. But dream-perceptions are not produced by the external organs which cease to function at that time, but they are produced entirely by the mind (*manomatraprabhavam*). And these dream-perceptions are not indefinite and indeterminate in nature, but they are definite and determinate in character (*paricchedasvabhava*). And these dream-perceptions are not valid but illusory, since they do not represent real objects present to the sense-organs "here and now".

Sivaditya defines a dream as a cognition produced by the central sensory perverted by sleep. Madhava Sarasvati points out the following distinctive marks of dream-cognitions as defined by Sivaditya. Firstly, they are produced by the central sensory or mind, and as such are different from the waking perceptions of jars and the like, which are produced by the external sense-organs. Secondly, they are produced by the perverted mind, and as such are different from the waking perceptions of pleasure and the like, which are produced by the unperverted mind. Thirdly, they are produced by the mind perverted by sleep, and as such are different from waking hallucinations which are produced by the perverted mind in the waking condition.

Prasastapada, Sridhara, Samkaramisra, Sivaditya and others recognize the central origin of dreams. Though they hold that certain dreams are produced by organic disorders within the body, they do not recognize the origin of dreams from the external sense-organs. But Udayana admits that in the dream-state the peripheral organs (at least the tactual organ which pervades the organism) do not altogether cease to operate; external stimuli, if not sufficiently intense to awaken the person, may act upon the peripheral organs and produce dream-cognitions. Thus Udayana recognizes both peripherally excited and centrally excited dreams, or in the language of Sully, dream-illusions and dream-hallucinations. Udayana also holds that though dream-cognitions are generally perceptual in character being produced by the central sensory or mind, sometimes, though very rarely, they assume the form of inference, when, for instance, a person dreams that he sees smoke in a particular place and from the sight of the smoke infers that there must be fire behind it. Thus the Vaisesikas generally advocate the presentative theory of dreams.

The ancient Naiyayikas also consider dreams as presentative in character. Gautama does not include dream-cognition in recollection. Vatsyayana regards dream as distinct from recollection. Udyotkara and Vacaspati also agree with Gautama and Vatsyayana. Thus the Naiyayikas and the Vaisesikas generally recognize the perceptual character of dreams. But there are some Nyaya-Vaisesika writers who hold that dreams are representative in character; they are recollections of past experience due to revival of subconscious impressions. We may designate this doctrine as the representative theory of dreams as contrasted with the presentative theory.

### *The Representative Theory of Dreams*

Among the Naiyayikas Bhasarvajna started the view that dream-consciousness is a kind of false recollection (*smrti*). We have already seen that Jayasimhasuri distinguishes between *anubhuyamanaropa* illusions and *smaryamanaropa* illusions. The former consist in the false ascription of a percept to another percept. The latter consist in the false ascription of an idea of memory to a percept. Jayasimhasuri includes dreams in the latter. So he regards them as representative in character. Jayanta Bhatta seems to regard dream-cognitions as recollections of past experience. Kesavamisra regards all dream-cognitions as false recollections. Jagadisa holds that dream-cognitions are produced by recollections of objects perceived in the past, *adrsta* or merit and demerit, and intra-organic disorders. Thus the ancient Naiyayikas regard dreams as presentative in character, while the majority of medieval and modern Naiyayikas, regard them as representative in character.

The Mimamsakas also recognize the representative character of dreams. Kumarila holds that even dreams have an objective basis; they are produced by external objects which are not present to the sense-organs but were perceived elsewhere in the past and now revived through their subconscious impressions. Parthasarathimisra says, "It is definitely known that dream-cognitions are of the nature of recollection." He holds that external objects perceived in some other time and place are remembered owing to the revival of their impressions through the agency of *adrsta* (merit or demerit); but they appear to consciousness as objects existing here and now owing to the perversion of the mind by sleep. Prabhakara also regards dream-cognitions as recollections of past experience. But he slightly modifies the doctrine of Kumarila. He advances his theory of obscuration of memory (*smrtipramosa*) to account for the apparently presentative character of dreams. His theory will be considered in the next section.

Samkara also is an advocate of the representative theory of dreams. He says, "Dream-consciousness is of the nature of recollection (*smrtt*)". "Dreams are reproductions of past waking perceptions owing to the revival of their subconscious impressions; so they have the semblance of waking perceptions." Though Samkara advocates the representative theory of dreams, his follower, Dharmarajadvarindra advocates the presentative theory.

***Prabhakara's Representative Theory of Dreams***

According to Prabhakara, dream-cognitions are really reproductions of past waking experience; but they appear to consciousness as direct and immediate sense-presentations owing to lapse of memory (*smrtipramosa*). In dream-consciousness memory-images of past experience appear to consciousness as percepts. It is due to lapse of memory which makes the distinctive character of the memory images, viz., their representative character drop out of consciousness; and thus the memory-images of past experience deprived of their representative character appear to consciousness as percepts in dream. The process may be represented as follows :

Memory-image–memory = percept; or re-presentation–memory = presentation.

Recollection is the apprehension of the previously apprehended (*grhitagrahanam smrtih*); and if the element of "the apprehended" sinks below the threshhold of consciousness, then recollection appears as a direct apprehension or perception, the representation appears as a direct and immediate presentation. Thus, according to Prabhakara, dream-cognitions are really representative in character, but they appear to consciousness as direct presentations owing to lapse of memory. Prabhakara explains both the waking illusions and dream illusions by the same theory of obscuration of memory (*smrtipramosa*).

### *The Nyaya-Vaisesika Criticism of the Prabhakara Theory*

Udayana discusses the nature of dream-cognitions in *Nyayakusumanjali* and criticizes the Prabhakara theory of dreams. In the dream-state, though the external sense-organs cease to function, yet we have direct and immediate presentations of objects not present at that time and place. This dream-consciousness cannot be of the nature of memory, inasmuch as during the state of dream we do not recognize dream-cognitions as reproductions of our past experience in such a form as "I remember this"; nor, on waking from sleep, do we remember our dream-cognitions in such a form as "I remembered this". But, on the contrary, during the state of dream we apprehend our dream-cognitions as actual perceptions, and not as mere echoes of our past experience; and on waking from sleep we remember our dream-cognitions as actual perceptions in the dream state. So dream-cognitions are not representative but perceptual in character.

But how can they be perceptual in nature, since the things that are presented to consciousness in dream are not present at that time and place, and the peripheral organs are not quite operative at that time, which are the channels of all perceptions, and the central organ too cannot apprehend external objects without the help of the peripheral organs ? Are dream-cognitions, then, illusions of memory (*smrti-viparyasa*) ? Do dream-cognitions appear as percepts, though, as a matter of fact, they are nothing but memory-images ? Do memory-images appear to consciousness as percepts in dream cognitions ? Are dream-cognitions the illusions of memory, as Prabhakara holds ? If by illusions of memory he means the illusory cognitions of the objects of memory, Udayana has no objection. But if by these he means the illusory appearance of memory as perception, then it cannot be maintained that dream-cognitions are the illusions of memory.

For if dream-cognitions were nothing but illusory appearances of memory-images as percepts, the perceptual character of dream-cognitions would be contradicted at some time or other and recognized as representative. But, in fact, in the dream state we never recognize dream-cognitions as reproductions of our past experience. Besides, in the dream-state we have cognitions of many things which have never been perceived before, e.g. the lopping off of our own heads. Moreover, it is not possible for one form of consciousness to appear as another, though an object may appear to consciousness as quite a different thing. If in dream-consciousness memory-images were illusorily cognized as percepts, we would never have a direct presentative consciousness in the form "I perceive this pot", but we would have a presentative consciousness in the form "I perceive that pot" (i.e. perceived in the past and reproduced in memory). As a matter of fact, in dream-cognitions we have a direct and immediate presentation in the form "I perceive this pot". Thisness is the special characteristic of perception alone, while thatness of memory. Hence, dream-cognitions must be admitted to be presentative or perceptual in character.

### *The Samkarite Criticism of the Prabhakara Theory*

According to the Samkarite, in an illusory perception of waking life we do not perceive an object as another, as the Nyaya-Vaiesika holds, but we perceive an illusory reality which is produced at that time and place; this reality is illusory (*pratibhasika*) and undefinable (*anirvacaniya*) as distinguished from the empirical (*vyavaharika*) reality which is the object of right perception. Likewise, according to him, dream-cognitions too are illusory perceptions, during sleep, of illusory realities produced at that time and place, like the illusory perceptions of our waking life.

But Prabhakara contends that dream-cognitions cannot be direct and immediate sense-presentations, because the peripheral organs cease to function during sleep and the central sensory or mind cannot apprehend external objects without the help of the peripheral organs; and because dream-cognitions are not presentations at all, it is quite useless to assume that they apprehend illusory realities produced at that time and place. In fact, Prabhakara urges that dream cognitions are nothing but representations of our previous waking perceptions; and because we cannot discriminate the dream representations from their originals in waking perceptions we mistake them for actual sense-presentations.

To this the Samkarite replies that dream-cognitions cannot be representative in character because in dream we are conscious that "we see a chariot", and on waking from dream we are conscious that "we saw a chariot in dream". This introspection clearly shows that dreams are perceptual in character and this fact of experience cannot be explained away by a dogmatic assumption. And, moreover, dream-cognitions cannot be mere recollections of our previous waking perceptions, for the objects of dream-cognitions (e.g. chariots, elephants, etc.) were never perceived in our waking life exactly in that place; hence dream-cognitions must be regarded as immediate presentations or perceptions.

### *The Samkarite Criticism of the Nyaya-Vaisesika Theory*

Though the Samkarite agrees with the Nyaya-Vaisesika in regarding dream-cognitions as presentative in character, and in refuting Prabhakara's doctrine of the representative character of dreams, yet he differs from the latter in the metaphysical implication of dreams. According to the Nyaya-Vaisesika, in an illusory perception we erroneously ascribe unreal silver to a nacre which is real in the illusory perception of the nacre as silver (*suktirajata*). But the Samkarite holds that unreal silver (*pratibhasika rajata*) is produced at that time and place, which is apprehended by the illusory cognition of silver. So, in dream-cognitions, too, according to him, unreal objects such as elephants, chariots, etc., are produced at that time and place and continue as long as dream-cognitions last.

The objects of dream-cognitions (e.g. chariots, elephants, etc.) cannot be erroneously ascribed to any real object (e.g. ground) present to the sense-organs, since the ground is not in contact with the peripheral organs. Nor can they be erroneously ascribed to an object such as ground reproduced in memory, since the ground is not reproduced in memory in dream but is an object of actual perception. Moreover, the objects of dream-cognitions cannot be perceived through the peripheral organs, since they do not really exist in that place, and consequently cannot come in contact with the sense-organs.

Nor can these objects of dream-cognitions be brought to consciousness in dream through association (*jnanalaksanasannikarsa*) with the ideas of other objects which are not present to the sense-organs at that time. Nor can they be perceived by the mind, since it cannot apprehend external objects which are not in contact with the external organs. Nor can they be cognized by inference, since they are distinctly felt as objects of direct perception. Moreover, the objects of dream-cognitions are perceived in the absence of recollection of any mark of inference. According to the Samkarite, therefore, the unreal objects of dream-cognitions are produced at that time and place and continue as long as dream cognitions last. Herein lies the difference between the Nyaya-Vaisesika and the Samkara-Vadanta in their explanation of dream-cognitions.

**Dreams, Illusions and Indefinite Perceptions**

Udayana distinguishes dream-cognitions from illusory perceptions of waking life and doubtful and indefinite perceptions. Though dream-cognitions are illusory perceptions, since they apprehend objects which are not present at that time and place, and as such resemble illusory perceptions of waking life, they differ from the latter in that they are produced when the peripheral organs are not quite operative, while the latter are produced by the peripheral organs. Then, again, dream-cognitions are not to be identified with doubtful and indefinite perceptions. For dream-cognitions are definite and determinate in character, in which the mind does not oscillate between alternate possibilities, while doubtful and indefinite perceptions are uncertain, because in them the mind is not fixed on a definite object but wavers between two objects without any definite decision. Bhatta Vadindra also describes a dream-cognition as an illusory, definite perception (*niyatakotika*) which does not waver between alternate possibilities and which is produced when all the peripheral organs cease to operate.

Sridhara also holds that dream-cognitions are definite and determinate perceptions as distinguished from indefinite and indeterminate perceptions. And also he clearly shows that dream-cognitions, arising either from the intensity of subconscious traces, or from intra-organic disorders, or from unseen agencies, are purely illusory, since they consist in the false imposition of an external form upon something that is wholly internal, and as such are not essentially different from the illusions of our waking life, the only difference lying in the fact that the former are illusory perceptions in the condition of sleep, while the latter are illusory perceptions in the waking condition.

Jayasimhasuri also holds that dreams are illusions in the condition of sleep. Dreams are illusions because in them things which were perceived in the past and in some other place are perceived here and now. Thus, in the language of James Sully, "Dreams are clearly illusory, and, unlike the illusions of waking life, are complete and persistent."

## Dreams and Hallucinations

Hallucinations are pure creations of the mind. And some dreams also are pure creations of the mind (*manomatraprabhava*). Both are centrally initiated presentations. Both are definite and determinate in character. And both are unreal. So there is a great resemblance between dreams and hallucinations. The only difference between them lies in the fact that the former are hallucinations in sleep, while the latter are hallucinations in the waking condition. This distinction has been pointed out by Madhava Sarasvati.

Frank Padmore says : "A dream is a hallucination in sleep, and a hallucination is only a waking dream, though it is probable that the waking impression, seeing that it can contend on equal terms with the impressions derived from external objects, is more vivid than the common run of dream." Wundt also regards dreams as hallucinations. They are as vivid as sensory experience and are projected into the external world as are sensations.

## Classification of Dreams

### *Caraka's Classification*

We find a crude classification of dreams in *Caraka-samhita.* Caraka says that a person sees various dreams through the mind which is the guide of the external sense-organs when he is not in profound sleep. Some of these dreams are significant; others are not. These dreams are of seven kinds, viz. dreams of those objects which have been seen, heard, and felt, dreams of those objects which are desired, dreams awakened by imagination, dreams that are premonitions of future events, and pathological or morbid dreams.

Caraka seems to suggest here the following psychological facts. Some dreams are mere reproductions of past experience (*anubhuta*) though they are apprehended as immediate perceptions. Some dreams involve constructive imagination (*kalpita*) though the material is supplied by memory. Some dreams are fulfilment of desires (*prarthita*). Some dreams are stimulated by pathological disorders within the organism (*dosaja*). And some dreams are prophetic in character (*bhavika*); they foreshadow future events. This fact is called dream-coincidence in modern western psychology. According to Caraka, dreams are experienced only in light sleep; they are produced by the central sensory or mind.

### *The Vasesika Classification*

Prasastapada, Sridhara, Udayana, Samkaramisra and others describe four kinds of dreams : (1) dreams due to intra-organic pathological disorders (*dhatudosa*); (2) dreams due to the intensity of subconscious impressions (*samskarapatava*); (3) dreams due to the unseen agency (*adrsta*), i.e. merit and demerit (*dharmadharma*); and (4) "dream-end cognitions" or dreams-within-dreams (*svapnantika jnana*).

### *The Buddhist Classification*

S.Z. Aung says that Ariyavansa-Adiccaransi attempted a systematic explanation of dream-phenomena from the Buddhist standpoint nearly a century ago in Burma. He recognized four kinds of dreams : (1) dreams due to organic and muscular disturbances, e.g. the flatulent, phlegmatic, and bilious humours; (2) recurrent dreams consisting in recurrence of the previous dreams, due to previous experiences; (3) telepathic dreams due to suggestions from spiritualistic agents, and (4) prophetic dreams due to the force of character of clairvoyant dreamers. "The first category includes the dreams of a fall over a precipice, flying into the sky, etc., and what is called "nightmare"; the second consists of the "echoes of past waking experiences"; the third may include dream coincidences; and the fourth is of a clairvoyant character."

Thus the Buddhists add to the Vaisesika list dreams due to spirit influence, or telepathic dreams. In addition to these various kinds of dreams, Caraka recognizes dreams which are wish-fulfilments.

Madhusudana and Samkara also recognize the influence of desires on dreams. These different kinds of dreams will be considered in the next section.

## Different Kinds of Dreams

We have seen that according to most Indian thinkers, dream-cognitions are presentative in character. They are felt as perceptions and are aroused by external and internal stimuli. They are sometimes produced by extra-organic stimuli, and sometimes by intra-organic stimuli in the shape of peripheral disturbances and other organic disorders. These dreams may be called dream-illusions. And there are some dream-cognitions which are produced by the strength of subconscious impressions of a recent experience coloured by an intense emotion. These dreams are centrally excited and hence may be called dream-hallucinations. Among the Western psychologists, Spitta, first of all, drew a distinction between these two kinds of dreams, and called the former *nervenreiztraume*, and the latter *psychische traume*. Miss Calkins calls the former presentation dreams, and the latter representation dreams. Jastrow calls the former presentative dreams and the latter representative dreams. Sully calls the former dream-illusions and the latter dream-hallucinations. And besides these two kinds of dreams, the Indian thinkers recognize prophetic or veridical dreams and telepathic dreams. The former are due to the merit and demerit of the dreamer, forecasting the future and so on; and the latter are due to the suggestive force of spiritualistic agents. In addition to these, there are dreams-within-dreams or "dream-end" cognitions. Let us consider the nature of these different kinds of dreams.

## Dreams Due to Peripheral Stimulation (Dream-Illusions)

Dream-illusions are those dreams which are excited by peripheral stimulation either internal or external. Udayana has discussed the question of the extra-organic and intra-organic origin of dreams. How can dream-cognitions arise in sleep ? What is the origin of dreams ? Dream-illusions are produced by the reproduction of those objects, the subconscious traces of which are resuscitated owing to certain causes. But how can the subconscious traces be revived without the suggestive force of similar experience ? What is the suggestive force here that revives the subconscious traces of past experience ? Udayana says that in dream-cognitions peripheral stimulation is not altogether absent. Dreams are not altogether without external stimuli; they are excited by certain external stimuli in the environment, and certain intra-organic stimuli. In the state of dream we do not altogether cease to perceive external objects, since the external sense-organs are not entirely inoperative. For instance, we perceive external sounds in dream, when they are not sufficiently loud to rouse us from sleep, and the faint external sounds perceived through the ears even during light sleep easily incorporate themselves into dreams. Even if all other external sense-organs cease to function in dream, at least the organ of touch is not inoperative, as the mind or central sensory does not lose its connection with the tactual organ even in dream, which is not confined to the external skin but pervades the whole organism according to the Nyaya-Vaisesika. This is the peculiar doctrine of the Nyaya-Vaisesika. In dream we can perceive at least the heat of our organism which serves to revive the subconscious traces of past experience. Hence certain extra-organic or intra-organic stimuli serve as the exciting cause of the revival of subconscious traces in dream.

Thus Udayana does not recognize the purely hallucinatory character of dreams. According to him, all dreams are of the nature of illusions because they are initiated by extra-organic or intra-organic stimuli. Thus he anticipates the more recent account of dreams in Western psychology. "Dream-appearances," says A.E. Taylor, "which Volkmann classes as hallucinations are more accurately regarded by Wundt as generally, if not always, based on illusion, i.e. they are misinterpretations of actual minimal sense-impressions such as those due to slight noises, to the positions of the sleeper's limbs, to trifling pains, slight difficulties in breathing, palpitations, and the like." Sully says, "Dreams are commonly classified with hallucinations, and this rightly, since, as their common appellation of 'vision' suggests, they are for the most part the semblance of percepts in the absence of external impressions. At the same time, recent research goes to show that in many dreams something answering to the 'external impression' in waking perception is starting point". Bergson says, "When we are sleeping naturally, it is not necessary to believe, as has often been supposed, that our senses are closed to external sensations. Our senses continue to be active." "Our senses continue to act during sleep they provide us with the outline, or at least the point of departure, of most of our dreams."

Prasastapada also describes the intra-organic stimulation of dream-illusions, which has been explained and illustrated by Udayana, Sridhara, Samkaramisra Jayanarayana, Tarka-Pancanana and others. There are some dreams which are due to intra-organic disturbances such as the disorders of the flatulent, bilious, and phlegmatic humours of the organism, which are supposed by the Hindu medical science to be the causes of all organic diseases (*dhatudosa*). Those who suffer from disorder of flatulency dream that they are flying in the sky, wandering about on the earth, fleeing with fear from tigers, etc. These are kinesthetic dreams of levitation. And those who are of a bilious temperament or suffer from an inordinate secretion of bile dream that they are entering into fire, embracing flames of fire, seeing golden mountains, flashes of lightning, meteorfalls, a huge conflagration, the scorching rays of the mid-day sun, etc. And those who are of a phlegmatic temperament or suffer from phlegmatic disorders dream that they are crossing the sea, bathing in rivers, being sprinkled with showers of rain, and seeing mountains of silver and the like.

**Dreams Due to Subconscious Impressions (Dream-Hallucinations)**

There are many dreams which are not excited by peripheral nerve-stimulation but by the intensity of the subconscious impressions left by a recent experience (*samskarapatava*). On the physical side, these dreams are due to central stimulation, and hence may be called dream-hallucinations. These dreams are generally excited by intense passions. For instance, when a man infatuated with love for a woman or highly enraged at his enemy, constantly thinks of his beloved or enemy, and while thus thinking falls asleep, then the series of thoughts produces a series of memory-images, which are manifested in consciousness as immediate sense-presentations owing to the strength of subconscious impressions. These dreams are purely hallucinatory in character.

We find a similar Buddhist account of dreams in Aung's Introduction to the *Compendium of Philosophy* in which he has summarized Ariyavansa-Adiccaransi's explanation of dreams. "When scenes are reproduced automatically in a dream with our eyes closed, the obvious inference is that we see them by way of the door of the mind. Even in the case of peripheral stimulations, as when a light, brought near a sleeping man's eye, is mistaken for a bonfire, it is this exaggerated light that is perceived in a dream by the mind-door. ... If these presentations do not come from without, they must come from within, from the 'inner' activities of mind. That is to say, if peripheral stimulations are absent, we must look to the automatic activity of mind itself for the source of these presentations; or, to speak in terms of physiology, we must look to the central activity of the cerebrum, which is now generally admitted to be the physical counterpart of the mind-door, the sensory nerves being the physical counterpart of the five-doors in an 'organized sentient existence' (*pancavokarabhava*)."

But Udayana surmizes that even these centrally excited dreams due to the revival of subconscious traces are suggested by extra-organic or intra-organic stimuli.

**Dreams as the fulfilment of Desires (Dream-hallucinations)**

Caraka says that some dreams are about those objects which are desired (*prarthita*). Madhusudana defines dream as the perception of objects due to the desires (*vasana*) in the mind (*antahkarana*) when the external sense-organs are inoperative. Samkara also recognizes the influence of desires (*vasana*) on dreams. Dr. M.N. Sircar truly observes: "Here the word 'desire' is significant, it introduces a volitional element in dream. It seems to hold that desires get freedom, in a state of passivity and acquire strength, finally appearing in the form of dream construction." This reminds us of the Freudian theory, according to which, dreams arise out of the unfulfilled desires of the unconscious. These dreams also should be regarded as dream-hallucinations, because they are not excited by peripheral stimulation, they are centrally initiated presentations or hallucinations.

**Prophetic or Veridical Dreams**

But all dreams cannot be explained by peripheral stimulation, due to the action either of external stimuli or internal stimuli, and by central stimulation. There are certain dreams which are prophetic in character; they are either auspicious or inauspicious. Auspicious dreams betoken good and inauspicious dreams forebode evil. The former are due to a certain merit (*dharma*) of the person, and the latter, to a certain demerit (*adharma*). Some of these prophetic dreams are echoes of our past waking experiences, while others apprehend entirely novel objects never perceived before. The former are brought about by the subconscious traces of our past experience, in co-operation with merit or demerit, according as they augur good or evil, while the latter, by merit or demerit alone, since there are no subconscious traces of such absolutely unknown objects. But merit and demerit are supernatural agents; so this explanation of prophetic dreams seems to be unscientific. But we may interpret the agency of merit and demerit as "the force of character of clairvoyant dreamers" after Mr. Aung.

Prasastapada and his followers recognized only three causes of dreams : (1) intensity of subconscious impressions, (2) intra-organic disorders, and (3) *adrsta* or merit and demerit of the dreamer. (*samskarapatavat dhatudosat adrstacca*)

**Telepathic Dreams**

And besides the peripherally excited dreams, centrally excited dreams, and prophetic dreams, Ariyavansa-Adiccaransi, a Buddhist writer, has recognized another class of dreams which are due to spirit-influence, or "due to suggestions from spiritualistic agents" in the language of Aung; these may include "dream-coincidences". They may be called telepathic dreams.

**Dreams-within-dreams**

Besides these dream-cognitions which we do not recognize as dreams during the dream-state, sometimes we have another kind of dream-cognitions which are recognized as dreams. Sometimes in the dream-state we dream that we have been dreaming of some thing; this dream-within-dream is called *svapnantika-jnana,* which has been rendered by Dr. Ganganatha Jha as a "dream-end cognition"; in this "dream-end cognition" a dream is the object of another dream. Such a "dream-end cognition" arises in the mind of a person whose sense-organs have ceased their operations, so it is apt to be confounded with a mere dream-cognition. But Prasastapada, Sridhara and Samkaramisra rightly point out that our "dream-end cognitions" essentially differ from mere dream-cognitions, since the former are representative, while the latter are presentative in character. The "dream-end cognitions" are recollections of dream-cognitions, while dream-cognitions resemble direct sense-perceptions. Dream-cognitions are presentative in character, though they arise out of the traces left in the mind by the previous perceptions in the waking condition; and these presentative dream-cognitions again leave traces in the mind which give rise to "dream-end cognitions". Thus dreams-within-dreams are representative in character.

**Physiological Basis of Dreams**

Caraka and Susruta describe various kinds of dreams which are the prognostics of impending diseases and death. Caraka suggests a physiological explanation of the morbid dreams which precede death. These horrible dreams are due to the currents in the *manovaha nadis* being filled with very strong flatulent, bilious, and phlegmatic humours before death.

From this we may infer that dreams are due to the excitation of the *manovaha nadi* which, in the language of Dr. B. N. Seal, is "a generic name for the channels along which centrally initiated presentations (as in dreaming or hallucination) come to the sixth lobe of the Manaschakra".

Samkaramisra says that dreams are produced by the mind when it is in the *svapnavaha nadi* and disconnected with the external sense-organs except the tactual organ; when the mind loses its connection even with the tactual organ and retires into the puntat there is deep dreamless sleep. Thus dreams are produced when the mind is in the *svapnavaha nadi*.

Thus, according to Caraka, the *manovaha nadi* is the seat of dreams, and according to Samkaramisra, the *svapnavaha nadi* is the seat of dreams. What is the relation between the *manovaha nadi* and the *svapnavaha nadi* ? Dr. B.N. Seal says that according to the writers on Yoga and Tantras, "the *manovaha nadi* is the channel of the communication of the *Jiva* (soul) with the Manaschakra (sensorium) at the base of the brain. It has been stated that the sensory currents are brought to the sensory ganglia along different nerves of the special senses. But this is not sufficient for them to rise to the level of discriminative consciousness (*savikalpaka jnana*). A communication must now be established between the *jiva* (in the *sahasrara chakra,* upper cerebrum) and the sensory currents received at the sensorium, and this is done by means of the *manovaha nadi.* When sensations are centrally initiated, as in dreams and hallucinations, a special nadi (*svapnavaha nadi*) which appears to be only a branch of the *manovaha nadi,* serves as the channel of communication from the *jiva* (soul) to the sensorium".

**Theories of Dreams**

Aung gives us a lucid account of the four Buddhist theories of dreams : "The first of these is clearly the physiological theory, which recognizes a source of dreams in the pathological conditions of the body. . . . The theory of the induction of dreams by peripheral nerve-stimulation, due either to the action of external objects on sense-organs, or to disturbances in the peripheral regions of the nerves, is but a branch of the physiological theory. The second may be called the psychological theory. It recognizes the induction of dreams by central stimulation due to the automatic activities of the mind. The theory of the induction of dreams by the agency of spirits may be stigmatized in the West as "the superstitious theory". "But as the *devas,* or mythical beings as they would be termed in the West, are, according to Buddhism, but different grades of sentient beings in the thirty-one stages of existence, the theory in question, merely recognizes the suggestive action of mind upon mind, and may therefore be aptly called the telepathic or telepsychic theory". The theory of the induction of prophetic dreams bý the agency of merit and demerit may be called "the clairvoyant theory". The theory which explains dreams as the fulfilment of desires may also be called the psychological theory. The different kinds of dreams described by Indian thinkers may be explained by these four theories.

# 16

# Abnormal Perceptions

## The Treatment in the Samkhya

Isvarakrsna mentions eleven kinds of anaesthesia of the sense-organs (*indriya-badha*) corresponding to the eleven kinds of sense-organs: five sensory organs, five motor organs, and one central sensory as distinguished from the peripheral organs. And besides these eleven kinds of sense-disorders and their effects on the intellect, he mentions seventeen other kinds of the disorders of the intellect (*buddhibadha*). Mathara says that *indriyabadha* means the incapacity of the sense-organs for apprehending their objects; the sense-disorders cannot produce right apprehension.

Vacaspatimisra explains the disorders of the five sense-organs as deafness (*badhirya*) or anaesthesia of the auditory organ, cutaneous insensibility (*kusthita*) or anaesthesia of the tactual organ, blindness (*andhatva*) or anaesthesia of the visual organ, numbness of the tongue and loss of the sense of taste (*jadata*) or anaesthesia of the gustatory organ, and insensibility to smell (*ajighrata*) or anaesthesia of the olfactory organ. He describes the abnormalities of the motor organs as dumbness (*mukata*) or paralysis of the vocal organ, paralysis of the hands or prehensory organ (*kaunya*) paralysis of the legs or the locomotive organ (*pangutva*), paralysis of the excretive organ (*udavarta*) and impotence or paralysis of the generative organ (*klaibya*). And he explains the anaesthesia of the mind as utter insensibility to pleasure, pain and the like (*mandata*). Gaudapada regards insanity (*unmada*) as the anaesthesia of the mind.

Corresponding to these eleven kinds of sense-disorders there are eleven kinds of intellectual disorders (*buddhibadha*) which consist in the non-production of psychoses corresponding to peripheral and central stimulations, or in the production of psychoses which are not in keeping with peripheral and central stimulations. And besides these eleven kinds of disorders of the intellect corresponding to the eleven kinds of sense-disorders, there are seventeen kinds of abnormalities which are purely intellectual due to some defects of the intellect, and do not owe their origin to the stimulations of the peripheral organs or the central sensory affected by pathological disorders. These intellectual disorders consist in the production of such psychoses as are contradictory to the nine kinds of *tusti* or intellectual complacence and eight kinds of *siddhi* or fruition of the peripheral organs or the central sensory affected by pathological disorders. These intellectual disorders consist in the production of such psychoses as are contradictory to the nine kinds of *tusti* or intellectual complacence and eight kinds of *siddhi* or fruition of intellectual operations. Thus altogether there are twenty-eight kinds of disorders of the intellect.

## The Treatment in the Ancient Medical Literature

In the medical works of the ancient Hindus we find a description and explanation of various kinds of sense-disorders and consequent abnormalities in sense-perception. Our account of abnormal perceptions would be incomplete without a reference to this account in the medical works. First we shall give an account of the abnormalities of visual perception as described by Susruta. But his account of the disorders of visual perception cannot be fully understood unless we understand his view of the mechanism of the visual organ. So we briefly refer to the mechanism of the eye described by him.

## Mechanism of the Visual Organ

The eye-ball (*nayana-budbuda*) is almost round in shape and about an inch in diameter. It is made up of five elements. The muscles of the eye-ball are formed by the solid elements of earth (*bhu*); the blood in the veins and arteries of the eye-ball is formed by the element of heat (*tejas*); the black part of the eye-ball (*iris*, etc.) in which the pupil is situated is formed by the gaseous element (*vayu*), the white part of the eye-ball (vitreous body) is made up of the fluid element (*Jala*); and the lachrymal or other ducts or sacs (*asrumarga*) through which the secretions are discharged, are made up of the ethereal element (*akasa*).

There are five *mandalas*, or circles, and six *patalas*, or layers, in the eye. The five *mandalas* are the following, viz. (1) the *drsti-mandala* (the pupil), (2) the *krsna-mandala* (the choroid), (3) the *sveta-mandala* (the sclerotic and cornea), (4) the *vartma-mandala* (the eye-lid), and (5) the *paksma-mandala* (the circle of the eye-lashes).

"The different parts of the eye-ball are held together by the blood-vessels, the muscles, the vitreous body, and the choroid. Beyond the choroid, the eye-ball is held (in the orbit) by a mass of sleshma (viscid substance capsule of tenon) supported by a number of vessels. The deranged *Doshas* which pass upward to the region of the eyes through the channels of the up-coursing veins and nerves give rise to a good many dreadful diseases in that region."

**Abnormalities in Visual Perception**

According to the Hindu medical science, all diseases are due to the provocation of three humours of the body, flatulent, bilious, and phlegmatic. So the disorders of visual perception are brought about by the bodily humours (*dosas*) attacking the different layers of the eye.

(1) "All external objects appear dim and hazy to the sight when the deranged Doshas of the locality passing through the veins (*sira*) of the eye, get into and are incarcerated within the first Patala (innermost coat) of the pupil (*drishti*)."

(2) "False images of gnats, flies, hairs, nets or cobwebs, rings (circular patches), flags, ear-rings appear to the sight, and the external objects seem to be enveloped in mist or haze or as if laid under a sheet of water or as viewed in rain and on cloudy days, and meteors of different colours seem to be falling constantly in all directions in the event of the deranged doshas being similarly confined in the second Patala (coat) of the *drishti*. In such cases the near appearance of an actually remote object and the contrary (Miopia and Biopia) also should be ascribed to some deficiency in the range of vision

(error of refraction in the crystalline lens) which incapacitates the patient from looking through the eye and hence from threading a needle."

(3) "Objects situated high above are seen and those placed below remain unobserved when the deranged Doshas are infiltrated into the third Patala (coat) of the *drishti*. The Doshas affecting the *drishti* (crystalline lens), if highly enraged, impart their specific colours to the objects of vision.... The deranged Doshas situated at and obstructing the lower, upper, and lateral parts of the *drishti* (crystalline lens) respectively shut out the view of near, distant and laterally situate objects. A dim and confused view of the external world is all that can be had when the deranged Doshas spread over and affect the whole of the *drishti* (crystalline lens). A thing appears to the sight as if cut into two (bifurcated) when the deranged Doshas affect the middle part of the lens, and as triply divided and severed when the Doshas are scattered in two parts; while a multifarious image of the same object is the result of the manifold distributions of movability of the Doshas over the *drishti*."

(4) When the fourth Patala of the eye is attacked by the deranged humours, we have a loss of vision (*timira*). When the vision is completely obstructed by the deranged humours, it is called *linganasa* (blindness). When *linganasa* is not deep-seated but superficial, we have only a faint perception of the images of the sun, the moon and the stars, the heaven, a flash of lightning, and such other highly brilliant objects. The *linganasa* (blindness) is also called *nilika* and *kaca*.

**Timira (Loss of Vision)**

There are various kinds of *timira* or loss of vision. In the type of *timara* due to the derangement of the flatulent humour (*vataja*) external objects appear to the sight as cloudy, moving, crooked, and red. In the type of *timira* due to the derangement of the bilious humour (*pittaja*) external objects appear to be invested with the different colours of the spectrum, of the glow-worm, of the flash of lightning, of the feathers of a peacock, or coloured with a dark blue tint. In the type of timira due to the derangement of the phlegmatic humour (*kaphaja*), all objects appear to the sight as covered with a thick white coat like that of a patch of white cloud, and look white, oily, and dull, and appear hazy and cloudy on a fine day, or as if laid under a sheet of water. In the type of *timira* due to deranged blood (*raktaja*), all objects appear red or enveloped in gloom, and they assume a greyish, blackish or variegated colour. In another type of *timira* (*sannipatika*), external objects appear to the vision as doubled or trebled, variegated and confused, and abnormal images of stars and planets float about in the vision. In the type of *timira* due to deranged bile in concert with deranged blood, which is called *parimlayi*, the quarters of the heaven look yellow and appear to the sight as if brilliant with the light of the rising sun, and trees appear as if sparkling with the flashes of glow-worms.

Besides these six types of *linganasa*, there are six other kinds peculiar to the *drsti* (pupil), which are called *pitta-vidagdha-drsti, slesma-vidagdha-drsti, dhuma-drsti, hrasva-jatya, nakulandhya* and *gambhirika*.

(1) In *pitta-vidagdha-drsti* all external objects appear yellow to the sight, and nothing can be seen in the day, but things can be seen only at night. It is due to an accumulation of the deranged bile in the third patala or coat of the eye.

(2) In *slesma-vidagdha-drsti* all external objects appear white to the sight, and they can be seen only in the day, but not at night; this is called nocturnal blindness. It is due to an accumulation of the deranged phlegm in all the three patalas or coats of the eye.

(3) In *dhuma-drsti* the external objects appear smoky. It is due to grief, high fever, excessive physical exercise, or injury to head, etc.

(4) In *hrasva-jatya* small objects can be seen with the greatest difficulty even in the day-time, but they can be seen easily and distinctly at night.

(5) In *nakulandhya* the external objects appear multi-coloured in the day-time, and nothing can be seen at night.

(6) In *gambhirika* the pupil is contracted and deformed and sinks into the socket, attended with an extreme pain in the affected parts.

Caraka says that when the cerebrum is injured the eye-sight is affected and we have disorders in visual perception. And he also says that *timira* or blindness is due to the excessive provocation of the flatulent humour.

## Abnormalities in Auditory Perception

Susruta describes three kinds of disorders in sound-perception, viz. *pranada* or *karna-nada, karna-ksveda,* and *badhirya.* In *pranada* or *karna-nada,* ringing and various other sounds are heard in the ear. In *karna-ksveda,* only a peculiar type of sound is heard in the ear. It differs from *karna-nada* in that in this disease only a sound of a special kind, viz. that of a wind-pipe, is heard in the ear, while in the latter various kinds of sounds are produced in the ear. In *badhirya* or deafness there is a complete loss of hearing.

Caraka holds that *badhirya* or complete deafness is due to the provocation of the flatulent humour. He mentions two other kinds of disorders in auditory perception, viz. *asabda-sravana* and *uccaihsruti,* which also are due to the provocation of the flatulent humour. The former is that kind of deafness in which a person can hear words uttered very softly or in whispers only. The latter is that form of deafness in which a person hears only such words as are uttered very loudly.

## Abnormalities in Olfactory Perception

Susruta describes many disorders of the olfactory organ, of which one may be regarded as a cause of the loss of the sense of smell. In *apinasa* (obstruction in the nostrils) there is a choking and burning sensation in the nostrils with a deposit of filthy slimy mucus in their passages, which deaden the sense of smell and taste for the time being. In a malignant type of *pratisyaya* (catarrh), too, there is an insensibility to smell.

Caraka also refers to *ghrana-nasa* which consists in the loss of the sensation of smell, and is due to the provocation of the flatulent humour.

## Abnormalities in Gustatory Perception

Caraka mentions *arasanjata* as a disease of the tongue in which there is a complete loss of the sensation of taste; it is due to the provocation of the flatulent humour. He also describes the different kinds of tastes owing to the provocation of different kinds of humours. Owing to the provocation of the flatulent humour, a person has an astringent taste in the mouth, and sometimes does not feel any taste at all. Owing to the provocation of the bilious humour a person feels in his tongue the presence of an acrid or sour taste. Owing to the provocation of the phlegmatic humour a person feels in his mouth the presence of a sweet taste. And owing to the simultaneous provocation of all the three humours, a person feels the presence of many tastes in his mouth. Caraka also refers to the disease of *tiktasyala* or a constant bitter taste in the mouth owing to the provocation of the bilious humour. He also refers to *mukhamadhurya* or a constant sweet taste in the mouth, and *kasayasyata* or a constant astringent taste in the mouth.

**Abnormalities in Tactual Perception**

Caraka and Susruta describe cutaneous affections as *kusthas*, which are of various kinds and which give rise to various kinds of disordered cutaneous sensations. According to Susruta, when the cutaneous affection is confined only to the serous fluid of the skin, there are the following symptoms, viz. loss of the perception of touch, itching sensation, etc.; when it is confined to the blood, it brings about complete anaesthesia; when it affects only the flesh, there are various symptoms such as excruciating pricking pain in the affected part and its numbness; and when it affects the fat, the body seems to be covered with a plaster. In the various kinds of cutaneous affections described by Caraka and Susruta there is partial or complete anaesthesia together with various kinds of disorders in cutaneous, organic, and muscular sensations.

Caraka also mentions various other abnormalities in tactile sensations (including organic and muscular sensations) such as *ekangaroga* (partial or local paralysis), *paksabadha* (side paralysis), *sarvangaroga* (complete paralysis), *dandaka* (stiffness of the whole body like a log of wood), *osa* (the disease in which the patient feels the sensation of fire being always placed very near to his body), *plosa* (the disease in which the patient has the sensation of his body being slightly scorched by fire), *daha* (a sensation of burning experienced in every part of the body), *davathu* (a sensation of every part of the body having been subject to painful inflammation), *antardaha* (a burning sensation within the body, generally within the thorat), *amsadaha* (a burning sensation in the shoulders), *usmadhikya* (excess of internal heat in the body), *mamsadaha* (a sensation of burning in the flesh), etc.

**Disorders in the Motor Organs**

Caraka refers to the abnormalities of the vocal organ such as *vaksanga* (temporary dumbness or difficulty in speaking, e.g. stammering) *gadgadatva* (slowness of speech), and *mukatva* (complete dumbness). When the cerebrum is injured, there are slowness of speech, loss of voice, and complete dumbness. Temporary dumbness (*vaksanga*) and complete dumbness (*mukatva*) are due to the provocation of the flatulent humour.

Caraka says that when the cerebrum is injured there is a loss of motor effort (*cestanasa*). According to him, the heart is the seat of the mind, the intellect, and consciousness. But the cerebrum is the seat of sensory and motor centres. He says that just as the rays of the sun have their seat in the sun, so the sensory and motor organs and the vital currents of the sense-organs have their seat in the cerebrum.

**Mental Blindness (Manobadha)**

According to Caraka, the heart is the seat of consciousness. So when the heart is injured, we have epilepsy (*apasmara*), insanity (*unmada*) delirium (*pralapa*) and loss of the mind (*cittanasa*). This paralysis of the mind (*cittanasa*) may be called "mental blindness" in the language of William James. "When mental blindness is more complete," says James, "neither sight, touch, nor sound avails to steer the patient, and a sort of dementia which has been called *asymbolia* or *apraxia* is the result."

According to Caraka, the *prdna* and the *udana*, which are biomorphic forces, the mind (*manas*) the intellect (*buddhi*) and consciousness (*cetana*) have their seat in the heart. So when the heart is overpowered by the provocation of the phlegmatic humour, consciousness is benumbed, and lapses into semi-unconsciousness (*tandra*). And when the heart is overpowered by the provócation of the flatulent humour, consciousness is suspended and lapses into torpor or unconsciousness (*moha*).

**Causes of Sense-disorders and Mental Disorders**

According to Caraka, there are four kinds of correlation or contact of the sense-organs with their objects, viz. *atiyoga*, or excess of contact, *ayoga* or total absence of contact, *hinayoga* or sparing or partial contact, and *mithyayoga* or contact of sense-organs with disagreeable objects. *Atiyoga* corresponds to over-use of a sense-organ, *ayoga,* to its non-use, *hinayoga,* to its under-use, and *mithyayoga,* to its misuse. This account of Caraka has a strangely modern ring. There is no doubt that sense-disorders are to a great extent due to the abnormal functioning of the sense-organs. So Caraka's explanation is very significant. He accounts for the disorders of the sense-organs and consequent abnormalities of sense-perceptions by the excess of correlation, absence of correlation, partial or insufficient correlation, and injudicious correlation of the sense-organs with their respective objects. *Tathayoga* or judicious correlation of a sense-organ with its object preserves the normal condition of the organ, and also keeps the perceptions produced by that organ unimpaired. But excessive exercise, absence of judicious exercise, insufficient exercise, and injudicious exercise impair the sense-organs, and consequently impair the perceptions produced by them. Caraka gives us some examples to illustrate the different kinds of correlation of the sense-organs with their objects. A continuous gaze at very bright objects is an example of excessive correlation of the visual organ. Total abstention from exercising the eye is absence of correlation. The sight of objects that are very minute or very distant, or that are hateful, terrible, amazing, repulsive, or extremely ugly is an example of injudicious correlation. All these impair the sense of vision.

Excessive correlation of the auditory organ arises from constantly exposing the ear to the stunning report of thunder or beat of a drum or loud cries. Total abstention from hearing by closing the ears is the absence of correlation. Injudicious correlation arises from hearing sounds that are rough, harsh, dreadful, uncongenial, disagreeable, and indicative of danger. These impair the sense of hearing.

Excessive correlation of the olfactory organ arises from constantly smelling very keen and powerful scents which call forth tears, excite nausea, produce stupefaction, etc. Total abstention from all scents is the absence of correlation. Injudicious correlation arises from smelling odours emitted by putrid objects, or objects that are poisonous, disagreeable, or repulsive. These impair the sense of smell.

Excessive correlation of the gustatory organ arises when the objects producing any of the six kinds of taste are taken in an excessive degree. Total abstention from tasting is the absence of correlation.

Injudicious correlation arises from tasting things which are made up of incompatible ingredients, or which are not suitable to the organism. These impair the sense of vision.

Excessive correlation of the tactual organ arises from exposure to excessive heat and cold, excesive indulgence in bathing and rubbing the skin with oil, etc., and indulgence in sudden changes of temperature. Total abstension from enjoying the sense of touch or from allowing the body to be touched is the absense of correlation. Contact of the body with poisonous objects or with untimely heat and cold is injudicious correlation. These impair the sense of touch.

# 17

# Super-normal Perceptions

## Introduction

In the last chapters we have dealt with indefinite perceptions, illusions and hallucinations, dreams, and abnormal perceptions. In this chapter we shall deal with super-normal perceptions, divine perception, the perception of the individual witness (*Jiva-Saksin*), and the perception of the divine witness (*Isvara-Saksin*).

The Indian treatment of super-normal perceptions is more descriptive than explanatory. Indian philosophers have distinguished between abnormal perceptions and super-normal perceptions, inasmuch as the former are disorders and aberrations of perception, while the latter are the higher grades of perception. Super-normal perceptions are above the general laws and conditions of normal perceptions. They transcend the categories of time, space, and causality, and apprehend the real nature of things divested of all their accidental associations of names, concepts, and so forth. So we cannot understand their nature by appealing to the facts of our ordinary perceptions. We must have a conception of these higher grades of super-normal perception on the basis of speculation, unless we ourselves attain the stage of higher intuitions. And Indian philosophers have tried to arrive at a conception of these super-normal perceptions by using speculative arguments and appealing to their own higher intuitions. Almost all schools of Indian philosophers believe in super-normal perceptions. Only the materialist like Carvaka cannot believe in any other source of knowledge than sense-perception. And the Mimamsaka also denies the possibility of super-normal perceptions, because according to him, the past, the future, the distant, and the subtle can be known only through the injunctions of the Vedas. But the Nyaya-Vaisesika, the Samkhya-Patanjala, the Vedantist, the Buddhist, and the Jaina believe in super-normal perceptions, though they give different accounts of them.

The modern science of hypnotism and other occult and esoteric sciences will find sufficient material for research and investigation in the Indian account of super-normal perceptions. They will find in it evidences of auto-suggestion, clairvoyance, clairaudience, hypersesthesia of vision, hearing, touch, etc., hypermnesia, though-treading, thought-transference or telepathy, and different kinds of trance or ecstasy.

**The Mimamsaka Denial of Yogi-Pratyaksa**

Yamunacarya, in his *Siddhitraya*, gives us a lucid account of the Mimamsaka argument against the possibility of yogic or ecstatic intuition. Is yogic perception sensuous or non-sensuous? Is it produced by the sense-organs or not ? If it is sensuous, is it produced by the external sense-organs or by the internal organ or mind ? The external sense-organs produce cognitions of their appropriate objects only when they come in contact with their objects. But as the external sense-organs can never come in contact with distant, past, and future objects, they can never produce cognitions of these objects. Hence yogic perception can never be produced by the external sense-organs. Nor can it be produced by the central sensory or mind. The mind can produce the perception of only mental states, e.g. pleasure, pain, etc., independently of the external sense-organs. But it cannot produce the perception of external objects independently of the external sense-organs. If the mind did not depend upon the external sense-organs to produce the perception of external objects, then there would be no need of the external organs at all in the perception of external objects, and no one would be blind or deaf. Hence the Mimamsaka concludes that external objects cannot be perceived through the central sensory or mind independently of the peripheral organs.

Nor can it be said that the external organs can apprehend objects even without coming in contact with them, when they attain the highest degree of excellence through the powers of occult medicines, incantations, and the practice of austerities and intense meditation or yoga; for all that these can do is to bring about a manifestation of only the natural capacities of the sense-organs, which are not unlimited, but strictly limited within their proper sphere. The ear can never produce the perception of colour or taste, even if it is extremely refined by the application of medicines. A sense-organ can never transcend its natural limitations, even when it attains the highest degree of perfection by intense meditation; the function of a sense-organ is always restricted within a limited sphere; so a sense-organ, even in its highest degree of excellence, cannot transcend its natural limits. Hence, sensuous knowledge can never apprehend past, distant, and future objects.

The perception of the yogin is said to be the result of intense meditation or re-representation. But though the cognition produced by constant meditation is manifested as a distinct presentation, does it cognize a thing as apprehended in the past or more than that ? If it apprehends exactly the same thing as was apprehended in the past, then the cognition produced by intense meditation is nothing but memory or reproduction of the past experience. And if it apprehends more than what was perceived in the past, then it is illusory as it apprehends something which has no real existence. Therefore, either the intuition of the yogin is not of the nature of perception, or if it is perceptual it is illusory. If it is regarded as perceptual in character, why should it transgress the general condition of perception that it must be produced by the contact of a sense-organ with its proper object ? Hence, the Mimamsaka concludes that there can be no yogic perception of past, distant, and future objects; these can be known only through the injunction of the Vedas.

### The Nyaya-Vaisesika View of Yogi-pratyaksa

Proof of the possibility of Yogi-Pratyaksa Sridhara proves the possibility of yogic perception by the following arguments :

1. In the first place, just as by constant practice we learn new things in different sciences and arts, so by the collective force of constant meditation upon the self, *akasa*, and other super-sensible objects we acquire true knowledge of these objects.
2. In the second place, the varying grades of the intellect must

reach the highest limit beyond which it cannot go, because they are varying grades, like the varying grades of magnitude. Jayanta Bhatta also offers the same argument. He says that just as there are various degrees of whiteness and other qualities, so there are various degrees of the faculty of perception and the highest degree of perfection is reached by man in yogic perception which apprehends all objects, subtle, hidden, remote, past, future, and the like; and there is nothing improbable in this. We see only proximate objects with the help of light. But cats can see objects even in utter darkness, and vultures can see objects from a very great distance. Why shall we not suppose, then, that we can acquire super-sensuous vision by constant practice in meditation ?

But it has been objected that the mere presence of the varying degrees of an object does not necessarily imply that it should reach the highest limit. For instance, there are varying degrees of heat when water is heated; but we never find it reaching the highest limit of heat and turning into fire itself; nor do we ever perceive the highest limit of jumping as there is no man who can jump over all the three worlds.

Sridhara replies that this objection does not apply to yogic practices. That property which has a permanent substratum, and which produces a peculiarity in it, gradually reaches the highest limit of excellence through constant practice or repetition. For instance, when gold is repeatedly heated and treated by the method of "putapaka" its purity gradually reaches the highest limit and acquires the character of the *raktasara*. As for the heating of water, it has no permanent substratum; so repetition cannot bring it up to the highest limit of perfection. That water has no permanent substratum is proved by the fact that it entirely disappears on the application of intense heat. Then as for the practice of jumping it does not produce any peculiarity in its substratum; because the first act of jumping is totally destroyed and leaves no such trace behind, so that the second and subsequent acts of jumping may be helped by the effect of the first act of jumping; all these acts of jumping are effects of different forces and efforts, and hence any subsequent excellence of jumping may not be due to the previous jumping. It is for this reason that when a man is tired by three or four jumps his limit of jumping begins to decline, owing to the decrease of strength. As for the intellect (*buddhi*), on the other hand, it has a permanent substratum and produces a peculiarity in it; since we find that though something is quite unintelligible to us at first, it becomes thoroughly intelligible when we repeatedly apply intelligence to it. Thus the more we practise meditation upon an object, the greater peculiarity is produced in it at each step of the practice, and when the practice is kept up continuously for a long time, the intellect acquires a fresh force due to the peculiar powers or merit (*dharma*) born of Yoga and must reach its highest limit of excellence. And there is nothing unreasonable in this.

Then, again, it has been objected that yogis cannot perceive super-sensuous objects because they are living beings like ourselves.

Sridhara says that this argument is not convincing. The yogis are, no doubt, living beings but they may be omniscient, too. The character of living beings is not inconsistent with omniscience; they are not mutually exclusive of each other. No inconsistency has ever been found between omniscience and the character of living beings. But since we cannot definitely ascertain whether our want of omniscience is due to our character of living beings, or due to the absence of the peculiar power of *dharma* born of yoga, which is regarded as the cause of omniscience, there is a doubtful concomitance of omniscience with the character of living beings. And because there is a doubtful concomitance between the character of living beings and omniscience, the former can never prove the inference that yogis cannot have super-sensuous knowledge because they are living beings. But the fact that the *dharma*, or a peculiar power born of yoga, is the cause of super-sensuous knowledge is well-known to us. So Sridhara concludes that our want of omniscience is due to the absence of the peculiar power of *dharma* produced by constant meditation.

### The Nature of Yogi-Pratyaksa

Jayanta Bhatta describes the nature of Yogi-Pratyaksa in *Nyayamanjari*. The yogis can perceive all objects past, distant, and future, hidden, subtle, and remote, and even *dharma* which is absolutely super-sensible to us. But do the yogis perceive all objects by one cognition or by many cognitions ? Not by one cognition, since contradictory qualities like heat and cold cannot be apprehended by a single cognition. Nor by many cognitions, since they cannot arise simultaneously owing to the atomic nature of manas; and if they are produced successively, then yogis would require infinite time to perceive all the objects of the world. Hence yogis cannot be omniscient.

Jayanta Bhatta refutes this objection by saying that yogis perceive all the objects of the world simultaneously by one cognition, and there is nothing unreasonable in it. It is found in actual experience that contradictory qualities like blue, yellow, etc., do appear in a single psychosis (*citrapratyaya*) and heat and cold are perceived simultaneously by a person with the lower part of his body plunged in water and the upper part of his body in the scorching rays of the sun. Thus Jayanta Bhatta concludes that yogis perceive all objects of the world simultaneously by a single intuition.

**Yogic Perception and Ordinary Perception**

Bhasarvajna divides perception into two kinds, yogic perception (*yogipratyaksa*) and non-yogic perception (*ayogipratyaksa*). He defines ordinary or non-yogic perception as direct and immediate apprehension of gross objects, produced by a particular relation between sense-organs and their objects with the help of light, time ("now"), space ("here"), merit or demerit of the person. And he defines yogic perception as direct and immediate apprehension of distant, past, future, and subtle objects.

**Yogic Perception and Divine Perception**

If yogis can perceive all objects of the world, past, present, future, hidden, subtle, and remote, and super-sensible objects like *dharma* etc., how do they differ from omniscient God? How does the perception of yogis differ from divine perception? Jayanta Bhatta says that the difference lies in that the omniscience of yogis is produced by constant meditation, while divine omniscience is eternal. Moreover, the divine perception of *dharma* (moral law) is natural (*samsiddhika*) to God; *dharma* constitutes the essential nature of God, which is the cause of the Vedic injunctions of dharma. But yogis at first learn the real nature of dharma from the Vedic injunctions and then by unceasing practice in meditation they come to perceive dharma , and when they acquire an intuition of *dharma*, the conception that the Vedic injunction is the ultimate standard of duty or moral obligation loses its hold upon their minds.

## Different Kinds of Yogi-Pratyaksa

### *Tukta-pratyaksa and Viyukta-pratyaksa*

Prasastapada divides yogic perception into two kinds, viz. (i) *yuktapratyaksa* or the perception of those who are in ecstasy, and (ii) *viyuktapratyaksa* or the perception of those who have fallen off from ecstasy. Those who are in a state of ecstasy can perceive their own selves, the selves of others, *akasa,* space, time, atoms, air, and the qualities, actions, generalities, and particularities inhering in these, and inherence itself through the manas aided by the peculiar powers or dharma produced by meditation. And those who have fallen off from ecstasy perceive subtle, hidden, and remote things, owing to the fourfold contact of the self, *manas,* sense-organs, and objects, and by virtue of the peculiar powers produced by meditation.

Bhasarvajna also follows Prasastapada in dividing yogic perception into two kinds : (1) ecstatic intuition or intuition in the state of ecstasy, and (2) non-ecstatic intuition or intuition out of the state of ecstasy. In the ecstatic condition there is no peripheral stimulation or intercourse of the external sense-organs with outward objects; but the perception of all the objects follows from the conjunction of the self with the internal organ or *manas,* aided by a certain dharma brought about by intense meditation and the grace of God. Thus in the state of ecstasy the internal organ or manas alone is operative, the external organs being entirely inoperative at the time. But in the non-ecstatic condition the yogic perception of super-sensible objects follows from the four-fold, three-fold or two-fold contact as required in different cases. When objects are perceived through the olfactory organ, gustatory organ, visual organ, or tactual organ, perception is brought about by the four-fold contact of the self with the *manas,* of the manas with the external sense-organs, and of these external sense-organs with their proper objects. In the perception of sound there is the three-fold contact of the self with the *manas,* and of the manas with the auditory organ. And in the perception of pleasure, etc., there is the two-fold contact of the self with the *manas.*

Similarly neo-Naiyayikas divide yogic perception into two kinds: (i) the perception of a yogin who has attained union with the supreme Being (*yukta*), and (ii) the perception of a yogin who is endeavouring to attain such a union (*yunjana*). The first yogin enjoys a constant perception of all the objects of the world, ether, atoms, etc., through his mind aided by a certain dharma born of meditation, while the second yogin can acquire perception of all the objects with a little effort of attention or meditation.

### *Savikalpaka and Nirvikalpaka Yogi-Pratyaksa*

Is yogic perception determinate (*savikalpa*) or indeterminate (*nirvikalpa*) ? Jayasimhasuri holds that the yogic perception in the state of ecstasy is indeterminate, since the complete focussing of attention in ecstasy cannot be brought about by a determinate or discriminative perception. There is no element of discrimination in the yogic intuition in the state of ecstasy. But it must not be supposed that the yogic intuition in ecstasy is the same as our indeterminate perception which apprehends the mere forms of objects and not their mutual relations. Our indeterminate perception marks the lowest stage of immediacy, while the yogic intuition in ecstasy marks the highest limit of immediacy. Our indeterminate perception is below determinate perception, while the indeterminate perception of the yogin in a state of ecstasy is above determinate perception and, indeed, above all determinate cognitions, presentative and representative, perceptual and conceptual. Our indeterminate perception is immediate "sense-perception", while that of the yogin in ecstasy is immediate "intellectual intuition". Our indeterminate perception apprehends the mere form of an object through an external sense-organ, while that of the yogin in ecstasy apprehends all the objects of the world simultaneously. Therein lies the speciality of the indeterminate perception of the yogin in a state of ecstasy. But the perception of a yogin out of the condition of ecstasy can be both indeterminate and determinate.

Dharmottara, the author of *Nyayatindutika,* also holds that the perception of a yogin in the highest stage is indeterminate.

### *Samprajnata Samadhi and Asamprajnata Samadhi*

Sridhara explains the meaning of yoga as ecstasy (*samadhi*) which is of two kinds, conscious (*samprajnata*) and supra-conscious (*asamprajnata*). The word *asamprajnata* has been translated by Dr. Ganganatha Jha as unconscious. And it has been translated by Professor Krishna Chandra Bhattacharya as supra-conscious, and by

Dr. S. N. Das Gupta as ultra-cognitive. The latter seems to be the better version. In the highest stage of ecstasy there is the most clear, most distinct, most vivid, and most concentrated consciousness of the self. It is supra-conscious rather than unconscious. The conscious ecstasy consists in the union of the *manas*, which has been controlled and concentrated on an aspect of the self, with the self in which there is a desire for true knowledge. And the supra-conscious ecstasy consists in the union of the controlled manas with an aspect of the self in which there is no desire or craving owing to its unruffled condition. The supra-conscious ecstasy is fully developed in the highest stage of the spiritual life of a person who has thoroughly suppressed all desires and cravings and seeks only deliverance, it does not produce any merit (*dharma*) as there is no desire in the self to acquire merit and avoid demerit; nor does it tend towards any external object as the manas is concentrated on the self alone. The conscious ecstasy, on the other hand, is always aided by a certain desire or craving, and as such brings about a true knowledge of the object for which there is a desire in the self.

## Other Kinds of Super-normal Perception

### *Arsa-jnana (Intuition of Sages)*

Prasastapada describes the nature of *arsa-jnana* which is kindred to *yogi-pratyaksa*. He says that the sages who are the authors of the sastras have a true intuitive cognition of all objects, past, present, and future, and also of *dharma* (moral law) and other supersensible objects, owing to the contact of the manas with the self and a peculiar dharma or power born of austerities; such an intuitive cognition is called *arsa-jnana*. This cognition is perceptual in character, since it is not produced by inferential marks and so forth; but it differs from ordinary perception in that it is not produced by the external organs, but by the manas with the help of certain powers acquired by learning, austerities, and meditation. This intuition is also called *pratibha-jnana* as it is a distinct and vivid perception which is not produced by the sense-organs, inferential marks, and so forth. It is a valid cognition as it is free from doubts and illusions. It is not a doubtful cognition because it does not oscillate between two alternatives. It is not an illusion as it is actually found to agree with facts.

Jayasimhasuri says that essentially there is no difference between sagic intuition (*arsa-jnana*) and yogic intuition (*yogi-pratyaksa*) as both of them are produced by a peculiar dharma or merit. The only difference between them lies in the fact that the former is produced by the practice of austerities (*tapojanita*), while the latter is produced by meditation (*yogaja*). Both of them are non-sensuous. The organ of both these kinds of higher intuition is the *manas*.

### *Siddha Darsana (Occult Perception)*

Besides the intuitions of yogis and sages, Prasastapada describes the perceptions of occultists who cannot perceive supersensible objects like yogis and sages, but can perceive only those sensible things which are too subtle or too remote for our gross sense-organs, and as such are hidden from our view. They can perceive these subtle, remote, and hidden objects not through the manas by meditation or austerities like yogis and sages, but through the external sense-organs refined by the application of certain unguents and the like which produce certain occult powers. And such an occult perception is purely sensuous, since it is produced by the external sense-organs with the help of certain occult medicines. Thus the difference between ordinary perception and occult perception lies in that the former is produced by the sense-organs unaided by any external applications, while the latter is produced by the sense-organs strengthened and refined by the application of occult medicines. But both of them are sensuous. Prasastapada and his commentators, Sridhara, Udayana and others, do not explain how occult powers are generated in the sense-organs by the application of occult medicines. They have simply recorded occult perception as a fact of experience.

### *Pratibhajnana (Flash of Intuition in Ordinary Life)*

Prasastapada says that *pratibhajnana* or higher intuition generally belongs to sages. But on rare occasions it belongs to ordinary persons also, as when a girl has a flash of intuitive perception that her brother will come tomorrow. Jayanta Bhatta also says that though yogis can perceive all objects, past, present, and future, ordinary persons like us are not entirely devoid of the power of perceiving the future. On rare occasions we also have a flash of intuition; for instance, when a girl perceives in her heart of hearts that her brother will come tomorrow. This flash of intuition must be regarded as a kind of valid perception on the following grounds :

(i) It is produced by an object;

(ii) It is not doubtful;

(iii) It is not contradicted;

(iv) Its causes are not vitiated by any defect.

It may be objected that the cognition is not produced by an object, since the object of the cognition does not exist at that time. Jayanta Bhatta says that this objection would be valid, if such a cognition were held to apprehend an object existing at that time, in fact, this intuitive cognition apprehends its object not as existing at that time but as existing in the future. Hence, it cannot be said that the cognition is not produced by an object.

But how can there be a perception of the future? Futurity is nothing but prior non-existence which will be destroyed; but how can there be a relation between this prior non-existence and the existent object (e.g. brother)? It is self-contradictory to say that existence is related to non-existence.

Jayanta Bhatta says that this objection is not sound. The object of the intuition (e.g. brother) is not non-existent, but its relation to that place. There is a prior non-existence not of the object itself, but of its relation to that place. The brother does exist, though not in that place. The girl is reminded of her brother for some reason or other, e.g. anxiety for feeding, etc., and when the "brother" flashes in her memory he is perceived as coming tomorrow. Thus the object of intuitive perception is reproduced in memory owing to a certain cause, and the reproduction of the object in memory is the cause of its presentation to consciousness. The intuition of the object, therefore, is the effect of its reproduction in memory. Thus it is a valid cognition, since it is produced by an object that has a real existence.

But how can it be regarded as perception, since it is not produced by peripheral stimulation? Jayanta Bhatta says that it is not of the nature of sensuous perception, but of the nature of "intuition" produced by the internal organ or manas. It is not an inference, since it is not produced by the knowledge of a mark of inference (*jingo*). It is not an analogy, since it is not produced by the knowledge of similarity. It is not a verbal cognition, since it is not produced by a word. It is a perceptual cognition produced directly by the *manas*, independently of the peripheral organs; it is an intuitive perception of a future object brought to consciousness by memory owing to a certain cause.

**Yogic perception of Dharma (Duty or Moral Law)**

Jayanta Bhatta discusses the question of the yogic perception of *dharma* or moral law in *Nyayamanjari*. Can the yogis perceive *dharma* which is regarded by all as super-sensuous ? Can the yogis acquire a vision of super-sensible *dharma*?

First, Kumarila argues that it is impossible; a sense-organ can never apprehend anything but its proper object; the eye can see only visible objects. It can never see odour or taste when it attains the highest degree of excellence by constant meditation, it can at best see subtle and remote objects, but it can never see dharma which is absolutely super-sensible. Jayanta Bhatta contends that it is not impossible for the yogis to acquire a vision of dharma which is super-sensible to us. If those things which are too remote for our vision, and which are hidden from our view by other things or concealed by utter darkness can be seen by other animals like vultures, cats, flies, etc., is it quite unreasonable to suppose that dharma which is not an object of our vision can be an object of the vision of yogis ?

Secondly, Kumarila urges that if dharma which is supersensible can be an object of the vision of yogis, then their eyes would perceive smell, taste, etc., which are not their proper objects. Jayanta Bhatta replies that this is an unwarrantable assumption, since the other sense-organs of the yogis, too, attain perfection and apprehend their proper objects. But similarly it cannot be argued that dharma cannot be an object of yogic vision, since it is not the proper object of vision like smell, taste, etc. For how do you know that dharma is not a proper object of the vision of the yogis? We know that an object is not the proper object of a sense-organ, if we cannot perceive it in the presence of that sense-organ. For instance, we cannot perceive sound even in the presence of the eyes; so we conclude that sound is not the proper object of the eyes. But how do you know that a yogin can not perceive dharma even in the presence of his visual organ?

Thirdly, Kumarila urges that dharma is above all temporal limits;

it is not determined by the past, the present, or the future. Is it then not absurd to suppose that it is an object of vision or sense-perception? Jayanta Bhatta replies that certainly it is absurd in the case of ordinary human beings whose perception is confined to "here and now" but not in the case of yogis who have transcended the limitations of time and space.

Fourthly, if the Mimamsaka insists that dharma can never be an object of external sense-perception, Jayanta Bhatta argues that it may be an object of internal perception. The yogis can perceive even super-sensible dharma through their internal organs or minds by constant practice in meditation. The mind can apprehend all objects; there is nothing which is not an object of the mind. Even those objects which are beyond the range of external sense-organs are found to be clearly perceived by the mind by constant practice in meditation. For instance, the lover mad in love for a woman perceives his beloved as present before his eyes, though not really present. But is it not a false analogy? Jayanta Bhatta says that though the perception of the lover is illusory and that of the yogin is perfectly valid, they agree in being clear and distinct presentations. Hence, even super-sensible objects like dharma can be perceived by yogis through the internal organ or mind, if not through the peripheral organs.

Lastly, just as we have flashes of intuition of future objects in *pratibhajnana,* so yogis can perceive all objects past, distant, and future, hidden, subtle, and remote, and even dharma which is absolutely super-sensible to us.

### The Samkhya

According to Samkhya, everything exists at the present moment nothing goes out of existence and nothing comes into existence. The various qualities of things are only modes of energy acting in different collocations of the original gunas or reals, mass (*tamas*) energy (*rajas*) and essence (*sattva*). "And these various energies are sometimes actual (*kinetic*), sometimes potential, rising to actuality, and sometimes sublatent, subsiding from actuality into sub-latency." Thus the so-called future objects are present as latent or potential,and the so-called past objects are present as sublatent; and only those things which are supposed to be present are actual. So the mind of the yogin can come in contact with past and future objects which are not non-existent at present, but exist only as sub-latent and potential respectively by virtue of certain peculiar powers produced by meditation. Certainly the Samkhya explanation of the yogic perception of past and future objects is more convincing than that of the Nyaya-Vaisesika. If the past and the future exist at present in some form or other, it is easier to conceive that the mind of the yogin can come in contact with them and produce a perception of the past and the future.

Vijnanabhiksu points out that the mind of the yogin can come in contact with distant and hidden objects by virtue of the peculiar power (*atisaya*) acquired by meditation. This peculiar power of the mind consists in its all-pervasiveness or its power of acting on all objects owing to the complete suppression of the inertia or matter-stuff (*tamas*) of the mind which prevents it from acting on all objects. He also points out that the inertia (*tamas*) of the mind is removed sometimes by the intercourse of the sense-organs with their objects as in ordinary sense-perception, and sometimes by the dharma born of meditation as in yogic perception.

Aniruddha says that the perception of a yogin is produced by the internal organ or mind and not by the external organs, and consequently, it is not like the perception of an ordinary person. The yogin alone, who has acquired peculiar powers through the favourable influence of the dharma born of yoga, can perceive objects in all times and places through the connection of his mind with Prakrti, the ultimate ground of all existence.

**The Patanjala**

Patanjali holds that ordinarily the mind is a continuous stream of mental functions. Vyasa says that it has five stages : (i) wandering (*ksipta*)) (ii) forgetful (*mudha*)) (iii) occasionally steady (*viksipta*), (iv) one-pointed (*ekagra*), and (v) restrained (*niruddha*). In the first stage, the mind being overpowered by energy (*rajas*) becomes extremely unsteady and constantly flits from one object to another. In the second stage, the mind is overpowered by inertia (*tamas*) and sinks into listlessness, drowsiness, and deep sleep. In the third stage, the mind, though unsteady for the most part, becomes occasionally steady when it avoids painful things and is temporarily absorbed in pleasureable objects. In the fourth stage, the mind is withdrawn from all other objects and concentrated on one object, either material or mental, and assumes an unflickering and unwavering attitude with regard to that object owing to the predominance of essence (*sattva*). In the last stage, all the mental functions are arrested and the mind retains only the potencies of its functions. In the fourth stage, the mind falls into conscious ecstasy (*samprajnata samadhi*). In the last stage, the mind reaches the highest stage of supra-conscious ecstasy (*asamprajnata samadhi*).

The mental functions can be arrested by constant practice of abstraction and concentration and extirpation of passion for objects of enjoyment. Trance or ecstasy (*samadhi*) is the ultimate result of the long and arduous processes of the inhibition of the bodily activities or perfect posture of the body (*asano*), regulation of breathing (*pranayama*), withdrawal of the mind from distracting influences (*pratyahara*), fixation of the mind on certain parts of the body (*dharana*) and constant meditation on the same object (*dhyana*). When the mind by deep concentration on an object is transformed into it and feels at one with it, that condition of the mind is called ecstasy (*samadhi*).

Patanjali recognizes two kinds of ecstasy : (i) conscious ecstasy (*samprajnata samadhi*), and (ii) supra-conscious ecstasy (*asamprajnata samadhi*).

Just as an archer at first tries to pierce a large object and then points his arrow at a small object, so a yogin at first concentrates his mind on gross (*sthula*) objects and then on subtle (*suksma*) objects. Thus the yogin rises to higher and higher stages of ecstasy according as he identifies his mind with subtler and subtler objects and at last reaches the highest stage of purely objectless and supra-conscious ecstasy. Let us explain the nature of the different kinds of conscious ecstasy in their ascending order.

1. *Savitarka samadhi* is the condition of the mind when by deep concentration it becomes one with a gross (*sthula*) object (*artha*) together with its name (*sabda*) and concept (*jnana*). This is the lowest stage of samadhi. In this stage, the object of contemplation does not appear in consciousness in its pure form but associated and identified with its name and concept, though, as a matter of fact, the object, the name, and the concept are quite distinct from one another. Thus *savitarka samadhi* cannot give us true knowledge of the real nature of an object;

it erroneously identifies the object of contemplation with its name and concept.

2. *Nirvitarka samadhi* is the condition of the mind when by deep concentration it becomes identified with a gross (*sthula*) object divested of all associations of name and concept. This is a higher stage than *savitarka samadhi*, because it gives us true knowledge of the real nature of its object free from all kinds of association, which serve to conceal its real nature. "The thing in this state does not appear to be an object of my consciousness, but my consciousness becoming divested of all 'I' or 'mine', becomes one with the object itself, so that there is no notion here as 'know this', but the mind becomes one with the thing, so that the notion of subject and object drops off and the result is the one steady transformation of the mind into the object of its contemplation."

The objects of the above two kinds of *samadhi* are gross material objects according to Ramananda Yati and Vacaspatimisra. But according to Bhojaraja, Nagesa, and Vijnanabhiksu, gross material objects (*sthulabhuta*) and gross sense-organs (*sthula indriya*) are the objects of contemplation in *savitarka samadhi* and *nirvitarka samadhi* which are comprehended under one name as *virtakanugata*. But Ramananda Yati and Vacaspatimisra regard the sense-organs as the objects of contemplation in *sananda samadhi*.

3. *Savicara samadhi* is the condition of the mind when by deep contemplation it becomes one with subtle objects such as atoms, *tanmatras*, etc., associated with the notions of time, space, and causality, qualified by many other qualifications and erroneously identified with their names and concepts.

4. *Nirvicara samadhi* is the condition of the mind when by deep concentration it becomes identified with subtle objects such as atoms, *tanmatras*, etc., in their pure state, divested of all the notions of time, space, and causality, and devoid of all qualifications and associations.

*Savicara samadhi* and *nirvicara samadhi* may have for their objects, atoms, *tanmatras*, the *ahamkara*, the *buddhi*, and the *Prakrti*. They are comprehended under one name as *wcaranugata*.

5. *Sananda samadhi* is the determinate state of the mind when by deep concentration it becomes identified with the gross sense-organs, the essence of which is *sattva* owing to their power of manifesting objects. This is the view of Ramananda Yati and Vacaspatimisra. But Bhojaraja, Nagesa, and Vijnanabhiksu hold that the sense-organs are the objects of *savitarka samadhi*. According to them, the object of *sananda samadhi* is extreme bliss arising from the predominance of *sattva* (essence), though *rajas* (energy) and *tamas* (inertia) are not entirely suppressed.
6. *Nirananda samadhi* is the indeterminate state of the mind when by deep concentration it becomes identified with gross sense-organs. But Vijnanabhiksu holds that ananda *samadhi* does not admit of two forms, viz., *sananda* and *nirananda*.
7. *Sasmita samadhi* is the determinate state of the mind when by deep concentration it becomes one with the *buddhi* (the cause of the sense-organs) which is identified with the self. This is the view of Ramananda Yati and Vacaspatimisra.

   According to Vijnanabhiksu, the object of *asmita* is the consciousness transformed into the form of the pure self. This kind of *samadhi* may have for its object either the finite self (*jivatman*) or the infinite self (*paramatman*). According to Bhojaraja, in this stage the *buddi* which is endowed with pure *sattva, rajas* and *tamas* being entirely suppressed, becomes the object of contemplation.
8. *Nirananda samadhi* is the indeterminate state of the mind when it becomes one with the *buddhi* which is identified with the pure self.

Ramananda Yati and Vacaspatimisra recognize the above eight kinds of *samprajnata samadhi*. But Vijnanabhiksu does not recognize two forms of samadhi each under *anandanugata* and *asmitanugata*. He recognizes only six kinds of *samadhi*.

Vacaspatimisra comprehends all the different kinds of *samprajnata samadhi* under three classes : (1) *grahya-samadhi* or concentration on external objects, (2) *grahana-samadhi* or concentration on the sense-organs, and (3) *grahitr-samadhi* or concentration on the ego.

In the different stages of *samprajnata samadhi* the yogin attains certain miraculous powers (*siddhis*) which strengthen his faith in the process of yoga. Different miraculous powers are achieved as the result of concentration on different objects. No reason is given why these powers are attained and why particular powers are attained as the result of concentration on particular objects. These are the facts of actual experience of the yogin, and they have been recorded as such. Some of these miraculous powers are clairvoyance, clairaudience, thought-reading, interpretation of veridical dreams, understanding the language of animals, memory of past lives, knowledge of the past and the future, the distant and the subtle, and knowledge of the self or *Purusa*.

The different kinds of *samprajnata samadhi* (conscious ecstasy) are called *savija samadhi* because they contain the seed of bondage inasmuch as they do not bring about true knowledge of the distinction between *Purusa* and *Prakrti*.

*Asamprajnata samadhi* (supra-conscious ecstasy) is produced by constant practice of extreme passionlessness which is the cause of the complete cessation of the mental functions. In this stage all the mental functions are arrested, leaving behind only their potencies or traces in the mind. Extreme passionlessness destroys even its own traces, and thus brings about the highest stage of *asamprajnata samadhi*, which is called *nirvija samadhi* because it is absolutely objectless and does not contain the seed of bondage.

## The Samkara-Vedantist

Sadanada Yati, the author of *Advaita-Brahma-Siddhi*, has accepted Patanjali's classification of *samadhi* in its entirety. He divides *samadhi* mainly into two kinds, viz. *samprajnata samadhi* and *asamprajnata samadhi*. And like Vijnanabhiksu he divides the former, again, into six kinds : (i) *savitarka samadhi*, (2) *nirvitarka samadhi*, (3) *savicara samadhi*, (4) *nirvicara samadhi*, (5) *sananda samadhi*, and (6) *sasmita samadhi*. From another standpoint, he divides *samprajnata samadhi* into three kinds : (1) *grahya-samadhi*, (2) *grahana-samadhi*, and (3) *grahitr-samadhi*. Here he agrees with Vacaspatimisra. Thus Sadananda Yati has incorporated the Patanjala system of yoga-practice into the Vedantic culture.

But Vedantists generally recognize only two kinds of *samadhi*, viz. *samaprajnata samadhi* or *savikalpa samadhi*, and *asamprajnata samadhi* or *nirvikalpa samadhi*. Mahadeva Sarasvati Muni, the author of

*Tattvanusandhana,* divides *samadhi* into the above two kinds. He defines *samprajnata samadhi* as an unbroken stream of mental functions having for their object the pure consciousness (*cit* or Brahman) without the distinction of subject and object. In this stage the mental modes are not entirely destroyed; they have for their object Brahman or pure consciousness and are transformed into it. In it the consciousness of subject and object drops off altogether, but the mental modes remain concentrated on and transformed into pure consciousness; it is the result of the utmost perfection of the practice of concentration.

Mahadeva Sarasvati Muni defines *asamprajnata samadhi* as the complete suppression of all mental functions (*saruadhnirodha*) on the suppression of the effects of *samprajnata samadhi.* Mahadevananda Sarasvati Muni explains it as the transformation of the mind into the form of Brahman or pure consciousness without the medium of mental modes which are entirely destroyed.

Sadananda, the author of *Vedantasara,* recognizes two kinds of iy viz. *savikalpa samadhi* and *nirvikalpa samadhi*. He defines the former as the mental mode which has for its object Brahman or pure consciousness into which it is transformed and in which the distinction of the knower, the known, and the knowledge is not destroyed. In this stage there is the consciousness of Identity (the pure self) through the medium of mental modes in spite of the consciousness of duality of subject and object. He defines the latter as the mental mode which has for its object Brahman or pure consciousness into which it is transformed and with which it is more completely identified. In this stage, though there is a mental mode which is transformed into Brahman or pure consciousness, there is no consciousness of the mental mode, but only the consciousness of pure Brahman.

But, then, what is the difference between *nirvikalpa samadhi* and dreamless sleep (*susupti*)? Sadananda says that though in both the states there is no consciousness of any mental mode, yet in the former there is a mental mode (*vrtti*) which is transformed into the form of Brahman, while in the latter there is no mental mode at all because the mind is dissolved into *avidya* in deep sleep.

Nrsimha Sarasvati, the author of *Subodhini,* a commentary on *Vedantasara,* describes two stages of *savikalpa samadhi*. In the first stage, there is the consciousness of Brahman through the medium of a mental mode (*vrtti*) which is interpenetrated by the authoritative knowledge that "I am Brahman". So, in this stage, there is a mental mode; its object is Brahman; there is the consciousness of Brahman through the mental mode; and there is the consciousness of the injunction of the *sastras,* "Thou art that." In the second stage, there is the continuous consciousness of Brahman through the medium of a mental mode which is not interpenetrated by the authoritative knowledge that "I am Brahman". So, in this stage, there is a mental mode, its object is Brahman : there is a continuous consciousness of Brahman through the mental mode; but there is no authoritative knowledge that "I am Brahman". In both there is the consciousness of the distinction between the knower, the known, and the knowledge. But though there is this consciousness of distinction or duality there is a consciousness of Identity. In both these stages there is a consciousness of Identity with the consciousness of duality. The only difference between them lies in that in the first stage there is the consciousness of the authoritative injunction "Thou art that", while in the second stage there is no such consciousness.

Nrsimha Sarasvati describes two stages of *nirvikalpa samadhi* also. In the first stage, there is the consciousness of Brahman through the medium of a mental mode (*vrtti*) which is transformed into and identified with Brahman with the aid of the subconscious impressions of the mental modes in the state of determinate ecstasy (*savikalpa samadhi*) devoid of the consciousness of the knower, the known, and the knowledge. In this stage, therefore, there are the following factors: (i) there is a mental mode having for its object Brahman; (ii) there are subconscious impressions of the mental modes in the state of determinate ecstasy, which colour and modify the present mode in the state of indeterminate ecstasy; (iii) there is no consciousness of the knower, the known, and the knowledge. In the second stage there is the existence of Brahman (pure consciousness and bliss) without the medium of any mental mode modified into the form of Brahman and thus manifesting it, in which there is no consciousness of the distinction among the knower, the known, and the knowledge, and in which there is no trace of subconscious impressions of mental modes, which are being completely destroyed by the constant practice of indeterminate ecstasy. In this state, therefore, there are neither any mental modes (*vrtti*) nor any subconscious impressions (*samskara*) of past psychoses, nor any consciousness of duality of subject and object; there is the existence of pure absolute consciousness and bliss (Brahman). This is the highest stage of *samadhi*.

According to Sadananda, there are mental modes in both determinate and indeterminate ecstasy. But in indeterminate ecstasy though there are mental modes there is no consciousness of them. According to him, in determinate ecstasy there is the consciousness of Identity (Brahman) together with the consciousness of duality of subject and object, while in indeterminate ecstasy there is the pure consciousness of Identity (Brahman) without the consciousness of duality of subject and object. According to Nrsimha Sarasvati also, in determinate ecstasy there is the consciousness of Identity together with the consciousness of duality, while in indeterminate ecstasy there is the pure consciousness of Identity (Brahman) divested of all consciousness of relativity of subject and object. But according to him, in the highest stage of indeterminate ecstasy all mental modes and their subconscious impressions are destroyed and there remain only the pure absolute consciousness and bliss. It is the pure, absolute, transcendental consciousness free from all empirical modes and determinations and devoid of all consciousness of relativity. This state of ecstasy alone should properly be called indeterminate ecstasy. All the other kinds of ecstasy in which there is empirical consciousness revealed through mental modes should be called *savikalpa samadhi*.

Mahadeva Sarasvati also holds that in the highest stage of ecstasy (*asamprajnata samadhi*) all mental modes and their subconscious impressions are totally destroyed and the mind is transformed into Brahman or pure consciousness and bliss, though devoid of all mental modes. But according to him, in *samprajnata samadhi* only there are mental modes which are transformed into Brahman or pure consciousness, but there is no consciousness of relativity of subject and object. But this is *nirvikalpa samadhi*, according to Sadananda.

The author of *Ratnavali* also describes *asamprajnata samadhi* as the condition of the mind in which all mental functions are completely arrested.

Ramatirtha Yati, the author of *Vidvanmanoraniani*, identifies conscious ecstasy (*samprajnata samadhi*) with determinate ecstasy (*savikalpa samadhi*) and supra-conscious ecstasy (*asamprajnata samadhi*) with indeterminate ecstasy (*nirvikalpa samadhi*).

**The Buddhist**

According to Dharmakirti, the author of *Nyayabindu*, the intuitive perception of a yogin is produced by constant contemplation of the ultimate truths when it reaches the highest limit of perfection. Dharmottara clearly explains the nature of yogic intuition in *Nyayabindutika*. There are four ultimate truths according to the Buddhists : (1) all is momentary, (2) all is void, (3) all is pain, and (4) everything is like itself. By constant contemplation of these four truths the yogin gradually attains a more and more distinct vision of them; and when he attains the highest and most perfect stage of contemplation, he acquires the most distinct vision or intuition of the ultimate truths. Until the yogin reaches the highest limit of distinct vision born of constant contemplation, he perceives the objects of contemplation as slightly indistinct, as if hidden behind mica. But when he reaches the highest limit of distinct vision by constant contemplation of the ultimate truths, he perceives the objects of contemplation most distinctly, as if they were within his own grasp. And because he has the most distinct vision of the ultimate truths at the highest stage of contemplation, his intuitive perception is indeterminate. According to the Buddhists, indeterminate perception alone is distinct and vivid; and the so-called determinate perception is not in itself distinct and vivid, but it acquires distinctness and vividness from its contact with indeterminate perception which is its immediate antecedent.

Anuruddha, the author of *Abhidhammatthasangaha*, describes the different levels of consciousness. He divides consciousness into two orders, viz. subliminal consciousness or subconsciousness below the threshold of consciousness (*manodvara*) and supra-liminal consciousness or consciousness above the threshold of consciousness (*manodvara*). He divides supra-liminal consciousness, again, into two orders, viz. normal consciousness and super-normal consciousness. Normal consciousness is called *Kama-citta* as it is generally confined to the *Kama-loka* or the plane of existence in which *kama* or desire prevails. Super-normal consciousness is called *Mahaggata-citta* or sublime or exalted consciousness. And this super-normal consciousness, again, is subdivided into *Rupa-citta*, which is generally found in the *Rupa-loka* or the sphere of visible forms which are not altogether immaterial, and *Arupa-citta*, which is concerned with *Arupaloka* or the sphere of the invisible or formless, and *Lokuttara-*

*citta* or transcendental consciousness which is above the three worlds, viz. *Kama-loka,* Rupa-loka, and *Arupa-loka.*

In order to pass from the *Kama-citta* or normal consciousness to the *Rupa-citta* or the lowest order of super-normal consciousness, a severe discipline and concentration of the mind are necessary. A monk (*bhikkhu*) must inhibit all physical and mental activity and concentrate his mind on a single selected object or sensation without changing the object of thought. After sometime the sensuous mark or symbol is replaced by the corresponding image. This concentration of the mind on a bare sensation or its image is called "preliminary concentration" (*parikamma-samadhi*). Then by more intense concentration of the mind the image is divested of its concrete, sensuous, or imaginal form, and is converted into an abstract conceptualized image, though not completely deindividualized. The concentration of the mind on this conceptualized image during the period of transition from normal consciousness to super-normal consciousness is still known as "access concentration" (*upacara-samadhi*). At this stage there intervenes the lowest order of super-normal consciousness known as the first *Rupa-jhana.*

The Pali word *jhana* corresponds to the Sanskrit word *dhyana,* which means "concentrative meditation", or "ecstatic musing". There are five *Rupa-jhanas,* which consist in the gradual elimination of the factors of consciousness and attainment of an "intensified inward vision" and on absolute equanimity or hedonic indifference,

1. The first *jhanic* consciousness of the *Rupa-loka* has five factors: (i) *Vitakka* or initial attention by which sloth-and-torpor (*thina-middha*) is inhibited, (ii) *Vicara* or sustained attention by which doubt (*vicikiccha*) is inhibited; (iii) *Piti* or pleasurable interest or zest by which aversion (*byapada*) is inhibited; (iv) *Sukha* or pleasure or happiness by which distraction and worry (*uddhacca kukkucca*) are inhibited; (v) *Ekaggata* or one-pointedness of consciousness or individualization which develops into ecstatic concentration (*appana-samadhi*) and inhibits all sensuous desire (*kamachanda*).
2. In the second *Rupa-jhana,* initial attention (*vitakka*) is eliminated, and it occurs together with sustained attention (*vicara*), pleasurable interest or zest (*piti*), pleasure (*sukha*), and individualization (*ekaggata*).

3. In the third *Rupa-jhana,* both initial attention (*vitakka*) and sustained attention (*vicara*) are got rid of; and it occurs together with pleasurable interest or zest (*piti*), pleasure (*sukha*), and individualization (*ekaggata*).
4. In the fourth *Rupa-jhana,* pleasurable interest (*piti*) also is eliminated; and it occurs together with pleasure (*sukha*) and individualization (*ekaggata*).
5. In the fifth *Rupa-jhana,* pleasure or happiness (*sukha*) is eliminated, and it occurs together with neutral feeling or hedonic indifference (*upekkha*) and individualization (*ekaggata*). Sometimes the fourth *jhana* and the fifth *jhana* are combined into one and only four *Rupa-jhanas* are spoken of.

The higher stages of samadhi in the yoga system are attained by concentrating the mind on subtler and subtler objects. But the higher stages of *jhana* in the Buddhist system are attained by eliminating the factors of consciousness gradually.

"Here we have," says Mrs. Rhys Davids, "a gradual composure and collectedness of consciousness gradually brought about by the deliberate elimination of : (1) the restless, discursive work of intellect, seeking likenesses and differences, establishing relations, forming conclusions; (2) the expansive suffusion of zest, keen interest, creative joy, (3) all hedonistic consciousness. The residual content of consciousness is admitted to be (a) a sort of sublimated or clarified satiy an intensified inward vision or intuition, such as a god or spirit might conceivably be capable of, (b) indifference or equanimity, also god-like."

Above the level of the *Rupa-citta* there is the *Arupa-citta* which is concerned with *Arupa-loka* or the world of the invisible or formless. The *Arupa-loka* is entirely non-spatial. And the experience of this world can never be sensuous. In the highest stage of the *Rupa-citta,* which is attained by the gradual elimination of the factors of consciousness, there is the abnormal clarity of inward vision or intuition together with hedonic indifference or equanimity. Above this stage there is no longer any elimination of factors of consciousness, but of all consciousness of distinctions or limitations. Just as there are four stages of *Rupa-jhana,* so there are four stages of *Arupa-jhana.*

1. At the first stage of *Arupa-jhana,* the mind transcends the

consciousness of matter and form distinctions and limitations, and being concentrated on the concept of infinite space, acquires "the blissful consciousness, subtle yet actual, of an infinite sensation of space". This may be compared to Kant's pure intuition of space as distinguished from his empirical intuition of space.

2. At the second stage of *Arupa-jhana*, the mind transcends the sensation of infinite space, and being concentrated on the concept of infinite consciousness "becomes conscious only of a concept, subtle yet actual, of consciousness as infinite".
3. At the third stage of *Arupa-jhana*, the mind wholly transcends the conceptual sphere of consciousness as infinite, and being concentrated on the concept of nothingness "becomes conscious only of a concept, subtle yet actual, of infinite nothingness".
4. At the fourth stage of *Arupa-jhana*, the mind wholly transcends the sphere of nothingness and attains the stage of an all but complete hypnosis or quasi-unconsciousness which may be described as "neither percipience nor non-percipience".

When the mind transcends all these different stages of super-normal consciousness concerned with the *Rupa-loka* and the *Arupa-loka*, it attains the highest stage of super-normal consciousness which is called transcendental or supra-mundane consciousness (*Lokuttara-citta*).

*Jhana*-consciousness is mystic consciousness. It is brought about by auto-suggestion. It consists in intensifying or concentrating consciousness on a single object. The object is first of all a percept, then an image, then a concept, so far the mind is in the preparatory stage. Then gradually the contents of consciousness are eliminated in the different stages of Rupa-jhana till the mind at last acquires super-normal clarity of vision and hedonic indifference. So long the mind is in the plane of visible forms (*Rupa-loka*) it is conscious of the ethereal but not of the immaterial or non-spatial. Then the mind comes in touch with the entirely immaterial world of the invisible or formless by gradually eliminating all consciousness of distinctions and limitations. The mind is, at first, concentrated on infinite space, then on infinite consciousness, then on infinite nothingness, and last of all attains the stage of complete trance or quasi-unconsciousness which may be described as neither consciousness nor unconsciousness. This is the highest stage of *jhana*-consciousness, but not the highest plane of consciousness. When the mind completely transcends even the plane of the invisible or formless (*Arupa-loka*), it attains the stage of transcendental or supramundane consciousness (*Lokuttara-citta*).

According to William James, ineffability, noetic quality, transiency, and passivity are the characteristics of mystical consciousness. As to transiency and ineffability, Mrs Rhys Davids says, "the former is markedly true concerning the momentary ecstasy of attainment or *appana* as also concerning the realization of great spiritual elevation generally. Touching the 'Fruit' of each '*Path*' of spiritual progress appears to have been a momentary (*khanika*) flash of insight. As to the latter, ineffability, it is also true that we find no attempts by brethren who were expert at *Jhana* to enter in detail into their abnormal experiences.... Language is everywhere too much the creature and product of our five-fold world of sense, with a varying coefficient of motor consciousness, to be of much use in describing consciousness that has apparently got beyond the range of sense and local movement.

As to the noetic quality, *Jhana*-consciousness is strongly characterized by it. It gives us insight into depths of truth unfathomed by the discursive intellect; it brings the mind into touch with higher and higher planes of existence. The chief intellectual result of the different stages of *Jhana*-consciousness is a super-normal clarity of inward vision or intuition "untroubled by either discursive intellection or hedonistic affection". The *Jhana*-process gives us the following powers :

1. Hyperaesthesia of vision or clairvoyance (*dibbacakkhuabhinna*) e.g. the super-normal vision of the past and the future history of a particular individual.
2. Hyperaesthesia of hearing or clairaudience (*dibba-sota*) e.g. super-normal hearing of sounds and voices, both human and celestial, the distant becoming near.
3. Thought-reading and thought-transference or telepathy (*cetopariya-nana* or *paracita-vijanana*).
4. Hypermnesia (*pubbenivasanussati*), or reminiscence of the past history of former lives.

According to William James, mystical consciousness has got another characteristic, viz. passivity. "When mystical consciousness has once set in," says James, "the mystic feels as if his own will were in abeyance, and indeed sometimes as if he were grasped and held by a superior power." This characteristic of passivity, however, is lacking in *Jhana*-consciousness and differentiates it from other kinds of mystical consciousness. It differentiates it from the eucharistic consciousness or the mystic sense of union with the divine one, and also from the Vedantic sense of identity of the individual soul with the world-soul. "There was, of course, this deep cleavage," says Mrs Rhys Davids, "between it and the eucharistic consciousness, that the self was banished, and no sense of union with the divine One, or any One, aimed at or felt. Herein, too, the Buddhist differs from the Vedantist, who sought to realize identity with *atman,* that is, the identity of the world-soul and his own self or *atman "Tat tvam asi"* (That are thou)."

But why is *Jhana*-consciousness wanting in passivity ? Mrs Rhys Davids offers a reason for it. She says, "it has the essential noetic quality too strongly to permit of passivity as a constant, intellect and volition, for Buddhist thought, are hardly distinguishable, and the *Jhayin* seems to be always master of himself and self-possessed, even in ecstasy, even to the deliberate falling into and emerging from trance. There is a synergy about this *Jhana,* combined with an absence of any reference whatever to a merging or melting into something greater, that for many may reveal defect, but which is certainly a most interesting and significant difference."

## The Jaina

The Jaina divides perception into two kinds : (1) empirical perception (*samvyavaharika pratyaksa*), and (2) transcendental perception (*paramarthika pratyaksa*). Empirical perception is what we have in everyday life. It is of two kinds : (1) sensuous perception (*indriya-nibandhana*) or perception derived from the sense-organs (i.e. external sense-organs), and (2) non-sensuous perception (*anindriya-nibandhana*) or perception derived from the mind which is not a sense-organ according to the Jaina. Transcendental perception owes its origin to the self alone; it is neither derived from the sense-organs nor from the mind. It is directly derived from the self owing to the destruction of the impediments to perfect knowledge. It is of two kinds, viz. imperfect or deficient (*vikala*) and perfect or complete (*sakala*). The former, again, is of two kinds, viz. clairvoyant perception of objects at a distance of time and space (*avadhi*) and direct perception of the thoughts of others, as in telepathic knowledge of the thoughts of other minds (*manahparyaya*). The latter is omniscience (*kevalajnana*) or the perfect knowledge of all the objects of the universe due to the complete destruction of the *karma-matter* which is an obstacle to knowledge. Thus the highest stage of transcendental perception, according to the Jaina, is omniscience (*kevala-jnana*). The Jaina does not believe in the existence of God and consequently in divine omniscience. But he holds that the *Jiva* or the individual self can attain perfection and omniscience by completely destroying the *karma-matter* which is an obstacle to perfect knowledge. The knowledge of all objects exists in the self. But it is veiled by *karma-matter*. When the veil of *karma-matter* is completely destroyed, the self realizes its omniscience. This perfect intuition of the whole universe is not produced by the external sense-organs, or by the internal organ of mind, as the Nyaya-Vaisesika holds. So before we discuss the nature of omniscience, let us briefly refer to the Jaina criticism of the Nyaya-Vaisesika doctrine of yogic intuition.

## The Jaina Criticism of the Nyaya-Vaisesika Doctrine of Yogic Intuition

According to some, the external sense-organs aided by the *dharma* or merit born of meditation (yoga) can apprehend past, future, distant, and subtle objects. But the Jaina (Prabhacandra) urges that the sense-organs can never be freed from their inherent imperfections, and so even the sense-organs of yogis can never enter into direct relation with supersensible objects (e.g. atoms), like ours because they are, after all, sense-organs. What is the nature of the aid rendered by the peculiar power or *dharma* born of meditation to the sense-organs? Does the dharma born of meditation increase the capacity of the sense-organs when they function with regard to their objects (e.g. atoms)? Or does it merely assist the sense-organs when they operate on their own objects? The first alternative is untenable, because the sense-organs by themselves can never operate on atoms, etc. If they do operate on atoms, etc., they do not stand in need of the aid of the dharma born of *yoga*; and if they operate on atoms, etc., only when they are aided by the *dharma* born of yoga, then there is a circular reasoning. The *dharma* born of yoga increases the capacity of the sense-organs, when they operate on their objects, e.g. atoms, etc.; and the sense-organs operate on atoms, etc., when they are aided by the *dharma* born of yoga. The second alternative also is impossible. If the *dharma* born of yoga cannot increase the capacity of the sense-organs, but merely assists them in operating on supersensible objects like atoms, etc., what is the use of the aid of *dharma* rendered to the sense-organs in their apprehension of supersensible objects ?

According to the Nyaya-Vaisesika, the internal organ of *manas* with the aid of the *dharma* born of yoga can simultaneously produce a knowledge of all the objects of the world, past, future, remote, and subtle. But Prabhacandra contends that the *manas* which is regarded as atomic by the Nyaya-Vaisesika can never enter into direct relation with all the objects of the world simultaneously, and therefore, cannot produce a knowledge of them at the same time, otherwise there would be a simultaneous perception of all the qualities of a cake, e.g. its taste, colour, odour, etc,, at the time of eating a cake, which is not admitted by the Nyaya-Vaisesika. In fact, the Nyaya-Vaisesika does not admit the possibility of simultaneous cognitions owing to the atomic nature of the mind. How, then, can it produce a knowledge of all the objects of the world at the same time, even when it is aided by the *dharma* born of yoga ? How can the atomic mind enter into relation with many objects at the same time by contradicting its very nature?

It is more reasonable to hold that it is the self which apprehends all the objects of the world independently of the mind by virtue of the specific powers born of meditation. What is the use of supposing that the self knows an infinite number of objects through the atomic mind at the same time ? If it is urged that the mind of a yogin enters into relation with all the objects of the world not simultaneously but successively, then there would be no difference between the perception of a yogin and that of an ordinary person. Hence Prabhacandra concludes that the atomic mind can never enter into direct relation with all the objects of the world at the same time.

But it may be urged that the mind of a yogin enters into relation with all the objects of the world, through its union with God who is ubiquitous and consequently related to everything in the world.

Prabhacandra contends that the mind of the yogin can enter into relation with the present objects alone through its union with God, but never with past and future objects, since they are non-existent at the time when the mind enters into union with God. Hence the Jaina concludes that omniscience, or a knowledge of all the objects of the world, can never be produced either by the external organs or the so-called internal organ of mind, though they are aided by the peculiar powers born of meditation.

**The Jaina Doctrine of Omniscience**

According to the Jaina, there is no eternal and omniscient God, but the finite self or *Jiva* can attain omniscience when all the *karma-matter* is totally destroyed, which is an impediment to right knowledge. And this omniscience is not derived through the channel of the external sense-organs or the internal organ of mind. And further, the Jaina holds that constant meditation cannot produce omniscience, until and unless the *karma-matter*, which is an impediment to right knowledge, is wholly destroyed. Herein lies the difference between the Nyaya-Vaisesika and the Jaina view.

Just as the Nyaya-Vaisesika proves the existence of yogic intuition by inference, so the Jaina also proves the existence of omniscience by the ontological argument. Just as heat is subject to varying grades and consequently reaches the highest limit, so right knowledge which is subject to varying grades owing to the various degrees of the *karma-matter* impeding it, reaches the highest limit of omniscience when the hindrance of the four kinds of *karma-matter* is completely destroyed.

What is the nature of this omniscience ? It is not derived from authority or scripture, because authority can never give us a direct and distinct presentative knowledge which characterizes omniscience. Nor can it be derived from inference for the same reason. Nor can it be derived from peripheral organs or the central organ of mind, as we have found already. Hence it is neither verbal, nor inferential, nor sensuous. It is a transcendental perception or pure intuition of the whole world, produced by the complete decay and destruction of the *karma-matter*. It is a distinct perception of all the supersensible objects of the world on the complete destruction of *karma*.

**The Mimamsaka's Objections to the Jaina View of Omniscience**

The Mimamsaka, however, does not advocate this view of omniscience. He asks : What is the meaning of omniscience ? Does it mean the knowledge of all the objects of the world ? Or does it mean the knowledge of certain principal objects? In the first alternative, does it mean the knowledge of all the objects of the world in succession or at the same time ?

1. If the former, then there can be no omniscience. The objects of the world, past, present, and future can never be exhausted, and so their knowledge also can never be complete. And since there can be no knowledge of all the objects of the world, there can be no omniscience.

2. If the latter, then also there can be no omniscience. All the objects of the world cannot be known simultaneously, because contradictory things like heat and cold cannot be apprehended at the same time by a single cognition.
3. Moreover, if all the objects are known at one moment by the omniscient self, then in the next moment it would become unconscious having nothing to know.
4. And further, the omniscient self would be tainted by the desires and aversions of others in knowing them, and would thus cease to be omniscient, since these are impediments to right knowledge.

   Thus, omniscience cannot mean the knowledge of all the objects of the world either at the same time or in succession. Nor, in the second place, can it be held that omniscience means the knowledge of certain principal objects or archetypal forms, because only when all the objects of the world are known can there be a discrimination of principal objects from subordinate objects.
5. Moreover, how can there be a knowledge of the past and the future, which are really non-existent? If the past and the future are known by the omniscient self, though they are non-existent, then its knowledge would be illusory. And if the past and the future are known as real and existent, then they are converted into the present; and if the past and the future are known by

the omniscient self as present, then its knowledge would be illusory. Thus the Jaina doctrine of omniscience is untenable.

### *The Jaina Refutation of the Mimamsaka's Objections*

Prabhacandra severely criticizes all these objections of the Mimamsaka in *Prameyakamalamartanda* in the following manner.

1. In the first place, it has been asked : Is omniscience made up of a single cognition, or many cognitions? Prabhacandra replies that it is a single intuition of the whole world. It does not depend upon the external sense-organs or the mind; so it need not be diversified by many cognitions. Our perception is produced by the external organs or the internal organ; so it cannot apprehend past, distant, future, and subtle objects. But the perception of the omniscient self is not produced by the external sense-organs or the mind; hence it can apprehend all supersensible objects. The pure intuition of the omniscient self is not produced successively; it knows all the objects of the universe simultaneously by a single stroke of intuition since it transcends the limits of time and space which are the necessary conditions of all sense-perception owing to the complete destruction of *karma*.
2. In the second place, it has been urged that contradictory things like heat and cold cannot be apprehended by a single cognition. Prabhacandra asks : Can they not be perceived by a single cognition, because they cannot be present at the same time, or because they cannot be apprehended by a single cognition, though they are simultaneously present? The first view is untenable because contradictory things like heat and cold can exist at the same time; for instance, when incense is burnt in a pot, the upper part of it is hot and the lower part is cold. The second view also cannot be maintained; because when there is a flash of lightning in the midst of darkness, we have a simultaneous perception of contradictory things like darkness and light.
3. In the third place, the Mimamsaka has urged that if the omniscient self knows all the objects of the world at one moment, in the next moment it would become unconscious

having nothing to know. Prabhacandra replies that the objection would hold good, if both the omniscient cognition and the whole world were destroyed in the next moment; but, in fact, both of these are never-ending. The omniscient self knows all the objects of the world by a single unending intuition.

4. In the fourth place, the Mimamsaka has urged that if the omniscient self knows the desires and aversions of the non-liberated souls, then it becomes tainted with these desires and aversions which hinder omniscience. Prabhacandra replies that desires and aversions are produced by changes or modifications (*parinama*). But the omniscient self is above all changes and modifications; so it cannot be tainted by the desires and aversions of others by merely knowing them. Moreover, desires and aversions are of sensuous origin; but the knowledge of the omniscient self is non-sensuous; hence it cannot be tainted by the imperfections of ordinary men.
5. In the fifth place, the Mimamsaka has urged that the omniscient self cannot perceive the past and the future, since they are non-existent. And if it knows them as existent, then the knowledge of the omniscient self is illusory. Prabhacandra replies that the past and the future are perceived by the omniscient self not as present, but as past and future respectively; so the knowledge of the omniscient self is not illusory.

But how can the past be perceived ? The past is not present; it is non-existent. Prabhacandra asks : Are past objects non-existent in relation to the past time ? Or are they non-existent in relation to the time when they are perceived by the omniscient self? The first alternative is untenable. The past objects are as much existent in relation to their own time, as the present objects which exist at their own time. The past objects as much exist in the past, as the present objects exist at present. The second alternative is true. The Jaina admits that the past objects are non-existent in relation to the present time when they are perceived by the omniscient self. The omniscient self knows the past as existing in the past; and it knows the future as existing in the future. In other words, the omniscient self knows the past as produced in the past; and it knows the future as to be produced in the future. Hence the knowledge of the omniscient self is not illusory.

But how can the past and the future be perceived by the omniscient self as past and future respectively, though they are not existent at the time of perception ? The Jaina replies that the omniscient self is absolutely free from the bondage of physical existence; its knowledge is not produced by the external sense-organs or the mind; so there is nothing to obstruct its knowledge of the past and the future. The Mimamsaka himself admits that recognition, which is a kind of perception according to him, can apprehend the past as well as the present, and a flash of intuition in ordinary life (*pratibhajnana*) can apprehend the future as future. Is it, then, impossible for the omniscient self who is entirely free from the fetters of *karma* and mundane existence to have a super-sensuous vision of the whole world, past, present, and future? So the Jaina concludes that the omniscient self directly and immediately knows all the objects of the world, past, present, and future, subtle and remote, by a single unending intuition without the medium of the external sense-organs or the so-called internal organ of the mind.

# 18

# Divine Perception

## Patanjali's Proof of Divine Omniscience

We have discussed the different orders of human perception, normal, abnormal, and super-normal. Now we shall briefly refer to the nature of divine perception as conceived by the Indian philosophers, apart from its value and validity.

Just as the possibility of yogic intuition has been proved by the Nyaya-Vaisesika, and the possibility of the omniscience of the individual self or *Jiva* has been proved by the Jaina by an appeal to something like the ontological argument, so the omniscience of God is proved by Patanjali by the ontological argument such as we find in Anselm in the West. Gradation in degrees of worth gradually leads to and implies as the terminus of the series and realism or the greatest reality which is omniscient, omnipotent, and all-perfect. Patanjali describes God as the Supreme Person untouched by all taint of imperfection, above the law of *Karma*, and above the processes of fulfilling and fulfilment.

We infer the existence of omniscient God from our knowledge of the supersensuous, whether in the past or future or present, whether separately or collectively, whether small or great. Our supersensuous knowledge is the germ of omniscience; so from this we infer the existence of omniscient God. When this supersensuous knowledge, which is the germ of omniscience, gradually increases and reaches the acme of perfection in a person, he is called omniscient, It is possible for the germ of omniscience to reach its highest limit of perfection, for it admits of degrees of excellence, as in the case of an ascending scale of magnitude. Whatever admits of degrees of excellence is capable of reaching the highest limit of excellence. We actually find that knowledge admits of degrees of excellence; it gradually increases in proportion to the degree to which the *tamas*, or matter-stuff, which covers the *sattva*, or pure essence of the mind is removed; therefore it must reach the highest excellence of omniscience. But here we are not concerned with the proofs of the existence of God. We are concerned only with the nature of Divine Knowledge,

### The Naiyayika View of the Nature of Divine Knowledge

Jayanta Bhatta has discussed the nature of divine knowledge in *Nyayamanjari*. He says that God is free from all taint of imperfection, and so He is omniscient. But we are corrupted by the impurities of cravings, aversions, etc., and so we cannot perceive all objects of the world.

Divine knowledge, which is all-embracing, is eternal; it is without a beginning and without an end. If there were a break in divine consciousness even for a moment, there would be a collapse of the whole universe, since it is created and sustained by the divine will which is inseparable from divine knowledge. Even at the time of the dissolution of the universe divine knowledge is not suspended, since there is no cause of its destruction at that time. And at the time of the creation of the universe, divine knowledge is not created, since there is no cause of its creation at that time. Hence divine knowledge is eternal. Herein lies the difference between the human omniscience and the divine omniscience; the former is produced, while the latter is eternal; the former is acquired, while the latter is natural and essential.

Divine knowledge is not diversified by many cognitions; it grasps all the objects of the universe, past, present, and future, subtle and remote, by a single all-embracing intuition. Were it not so, God would have many cognitions either successively or simultaneously. But He cannot have them in succession, for, in that case, he would have discrete, discontinuous cognitions, and consequently, He would be unconscious at intervals, and thus would bring about a collapse of the universe at intervals, which would make all human activities impossible. How can God have many cognitions simultaneously, for, in that case, there would be no cause of the difference of divine cognitions?

Divine Knowledge is perceptual in character as it satisfies the essential conditions of perception. Visvanatha defines perception as a cognition which is not derived through the instrumentality of any other cognition. Inference is derived through the medium of the knowledge of invariable concomitance. Analogy is derived through the medium of the knowledge of similarity. Verbal knowledge is derived through the medium of the knowledge of the import of a term or a proposition. Thus perception alone is direct, immediate, and presentative knowledge. And divine knowledge is perceptual in character as it consists in direct and immediate apprehension of the whole universe. Divine perception is not produced by the intercourse of the sense-organs with their objects, as God has no sense-organs at all. In fact, divine perception is not produced at all; it is beginningless and endless; it is eternal. Divine perception, therefore, is not of the nature of sensuous perception, but of the nature of "creative intuition". God evolves the materials of His consciousness by the divine will, and perceives them all by a single all-embracing intuition, even as the sun illumines all the objects of the universe, though it is not produced by them. Thus the knowledge of God is not determined by its objects; but the objects are determined by the knowledge of God.

Thus divine knowledge is perceptual in character and is eternal. And because divine perception is eternal, God has no subconscious impression (*samskara*). He is never subconscious or unconscious. And because He has no subconscious impression, He has no memory. And because He has no memory, He has no inferential knowledge which depends on memory. He has no need of inference as it is a mark of limitation or finitude. God does not know things in a fragmentary and piecemeal fashion. He knows all the objects of the universe, past, present, and future in one intuitive glance; He is above the limitations of time and space; so He has no need of inferential or discursive knowledge. For the same reason He has no analogical or verbal knowledge.

## Divine Knowledge and Human Knowledge

Human knowledge is finite and limited, while divine knowledge is infinite and unlimited. Human knowledge is produced by many causes, while divine knowledge is eternal. Human knowledge is tainted by errors and illusions, while divine knowledge is free from errors and imperfections. Human knowledge is conditioned while divine knowledge is unconditioned. Human knowledge admits of degrees of excellence, while divine knowledge is unequalled and unexcelled.

Human knowledge is derived from perception, inference, analogy, and authority, while divine knowledge is neither inferential, nor analogical, nor verbal, but only perceptual in character. In human knowledge there is memory produced by subconscious impressions, while in divine knowledge there is no subconscious impression at all, and, therefore, no memory. There are breaks in human knowledge, while divine knowledge is unbroken and continuous. Man is sometimes subconscious or unconscious; but God is never subconscious or unconscious.

Human perception is sensuous, while divine perception is non-sensuous. Human perception is determined by its objects, while divine perception is not determined by its objects, but it determines its own objects. Human perception is limited by space and time, while divine perception is above the limitations of space and time. Human perception is confined to "here and now" while divine perception grasps the past, the present, the future, and the remote in an Eternal Now. Man has sometimes a flash of intuition of the future, and can attain omniscience by constant meditation, practice of austerities, and so on, but divine omniscience is natural and eternal. This higher intuition of man is acquired through the internal organ of mind. But divine intuition depends neither upon the external organs nor upon the internal organ.

**Divine Omniscience and Human Illusions**

This interesting question has been raised by Udayana in *Nyaya-Kusumanjali* in connection with the validity of divine knowledge.

God is omniscient. There is nothing in the universe which is unknown to God, so there is nothing in human experience which escapes divine knowledge. And since there are illusory cognitions in human experience, these, too, must be objects of divine knowledge. And if God knows human illusions. He must know also the objects of these illusions, since there cannot be a cognition of another cognition without apprehending the object of that cognition. Just as there cannot be a cognition without apprehending an object, so there cannot be a cognition of another cognition without apprehending the object of the latter cognition. So, if human illusions are objects of divine knowledge, the objects of these illusions, too, must necessarily be objects of divine knowledge. In other words, God being omniscient, must perceive certain objects as different things, and thus God must be subject to illusions like human beings.

It cannot be said that God does not know the errors and illusions of human experience, for God is omniscient. But God cannot be subject to illusions as a penalty for His omniscience. His knowledge of human illusions is not itself illusory. When we perceive silver in a nacre, our perception is illusory; but when God perceives our illusory perception of silver. He does not perceive silver in a nacre, but He perceives silver as the real object of the cognition of silver, and so His cognition is not illusory. When we perceive that we have a perception of silver, though we do not know that it is illusory, this second perception, viz. the perception of the perception of silver, is not illusory. A cognition of silver in a nacre is illusory; but when it is appropriated by the self, the cognition of this illusory cognition is not illusory. Likewise, God never perceives silver in a nacre. He perceives everything as it really is; but when we perceive silver in a nacre God perceives that we have an illusory perception of silver in a nacre. Hence, God can never be subject to the illusions and imperfections of human experience. Divine knowledge is absolutely free from limitations and imperfections, illusions and hallucinations. It is the supreme norm and ultimate criterion of the validity of human knowledge.

# 19

# Jiva-Saksi-Pratyaksa and Isvara-Saksi-Pratyaksa

## The Samkara-Vedantist

The author of *Vedanta-Paribasa* not only distinguishes between the *Jiva* (finite self) and Isvara (God), but also between the *Jiva-Saksin* and the *Isvara-Saksin*, and consequently he distinguishes between the perception of the *Jiva-Saksin* and the perception of the *Jivara-Saksin*. This view is peculiar to the Samkara-Vedanta.

## The Jiva and the Jiva-Saksin

According to the Samkarite, there is one, undifferenced, eternal consciousness (*caitanya*). And this universal consciousness is particularized by certain determinants. There are two classes of determinants, namely, qualifying adjuncts or qualifications (*visesana*) and limiting adjuncts or conditions (*upadhi*). A qualification (*visesana*) is intimately connected with and inseparable from the qualified object, and as such distinguishes it from other objects. For instance, the particular colour of a jar qualifies it in such a way that it cannot be separated from the jar, and as such it distinguishes the jar from all other objects. A limiting adjunct or condition (*upadhi*) on the other hand, does not qualify an object in such a way that it cannot be separated from it, but simply limits the object to a particular time and space. For instance, the ear-drum is the limiting adjunct or condition of ether (*akasa*), because it is not inseparable from *akasa*, but simply limits it to a particular time and space, and can be separated from it. Thus there are two kinds of determinants which particularize the one eternal consciousness.

According to the Samkarite, *antahkarana*, or the internal organ, is the principle of individuation; it particularizes the eternal consciousness in two different ways. When the universal consciousness is determined by *antahkarana* as a qualifying adjunct or qualification (*visesana*) it is called the Jiva or the individual self, and when it is determined by *antahkarana* as merely a limiting adjunct or condition (*upadhi*), it is called the Jiva-Saksin or the Witness Self. *Antahkarana* is not separable from the individual self (Jiva) because it enters as a constituent element into the individual self; but it is separable from the Witness Self (Jiva-Saksin), because it limits it merely as an adventitious condition. In both the individual self (Jiva) and the Witness Self (Jiva-Saksin) the presence of *antahkarana* is necessary as a determining condition. But in the case of the individual self (Jiva), it is a qualification (*visesana*) of the universal consciousness (*caitanya*) while in the case of the Witness Self it is merely a limiting adjunct or condition (*upadhi*) of the universal consciousness. Thus *antahkarana* is a constituent factor of the individual self (Jiva), but it is merely an adventitious condition of the Witness Self (Jiva-Saksin).

It is the Jiva or the individual self that is the knower (*jnatr*), doer (*kartr*) and enjoyer (*bhoktr*), but that in the individual self through which there is the manifestation (*avabhasa*) of consciousness (*caitanya*) is the Jiva-Saksin or the Witness Self. *Antahkarana* or the internal organ is material and unconscious, and hence it cannot manifest consciousness in the individual self. It is the Jiva-Saksin or the Witness Self which manifests consciousness and all objects of individual experience. This Jiva-Saksin is not one, but it differs in each individual self for otherwise there would be no compartmental division of individual experiences.

But what is the use of the distinction between the Jiva and the Jiva-Saksin ? The empirical ego is the object of consciousness. But who is the cognizer of the empirical ego ? There must be a Saksin (Seer or Witness) of the empirical ego, otherwise there would be no unity of apperception in our knowledge of external objects and that of the empirical ego. But the Jiva-Saksin is not known as an object of knowledge, it is the presupposition of all knowledge, the knowledge of objects and the knowledge of the empirical ego or the subject. It is the Transcendental Ego as distinguished from the Empirical Ego. Thus the Jiva is the Empirical Ego, and the Jiva-Saksin is the Transcendental Ego.

The Jiva which is manifested either as a knower (*jnatr*) or a doer (*kartr*) or an enjoyer (*bhoktr*) is a psycho-physical organism; it is intimately connected with the material *antahkarana* which enters into it as a constituent factor. But the Jiva-Saksin is the universal consciousness only limited by *antahkarana* to a particular individual and thus individualized by it; it is not qualified by *antahkarana* as a constituent factor, and hence it is not a psycho-physical organism. But it is not altogether free from connection with organism (e.g. the internal organ); it is limited and individualized by the internal organ. The Jiva-Saksin may be regarded as the super-organic self, but limited by *antahkarana* to a particular individual, while the Jiva is the psycho-physical organism of which *antahkarana* is a constituent factor. The Jiva is the Empirical Ego which is the centre of all feelings of "me" and "mine" intimately connected with the organism, while the Jiva-Saksin is the Transcendental Ego which lights up all the experience of the individual self, the experience of the known objects and the knowing subject.

**Isvara and Isvara-Saksin**

According to the Samkara-Vedantist, just as the universal consciousness is particularized by *antahkarana* in two different ways, so it is determined by Maya (cosmic nescience) in two different ways. When it is determined by Maya as a qualifying adjunct (*visesana*) it is called Isvara (God); and when it is determined by Maya as a limiting condition (*upadhi*) it is called Isvara-Saksin (the Divine Witness). In other words, when Maya enters as a constituent factor into relation with the universal consciousness, it is called Isvara; and when Maya enters into relation with the universal consciousness merely as an adventitious condition, it is called Isvara-Saksin.

Isvara-Saksin is the connoisseur before whom the cosmic panorama unfolds itself. Though there is a difference between the character of Isvara and the character of Isvara-Saksin, according as the determinant Maya enters into relation with the universal consciousness either as a constituent factor (*visesana*) or as an adventitious or limiting condition (*upadhi*), yet there is no difference whatsoever in the substrata of these two characters, namely, Isvara and Isvara-Saksin. Just as one and the same person, viz. Devadatta may be a cook as well as a reader, so one and the same universal consciousness may be Isvara and Isvara-Saksin. Just as there is a difference between the two functions of Devadatta, viz. cooking and reading, but there is no difference in their substrata, viz. the cook and the reader, they being one and the same person, viz. Devadatta, so there is a difference between the two characters of the universal consciousness, viz. those of Isvara (*Isvaratva*) and Isvara-Saksin (*Isvara-Saksitva*), but there is no difference in their substrata, viz. Isvara and Isvara-Saksin, they being one and the same universal consciousness.

Though there is a plurality of Jiva-Saksins owing to the plurality of the limiting conditions, viz. *antahkaranas* or internal organs, there is only one Isvara-Saksin owing to the oneness of its limiting condition, viz. Maya or cosmic nescience; and this Isvara-Saksin is eternal as its limiting condition, Maya, is eternal. Thus according to the Samkarite, there is not only a difference between human perception (*Jiva-pratyaksa*) and divine perception (*Isvara-pratyaksa*), but there is also a difference between the perception of the Jiva-Saksin or the Witness Self and that of Isvara-Saksin or the Divine Witness, The author of *Pedantaparibhasa* does not specify the distinctive characters of these different kinds of perception, viz. *Jiva-pratyaksa, Jiva-saksi-pratyaksa, Isvara-pratyaksa, Esvara-saksi-pratyaksa.*

# Index